W9-DBS-857

Women
and
Resistance
in South Africa

Women and Resistance in South Africa

CHERRYL WALKER

MONTHLY REVIEW PRESS
NEW YORK

SCCCC - LIBRARY
4601 Mid Rivers Mall Drive
St. Peters, MO 63376

WITHDRAWN

Copyright © 1982, 1991 by Cherryl Walker
All rights reserved

Library of Congress Cataloging-in-Publication Data

Walker, Cherryl.
    Women and resistance in South Africa / Cherryl Walker.
        p.   cm.
    Reprint, with new introd. Originally published: UK: Onyx
Press Ltd.
    Includes bibliographical references ind index.
    ISBN 0-85345-829-4 (cloth): $36.00.—ISBN 0-85345-830-8
(pbk.): $18.00
    1. Women—South Africa—History.   2. Women in politics—
United States—History.   3. Women—South Africa—Societies
and clubs—History.   4. Women's rights—United States—
History.   I. Title.
    305 42'0968—dc20   91-22563
                                                                  CIP

Monthly Review Press
122 West 27th Street
New York, NY 10001

Printed in United States of America

10   9   8   7   6   5   4   3   2   1

CONTENTS

ABBREVIATIONS

AAC	All African Convention
AME	American Methodist Episcopal (Church)
ANC	African National Congress
ANCWL	African National Congress Women's League
APO	African People's Organisation
COD	Congress of Democrats
CPSA	Communist Party of South Africa
CYL	Congress Youth League
FCWU	Food and Canning Workers Union
FSAW	Federation of South African Women
GWU	Garment Workers' Union
ICU	Industrial and Commercial Workers' Union
NCAW	National Council of African Women
NCW	National Council of Women
NEC	National Executive Committee
NEUM	Non-European Unity Movement
NCC	National Consultative Committee
NIC	Natal Indian Congress
NLL	National Liberation League
PAC	Pan-African Congress
SACPO	South African Coloured People's Organisation
SAIC	South African Indian Congress
SACTU	South African Congress of Trade Unions
SAP	South African Party
TCC	Transvaal Consultative Committee
TIC	Transvaal Indian Congress
TLC	Trades and Labour Council
WEAU	Women's Enfranchisement Association of the Union
WIDF	Women's International Democratic Federation

PREFACE TO THE SECOND EDITION

March 1991 is an extraordinary time to be writing a new introduction to this book. When *Women and Resistance* first appeared in book form, in 1982, South Africa was locked into the fortress of apartheid. For me, as for many others, there was a strong sense of continuity and identification with the past that this book describes. The 1950s were becoming mythologised as the decade of glorious resistance: and nowhere was resistance more glorious than the women's anti-pass campaign described in this book. In the early 1980s progressive politics were the politics of resistance – urgent, often heroic, but essentially oppositional, attuned to the past rather than the future.

Today the brutal yet familiar certitudes of the apartheid state are crumbling. Now the challenge facing progressives is to move away from the politics of resistance to the politics of engagement: with the state, with constituency-building, with policy – with the whole process of transition to a post-apartheid society. We are living in a time of unprecedented flux politically. The mind-boggling events of the past year do not need review here – the unbanning of the African National Congress (ANC), South African Communist Party (SACP) and the Pan-Africanist Congress (PAC), the return of exiles (some of them key actors in the events of the 1940s and 1950s), the talks about talks, about constituent assemblies, about a bill of rights. Major apartheid laws – the Land Act, the Group Areas Act, even the Population Registration Act – are on the brink of being repealed. The hated influx control laws have already been abolished, in 1986, and a new generation of South Africans is growing up for whom the pass laws are indeed history. Society is being restructured, but what will emerge out of this period of transition is not at all certain, as we teeter between the promise of fundamental reform and the spectre of civil chaos. It is clear that the mere repeal of apartheid legislation will not, by itself, guarantee either stability or economic and political justice.

In this unsettled time, women, as a new commonplace will have it, are finally 'on the agenda' (at least in the anti-apartheid movement) in a way that was unimaginable in 1982. The ANC Women's League (ANCWL) has been relaunched within the country (on Women's Day, 9 August 1990) and there is talk of putting together an independent national women's alliance. Within the Congress of South African Trade Unions (COSATU) women are organising themselves in forums set up specifically to address the problems faced by women on the factory floor and within worker organisations. Several major conferences in the past eighteen months have highlighted women's subordination and urged recognition of the need to address the issue of gender inequality in a post-apartheid society.[1]

Gender is now an acceptable term. When *Women and Resistance* was first being researched, the word had not yet entered the lexicons of even the most progressive of South African academics, let alone politicians and activists. Even 'feminism' is no longer quite the bogey term that it was; though there are many on the left who still stumble over the word and many more who do not embrace it as a serious political project.

In this context, the 1950s and the decades of resistance and organisation that preceded them take on a new meaning. In some senses they are more firmly 'history'; we are able to look more critically, less nostalgically, at them than before. But the battles of the 1950s should be of more than mere academic interest. For women there is still much of direct political import to learn from the strategies and organisational structures of these struggles in the past. The broad goals of the women's organisations described in this book have not yet been achieved: neither the drive for national liberation, nor, in the words of the Women's Charter of 1954, 'the removal of all laws, regulations, conventions and customs that discriminate against us as women, and that deprive us in any way of our inherent right to the advantages, responsibilities and opportunities that society offers to any one section of the population'. While some form of settlement with African nationalism appears on the cards, the struggle against a male-dominated social order has barely begun.

Thus the reissue of this book appears particularly timely. Inevitably, some of the analysis is dated while new research has enlarged the body of information about women's past political organisations and activities, adding to and sometimes modifying this account, as well as providing alternative emphases and interpretations. This makes the prospect of placing it under scrutiny somewhat daunting. Nevertheless, as a history of the Federation of South African Women (FSAW) and the many organisations that could, in some sense, be seen as its forebears, *Women and Resistance* does, I believe, remain a key resource. Hopefully its reissue will place before a larger readership a history of women's organisation within the broad national liberation movement, and, directly or indirectly, raise pertinent questions about the nature and goals of political organisation by and for women.

Were I to research and write this history in the 1990s, I would undoubtedly produce a different book. It is, however, neither possible nor probably desirable to revise the text, which must stand as a document of its time. Nor does it seem particularly useful to take a lot of space in this introduction detailing what I would do differently. I hope some of that, at least, is implicit in what I discuss below. What I want to do, rather, is use this opportunity, firstly, to sketch developments in the 1980s in the literature on women and resistance, and then to review three issues raised directly or indirectly in the text, that strike me as of special interest today. These are (1) developments in the analysis of the relationship between the struggle against women's subordination and the struggle against national and racial oppression in South Africa, and, linked to that, the need for an autonomous women's movement; (2) the idea that historically black women's political involvements have been essentially conservative as far as gender relations are concerned, as evidenced in their perceived defence of 'the family' and endorsement of 'motherhood'; and, finally, (3) the legitimacy of a feminist historiography in South African studies. Because the 1950s and the FSAW have proved to be especially rich as topics of debate in all three areas, I will be paying more attention to the second half of *Women and Resistance* in what follows than the first.

Women, resistance and women's studies

When *Women and Resistance* first appeared, very, very little had been published on the subject. It may be hard to imagine today, but when I started researching the subject, in 1976, there was almost total indifference to the idea of women's studies within the academic community, and virtually no local body of scholarship on women's roles historically or on theories of gender on which to draw. This indifference on the part of academics was compounded by the hostility of, firstly, the state which banned the book for distribution, and secondly, many political activists who regarded this work with suspicion as a 'feminist' misappropriation of women's contribution to the national liberation movement (a hostility that was not confined to male activists alone).

Since then the body of information about women's political organisation and the history of their resistance to the pass laws, as well as to other forms of oppression, has grown considerably – although significant gaps remain. While it is not possible to do justice to this work here, certain key texts must be acknowledged.[2]

Julie Wells's thesis, 'The history of black women's struggle against pass laws in South Africa, 1900–1960', covers similar terrain to *Women and Resistance.*[3] Her focus is the anti-pass campaign rather than women's organisation more broadly, and her detailed account of women's organisation against passes in the early twentieth century, in the Orange Free State and on the Rand, is particularly useful, filling in many of the gaps in my account. She begins to analyse the social origins of participants and leaders in these campaigns, distinguishing between a small, literate elite, who took leadership roles, and the mass of participants who were 'neither highly educated nor skilled'.[4] She also problematises the question of 'why women rebel' and in this her work points beyond the rather simple model of resistance as the almost mechanical consequence of oppression that informs the discussion in *Women and Resistance*. More recently Kathy Eales's work has brought into view the complex ways in which class, gender and age affected people's responses to the imposition of a curfew for African women in Johannesburg in the 1920s. She points to the outrage of the tiny African middle class at this further erosion of their status but also notes that 'while it would be facile and presumptuous to suggest that the majority of Africans supported the curfew, one should bear in mind that it could benefit sectional interests', such as those of parents and husbands anxious to bolster a crumbling control over their daughters and wives.[5]

Jenny Schreiner's thesis, 'Women working for their freedom: FCWU and AFCWU and the Woman Question',[6] looks at the operations of a key component of the Federation of South African Women in the Western Cape. Her analysis is rooted in the classic Marxist tradition of 'the woman question' and specifically rejects the considerable range of feminist theorising which falls outside these boundaries. While her approach may seem unduly purist today, she does open up a useful debate by arguing, essentially, that the Food and Canning Workers' Union and the FSAW were correct to organise women around the issue of motherhood. Hers remains the only detailed regional history of women's organisation in the 1950s to date, although Iain Edwards's thesis on Cato Manor provides valuable material on a centre of women's resistance in Natal in the late 1950s.[7]

In these more focused studies the broad, undifferentiated category of 'women' begins to break down so that one can start to see the operation on the ground of important divisions of class, age and marital status amongst women, as well as their effects on organisation. Needed are similar in-depth studies of women's organisations in other regions, in particular the Eastern Cape, a stronghold of the ANCWL and of the Congress Alliance in general but badly under-researched.

Recently, Frene Ginwala has published an account of the early history of the ANCWL which adds to and in some details corrects the material presented in *Women and Resistance*. She argues that women's exclusion from full membership within the ANC before 1943 contrasted with their *de facto* participation 'in the deliberations, decision making and campaigns of the organisation', at branch level but also at national conferences.[8] While she criticises me for misrepresenting this relationship, her overall conclusion does converge with mine, that the eventual incorporation of women as full members of the ANC after 1943 still fell far short of their achieving equal power and status with the men. Similar attention to other structures in which women participated in the early twentieth century, for instance the Communist Party of South Africa, the labour movement and the Indian Congresses,[9] would help flesh out the skeletal history of women's activities in the pre-apartheid era in *Women and Resistance* still more.

In addition several recent biographies and autobiographies of important activists have added their perspectives on women's struggles to the literature, notably Helen Joseph's *Side by Side*[10] and Frances Baard's *My Spirit Is Not Banned*.[11] These are invaluable records, melding together first-hand perspectives of past events and direct and indirect insights into the diverse routes women followed into political activism. There is enormous scope for further in-depth biographical studies, ones that go beyond the useful but limited pen sketches of 'heroines of the struggle', to probe in more analytical fashion the place and meaning of political activism in these women's lives. What about the life of Lilian Ngoyi, for a start?[12] It would be very useful, although even more difficult, for the lives of less prominent activists to be documented and explored in this way as well.

Complementing this political history has been a great flowering of work in the broad field of 'social history' since the 1970s, which has added considerably to our understanding of the processes of urbanisation and proletarianisation, the backdrop to much of the discussion in *Women and Resistance*. Some of this work has important things to say about women as well.[13] Debbie Gaitskell's study of women's organisation within the churches serves as a useful counterpoint to interpretations of women's political activism. Her work explores the impact of Christian ideas about womanhood and motherhood on gender and inter-generational relations, while also pointing to the need to examine critically one-dimensional notions of religious women's conservatism and acquiescence to patriarchal authority in the church.[14] Work by William Beinart and by Helen Bradford has begun to show the extent of women's organisation and resistance in rural areas in the 1920s.[15] Collectively this work broadens the context in which the political organisations described in *Women and Resistance* need to be viewed, and extends our understanding of the diverse forms of women's organisation.

At the same time, the scope of the analysis has widened. A growing body of literature is beginning to probe the meaning of and role assigned to motherhood and mothering within the liberation movement, both historically and in the contemporary period;[16] this is touched on further below. Finally, writing about women in South African history has begun to move beyond the early 'rectificatory and recovery' preoccupations that to some extent determined my original interest in the history of women's political organisation, to look at the workings of gender and its significance in shaping political practice and theory. Belinda Bozzoli's seminal 1983 article, 'Marxism, Feminism and South African Studies',[17] remains a key point of entry into these debates. More recently, Michelle Friedman and Shireen Hassim have begun to raise important questions about the gendered nature of politics and women's formulation of their organisational priorities, while Deborah Posel has redirected critical attention to the concept of 'patriarchy' in South Africa and 'the apparent contradiction of African women's defiance of, and submission to, patriarchal values'.[18] It would be a fine project to re-examine the source material for *Women and Resistance* in the light of these theoretical developments.

'Women's Studies' is, itself, becoming a subject of analysis and debate.[19] At the recent conference on 'Women and Gender in Southern Africa' at the University of Natal, a highly contentious issue was the racial division of labour that is very evident in this (as in other) fields of academic work.[20] Black women are voicing their frustration that they remain so often the objects rather than practitioners of research. A decade after *Women and Resistance* was published, there is still no major historical study of the anti-pass campaign by those with the most direct connection to the issue and the experience, African women – a tremendous gap and a reflection of the dearth of African women historians more generally. Elsewhere I have argued against the position that 'only blacks can write about black experience, or women about women's experience – or French people about French history' while affirming the critical importance of the perspectives of historians who are black.[21] It is obvious that women's and gender studies are experiencing something of a lift-off; the interest in the 'Women and Gender' conference in Durban at the end of January 1991 is testimony to that. However, until black women are fully engaged in the process of recovery and, more important, theorising of gender relations in both the past and the present, the reach of this work will remain limited, its potential for radical transformation of knowledge only partially realised.

Women's emancipation and national liberation struggles

Women and Resistance raises what is today a central strategic issue in the debates about gender subordination in South Africa: to what extent can and should women look to the national liberation struggle to eradicate sexism and the oppression of women. When it was first published, the implication that national liberation movements did not and could not address the problem of patriarchy, thereby necessitating an independent women's movement, was seen as divisive within the liberation movement. Today, as victory over apartheid moves into the realm of feasible rather than utopian politics, so, finally, more serious attention is being given to what the most appropriate ordering of the relationship between women's and national liberation should be.

In the preface to the first edition of *Women and Resistance* I noted that it 'is not a general history of all political organisations among women, nor is it a history of feminism in South Africa'. Rather, I saw it as 'a history of a movement that in its preoccupations and aims reflected the dominant concerns of the majority of South African women' (p. xxvi). In its formal statements, the FSAW saw the women's struggle in South Africa as a two-pronged one: first and foremost, the struggle for national liberation and the overthrow of apartheid structures, and second, coupled to the former in some hazy way, the struggle by women against the 'laws and institutions' that discriminated against them as women. This 'prong' achieved its clearest articulation in the Women's Charter which the FSAW adopted in 1954 at its inaugural conference, and tended to be pushed to one side thereafter. The nature of the link between the two was never theorised, and, as *Women and Resistance* makes clear, the first aim dominated the FSAW's programme. For most members it was their blackness rather than their femaleness that ultimately determined their political practice – although the power of the pass campaign to mobilise women undoubtedly lay in its fusion of these two elemental strands of African women's identity around a single issue, and much of the FSAW's programme was directed at women in their role as mothers.

Inasmuch as discrimination against women was looked at, it was often as the barrier to women's full participation in the national struggle – i.e., as a means to an end rather than an end in itself. Very few of the FSAW's members would have described themselves as feminists, and the formal commitment to women's emancipation was overshadowed by practices and ideas that could only be described as patriarchal. As I tried to show in *Women and Resistance* and as I discuss further below, this does not mean that there were not moments of explicit feminist consciousness or less articulate murmurings of resistance to male domination and exploitation within the organisation and among individual members: the very process of organising as women involved a conscientising exposure to the power imbalances between men and women within the Congress Alliance and society at large.[22] But such moments were always subordinated to the claims of national liberation. Women's struggles against male domination, whether in their families, workplace or political life, were for the most part private and riddled with ambiguity. Few would have acknowledged them as 'political'. These were struggles 'without a name', to adopt the phrase used by Betty Friedan to describe the roots of the contemporary women's movement in the United States.[23]

Thirty-five years later, with the experience of women in post-colonial situations in the region – most notably Zimbabwe and Mozambique – before one, the limitations of this easy coupling of gender and national struggles have become more apparent. A recent, telling development, which serves to crystallise the issues involved, has been the decision by the Organisation of Mozambican Women (OMM) to separate from FRELIMO, in order to better represent women's gendered interests in independent Mozambique. This comes after years of loyal obedience to FRELIMO's formally gender-neutral but actually gender-biased programme to build socialism in this war-ravaged country.[24] Criticisms of national liberation movements for failing to deliver the promise of women's emancipation have now moved out of academic journals into organisational position papers. Today the ANC acknowledges that the emancipation of women is a worthy goal in itself and, crucially, not an inevitable corollary of victory against colonialism and white supremacy. For many it has come as a bitter disappointment that this is not so. Nevertheless, its recent (some might say belated) recognition by the major liberation movement in South Africa remains a breakthrough of enormous strategic significance for a feminist women's movement in this country.

The 'Statement of the National Executive Committee of the African National Congress on the emancipation of women in South Africa' of 2 May 1990 spells out this new understanding explicitly; it is a pathbreaking document. 'The experience of other societies has shown that the emancipation of women is not a by-product of a struggle for democracy, national liberation or socialism. It has to be addressed in its own right within our organisation, the mass democratic movement and in the society as a whole.'[25] The NEC goes on to propose a national debate around a Charter of Women's Rights 'which will elaborate and reinforce our constitution, so that in their own voice women define the issues of greatest concern to them and establish procedures for ensuring that the rights claimed are made effective'.[26]

This statement has been met with considerable enthusiasm and satisfaction by feminists within and without the ANC, and deservedly so. It legitimates struggles against gender hierarchy in a way that is new for mainstream political organisations. But, as hardly needs to be pointed out, the gap between rhetoric and practice remains a large and difficult one to bridge. There is a real danger that this document will remain ghettoised in the realm of 'women's policy issues' rather than inform ANC planning at all levels. Such discussions as it has generated have taken place largely at women's forums. While today it would be really crass for leadership within the ANC to belittle the struggle against sexism, the reticence on gender issues in any but the most obviously women-centred contexts is disturbing. As Hassim points out, 'neither the Women's Charter nor the May 2 statement have had the kind of attention they deserve, either from the Women's League or from the NEC [National Executive Committee of the ANC]. Why, for example, has the Harare document received such widespread coverage in the alternative media and the May 2 statement been ignored?'[27]

Furthermore, lurking within the document is a familiar tension between the old, instrumentalist reasons for emancipating women – as a means to an end, the strengthening of the movement – and a new, more coherent and essentially feminist commitment to gender equality in all areas of society. Thus, on the one hand, the NEC notes: 'The absence of sufficient numbers of women in our organisations, especially at decision-making levels, and the lack of a strong mass women's organisation has been to the detriment of our struggle. As a consequence the particular concerns of more than half of our people are hardly heard when we define our strategies and determine our tactics. ... The realisation of *our objective of a non-racial and democratic South Africa* is dependent upon the extent to which we are able to address and mobilise all the people of South Africa, men and women.'[28]

In similar vein, a little later: 'we believe it is imperative to address the inequalities women face in every aspect of our work. By adopting such an approach we will bring women in their millions into active participation in all our forms of struggle and at all levels.' On the other hand, the NEC acknowledges the importance of 'the formulation of national policy regarding the emancipation of women and the promotion of women's development in our country' and talks favourably about constitutional guarantees against 'laws, customs, traditions and practices which discriminate against women'.[29]

Clearly black women have a dual interest – in national liberation and in women's emancipation – so these positions are not in themselves incompatible: their articulation within the document can be interpreted as the restatement of the two-pronged set of goals which women have themselves repeatedly identified for so long. Women's interests, as Maxine Molyneux has pointed out, are broader than gender interests.[30] What needs to be addressed, however, is how these different emphases will translate into organisational priorities and practice: whether the national struggle will continue to dictate the terms on which women's gender struggles can be waged or not. Given the strongly patriarchal character and history of the ANC one cannot take its conversion to feminism for granted. But even were these statements coming out of a different tradition, it is still doubtful that a nationalist movement is the best vehicle through which women can struggle for their emancipation from patriarchy.

Key thinkers on gender issues within the ANC are aware of the limitations of the ANCWL as an instrument of women's emancipation. In the words of Frene Ginwala:

> I don't think the ANC Women's League *can* liberate women. To assume that it can, that is ignoring political reality. It is true that as a national liberation movement the ANC's priority is national liberation. ... But we have progressed by moving to integrate into it, an understanding of gender oppression and a commitment to the emancipation of women. And the Women's League has taken on an autonomous role. But being realistic we have got to accept that when it comes to a choice, either or, the decision is more than likely to fall towards national liberation. I mean that is by virtue and definition of what the organisation is.[31]

She goes on to propose a structure that she believes could push for 'a real challenge to gender oppression and the real emancipation of women': a national women's organisation to which a whole range of women's organisations, including the Women's League, could affiliate. In this way, she argues, 'women's interests' would not be pushed aside by the pressing claims of the national liberation movement.[32]

What has not yet been thoroughly debated, however, is the degree to which such a structure would be independent of indirect ANC control and pressures to conform to the priorities of the national struggle anyway. The proposed organisation has much in common with the FSAW of the 1950s – where, as I show in *Women and Resistance,* the ANC remained the ultimate source of authority, with the power and the status to override the FSAW's own decisions at key moments, such as in the handling of the anti-pass demonstrations in

Johannesburg in 1958 (see chapter 18). For these reasons the parallels with the organisations of the 1950s warrant serious attention.

In the mid-1950s there was vigorous debate amongst the founders of the FSAW about the best membership structure for the fledgling organisation. The Cape leadership, centred around Ray Alexander and Dora Tamana, wanted an individual membership, while the Transvaal region pushed, successfully as it turned out, for a federation of affiliated organisations (see chapters 14 and 20). It is significant that one of the staunchest advocates of individual membership was Ray Alexander, a committed feminist. For the proponents of a federation two key and somewhat contradictory motivations dominated: the fear that an autonomous organisation would compete with the ANCWL, and the conviction that an autonomous women's organisation was not feasible: there would not be the support to sustain it. A proponent of individual membership noted: 'We believe that this opposition to individual membership is due to a fear that if our organisation becomes a mass organisation, it will draw women away from the ANC and perhaps lead to divided loyalties. We do not think there is any justification for this fear, but we might not be able to dispel it easily or quickly.'[33] For the advocates of federation, 'Any women's organisation that stands outside this [the national liberation] struggle must stand apart from the mass of women.'[34] The hegemony of the national struggle in the construction of oppositional politics was clear.

This decision had significant consequences for the subsequent operation of the FSAW. It meant that the basis of the FSAW's membership was the ANCWL, whose priorities and internal organisational commitments inevitably exerted enormous influence over the new women's organisation. The space for women to raise and address issues of concern that fell outside the agenda of the national liberation movement was, as a result, that much more circumscribed. In practice, major conflict did not arise – the women felt their primary loyalty to be to the national liberation movement, and whenever there was a potential conflict of interest, it was this that overrode other considerations, as in the 1958 anti-pass campaign in Johannesburg. Nevertheless, the agenda for the FSAW was *structurally*, not just by choice of its members, submerged in that of the ANC; its structure made it that much more difficult for those struggles 'that have no name' to be identified and inserted on the agenda of liberation as legitimate political issues. At the same time, decision-making within the FSAW was complicated and at certain critical moments handicapped by the fact that the ANCWL was accountable in two different directions: to the NEC of the ANC, and to the FSAW.[35]

The intention today is not to replicate the FSAW. For one thing, a much broader range of women's organisations, including specifically feminist ones such as Rape Crisis, is being mooted. For another, the Women's League of today is constituted in such a way as to have far greater autonomy within the ANC than before. No longer 'a department or sub-section as it has been in the past', it will 'engage in its own decision-making within overall ANC policy, it will have its own funding, the right to own property, control bank accounts, in other words, the real mechanisms of power.'[36] According to Ginwala, the only structural link between the ANCWL and the NEC will be through the head of the League, who is automatically a member of the NEC.[37] Furthermore, as already noted, the commitment to women's emancipation within the ANC is far more developed than it was in the 1950s.

The degree to which the Women's League will in fact be able to develop as an autonomous body, as well as the degree to which it will be able to develop a more explicitly feminist agenda, has still to be established. Developments to date are not encouraging, but it has to be recognised that in its reconstituted form it is still a very young organisation. But even were it to consolidate itself quickly, the question of its political priorities remains an issue for proponents of the women's alliance to confront.

Implicit in the NEC statement is that the ANC, through the Women's League, will take the lead in the struggle against women's oppression: thus the ANCWL must initiate the campaign for a Charter of Women's Rights 'which will elaborate and reinforce our constitution, so that in their own voice women define the issues of greatest concern to them'.[38] But can the ANCWL be the most effective body to take on this role? Without in any way downplaying its political significance or the importance of its commitment to gender equality, there are cogent reasons for thinking it is not. One major limitation has to be its partisan location within the violently divided terrain of black oppositional politics, which will hinder the incorporation of women who are not ANC supporters into the proposed alliance. Another is the continued demands of the national liberation struggle on Women's League members and organisational resources. Given the enormous task of 'mobilising and organising women into the liberation struggle',[39] how independent can the ANCWL be in its formulation of its aims and tactics and the leadership it offers to the women's movement? Since the primary goal of the ANCWL must, as Ginwala has pointed out, be the national liberation struggle, this will surely shape the concerns that it will bring to the alliance, where it will dominate as it did the FSAW in the 1950s. Already its political priorities extend beyond the dismantling of white supremacy, to the establishment of an ANC government in a future constitutional dispensation. Furthermore, despite the greater autonomy of the ANCWL today, the problem of dual accountability that the FSAW experienced in the 1950s can be anticipated in the national alliance that Ginwala and others are proposing.

On the other hand, the critics of individual membership in the 1950s were probably correct. Given the meagre resources at the women's disposal, as well as the enormous legitimacy of the national struggle, it would have been very difficult, if not impossible, to mobilise women in significant numbers into a women's movement outside the ambit of the liberation movement then – and the same is most probably true of today. While there is greater organisational commitment to women's emancipation now than in the past, this is still not a project with a mass following or unquestioned political credibility and urgency. It is instructive that the OMM has only broken away from FRELIMO long after independence had been won in Mozambique, when FRELIMO's transformation from a liberation movement into a government is complete. At this stage, an autonomous, mass-based women's movement with an explicitly feminist agenda appears outside the realm of feasible politics. Given the current situation, alliance politics, as in the proposed national women's organisation, is probably the best way for feminists to build upon the concern with women's issues and problems in current political debate. This, however, means that feminists have to establish some way of consolidating their presence as an advocacy group within the broader alliance, so that they can play a constructive role of education and challenge around gender issues. It also means that the nature of the alliance and its programme has to be carefully considered, to be as inclusive of progressive women's groupings as possible.

Motherhood, the family and the conservatism of women

Recently researchers have begun to examine the role of motherhood within the national liberation movement and what Julie Wells identifies as 'mother-ism' – 'a women's politics of resistance [which] affirms obligations traditionally assigned to women and calls on the community to respect them'.[40] To date the debate has centred on two related issues: (1) the way in which motherhood has been perceived and utilised by political organisations, and (2) the way in which African women have themselves organised politically around the notion of motherhood, the aspect I wish to develop here. This identification with motherhood has generally been interpreted as evidence of women's conser-vatism and defence of patriarchal values and institutions. Thus Wells: 'Mother-ism is clearly not feminism. Women swept up in motherist movements are not fighting for their own personal rights as women, but for their rights as mothers. ... Motherist movements must be recognised as limited in scope, duration and success in achieving their goals.'[41] This in turn has led to attempts to under-stand the apparent paradox of women's militancy in protest coupled to their apparent conservatism in formulating their goals.[42]

The essential conservatism of women in the anti-pass campaign *vis-à-vis* patriarchy is a view I adopt in *Women and Resistance*. Thus in describing the anti-pass demonstrations in Zeerust in 1957, I state (p. 264):

> For the most part, opposition to passes was bound up with a conservative defence of traditional institutions – chieftainship, the patriarchal family, established sex roles. The women who defied the reference book units were not demonstrating consciously for freedom or equality; one of the strongest reasons why women were opposed to passes was that they were seen as a direct threat to the family.

In assessing the FSAW I state (p. 264):

> Patriarchal ideology ran deep and was not confined to male members of the Congress Alliance only.... The conservative defence of home and custom which had charac-terised much of the protests by rural women in the 1950s helped shape urban women's anti-pass protests too: 'Verwoerd is to break our homes with this [*sic*] pass laws,' commented one woman at an ANCWL meeting at Moroka township, Johannes-burg, in 1955.
> Within the FSAW, the degree to which the importance of the battle against sex discrimination was stressed varied from woman to woman and from occasion to occasion. Even amongst the FSAW leadership, where women's rights and the aboli-tion of sex discrimination were strongly endorsed, women's domestic role as wife and, more often, mother was continually being stressed. Frequently 'mother' and 'woman' were interchangeable terms in the FSAW rhetoric.

Today I would wish to look more carefully at the assumption that women's defence of their maternal roles constituted a negation of their rights as women

– that women's rights are somehow at odds with the maternal role – and that organisation around the latter is evidence of an unproblematic conservatism and defence of patriarchy. What follows is tentative and sketchy; this is, I believe, an area requiring both more research and further analysis. It is an area where the contribution of black women historians who are alive to the subtleties of South African languages and culture would be particularly valuable.

That African women have frequently been organised around appeals that were addressed to them as mothers is not in question. As I note above, 'women' and 'mothers' were often used interchangeably in the rhetoric of the FSAW and the organisations that preceded it. That confining women to the role of mother is restrictive and also marginalises the large numbers of women who, by choice, circumstance or age, are childless is also not being disputed.[43] What needs to be more carefully looked at, however, is the content and meaning of 'mother' and 'motherhood' for the women who became involved in the FSAW, the nature of 'the family' they were defending, as well as the role of other factors, such as economic self-interest, in pushing women to rebel against the pass laws. What set of relationships and interests was at stake for women when they rallied in defence of 'motherhood' and 'the family' in the anti-pass campaign and how might these have differed for different groups of women? What did 'mother' mean, and why did the term resonate so deeply with women, that 'woman' and 'mother' could be used interchangeably? How might the meaning have varied according to class, religious affiliation and age and between urban and rural dwellers? Are motherhood and its defence necessarily incompatible with progressive politics and especially a feminist politics, as Wells's formulation suggests? These are the sorts of questions I think would be revealing to ask more critically of my sources today. To answer them requires an understanding of the complex, often fractured nature of ideology as well as an appreciation of women's own, gendered interests.

A start in unravelling the many strands in the ideology of the family and motherhood has been made in the collection of essays I edited on *Women and Gender in Southern Africa to 1945,* which begins to look at the complex interaction historically between what is termed 'settler' and 'indigenous' ideologies of gender. Jeff Guy's analysis of the central role of women's fertility in precapitalist society, and the 'social standing and social integrity' that this accorded to women, suggests that historically motherhood in African society cannot be equated with submission and passivity.[44] The association of mother with these qualities is a feature of Western rather than African society; and the unexamined assumption that this is what 'mother' must have meant to female anti-pass protesters in the 1950s and before suggests a Eurocentric interpretative bias. A further implication is that the women's militancy is neither as surprising nor out of character as both contemporary and subsequent commentators have tended to portray it. Certainly by the mid-twentieth century Western and specifically Christian notions of motherhood and male authority within the household had, as I express it in *Women and Gender in Southern Africa to 1945,* 'been grafted onto the stump of indigenous formulations'[45] so that these earlier ideas were no longer pre-eminent: but, as the various essays in that collection indicate, the settler sex–gender system that came to dominate was neither pure nor uncontested. What this meant for women in the FSAW individually and collectively, how older meanings about womanhood and more specifically motherhood might have persisted and in what forms, and whether there were any differences between leadership and members in this regard, are all aspects that need to be further investigated. I am proposing that for many women there was not a major contradiction between their self-identification as mothers and their involvement in political protest.

We also need to look more critically at 'the family' that women in the anti-pass campaign were defending. The designation of this defence as conservative suggests that what was at risk was the classic patriarchal family of male head of household, wife and dependent children. But can we assume this was always, even generally, the case? Being clearer about what family form or forms women were defending in turn requires more information than I put together about the range of women in the FSAW and in the anti-pass campaigns: their class, marital, occupational and religious locations, as well as the variations between rural and urban contexts. What we do know is that the twentieth century saw a marked increase in female-headed households among the African population[46] and that for significant numbers of women, the process of proletarianisation and urbanisation provided opportunities to escape domestic relationships that were experienced as onerous and restrictive. What is also of note here is precisely the identification of women within the FSAW with the role of mother, rather than that of wife: the central concern that they articulated was most often the defence and protection of their children, not of their husbands or of the institution of marriage *per se.*

Furthermore, when women migrated to the cities, economic imperatives mingled with and often dominated emotional ties and needs. This was true even of those who were going specifically to search for or join their husbands. The institution of marriage (whether a marriage recognised as such by the state or not) is a fundamentally economic institution, as feminists and Marxists have long recognised. This is not to deny the part played by emotional and sexual ties in marital relationships, nor to disregard the tremendous damage that segregationist and apartheid policies have wreaked on African families, but to place these in a larger context. That the explanation of these illegal or rebellious acts was often couched in terms of upholding the family and the sanctity of the marriage relationship does not exclude the operation of other more individualistic motives, nor eclipse the priority women accorded the maternal rather than the conjugal role. The precise configuration of motives no doubt varied considerably and would need to be investigated further, but the assumption that what was at stake for women in the anti-pass campaign was a simple defence of the implicitly Western and explicitly patriarchal family needs to be rejected. We cannot presume that in organising as mothers (or potential and future mothers) women were simply endorsing the gender relations of the patriarchal family.

Even were this the case, I believe it is still inadequate to categorise a women's politics constructed around the maternal and familial role as inherently conservative and leave it at that. This labelling seems to rest on an uncritical acceptance of conventional views (which one might describe as masculinist) of what the domain of the political is, with its corresponding designation of the domestic as the realm of the personal and therefore, by definition, the apolitical. Feminists have long criticised both the notion that the personal is not political, and the assumption that domestic issues and family relationships are private rather than social (and political) matters. Hassim's insistence on the gendered nature of politics is useful here, in reminding us that women and men perceive their political priorities and interests in different, gendered ways.[47] Women invest in motherhood (and the family) and this needs to be recognised and understood – understood not simply as the product of their socialisation or patriarchal ideology but as something mediated by their own experience of this role.

Regardless of the way in which the sexual division of labour in the family underwrites women's general subordination in society, for many women motherhood brings with it both a degree of social power and emotional satisfaction. At the same time, the severe restrictions on women's mobility and entry to the cities imposed by influx control threatened directly their access to resources, both for themselves and for their children. Thus the anti-pass campaign represented a gendered politics that was, in part at least, of the women's own making. What I am proposing is that the women in the FSAW had an essentially positive understanding of the value and power of mother-hood, at least partly rooted in their own experience of it and sanctioned by the past, and that in defending this they were defending their gendered interests, rather than patriarchy as such.

I am not suggesting that women have not suffered oppression or that patriarchal ideology has played an insignificant role in shaping women's roles and views of themselves. Rather, I am wanting to question the explanatory force that I and others have attributed to this with regard to women's political behaviour. What needs to be further developed, it seems to me, is the way in which our very understanding of the nature of politics and, by extension, what is or is not conservative, has been structured by an essentially male interpreta-tion of the world. What I am trying to develop is a view that recognises women's agency and begins to take their demands seriously, on their own terms, as an expression of their particular location in society and their active engagement with that.[48] This may be a more fruitful way of dealing with the superficially contradictory relationship between women's political methods (their appar-ent 'militancy') and goals (their apparent 'conservatism') and explaining 'why women rebel'.

Feminism and South African history

Finally, I wish to address an issue which is only just becoming a subject of serious discussion: the legitimacy of a feminist critique in South African studies. The formulation of a feminist theory and methodology appropriate to South Africa's highly complex social order has barely begun. As a result of a very narrow reading of feminism as either 'bourgeois' or 'separatist', academ-ics and activists alike have, until recently, generally been chary of the notion of feminism and towards attempts, such as *Women and Resistance*, to use a feminist lens when looking at women's organisations historically and in the present. Thus, when this book first appeared, it was criticised for its 'feminist teleology' and for erroneously depicting the FSAW as a feminist organisation.[49] Although today I would want to refine and extend what I understand by feminist scholarship, I think the attempt to look at women's organisation in the twentieth century through a feminist lens was a valid one. If anything, my feminist lens was not sharp and powerful enough to do justice to all the conceptual, methodological and political issues involved; today I would want to argue that as an example of 'feminist' history, *Women and Resistance* does not go far enough.

But first of all, some definitions are needed. What does one mean by feminist and feminism? Rosemary Tong has noted that 'feminist theory is not one, but many, theories or perspectives and ... each feminist theory or perspective attempts to describe women's oppression, to explain its causes and consequences, and to prescribe strategies for women's liberation'.[50] In other words, a feminist is someone who perceives that women in a given society are oppressed *as women*, and believes that this should be changed. This is a very broad definition, one that does not presuppose the answer to the question *why* women should be oppressed, nor, even, how they are oppressed; hence the possibility for different types of theoretical traditions to exist under the broad rubric of feminism (and hence the fallaciousness of arguing that feminism equals 'bourgeois' feminism). Feminism is essentially a political project. It is this political commitment that gives to the best academic feminism its intensity and topicality, even when the matter under scrutiny is not a contemporary one. It is not, as Tong points out, a single theory of society or even of gender relations. Often something called 'feminism' is contrasted or related to a body of theory such as Marxism, but it seems to me that the two are not equivalent, any more than anti-racism and Marxism are – anti-racism, like feminism, cannot constitute a theory of society on its own.

Similarly, I do not believe there is a uniquely feminist methodology. Much of what has been put forward as distinctly feminist in research methodology has in fact been used by social scientists and historians who are not specifically feminist – trying to break down the hierarchical relationship between researcher and researched; moving away from quantitative to qualitative data; probing the ordinary, the social, even the personal, etc. What makes research feminist lies rather in the type of questions one is asking, the concern with the political project outlined above, as well as careful attention to gender stratification and the sexual division of labour in one's analysis of social relations and hierarchies.

A feminist history, then, is one that sees the subordination of women in a given society as a problem, requiring explanation and challenge; it is not something to be taken for granted, as part of the natural order of things. It is one that uses gender as a major category of social analysis. Furthermore, a feminist academic attaches real importance to this project: which is not to say that other issues, for instance the struggle against racism or colonialism, or other social categories such as race and class, are irrelevant or necessarily less important. Nor does a feminist perspective have to lead to sloppy and ethnocentric assumptions of 'global sisterhood' and the universality of Western-style patriarchy. Much of the most interesting feminist work and criticism in recent years, spurred by the criticisms of black feminists and nationalists, has been precisely to show up the limitations of these assumptions and the need for the existence of women's subordination, as well as the form it takes, to be established in each case. A feminist approach to the study of society does mean that the position of women in the society under investigation will be brought into focus, and that gender-sensitive questions will be asked of one's material. Depending on the subject being studied, such questions might include: Where were the women? How did they perceive their interests? What were their ideas on women's position? Was there a commitment to women's emancipation? To what extent were women's organisations aware of the oppression of women and how did they respond to that? How did men and women relate to each other? What was the nature of the sexual division of labour? Until very recently these were not questions that occurred to most historians; making the invisibility of women in history visible is a political achievement of the broad women's movement.

What needs to be made clear is that asking such questions is not at all the same as imposing feminist answers on the material, in the sense of insisting on a feminist consciousness where there is not one. This is one of the criticisms that has been levelled, unfairly I believe, at *Women and Resistance*. An analogy can be made with the way in which Marxist historians have used the theoretical construction of class to examine the extent or lack of class consciousness among workers and worker movements in the past. The concept of class interests has been a guiding one in probing how workers have actually organised themselves in specific circumstances. Thus, in the case of South African worker history, the notorious slogan of the white mineworkers of the 1920s, 'Workers of the World Unite, and Fight for a White South Africa', has been used again and again to reveal the lack of an overriding class consciousness and the depth of racial cleavage among South African workers: to demonstrate, in other words, the existence of other forms of stratification and consciousness.

Thus in analysing the anti-pass campaign and the women's organisations that were involved in it, there are two issues that need to be untangled and separated out. The first is the methodological one outlined above – the legitimacy of asking these feminist questions of the material, even if the subjects of research do not perceive themselves as feminists. This is what I tried to do in *Women and Resistance* and, as I indicate above, I believe this is not simply a legitimate but a necessary exercise if we are to understand gender relations and the position of women historically. The second issue is an interpretative one – the extent to which one can perceive a feminist consciousness, in the sense outlined above, in the women and organisations studied here. Here the evidence is, I believe, far denser and less amenable to a simple negative than some of the critics of *Women and Resistance* have suggested.

What *Women and Resistance* documents, I believe, is the existence of those feminist 'moments' already referred to: moments when patriarchal relations were directly called into question and challenged. It makes very clear that for the women involved in the FSAW (to limit the discussion to that organisation) their primary commitment was to the national liberation movement. It also makes clear that the FSAW generally endorsed what are described as conventional views on the sexual division of labour and male authority in society.

Nevertheless, it also documents examples of direct resistance to male domination – the discussion surrounding the adoption of the Women's Charter, for instance, as well as the challenge that the FSAW threw out to the NEC of the Congress Alliance from time to time, most notably over the handling of the anti-pass demonstrations in Johannesburg in 1958. Another significant episode, the treatment of which highlights both the interpretative and the methodological issues involved, concerns the document 'What Women Demand' which was discussed at the 'Congress of the Mothers' meeting in Johannesburg in 1955. In the heated discussion which took place over a proposal for birth control clinics, those members of the audience who supported the demand were voicing a challenge to men's control over their sexuality and reproductive powers (see p. 183).[51] *Women and Resistance* also documents distinctly anti-feminist moments or, rather, eruptions in the operations of the ANC and other organisations documented here, such as the circumstances surrounding the publication in 1956 of the *Sechaba* article 'Don't stifle the work of the Women's Federation'.

Within the FSAW there were some women, such as Ray Alexander, with a strong commitment to the emancipation of women, who did not shy away from the feminist label; Alexander's influence in formulating explicitly feminist policy positions, such as in the Women's Charter, is clear. There were many more for whom the term 'feminist' was an unfamiliar, even perhaps a threatening one. Nevertheless these were the women who cheered Lilian Ngoyi when she said from the floor at the opening conference that 'the husbands talked of democracy but did not practise it' (see p. 158). This incident cannot be explained away as the manouevrings of a leader out of touch with her membership, whose thinking was in advance of her time.

Describing these events as 'feminist' or 'proto-feminist' is not an imposition on the material, once one ceases to see feminism as involving a single theoretical paradigm and allows for the ebb and flow of moments of anti-patriarchal consciousness. Explaining them and their relationship to the dominant discourse and to women's submission to patriarchal relationships in other situations is another matter. *Women and Resistance* does not present a coherent theory of gendered politics in twentieth-century South Africa; it is, as already noted, a task that has just begun. As suggested in the previous section, I believe that developing this theory requires taking seriously women's own understandings of their roles and priorities – moving beyond seeing them as mere victims of patriarchal domination to an appreciation of their own, gendered interests. It also requires taking their history seriously. This *Women and Resistance* attempts to do.

Notes

My thanks to Michelle Friedman, Shireen Hassim and Gerry Maré for their helpful comments on an earlier draft.

1. These include the 'Malibongwe conference', Amsterdam, 8–19 January 1990; 'Putting women on the agenda', Lawyers for Human Rights, University of the Witwatersrand, 23–25 November 1990; 'Women and gender in southern Africa', Gender Research Group, University of Natal, 30 January–2 February 1991.

2. For a full listing of material, readers are referred to the revised edition of *Women in Southern Africa: A Bibliography* (Durban: Durban Women's Bibliography Group, 1991).

3. Julie Wells, 'The history of black women's struggle against pass laws in South Africa, 1900–1960', unpublished Ph.D. thesis, Columbia University, 1982, which is to be published by the University of the Witwatersrand Press. See also her 'Why women rebel', *Journal of Southern African Studies*, 10, 1 (1983).

4. Wells, 'Why women rebel', p.63. I think a fuller answer to why (and which) women rebel awaits (1) more empirical work on the range of locations of demonstrations and the background of participants, and (2) a conceptual and theoretical framework that utilises the notion of gendered politics referred to below.

5. Kathy Eales, 'Patriarchs, passes and privilege' in Philip Bonner *et al.* (eds), *Holding Their Ground* (Johannesburg: Ravan Press and Witwatersrand University Press, 1989).

6. Jenny Schreiner, 'Women working for their freedom: FCWU and AFCWU and the women question', unpublished M.A. thesis, University of Cape Town, 1986.

7. Iain Edwards, 'Mkhumbane our home. African shantytown society in Cato Manor Farm, 1946–1960', unpublished Ph.D., University of Natal, Durban, 1989.

8. Frene Ginwala, 'Women and the African National Congress 1912–1943', in *Agenda*, 8 (1990), p.77.

9. The role of Indian women in political organisation has begun to receive attention. See for instance D. Chetty, '"Sammy" and "Mary" go to gaol: Indian women and South African politics in the 1940s', and also Uma Mesthrie-Dhupelia, 'From Rose Day shows to social welfare: White and Indian women in joint cooperation in the 1930s', both papers presented at the 'Women and gender in southern Africa' conference, University of Natal, 1991.

10. Helen Joseph, *Side by Side: The Autobiography of Helen Joseph* (London: Zed Books, 1986).

11. Frances Baard, *My Spirit Is Not Banned: As Told by Frances Baard to Barbie Schreiner* (Harare: Zimbabwe Publishing House, 1986).

12. A biography of Ray Simons (Alexander), by Muff Anderson, is in preparation.

13. See, for example, Paul la Hausse, 'The message of the warriors: The ICU, the labouring poor and the making of a popular political culture in Durban, 1925–1930' and Hilary Sapire, 'African settlement and segregation in Brakpan, 1900–1927', both in Philip Bonner *et al.* (eds), *Holding Their Ground* (Johannesburg: Ravan Press and the Witwatersrand University Press, 1989); Phil Bonner, '"Desirable or undesirable Basotho women?" Liquor, prostitution and the migration of Basotho women to the Rand, 1920–1945' in Cherryl Walker (ed.), *Women and Gender in Southern Africa to 1945* (Cape Town: David Philip, 1990); Shula Marks, *Not Either An Experimental Doll: The Separate Worlds of Three South Africa Women: Correspondence of Lily Moya, Mabel Palmer and Sibusiswe Makhanya* (Durban: University of Natal Press, 1987).

14. Deborah Gaitskell, 'Female mission initiatives: black and white women in three Witwatersrand churches, 1903–1939', unpublished Ph.D. thesis, University of London, 1981. A revised version is to be published by the University of the Witwatersrand Press. See also her '"Wailing for purity": Prayer unions, African mothers and adolescent daughters, 1912–1940' in S. Marks and R. Rathbone (eds), *Industrialisation and Social Change in South Africa* (London: Longman, 1982), and 'Devout domesticity? A century of African women's Christianity in South Africa' in C. Walker (ed.), *Women and Gender in Southern Africa to 1945.*

15. William Beinart, 'Amafelandawonye, the die-hards: Popular protest and women's movements in Herschel district in the 1920s' in William Beinart and Colin Bundy (eds), *Hidden Struggles in Rural South Africa: Politics and Popular Movements in the Transkei and Eastern Cape, 1890–1930* (London: James Currey, 1987), and Helen Bradford, '"We are now the men": Women's beer protests in the Natal countryside,

1929' in B. Bozzoli (ed.), *Class, Community and Conflict: Southern African Perspectives* (Johannesburg: Ravan Press, 1987).

16. See, for example, Deborah Gaitskell and Elaine Unterhalter 'Mother of the nation: A comparative analysis of nation, race and motherhood in Afrikaner nationalism and the African National Congress' in Nira Yuval-Davis and Floya Anthias (eds), *Woman–Nation–State* (London: Macmillan Press, 1989); Julie Wells, 'The rise and fall of motherism as a force in black women's resistance movements', paper presented at the conference on 'Women and gender in southern Africa', University of Natal, 1991.

17. In *Journal of Southern African Studies*, 9, 2 (1983).

18. Michelle Friedman, 'Gender, geography and urban form: A case study of Durban', unpublished M.Soc.Sci. thesis, University of Natal, Durban 1987; Shireen Hassim, 'Black women in political organisation: A case study of the Inkatha Women's Brigade', unpublished M.A. thesis, University of Natal, Durban, 1990; Deborah Posel, 'Women's powers, men's authority: Rethinking patriarchy', paper presented at the conference on 'Women and gender in southern Africa', University of Natal, Durban, 1991.

19. See, for instance, Ireen Dubell, 'Whither South African women's studies?', paper presented at the conference on 'Women and gender in southern Africa', University of Natal, 1991.

20. See the fothcoming report on the conference, produced by the Gender Research Group, University of Natal, Durban.

21. In 'Women and Gender in Southern Africa to 1945: An overview' in C. Walker (ed.), *Women and Gender in Southern Africa to 1945*, pp. 6-7.

22. Later in this Preface I define 'feminist' as someone who perceives that women are oppressed as women and believes that this should be challenged.

23. In *The Feminine Mystique* (New York: Dell, 1970).

24. On this relationship (written prior to OMM's decision to separate) see Signe Arnfred, 'Women in Mozambique: Gender struggle and gender politics' in *Review of African Political Economy*, 41 (1988).

25. 'Statement of the National Executive Committee of the African National Congress on the emancipation of women in South Afrca', reproduced in *Agenda*, 8 (1990), p. 19.

26. Ibid., p. 23.

27. Shireen Hassim, 'From handmaiden to comrade: The ANCWL and the question of political power', paper presented at the conference on 'Putting women on the agenda', Lawyers for Human Rights, University of the Witwatersrand, November 1990, p. 2.

28. 'Statement', *Agenda*, 8 (1990), p. 21. Emphasis added.

29. Ibid., p. 22.

30. Maxine Molyneux, 'Mobilization without emancipation? Women's interests, the state and revolution in Nicaragua', *Feminist Studies*, 11, 2 (1985).

31. In '"Picking up the gauntlet": Women discuss ANC statement' in *Agenda*, 8, p. 13.

32. Ibid.

33. FSAW correspondence 6.11.54, FSAW BII.

34. 'Report to the WIDF' p. 1, FSAW E.

35. The awkwardness of the FSAW's structure was compounded by the fact that some of its affiliates were not clearly constituted women's organisations but, rather, even more clumsy, female memberships of organisations (as in the case of the Congress of Democrats), also owing their primary loyalty to their parent body. See the discussion on the disagreement about the ratification of the FSAW constitution between the FSAW and the Congress of Democrats, chapter 16. There was also the problem that the banning of affiliated organisations by the government had on the

membership, such as the FSAW experienced after the banning of the ANC in 1960, described in chapter 22. This is not an issue for women's organisation at the moment, though probably few would be willing to declare yet that the spectre of bannings of organisations has been eradicated from the South African scene forever.

36. Ginwala in '"Picking up the gauntlet"', in *Agenda*, 8, p. 11.
37. Ibid., p. 11.
38. 'Statement of the National Executive of the African National Congress', *Agenda*, 8, p. 23.
39. Ibid., p. 21.
40. 'The rise and fall of motherism as a force in black women's resistance movements', citing Sara Ruddick, 'Maternal peace politics and women's resistance: The example of Argentine and Chile', *Barnard Occasional Papers on Women's Issues*, iv, 1 (1989).
41. 'The rise and fall of motherism', pp. 4-5.
42. See, for example, Deborah Posel, 'Women's powers, men's authority: Rethinking patriarchy'. In this she proposes that we utilise the distinction between 'power' ('the capacity of the individual or group to further their interests in the face of actual or potential resistance from others') and 'authority' ('power which is legitimised in terms of the hegemonic ideology of the society in question') to distinguish between women's struggles which challenge the patriarchal order and those which do not. While this is an important attempt to advance the analysis of gender relations, missing from it is the notion of gendered interests I develop here; it also reproduces the assumption that organisation as mothers necessarily involves a defence of patriarchy.
43. On this see Hassim, 'Where have all the women gone? Gender and politics in South African Debates', paper presented at the conference on 'Women and gender in southern Africa', University of Natal, 1991, p. 12: 'a discourse in which motherhood is the ultimate symbol of women's political heroism is in fact disempowering for women. Women's legitimate concerns become their *sole* concerns...' I make a similar point in a review of the article by Gaitskell and Unterhalter, 'Mothers of the nation: A comparative analysis of nation, race and motherhood in Afrikaner nationalism and the African National Congress'. In this I argue that 'one of the essential components of that struggle [for women's emancipation] is precisely to challenge the assumption that women and mother are interchangeable categories – to force recognition of other roles and identities for women.' See *Agenda*, 6 (1990), p. 47.
44. Jeff Guy, 'Gender oppression in southern Africa's precapitalist societies', in Walker (ed.), *Women and Gender in Southern Africa to 1945*.
45. C. Walker, 'Women and gender in Southern Africa to 1945: An overview' in Walker, *Women and Gender in Southern Africa to 1945*, p. 8.
46. Posel, 'Women's powers, men's authority', p. 3.
47. Shireen Hassim, 'Where have all the women gone? Gender and politics in South African debates'.
48. This is obviously a project that would also have to take into account the ways in which political organisations have appropriated and attempted to use for their own purposes ideas about motherhood and marriage.
49. Debbie Budlender *et al.*, 'Women and resistance in South Africa: review article' in *Journal of Southern African Studies*, 10, 1 (1983), pp. 134-5, and 'Women and resistance: A critical review' in *Work in Progress*, 34 (1984). I have already responded in detail to the issues raised in these reviews and do not wish to pursue all the points here. The interested reader is referred to my reply, 'Women and resistance: In search of South African feminism' in *Work in Progress*, 36 (1985). For an analysis of the context in which this debate took place, see Josette Cole '*Women and Resistance in South Africa* and the debates surrounding it: Coming to terms with its historiographic and political implications', unpublished paper, Department of Economic History,

University of Cape Town, 1985.

50. Rosemary Tong, *Feminist Thought. A Comprehensive Introduction* (London: Unwin Hyman, 1989), p. 1.

51. Helen Joseph has dismissed this incident as a product of her 'social work approach' which 'drew lively protest from both men and women' (in *Side by Side*, p. 44). Her assessment is taken up by Budlender *et al.* in their review of *Women and Resistance*. This account ignores the fact that some women at the meeting supported the call, and also misrepresents my own account of the discussion and its significance. See the discussion in my reply to Budlender *et al.* (in *Work in Progress*, 36) and the assessment in Cole, '*Women and Resistance in South Africa* and the debates surrounding it'.

PREFACE TO THE FIRST EDITION

This book is based on an MA thesis I submitted to the University of Cape Town in 1978[1] and have since revised and amended. It traces the development of a women's movement in South Africa, within the context of the national liberation movement, from 1910 to the early 1960s. By 'national liberation' is understood the liberation of the black majority of South Africans from the burden of white supremacy, the replacement of a white minority government with majority rule. This was the minimum political programme of the Congress Alliance, a loose alliance of black nationalists, trade unionists and white radicals which came together in the early 1950s under the leadership of the African National Congress [ANC].

The women's movement with which this book is concerned, developed out of the organisations that contributed, in varying degrees, towards the emergence of that Alliance—the ANC, the Communist Party of South Africa [CPSA], the South African Indian Congress [SAIC] and various trade unions and grassroots political organisations. It came to maturity with the establishment of the Federation of South African Women [FSAW], formed in 1954 within the ambit of the Congress Alliance. It is thus a specific kind of women's movement that is being considered. This is not a general history of all political organisations among women, nor is it a history of feminism in South Africa. It is, however, a history of a movement that in its preoccupations and aims reflected the dominant concerns of the majority of South African women. As Helen Joseph, National Secretary of the FSAW, said in 1957, 'The fundamental struggle of the people is for National Liberation and. . . any women's movement that [stands] outside this struggle must stand apart from the mass of women.'

The book is divided into three parts. The first two parts look at the growth of political organisations among women from 1910 to 1939 and 1939 to 1953, against the background of the economic changes restructuring their position in society. The third part concentrates on the history of the FSAW after 1954. This is not a theoretical study. Nevertheless, since it is impossible to look at the women's movement in a theoretical vacuum, I have included a brief introduction which offers some general perspectives on the position of women. There is currently an enormous interest in the history of resistance in South Africa, but very little is known about the role that women and women's organisations have played within that. It is hoped that this study will help redress the balance and suggest further areas of research.

The reasons why so little is known about women's role in history are instructive. They reflect on the subordinate position that women have occupied in society, both historically and currently, as well as on the restrictions on knowledge that operate in South Africa. There is a dearth of both primary and secondary material on women. Partly, this is a product of most historians' preoccupation with political and constitutional rather than social history. Given their subordinate status within society, as well as their primarily domestic preoccupations, women have generally been excluded from the institutions of political power and, as a result, excluded from much orthodox historiography as well. The neglect of women is also a product of historians' own, often unconscious, bias against women, in itself a product of the very social attitudes that reinforce and perpetuate women's subordinate position within the larger society. This bias means that for many historians—female as well as male—women are, historically, invisible. Either their experiences and activities are not considered sufficiently important an area of research, or else the presence of women at particular historical junctures is simply not noticed.

Even when women have been politically active, as in the case of the FSAW, they have been ignored or overlooked by researchers. The anti-pass protests of African women in South Africa in the 1950s (in which the FSAW played a prominent part) were probably the most successful and militant of any resistance campaign mounted at that time. They were also an indication of the degree to which black women of the 1950s were throwing off both traditional and modern restraints on their independence and assertiveness. Yet in one of the major general histories of black opposition in South Africa for this time, E. Roux's study, *Time Longer than Rope*, the women's anti-pass campaign warrants barely a mention. Roux does not record the foundation of the FSAW in 1954. Even more remarkable, his year-by-year synopsis of major political events does not include the huge anti-pass demonstration by women which took place in August 1956 outside the Union Buildings, Pretoria. This demonstration, which brought together a crowd of women estimated at between ten and twenty thousand from all over the country, was a political highpoint of 1956, not only for the women who took part but for the entire Congress Alliance. Nevertheless, it is not featured in Roux's chronology—a chronology that is regarded as authoritative by many students of the period.

One of the premises underlying this book is that the study of history needs to be broadened to incorporate the female world as a legitimate area of research. Such a step will deepen our understanding not only of the position of women—50 per cent of the population—but of the workings of the total society at any one time as well. This does not mean that one can delineate a 'women's history' that forms a separate study from the history of society in general. Women do not form an isolated and homogeneous category that can be studied apart from society as a whole, any more than men do. Just as women need to be drawn into a more equal participation in the economic, social and political institutions of our society, so, too, 'women's history' needs to be integrated into our general histories. Yet at the same time, since women have, by and large, been bypassed by historians and since, moreover, their position in society has been stamped with its own, distinctive features, there is a place for detailed and specialised studies on women, their organisations and the sweep of their experience in those social spheres in which they have been active.

There are, however, more reasons than a simple lack of research why so little is known about this period. 'History' is not a neutral, objective collection of 'all the facts', the writing of history has an ideological dimension which can be used to serve political ends. In South Africa much of the history of popular resistance and organisations has been deliberately suppressed by the state in order to maintain and extend its domination and control of the people. Thus, access to much of the primary and secondary material that does exist, and is essential for any thorough study of the period, is restricted or even denied completely by various security laws and regulations operating in this country. To give but one example, during the course of my own research, the regulations allowing post-graduate students access to banned material in public libraries were tightened up. As a result, I was unable to complete reading through all the issues of the newspaper *New Age* (banned in 1962) which the South African Library in Cape Town holds. Since *New Age* was the only newspaper to give regular and comprehensive coverage to affairs and organisations linked to the Congress Alliance, this was a major setback.

The frustrations of conventional library research are compensated for, however, by the richness of research in the field. One of the most exciting and personally rewarding sources of information has come from interviews with women who took part in the events described. Oral history and oral evidence are only just beginning to be recognised as legitimate and valuable sources of material by South African historians, yet this kind of research is essential if our lost history is to be retrieved and preserved.

The restrictions on research into women do not come only from the state. Even within the national liberation movement there is sometimes hostility towards any study that smacks of 'women's liberation'. The women's movement is equated with bourgeois feminism; it is regarded as a threat, a reactionary movement that will divide men from women and weaken the combined struggle of both against their common enemy. This view fails to do justice to either the commitment the women's movement in South Africa has shown to the common struggle, or the intimate relationship that exists between the women's movement and the struggle for liberation. As the following pages will show, black women in this country suffer a triple oppression—colour, class and sex. One of the major contributions of the FSAW to the national liberation movement was to point that out and to insist that only when all three categories of exploitation and oppression have been removed will true liberation, for all the people, have been achieved.

Finally, it becomes necessary to point out that since this study deals with an area and a period that is still politically sensitive today, certain difficulties have been encountered with the citing and acknowledging of sources. Where possible I have identified my source; occasionally, however, I have been obliged to respect my informant's desire for anonymity. In addition, it is necessary to state that responsibility for all opinions expressed and material used rests with me alone.

[1]   The financial assistance of the Human Sciences Research Council and the University of Cape Town Council towards this research is hereby acknowledged.

Women
and
Resistance
in South Africa

INTRODUCTION

'To Be Born Branded'—Some General Perspectives on the Position of Women

Women Under Capitalism

In 1883 Olive Schreiner, perhaps South Africa's most famous feminist, cried out in frustration: 'But this one thought stands, never goes—if I might but be one of those born in the future, then perhaps to be born a woman will not be to be born branded.'[1] It is a cry that almost a hundred years later has still not been answered. Socially, economically, legally—in all spheres of society—women occupy a distinct and subordinate position to men. Changes and developments there have been since Schreiner's day. Nevertheless, the subordinate position of women has remained a basic fact throughout the twentieth century.

For many feminists this statement is the starting point in their analysis of society and hence their political theory. They argue that it is the sexual division between men and women which is the fundamental contradiction in society and the source of their oppression as women; the removal of this division is thus the key task in the emancipation of women.

This position fails to do justice to the complexities that mark the status and role of women within society. Nowhere do all women share a uniform and unambiguous subordination to all men. Even though their subordination is general, it was—and is—not possible to talk of women as if they make up a single category of individuals with a common unified experience. While it is true that women, as a *general* category, occupy a subordinate position to men, and that this sex-based division of society means women have areas of experience in common, sex is not the only or even the dominant determinant of a woman's place in society—a statement which the history of women's organisations in South Africa bears out. In societies where the capitalist mode of production is predominant—as it was in South Africa by the beginning of the twentieth century—the basic division of society into conflicting classes has a crucial bearing on the position of women as well. As a glance at any anthropology textbook will show, the sex-based division of labour in society has preceded a class-based one. However, under capitalism, this sex-based contradiction is both overshadowed and transformed by the dominant contradiction between capital and labour, between the owners of the means of production and the workers. Women are distributed throughout the class spectrum and it is this, their different class positions, rather than their shared sex, that, finally, determines their basic and varied political allegiances.

However, for the very reason that a sex-based division of labour is maintained under capitalism, women overall still have important areas of experience in common, experiences which in certain situations can

1

transcend the barriers of class (and colour) division. This amounts to more than simply a shared inferiority to men within the different and separate strata of society. As well as suffering from sexual discrimination, women at all levels share the role of reproducers and socialisers of children; their responsibility is caring for the family. This has stamped some common features on their experience of the world and allowed the development of a kind of broad 'women's consciousness'.

'We are the women who know the joy of having children and the sorrow of losing them. We know the happiness of rearing our children and the sadness caused through illness and ignorance.'[2] This statement, issued in 1955 by the Federation of South African Women, formed part of an appeal for the support of all the women of South Africa. The call for solidarity was not merely rhetoric, nor a cynical political stratagem, but flowed out of the recognition that for most women motherhood is a central and unifying experience in their lives.

The manner in which the sex-based division of labour has been incorporated within capitalism has been twofold. Firstly, women are responsible for the reproduction of the work-force, both on a daily and on a 'generational' level—ie they look after their families (including their husbands and fathers—the 'workers') on a day-to-day basis, as well as rearing the children, the next generation of workers. The old cliché, 'a woman's place is in the home', is more than a moral injunction. It has always been a basic factor in the continued reproduction of capitalist relations of production.

Secondly, with the growth of a mature, industrial economy, women have been drawn into the sphere of production in increasing numbers, for the most part as a distinct category of workers. Here they have been used as a source of cheap labour—a situation that the sex-stereotyping of jobs frequently disguises, and the view of women as still primarily home-oriented condones. (Their wages are just for 'extras', wage employment for women is not a lifetime undertaking as it is for men, etc.) In addition, because their domestic role continues to be seen as primary, women have also made up a large part of the so-called 'reserve army' of labour. In times of economic expansion they are drawn out of their homes into wage employment; in times of recession they can be phased out of employment and channelled back into the home, without seriously disrupting industrial relations in the way that the rise in unemployment among men would do. This was most dramatically illustrated in Europe during and after the world wars.

In recent years another dimension has been added to the role of women, further modifying their position without fundamentally challenging their subordinate and dependent status. This has been the growing importance of women as consumers. Within mature capitalist societies, as more and more of the domestic functions have been taken over by capitalist industry and business—the manufacture of food and clothing, laundry facilities, household cleaning gadgets—the function of women has shifted from being the producers of these necessities within the home, to being the consumers of these commodities on their families' behalf. Their reproductive role has been transformed but not eliminated. Along with this has gone a growing emphasis on women themselves as objects of consumption—women as sex objects, female sexuality as the means by which commodities ranging from the classic example of the motor car, to cigarettes, deodorant, and life insurance, are promoted for sale.

Although women have remained subordinate to men, this does not mean that their position in society has been without change or contradiction. The twentieth century has been a time of rapid change and flux, powered by far-reaching economic developments in the capitalist world. Since the first world war, women have been drawn upon by industry in increasing numbers as a source of cheap labour. This has promoted their economic independence and shattered their isolation as housebound mothers. At the same time, as already pointed out, the nature of their reproductive role within the home has been transformed by the growing commoditisation of domestic labour. In both reproductive and productive capacities, women occupy a special sex-typed role which the ideological structures of society—the law, the schools, the media, etc.—have sought to maintain, by promoting women's domestic and supportive role and reinforcing their subordinate status.

Related to these economic developments, the growth of towns, the centre of the economic changes transforming society, has also undermined many of the structures previously supporting women's subordinate position. The impact of industrialisation and urbanisation has affected the total society, urban and rural. In South Africa the relationship that developed between town and country has been particularly destructive on the social order of the latter, as the subsequent discussion will make clear. Thus rural women have not been totally isolated from political developments and the pressures on them have, on occasion, led to protests and behaviour which assumes political form. Nevertheless, the scope and opportunities for sustained political organisation are far smaller, and more tightly contained within traditional limits, in the countryside. It is in the towns that women have staked their claim for equality most strongly.

Economic life in town is based on the individual worker rather than the family unit, so the extended patriarchal family of the countryside, and its authority, have been whittled down as a result. Education opportunities are far greater, the range of organisations—political, social, cultural—open to women considerably enlarged. Urban women have thus generally gained in independence and mobility, although this has never been a simple and inevitable development. At the same time, urban life has produced new stresses, new problems which demand new forms of organisation from those existing in the countryside. These developments have, in turn, brought urban women into conflict with an ideology that continues to define them as passive, domestic, apolitical. The various movements in all the advanced capitalist countries in the late nineteenth and twentieth centuries to emancipate women from their position of inferiority to men, have been expressions of such conflict.

The related processes of industrialisation and urbanisation have thus been two major factors in the changing position of women in the twentieth century. This does not mean, however, as communists in the early part of the century simplistically assumed, that the key to women's emancipation lies merely in their greater involvement in production. Psychological and ideological barriers are more deeply entrenched than that and can in fact be bolstered up by new transformations of sexual inequalities and the division of labour within production—for instance, by sex-typing particular industries (textiles, food processing) as 'women's work' which is lower paid, less skilled, and lower in status. Nevertheless, the direct participation of women in the wider, non-domestic economy remains an important precondition for any movement aiming to destroy the inferior position of women in society.

Women in South Africa

The above represents, very briefly, a general outline of the factors affecting the position of women. In South Africa, these general features have assumed specific forms which have provided a particular slant to the way in which women have become politicised. Subsequent discussion will enlarge upon this. Here only a brief outline of the most pertinent features will be sketched.

The first and most glaring of these is that the broad divisions of society along class lines have been further compounded by cleavages based on colour and ethnic considerations. In South Africa the colour of one's skin—one's 'race', in the popular terminology—is a crucial determinant in ordering people's lives. It determines where one may live, whom one may marry, the schools one may attend and the wages one receives. It determines whether one can vote for the central and provisional governments, whether one has freedom of movement within one's country and between jobs, or not. If one is white, one belongs to a minority of privileged people in whom economic and political control is vested. If one is black, one is a second-class citizen.

The broad polarity between white and black in society has corresponded roughly, but not entirely, to that of class. The bulk of the working class and all the peasantry have been black, the bourgeoisie almost exclusively white. Yet here, too, the actual distribution of the different colour groups along the class spectrum has been complex. There has never been a simple homogeneity of class position amongst whites or blacks or even within each dominated racial group. And, as the economy has become more sophisticated, the range of subtleties of class membership have become still more extended. The experience of a daughter of a 'poor-white' bywoner struggling to find employment in a factory in the 1920s was far removed from that of the wife of a mining magnate or one of the handful of women doctors practising at the same time. A rural tribeswoman has little in common with a shebeen-queen or nurse in the urban locations and that nurse has, in certain situations, more in common with her white counterpart in the hospital than her black neighbour in the township.

Recent work on the relationship between class and race in South Africa has begun to show how racism has been manipulated in the interests of the capitalist state, particularly in underpinning a cheap black labour force and winning to the state the allegiance of almost the entire white population group. Colour consciousness and ethnic divisions have formed a basic part of the ideologies of successive governments since Union in 1910. This reached a peak of refinement in the apartheid era that was launched after the National Party came to power in 1948. These dogmas of white supremacy and 'racial' purity have tended to blur the economic realities which underly them. One effect has been to obscure the existence of class divisions within each of the four so-called races (white, African, 'Coloured'[3] and Asian), prompting the growth of political ideologies that appeal to colour solidarity—white supremacy and, more recently, black consciousness. The division into African, 'Coloured', and Asian (mostly Indian) groups has corresponded to, and perpetuated, real differences in political, economic and legal status as well as culture, which historically have obstructed the development of a political unity based on their common blackness. Another effect of racial ideology has been to obscure the existence of common class interests that cut across colour lines, and hence to obstruct the emergence of a non-racial working-class consciousness among both white and black workers. This process could be seen at work in the trade union movement in the 1930s and 1940s.

Very clearly, the colour stratification of society has also informed the manner in which women have participated in the economy. Here the link between class and race as outlined above can be seen to have had a diversifying effect on women's economic position, with far-reaching repercussions on their political outlook. For instance, within manufacturing, upward job mobility by women took place along colour lines. Initially white women formed the bulk of the female industrial labour force. Then, as industry expanded, more and more black women were proletarianised and drawn into the labour force. White women tended to move up the scale into clerical and administrative work, leaving black women on the factory floor. A sexual hierarchy between male and female labour was still maintained—and so was the colour hierarchy of white over black.

While more attention is now being given to racism as a tool of capitalism in South Africa, what has not yet been investigated in any depth is the way in which sexism has been manipulated in the interests of capitalism. In South Africa, as elsewhere, women's reproductive function has remained fundamental throughout the twentieth century. This, too, has been structured on distinct lines. A major divide has existed between non-African women, whose reproductive role has been located within the modern industrial sector of society, and African women. Until the late 1940s, the majority of African women (who formed nearly 70 per cent of the female population in South Africa) were living in the tribal, precapitalist societies of the so-called 'Native Reserves'. Their reproductive role within capitalism was thus located primarily in the precapitalist reserve economies, with crucial implications for their position in the wider society.

The reserves were made up of the fragments of land set aside for African ownership (generally communal) once the process of white conquest in Southern Africa had been completed. In 1913 the all-white parliament set their outer limits at 13 per cent of the land mass of the country, and thus laid the basis for a coherent policy of labour exploitation.

The maintenance of and dominance over the precapitalist reserve economies were a major feature of the growth of capitalism in South Africa, prompting much of the repressive legislation that has characterised its development. It was apparent from the start that the amount of land set aside was totally inadequate for an independent African subsistence—and this was always the intention. The industrial revolution of the late nineteenth century was based largely on the use of cheap black migrant labour flowing from the subsistence economies of the African reserve areas to the dominant industrial and agricultural sector in so-called 'white' South Africa, and back. This flow of labour was controlled by a cumbersome but increasingly far-reaching system of control in the form of passes—documents which African men were required to carry with them at all times and produce on demand, on pain of arrest. Passes identified who the bearers were, showed who they worked for and where, and established whether or not they had official permission to be living and working or travelling in the area. These notorious and deeply hated documents underpinned the entire system of cheap black labour. During the twentieth century the pass laws were extended and increasingly refined as the demand for cheap labour grew and different fractions of capital—mining, industrial, agricultural—dominated successive governments. In the 1950s the ANC correctly described them as 'the foundation of the whole cheap labour system of South Africa'.

The base that the worker retained in the reserve economy meant an enormous saving for the capitalist sector, on wages and in the social services of the state in general. Because his family could eke out an existence in the reserves, the worker could be paid a single man's wages, while the young, the old, the sick and disabled were cared for by the community 'back home'. Until the 1940s (by which stage their economic resources were more or less exhausted), the reserves were the main location for the reproduction of South Africa's cheap (black) labour force.

The effects on the position of African women (and ultimately on the forms of political organisation that developed amongst women generally) were profound. The maintenance of the reserve economy, and hence of the tribal institutions which reproduced it, became priorities for the state in the early years of the century. As more and more men were sucked into the migrant labour machine, the women left behind came to play an increasingly important part in keeping the subsistence economies of the reserves functioning and, thereby, reproducing the supply of migrant workers. Within the tribal economy women had always taken an active part, but with the expansion of the migrant labour system this grew enormously, so that they came to bear the main brunt of keeping the subsistence economy operating.

The state, therefore, was not anxious to see a widespread migration of women from the reserves to the towns. Nor was it anxious to see greater equality between the sexes. It had a vested interest in preserving women's traditional junior role within the African family, since this was one of the basic institutions of tribal society and tied them to the rural areas. The subordinate status of women was accordingly entrenched in the system of customary law applied to Africans. Under it, women were deemed perpetual minors, always under the guardianship of their nearest male relative, regardless of their age, marital status or any other consideration. These factors combined to isolate a major sector of African women from the main radicalising forces affecting women—urbanisation, industrialisation—until well into the twentieth century. Sexual discrimination was thus built into the system of labour exploitation from the start.

By the 1940s, however, the ability of the precapitalist sector to function as a reproductive base for migrant labour had largely broken down under the impact of sustained contact with the dominant capitalist sector. One index of this breakdown lay in the increasing number of African women migrating from the reserves to the towns. This had important consequences on the attitude of the state towards African women. As the institutions of tribal society fell into greater disarray, the state came to play a more direct and coercive role in maintaining the migrant labour system. At the same time, the reserves came to play an increasingly important political role after 1948, as areas into which the more insistent political demands of Africans could be channelled and diffused. To bolster the myth of the reserves as the true 'homelands' of the African people, it was essential that women be forced to remain there in large numbers. The state's increased formal control over African women's mobility after 1948, in the form of refined urban influx control measures and passes, was at least in part an expression of these concerns.

Thus, the position of women in South Africa has been far from uniform: the nature of the cleavages among them is complex. White women have been separated from black women by a very wide gulf, one located in the basic structures of white supremacy. For most women this colour-based divide cuts through any experience of common womanhood they might share. Furthermore, for the majority of women who are black, the disabilities they suffer as blacks rather than as women have been felt to press most heavily upon them. At the same time, the experience of their 'blackness' has varied considerably among different sections of black women.

It is in this context that the growth of a women's movement in South Africa has to be considered.

> [W]omen must not be seen as a homogeneous group. Women must be analysed both separately and as part of the social groups, castes or classes to which they belong. In doing so, the nature of these groups, castes and classes will be illuminated.[4]

The specific interaction of sex, class and race has taken different forms for different women at various times. It is this interaction that has defined their shifting, diverse positions and thus, ultimately, determined their political organisation.

Notes

1. O. Schreiner, *The Story of an African Farm,* p. 197.
2. 'Meeting of Congress of Mothers: Sunday 7th August, 1955', Treason Trial exhibit G 838, p. 1.
3. Since 'Coloured' is not a neutral, descriptive term but has strong political connotations, I have chosen to place it in inverted commas throughout the text.
4. M. Mackintosh, *The Study of Women in Society* (mimeo), p. 1.

PART ONE: POLITICAL ORGANISATION AMONG WOMEN, 1910–39

1

'A Not Unsatisfactory State of Affairs': The Position of Women in South Africa Before 1939

The late nineteenth century and early twentieth century was a period of enormous change and flux in Southern Africa. The conquest of the independent African polities by the white settlers had been taking place throughout the nineteenth century. By the turn of the century this process had been completed. All land was under white jurisdiction; vast areas had been opened up for white settlement. The formerly independent African tribesmen were being transformed into labourers on the farms, in the mines, in the infant cities and industries—their economic independence had been shattered as thoroughly as their political independence.

In 1910 the political boundaries of the modern South Africa were established. The leaders of the white settlers of the four British colonies— the Cape, Natal, Transvaal, and Orange Free State—met and agreed to form the Union of South Africa. Between 1899 and 1902 Afrikaners in the two inland republics of the Transvaal and Orange Free State had fought the British for their independence and lost, but in 1910 the basis for their future hegemony over the whole of South Africa was laid. The Union of South Africa was founded unequivocally on the principle of white supremacy. Only in the Cape Province were a tiny proportion of black men who met stringent educational and property requirements allowed to retain the franchise.

Underriding these political developments were the revolutionary economic changes unleashed in the subcontinent by major mineral discoveries; first, diamonds in Kimberley in 1867 and then, even more important, gold on the Witwatersrand in 1886. The mineral discoveries launched a backward, pastoral society—or number of societies—on the road to a modern capitalist state. They fuelled the political conflict between Briton and Afrikaner and created a voracious appetite for a cheap and docile labour force to work the mines and then the industries that grew up around them. Almost overnight the city of Johannesburg grew up from the tents and covered wagons of the first gold-mining camps.

It was a dynamic and formative period in the history of South Africa. Yet women seem hardly to have featured in the surge of events. Those who appear in the history books are all men; the wars fought over land were between men; the politicians who assembled in 1909/10 to lay down the foundations of the South African state were all men; the masses who worked the first mines and factories, anonymous and blurred though their features are, were men.

There are very few recorded utterances by South African women in

9

the nineteenth century. One that survives is a defiant statement of independence made by a group of Voortrekker women shortly after the British had annexed their short-lived Republic of Natal in 1843. They scandalised the British Commissioner by asserting that they regarded themselves to be as eligible for involvement in the political future of the territory as their men. 'I endeavoured (but in vain) to impress upon them that such a liberty as they seemed to dream of had never been recognised in any civil society', Cloete, the Commissioner, reported to the Governor at the Cape, '. . . and that however much I sympathised in their feeling, . . . I considered it a disgrace on their husbands to allow such a state of freedom'.[1]

Another outspoken proponent for women's advancement in the nineteenth century was the writer Olive Schreiner. Her writings were of considerable significance in the development of the women's suffrage movement, both in South Africa and internationally. Her first novel, *Story of an African Farm*, appeared in 1883 and created something of a stir, not least because of its outspoken rejection of women's inferior standing in society. This was followed by the establishment of the Women's Christian Temperance Union in 1889, which in 1895 established a Franchise Department to champion the cause of women's suffrage.

These women were, however, far in advance of their times. They were exceptional women whose claims could easily be dismissed by contemporary observers as irrelevant and absurd. The audience they reached was tiny, confined almost exclusively to white, upper-class women in the towns, women who had had some access to higher education and were beginning to rebel against the strictures placed on them by society. They did not speak to most white women, and not at all to the great majority of women who were black, nor did they choose to—the women's suffrage society which grew out of these beginnings was concerned with the enfranchisement of white women only.

Yet, though women were not in the forefront of events, they were not removed from the impact of the political and economic developments either. The domination and incorporation of the independent African polities into the boundaries of a single capitalist economy had particularly profound consequences on the position and status of African women. It is a subject calling for far greater research, research that is free from either the romanticism of those who look back to the pre-conquest societies as to a golden age, or the cultural myopia of those who regard Africa before the whites as a sea of barbarism.

Although women's part in the history of these times has been overlooked or ignored, yet they were an integral component of their society, with important parts to play in its development. As has already been argued, the reproductive role of women plays a crucial part in maintaining or transforming the social and economic relationships of any society. By the late nineteenth century in South Africa this role, in town, country, and the reserves, had begun to be restructured by new economic needs. As yet the signs of this were not overt, and the role of women in the public life of society—that part which receives the most attention from contemporary observers and conventional historiography—was minimal. In 1904 the Cape census set out to establish 'to what extent the married women of the European race are employed in occupations which are likely to interfere with the proper performance of their home duties'. Having established how few women were 'absorbed in occupations other than those which are entirely or partially of a household nature', it concluded complacently, 'On the whole, these figures may be said to point to a not unsatisfactory state of affairs.'[2] These attitudes and the conditions they described were to prevail for some time to come. But already the foundations of change had been laid.

The Position of Women in the Early Twentieth Century

In the early twentieth century the lives of most women were bounded by their domestic responsibilities, defined in terms of their role within the home and family. Few women were working outside the home, and those that were, were to be found mainly in domestic employment. Women's direct contact with the public sphere of the economy and politics was very limited.

Most women were living a rural existence, under conditions which did not immediately challenge this position. In 1921, the year of the second national census, the urban population for the Union as a whole was only 28 per cent of the total, and, because of the migrant labour system, the percentage of women living in the towns was even less. The bulk of the rural population was African, and the disparity between the proportions of African and non-African women living in the towns was very marked. Thus, while between 50 per cent and 60 per cent of the white, 'Coloured' and Asiatic groups (who together made up a little over 30 per cent of the total population) were classified as urban, only 14 per cent of Africans—and less than seven per cent of African women (approximately 147,000)—were living in the urban areas by 1921.[3] African women, by far the largest racial group among women, were thus the least urbanised of any sex-race category.

Already migrant labour had driven a wedge between the experience of African and non-African women. The security and stability of marriage and family life which, for all its restrictions, most non-African women could reasonably expect, was no longer something African women could take for granted. In both town and country the system of migrant labour was destroying the traditional pattern of the African family. Statistics for the sex ratios of the different groups show this up crudely. Amongst non-Africans in both town and country this ratio was more or less equally balanced between males and females. Amongst Africans, however, it was heavily distorted. In the towns, African men outnumbered women by approximately three to one as an average. The greatest disparity between men and women was found on the Rand, where in 1921 the masculinity rate (males per 100 females) was a staggering 863—almost nine males to every female. This figure was followed by that of Durban (624) and then

Cape Town (389).[4] The three largest urban centres had the smallest
proportion of women in their populations. Since it was in the larger towns
that political activity was most developed and the incipient struggle by
blacks for political rights most firmly based, this was a significant brake
on the momentum of African women's politicisation at the time.

In the reserves the obverse of the situation in the towns prevailed, and
women outnumbered men. The 1921 census returns showed there were
1,345,421 female as opposed to 1,036,856 male 'peasants', a blanket term
that was used to describe all Africans, including children, living in the
reserves at the time. This preponderance was most marked at the most
productive age levels, ie between 15 and 60 years of age.

In the 1920s, then, African women by and large occupied a distinct
place in society compared to other women. The majority—just over
58 per cent of their total in 1921—were living in the so-called Native
Reserves under tribal conditions.[5] These women constituted almost
40 per cent of the total female population in South Africa at the time.
Since they made up such a large and significant proportion of the female
population, it is worth considering the dominant features of the world
they inhabited.

Women in the Reserves

Life in the reserves was tough, and rooted in traditional customs and
values. Dora Tamana, a leading ANC and FSAW activist in Cape Town in
the late 1940s and 1950s, grew up in the Transkei in the early years of
the century. She was born in 1901. From her description of her childhood, a picture emerges of an austere and isolated existence.[6] In its broad
outlines it can be duplicated many times to describe general conditions in
the impoverished and backward reserve areas at the time.

The Tamanas lived in a scattered community called Hlobo. The
nearest town, Idutywa, was a three to four hours' walk away, the nearest
shop an hours' walk. There were no buses, and such roads as there were
were extremely rough. In Hlobo, modern medical facilities were non-
existent. There was a two-room mission school which catered up to
Standard 6. Dora herself went up to Standard 4. Her father worked a
small allotment on which she and her four sisters helped before and after
school. Although she describes her family as having been poor, she
remembers other families who had no fields at all.

> The chiefs had to give the people lands. But the lands were finished so that
> others couldn't get land. The others had to go to other places, such as my
> cousin who went to Mafeking to get fields there, because there were no fields
> at Hlobo. . . Others had to go to people with fields and ask for a piece of ground
> to plough.

The nearest water supply for the family was a spring about half a mile
away. Every day Dora and her sisters would have to make several trips to

collect domestic water; during summer, when vegetables needed watering, the trips became more frequent. Into this isolated community, developments in the outside world barely penetrated. The establishment of Union in 1910, the Land Act of 1913, the coming of the first world war were distant, hazy events without apparent substance or meaning, if they were known at all. As Dora describes it, there were 'no politics' at that time.

Within tribal society women traditionally occupied a junior position in the basic unit of that society, the patriarchal and extended family. This position, for reasons already outlined, white jurists and courts had entrenched in their codification and interpretation of tribal laws during the course of the nineteenth century. In the process, they had exaggerated and ossified the inferior status of women. The Natal Code of Law of 1891 was the most glaring example of this: 'The code stereotypes a concept of feminine inferiority unknown to the traditional society and burdens women in Natal with disabilities that they do not suffer in other provinces', commented H.J. Simons in his study of the legal status of African women.[7] As this and several other studies have pointed out, women in the pre-conquest societies had had a clear economic function. With it had gone a degree of economic independence and hence a relatively high personal status. Under white domination much of this was lost. Apart from the downgrading of women's legal status, the acute pressure that developed on land in the reserves meant that married women and widows were rarely allocated fields of their own; previously this had been an accepted procedure. Yet, increasingly, the burden of all agricultural work was falling on women, and this responsibility sat uneasily with their proclaimed, and largely internalised, position of inferiority to men.

From an early age, reserve women were working in and around their homes. From the age of about twelve, Dora was fully occupied with these responsibilities.

> I was looking after the calves. . . And I was also doing the cooking at home and cleaning the floor with mud and also plastering our house with mud. . . I was looking after my sisters also. When my mother had gone to the field, I had to look after the baby. . . and do some cooking—cooking mealies. . . there were no trees in Hlobo. We were making fire with manure. . . We had to look after the manure and make it dry and if it was not enough, we had to go to the field where the cattle eat grass and pick it up. No wood, no wood.

By the 1920s the position of African women was still broadly contained within the traditional tribal limits. However, already there were signs of contradiction. The system of migrant labour, which depended on the preservation of the reserves as a subsistence base, was in fact undermining the very basis of tribal society. In the reserves women were being obliged to assume an increasing degree of *de facto*, if not *de jure*, responsibility and authority as heads of their households. The sexual imbalance in both town and country (one of the most distinguishing features of African family life in the twentieth century) was undermining the stability and organisation of the traditional family structure. Already, too, women were showing signs of breaking away from the oppressive conditions in the reserves and moving to the urban areas. In the early 1920s there were not yet any restrictions, in the form of passes, on the mobility of African women largely because their townward migration was on so small a scale. Yet, while it was still small, it was beginning to increase. In the ten years between 1911 and 1921 the percentage of women in the African urban population rose from 19 per cent to 25 per cent. As yet the destructive effect of these developments on the position of African women was barely noticeable, but pressure on such institutions as tribal marriage and the extended family was beginning to mount.

The Pattern of Female Employment Outside the Reserves

Outside the reserves, women's lifestyles and the economic opportunities open to them were more diversified. But here, too, women's domestic role was still clearly paramount. At this stage the number of women 'economically active' was very small. Most non-African women were classified as dependants occupied with 'household duties'. In the 1921 census only approximately 23 per cent of all 'Coloured', Asiatic, and white women over the age of fifteen were in the economically active category, compared to 92.4 per cent of the same sample of men. In terms of numbers, economically active white women outnumbered 'Coloured', but the proportion of 'Coloured' women working was the highest among the four race groups, at 37.4 per cent. White women followed, with 19.2 per cent economically active. Asian women, numbering a mere 4,368, or 12.6 per cent of their total fifteen years and older, were an insignificant fraction of the female labour force.

The available figures for African women are not strictly comparable, since no distinction was made as to age in enumerating those employed. Furthermore, as we have seen, all African females in the reserves were classified as peasants and included within the economically active category. Once the peasant category is excluded, then a mere 10 per cent or 11 per cent of the rest of African women were to be found in wage employment.

The pattern of female employment followed lines that much research has shown to be typical of other capitalist economies. Women were clustered in the least paid, least skilled jobs. In most cases these jobs were merely an extension of their domestic work into the public wage sphere. The largest single area of employment was domestic service—fully 56 per cent of all female workers fell within the service category, almost all of them as domestic workers. For black women the predominance of domestic work was especially marked. Almost 65 per cent of all African women workers and 85 per cent of 'Coloured' were in domestic service. Probably more than any other single type of work, domestic service has had a formative influence on the way black women are viewed within white society. It has played a major socialising role in black/white relationships, and also conditioned the way many black women see both themselves and their white employers. The relationships established between employer and employee in the domestic service situation carry an intimacy and degree of personal interaction that no other field of employment has. White men and black women and, more pertinent for the women's movement in South Africa, white women and black women are brought into a close and daily contact. This allows for the development of personal relationships which in some ways transcend the rigid social colour bar in society, yet finally remain bound by its parameters. The objective relationship that exists between boss and worker is smudged, sometimes hidden, but not destroyed. Very few white children have grown up without a black nanny who in many important respects takes the place of the mother—yet remains a servant. Many of the reported (and no doubt unreported) cases of 'immorality'—illicit sexual intercourse between black and white—take place between white master and black maid. Few white women have not had a black woman servant on call to free them to take up outside employment or leisure-time activities. This last is a contradiction that the middle-class 'women's liberation movement' has yet to come to terms with.

After domestic work, the next largest area of employment for women in the early twentieth century was agriculture. By the 1920s, this accounted for close on 19 per cent of the female labour force. (This figure excludes peasants.) Agriculture was virtually the only area of employment for women, white and black, in the so-called 'white' countryside outside of the reserves. Even so, relatively few women were employed in it. In 1921, 66,868 African women were returned as farmworkers. Compared to other categories of employment, this was a large figure. Nevertheless, it amounted to only 8 per cent of the total African female population then living outside of the reserves and urban areas.[8] At that stage, labour tenancy was the chief form of labour on most of the country's white farms.[9] According to the *Native Farm Labour Committee Report* of 1937–39, the female members of a labour tenant's family did not generally participate regularly in farm labour, but rather on a casual or part-time basis.[10] Here too the major function of women on farms would seem to have been reproductive—rearing and caring for the present and future generations of farmworkers.

The third most important area of employment for women was in industry. This accounted for approximately 7 per cent of the total female labour force in 1921. In the sphere of manufacturing, women as yet made up only a small percentage of its total labour force—12 per cent in 1924/25. Already, however, there were signs of changes in the sex composition of the industrial labour force. In view of the importance of productive work in the emancipation and politicisation of women, these were of far-reaching significance.

Women, it has been said, played little part in the first stage of South Africa's industrial development, that associated with mining. Once secondary industry began to be established, however, in the early years of the century, there was a new demand for female workers. The coming of the first world war in 1914, and later the protectionist policies of the Pact

Government in the 1920s, greatly boosted the growth of manufacturing industry, and the numbers of women entering factory work grew rapidly. At this stage white women predominated on the factory floor, accounting for roughly one half of the female manufacturing labour force in 1924/25. The bulk of these were young Afrikaner girls who were streaming to town from the countryside to escape rural poverty and depression—the so-called 'poor whites', without education or marketable skills. 'Coloured' women accounted for almost all the black women in industry at the time. African and Asian women were barely represented in manufacturing at all. Thus, in the earliest trade unions that developed among white women, white Afrikaner women dominated. The Garment Workers' Union, which is dealt with in subsequent chapters, was a notable example.

Sex-typing of manufacturing jobs was already clearly visible. The clothing industry was the important area of female industrial employment and rapidly growing more so. In 1923/24, 86.4 per cent of all white women employed in industry were to be found in four areas—the textile and clothing industry; the food, drink, and tobacco industries; books and printing; and the leather industry. Conditions of female employment were generally extremely poor—low wages, long hours, and inadequate facilities were the norm. The trade union movement was only just beginning to get under way. The new female recruits to industry were mostly ignorant, unsophisticated newcomers to city life, at the mercy of their employers. The contrast between the reality of how working women were treated in industry and popular stereotypes of women as the fair and weaker sex, the ideal of chivalry and suchlike, was a harsh (and instructive) one. In 1911 Olive Schreiner commented sharply on the hypocrisy of those who urged that women's place was in the home and therefore justified their continued political and social subordination, yet at the same time condoned the most ruthless exploitation of working class and peasant women. In her pioneering study, *Woman and Labour*, she asserted,

> at the present day, when probably more than half the world's most laborious and illpaid labour is still performed by women, from tea-pickers and cocoa tenders in India and the islands, to the washerwomen, cooks and drudging labouring men's wives. . . it is somewhat difficult to reply with gravity to the assertion, 'Let woman be content to be the "Divine Child Bearer" and ask no more.' [11]

As in many other respects, however, Schreiner was ahead of her times. Conditions in the factories were slow to improve. Women had first to be mobilised into effective trade unions, and this took time to achieve.

The fourth category of employment for women, that of 'professional and technical', accounted for a mere 5.8 per cent of the total female labour force in 1921. Here the general features of women's employment—sex-typing of jobs, lower status, less specialised work etc.—were all apparent. Teaching and nursing, in many ways extensions of women's maternal role, were by far the largest areas of employment in this field. The 1921 census made no detailed breakdown of the 'professional and technical' category for black women, but amongst whites, out of a total of 20,341 women returned in this group, fully 14,035 were 'professors and teachers' and 4,558 'medical'. Women were almost completely absent from any of the more specialised, high-status professions. In 1921 there were only 35 white women 'physicians, surgeons, medical practitioners' in the country, and no female architects, engineers, chartered accountants, barristers or solicitors. Until 1923 and the passage of the Women's Legal Practitioners Act, legislation actually prohibited women from practising law.

The gulf separating white women from black was extremely marked in the professional category. White women, less than a quarter of the female population, greatly outnumbered blacks in this category. The ratio of white women professionals to black was in the vicinity of 7 to 1. The ranking of occupational categories for white and black women in 1921 revealed clearly how race and class mediated with sex to assign women to different levels in society. While almost all women were found in sex-typed employment, white women were concentrated in the more skilled and better paid jobs within this division. For them the ranking of occupational categories was first, professional and technical, second, clerical work, third, service, and only then industry. For black women, service, then agriculture and then, trailing a long way behind, industry were the three most important areas of employment.

From this brief survey it is clear that, over all, the economic opportunities open to women in 1921 were still very restricted. Women's primary function was reproductive. Yet, already, in the ten years that had elapsed since the first population census for the Union, in 1911, the pattern of female employment had begun to show signs of change. Between 1911 and 1921 clerical and typing work outstripped teaching as the largest area of white female employment. Saleswomen had become a considerably more important group of working women than previously and several new jobs employing appreciable numbers of women had appeared—waitress, tailor, machinist, telephonist. Prejudice against women in the professions showed a few signs of being on the wane, the 1923 act which enabled women to practise law being one such indication. Furthermore, the manufacturing industry was beginning to get established, and with it the demand for female labour, particularly in the clothing and textile industries, was on the increase.

The Legal and Educational Systems and Women

Both the legal and educational systems were geared towards perpetuating the domestic and subordinate status of women. Two systems of civil law operated in South Africa—Roman-Dutch, the general law of the land, and tribal or customary law. This latter was applied by special Native Courts to the African population in matters falling outside the scope of Roman-Dutch law (for instance, in *lobola* suits). Both systems were imbued with a strongly patriarchal system of values. Customary law, however, was the far harsher of the two in the restrictions it imposed on African women. Under Roman-Dutch law, women became legal minors upon marriage. Unless an antenuptial contract was signed, marital power was vested in the husband. This made the husband the legal guardian of his wife, allowing him, *inter alia*, to exercise sole control over their joint estate. The father was the legal guardian of all legitimate children. In the eyes of the law it was the husband who had the right to decide on the place of domicile of a married couple. Thus, a woman who refused to comply with her husband's wishes about where they should stay was technically guilty of desertion. However, single women over the age of 21, or widowed and divorced women, enjoyed the same legal status as men.

The system of customary law in the early 1920s was confused and confusing. It varied from province to province, a legacy of the days before Union. It was not till the passage of the Native Administration Act in 1927 that a more uniform system was imposed on the tribal law courts throughout the country. Far from modernising the legal status of African women to conform with the decay of tribal society, the 1927 legislation endorsed the very conservative views on the position of women that were already embodied in the Natal code of law. The fact that the state chose to maintain this interpretation reflected the importance that it attached to preserving the subordinate position of women within reinforced tribal structures. Under customary law, women were deemed perpetual minors— at no stage could a woman escape the guardianship of her nearest male relative, whether father, husband or son. In the 1920s, very few women qualified for exemption from these provisions. At that stage, with the vast majority of African women still living in the rural areas, the contradictions between their subordinate legal status and the demands of a modern, industrial society were not yet so acute. However, during the course of the twentieth century, women would find their inferior legal status a tremendous handicap in dealing with a rapidly changing society.

Discrimination against women was particularly apparent in the field of education. Fewer girls than boys attended school, the gap between the enrolment figures becoming wider the higher up the school system one went. Figures for the 1920s are not available, but in 1933 (the first year of separate school enrolment figures for whites), white boys in school outnumbered white girls by approximately 16,000. In the final year of school, standard 10, roughly 60 per cent of the total enrolment were boys. By the time one reached university level, girls had fallen even further behind. In 1917 almost 75 per cent of the total student population in South Africa was male—out of a total of 1616 students, 1214 were men.[12]

In education, the race-class schism cut across the sexual division as well. Even though their education was geared toward a particular sex-stereotyped end, whether in the home or at work, white women were far more privileged than blacks generally, in both the scope and the quality of the education they received. Thus, in 1935 the total number of all black matriculants amounted to a mere 144, little over 5 per cent of all the white girl matriculants at the time. Unfortunately, no separate figures for black male and female students are available for this period, but in education, as in other spheres, black women were pushed to the very bottom of the pile. As late as 1958, by which time separate figures for boys and girls are available, there were only 317 'Coloured' and Asiatic girls, compared to 1293 boys in standard 10, and 215 African girls compared to 723 boys. These national figures are meagre indeed. The comparable figures for whites were 9310 boys and 7563 girls.[13]

In general, school curricula were geared towards training girls for domestic or menial occupations. This was reflected in the almost complete absence of women from any of the more specialised professions, other than teaching and nursing. The conventional view on what education for women should aim at was implicit in the following discussion in the *Carnegie Commission Report* (1932) on adult education as a means of combating the 'poor white' problem:

> The welfare and progress of poor families is influenced by the activities of women to a degree that is not always fully realised. Our measures of social welfare ought therefore to be designed far more with reference to the women and their power of raising the social level of the family. A system of adult education ought to devote earnest attention to the mothers and daughters of indigent families. They should be trained not only in matters of health and nursing and the care of infants, but also in the economics of housekeeping and the upbringing of children.[14]

The commission recommended that further steps be taken to promote such skills amongst women, 'in addition to the ordinary activities of schools and churches'.

The limitations were even more startling when one looks at the education of black women. In the reserves, despite the fact that to an ever-increasing extent most of the farming was carried out by women, the few agricultural colleges that did exist were only for men. Thus, the objectives of the Fort Cox Agricultural School were described as 'to give a thorough, practical and theoretical training in general agriculture and stock farming to young native men, so as to enable them to make better use of their own land or to take up posts as skilled agricultural labourers in the European industry'.[15] In a similar vein, the *Report of the Native Affairs Department, 1919-21*, stressed the importance of agricultural training in African schools 'in the case of boys', but only 'practical domestic training for girls'.[16]

Women in Politics: the Women's Suffrage Movement

Given the general position of women, it is not surprising that the scope for women in political work was very restricted. Until 1930 no women in South Africa had the vote, and their participation in political parties, both white and black, was very limited. Most people accepted that women were first and foremost mothers and, furthermore, that motherhood in some way set women apart from a full and equal participation in all spheres of society. Until women became a more prominent and active part of the country's labour force, there was little public debate on established assumptions of male superiority. Thus, throughout this time, none of the major political parties regarded women as an important area for political work and propaganda. In the early years of the century most politicians accepted without much thought that it was not 'natural' for women to meddle in politics. The structural reasons that lay behind this attitude, in the form of the important reproductive function that women served, have already been outlined. The handful of women who took up the question of women's suffrage in the early twentieth century were regarded by almost all white politicians as eccentrics at best, dangerous subversives or lunatics at worst.

In March 1911, suffragists met in Durban to establish a national women's suffrage society, the Women's Enfranchisement Association of the Union [WEAU], to lobby their cause. Their conference drew forth the following editorial in the local newspaper, the *Natal Mercury:*

> We hope the women suffragists have enjoyed their picnic in Durban, but we do not think the political effect of their visit can have rewarded their endeavour, and we cannot pretend that we have any regrets for their non-success.[17]

Amongst black politicians, women's suffrage was even less of an issue. Black leaders in this period were preoccupied with defending the limited rights that Africans still possessed, notably their franchise rights in the Cape, not with extending them into the uncharted area of women's rights.

The attitudes towards women that were current in black political organisations, and the development of a women's movement within them, form one of the major themes of this history. It is examined in detail in subsequent chapters. The remainder of this chapter will therefore look briefly at the white women's suffrage movement. This was one of the main political campaigns by women in the early twentieth century and throws light on their general position in society at the time. Although it stood apart from the great mass of black women, those with whom this book is primarily concerned, its history has much to tell about the nature of women's organisations in South Africa, as well as the different priorities that have divided white women from black. It illustrates clearly how class and colour divisions have interacted to shape the political conscious-ness of South African women.

In the early twentieth century the women's suffrage movement was the only political movement that was actively concerned with women's rights. Yet even it was at pains to point out that the enfranchisement of women would not upset established sexual relations in the home. In 1913 the suffrage journal, *Women's Outlook*, argued that,

> The home, as has so often been said, is the woman's sphere. We must show other women what we already know so well, that it is the very things pertaining to the well-kept happy home that need their combined operation.

At that stage no women had the vote. In this respect they were classified on the same plane as children, lunatics, and criminals. They shared this fate with most black men—and it was largely because the question of the franchise raised such explosive issues about black political rights, that the suffrage movement was always a muted one and the eventual enfranchisement of white women was delayed till some ten years after the suffrage movement had triumphed in Europe and North America.

As already mentioned, the roots of the suffrage movement can be traced back to Olive Schreiner and later to the Women's Christian Temperance Union in the late nineteenth century. The WCTU's Franchise Department was followed by a number of tiny, separate societies that established themselves in all the main urban centres of the country in the first decade of the twentieth century. Their membership was small, exclusively white, and almost entirely English-speaking; these were to remain dominant characteristics of the movement throughout its history. The majority of suffragists were drawn from the most privileged strata of society. They were women who had both the education and the leisure to query their restricted role in society: energetic and capable women, restless for all the opportunities that society offered to their class but denied to their sex.

In 1911 the various local suffrage societies affiliated to form a national body, the WEAU (to the scorn of the *Natal Mercury*). For the next twenty-odd years this was the premier suffrage organisation in the country, campaigning and lobbying for support through public meetings, newspaper articles and letters, deputations to the authorities, petitions, and public statements. Compared to the suffrage campaign being waged by Emily Pankhurst's Women's Social and Political Union in England, the South African campaign was a timid and decorous affair. On occasion, frustrated suffragists hinted darkly that perhaps the time was approaching when 'more militant tactics' would be required. These remarks never amounted to more than a fairly transparent attempt at political blackmail, and the campaign continued on its constitutional path.

'This is no country in which to refuse to pay taxes without direct parliamentary representation', commented the *Cape Times* caustically on the one occasion when an individual suffragist, Edith Woods, had resorted to defying the tax authorities as a method of protest. 'The white women who can plead that injustice are an infinitesimal fraction of the inhabitants of this country who have it as a basic condition of their lives.' It was a point of view with which most suffragists concurred.

Largely because their tactics were so mild, and their numbers always so small, the suffragists had to wage a long, uphill struggle. Parliament, on which the WEAU focused its attention, was preoccupied with other issues. For the white political parties, the question of women's suffrage was swamped by other and more pressing concerns—workers' unrest on the Rand, the proper relations with 'the natives', the coming of the first world war, an attempt at rebellion by die-hard Afrikaner nationalists, and constitutional developments within the British Empire. At the same time, many members of parliament came from a deeply conservative and

staunchly patriarchal background. 'The question of why are women
without votes is on a par with why are women without beards', was
how one MP summed up the matter. In the first decade after Union only
the tiny South African Labour Party actively championed the cause of
women's suffrage. The ruling South African Party was divided on the
matter, and the opposition National Party was almost uniformly hostile
to it.

By the 1920s, however, women's suffrage had divested itself of
much of its earlier radical connotations. The movement of women into
greater public employment and higher education had begun to show
by then. At the same time, the sudden influx of Afrikaner women into
the cities and into new areas of work was prompting the National Party
to re-evaluate its own attitude to women; in the 1920s it came to adopt
a more flexible attitude towards the question of women's suffrage. In
addition, many opponents of women's suffrage were reassured by the
example of Europe, where the enfranchisement of women in a number
of different countries in the wake of the first world war had not led
to the collapse of the entire social order, as was previously predicted.

But still, women's suffrage was not an issue to carry much importance.
By 1921 the WEAU presented the Prime Minister, Smuts, with a petition
of nearly 54,000 signatures in favour of women's suffrage. His reply
showed that, while he accepted the idea of the eventual enfranchisement
of women, it was by no means a matter of urgency. 'If it does not win this
session, it may win the next session, or the session after.'

Up until this time, the suffrage movement had managed to steer
fairly clear of the question of black women's suffrage. Its call for the
vote was couched in apparently non-racial terms: it wanted women to be
enfranchised 'on the same terms as for men'. Its claim to being a non-
racial organisation was a very superficial one, however, since only in the
Cape were any black men enfranchised (and there they were a tiny and
increasingly beleaguered section of the voting public). So only in the
Cape were any black women encompassed by the suffrage claim. The
WEAU never had any intention of challenging the *status quo* as regards
political relationships between white and black. It was not called upon
to define its stance with any degree of exactitude, although a fair number
of suffragists, if pressed, did believe that 'qualified' black women should
be enfranchised in the Cape.

By the 1920s, however, once the principle of women's suffrage
had been gradually conceded, the focus of the suffrage debate sharpened.
Henceforth it centred more and more upon the implications for the
African franchise and whether black women should be enfranchised
or not. 'After all, we who are opposed to women's suffrage are opposed
to it not on account of the unfitness of women, but on the grounds of
the difficulty in the coloured and native vote.' Thus Brand Wessels, a
Nationalist member of parliament who was appointed to a select committee
on women's enfranchisement in 1926, explained his position. As the
debate narrowed, the WEAU's own position came under close scrutiny.
It began to equivocate on its earlier claim, with leading members arguing

that half a loaf (the enfranchisement of white women) was better than none: 'We know in our hearts we shall not get all that we ask, but we are very anxious for the half-loaf. The other may come.' So said Lady Rose-Innes, a leading suffragist, in 1926, at a hearing by the select committee.

Finally, women's suffrage became a weapon with which the National Party of General Hertzog, which came to power in 1924, could attack the limited black franchise that still existed. The elimination of the African vote in the Cape had been one of General Hertzog's major aims when he took office as prime minister in 1924. The franchise clause had, however, been entrenched in the Union constitution in 1910 and could not be amended without a two-thirds majority of both houses of parliament sitting together. Although Hertzog commanded a majority of seats in parliament, he did not control sufficient votes to achieve his aims of amending the constitution. Frustrated in repeated attempts to secure this majority, Hertzog then turned to women's suffrage to launch his attack from another direction. In 1930 he piloted a Women's Enfranchisement Bill through parliament that applied to white women only. With his support the matter was never in question, and the bill became law. Henceforth all white women were eligible to vote and stand for parliament. With this act, Hertzog managed to double the electorate at one stroke and thereby drastically reduce the importance of the black vote in the Cape. The percentage of black voters was slashed from 19.9 per cent of the total electorate in the Cape in 1929 to 10.9 per cent in 1931.

While it is incorrect to analyse the women's suffrage movement purely in its relationship to the Cape African franchise, as most historians have done, it is also clear that this was the dominant concern in Hertzog's mind in 1930. The changing position of women and the suffrage campaign itself had made their eventual enfranchisement inevitable by the late 1920s; the specific timing and the scope of the legislation that finally brought this about, however, had little to do with women's rights and far more to do with black rights or, rather, the removal of such rights.

The suffrage movement was thus used by Hertzog—but it allowed itself to be used. Very few of its members were in fundamental disagreement with the principle of white supremacy implicit in the enfranchisement act. The history of the WEAU supports the argument already advanced, that the basic political allegiance of South African women has been shaped not by their sex, but by their class position and their colour. White and middle class, the suffragists were women who were wanting to expand the existing political structures of society to incorporate themselves. They were not wishing to overthrow the structures on which, ultimately, their privileges rested. Said Mrs Grant, a leading Cape suffragist, in 1926,

> Well, in this country it is no use talking of justice. If we talk of justice, we are told we shall go under. Such native policy as we have is based on injustice. . . Should we women be so wonderfully just, when after all, the white men in this country are not entirely just to native men?

Although the demand for the enfranchisement of women was an explicitly feminist one, the suffrage movement was a racist movement that ignored three-quarters of the women in the country. The great majority of suffragists placed the protection of their privileges as members (albeit subordinate members) of the ruling class before the elimination of sexual discrimination. A comment another suffragist, Aletta Nel, made at the 1926 select committee hearing on women's suffrage expressed this succinctly. When asked if she favoured extending the vote to black women, she replied, 'As a woman, sir, yes. . . but as a South African born person, I feel that it would be wiser if we gave the vote to the European woman only'. It was an attitude that would characterise the bulk of white women's organisations throughout the twentieth century.

Notes

1. Henry Cloete, British High Commissioner in Natal, to the Governor of the Cape, describing a deputation of Voortrekker women in Pietermaritzburg, August 1843. Quoted in A.P. van Rensburg, *Moeders van ons Volk*, p. 111.
2. *Census of the Colony of the Cape of Good Hope, 1904*, p. cxiv.
3. Statistical material in the following sections have been drawn from many sources, including the census reports as cited, the useful compendium *Union Statistics for 50 Years*, the *Report of the Carnegie Commission*, vol. 1, and S. van der Horst's paper, 'Women as an economic force in Southern Africa'. In many cases, I have calculated the specific figures and percentages for women from the available data.
4. *Industrial Legislation Commission*, 1951, p. 14, Table 16.
5. Although a detailed breakdown of the distribution of the rural African population between white farms and 'Native Areas' is not available before 1936, in 1921 all African females living in the reserves were classified as peasants. This figure (1,345,421) in the occupations census amounts to just over 58 per cent of the total African female population. *Union Statistics for 50 Years*, Tables A-5, A-33.
6. The following account is based on interviews with her over several months.
7. H.J. Simons, *African Women, their Legal Status in South Africa*, p. 26.
8. This has been calculated from figures for the total of African women in the country, less the 'peasant' category and the total number of African female farm workers, *Union Statistics for 50 Years*, Table A-33.
9. Under this system, a man and his family worked at a nominal wage for the landowner for part of the year as a form of rent. This entitled them to occupy and farm a piece of land for themselves during the remainder of the year.
10. *Report of the Native Farm Labour Committee*, 1937–39, p. 37.
11. O. Schreiner, *Women and Labour*, p. 200.
12. *Union Statistics for 50 Years*, Tables E-12, E-13, and *Official Yearbook of the Union*, no. 2, 1918, p. 252.
13. *Union Statistics for 50 Years*, Tables E-13 to E-22.
14. *Report of the Carnegie Commission*, Vol. 5, p. xv.
15. *Report of the Department of Native Affairs*, 1935–36, p. 50.
16. *Report of the Native Affairs Department*, 1919–21, p. 22.
17. This and the following quotations and comments to do with the women's suffrage movement are taken from my study, *The Women's Suffrage Movement in South Africa*.

2

'Equal Rights to All Civilised Men': Women and the ANC Before 1939

The fact that until 1930 no women had the vote was both a reflection of their inferior status and a factor in perpetuating it. Although the enfranchisement of women did not bring about the profound changes that many suffragists had anticipated—and their opponents feared—it was also true that not until women were enfranchised did parliament begin to debate such issues as the legal disabilities of women. Nevertheless, the women's suffrage movement stood apart from black women, and the enfranchisement of white women as a distinct category only drove a further wedge between the two groups. Before black women could campaign for the vote for women, they had first to establish the right for blacks to vote—a right that by 1930 was coming under very heavy fire.

The issues that stirred black women to political activity at this time were not primarily 'women's issues'. They were basic bread and butter issues that affected the entire community—passes, rents, the cost of living, and laws that discriminated against blacks. In the 1930s and again later, in the 1940s, some women attempted to establish a suffrage league amongst 'Coloured' women in Cape Town, but failed to attract significant support; it was an issue of scant relevance to most black women.

It was the organisations prepared to take up community issues that attracted black women into politics, and it was in the general political context of the national liberation movement against white supremacy that a truly representative women's movement took shape. In the period before the second world war, the three most important organisations to deal with women politically, within this general context, were the African National Congress [ANC], the Communist Party of South Africa [CPSA], and the trade union movement. There was contact and overlap between all three organisations, most marked in this early stage between the CPSA and various of the trade unions. However, for the sake of convenience, but also because the position of women varied within each, these three areas will be, dealt with separately in the ensuing chapters.

In assessing the scope of black women's political activity in this period, the general discussion of the position of women, and of black women in particular, must be borne in mind. There were many barriers preventing black women from taking an active part in political affairs. The period before the second world war, though an important and formative one, was not characterised by coherent and sustained, large-scale participation of women in politics.

The Establishment of the ANC

In the 1950s the ANC would be the single most important source of membership for the FSAW, through its women's section, the ANC Women's League [ANCWL]. However, in 1912, when it was formed, women were completely peripheral to the organisation. At that stage, as already described, the public sphere of politics and political parties was a male domain. Pixley ka Izaka Seme, who played a leading part in the convening of the first conference of the ANC, set out its concerns as follows:

> Chiefs of royal blood and gentlemen of our race. . . we have discovered that in the land of their birth, Africans are treated as hewers of wood and drawers of water. The white people of this country have formed what is known as the Union of South Africa—a union in which we have no voice in the making of laws and no part in their administration. We have called you therefore to this conference so that we can, together, devise ways and means of forming our national union for the purpose of creating national unity and defending our rights and privileges.[1]

While this gathering of 'chiefs and gentlemen' was opposed to its own exclusion from the process of lawmaking, it had no quarrel with the exclusion of women. Women were not immediately and automatically granted membership in the new organisation. Nor were women included in its earliest franchise claim. In 1912 the ANC's call for political rights was an echo of Cecil Rhodes' dictum, 'equal rights to all civilised men from the Cape to the Zambezi'.[2] Only in the 1940s did it come out unequivocally in support of a universal suffrage that included women too.

There are some striking parallels between the early ANC and the WEAU. Both were composed of people who were seeking to extend rather than overthrow the existing power base in society, so as to incorporate themselves. The leaders of the ANC were drawn from the tiny westernised and educated African elite—the lawyers, ministers, teachers. Very few black women qualified in terms of education or economic standing for inclusion within this category. Conservative men, reared in a strongly patriarchal tradition, the early ANC leaders aspired to full partnership within a parliamentary democracy with the whites. They had embraced the system of values of the dominant group within society, the white middle class. In the process they adopted without questioning its views on the subordinate place of women, views which did not conflict with their own patriarchal tradition. Right up to the 1950s and beyond, the ANC continued to see women primarily as mothers and wives. This view conditioned the outlook of its female members as well.

Politics in the early twentieth century was thus a male-defined occupation. However, in 1913, African women themselves burst on to the public political stage in a fierce and unexpected campaign against pass laws for women in the Orange Free State. Opposition to passes was a key issue round which African women in the twentieth century would rally. The anti-pass campaign in the Free State was an early example of this and one of the earliest expressions of discontent by black women in modern

South Africa. As such, it came to assume a symbolic importance in later years. At the same time, it forced the ANC to pay greater attention to women, and provided the momentum for the establishment, in 1913/14, of a Bantu Women's League within the ANC. This was the first national organisation of black women to attempt to operate within the framework of non-tribal political institutions. For all its shortcomings, it stands as a landmark in the development of the women's movement.

The Anti-Pass Campaign in the Orange Free State, 1913–20

The pass laws in South Africa have been one of the crucial mechanisms of state control over the African population. However, as already mentioned, until the 1930s women were generally exempt from any systematic attempt at pass control. Since so few African women were living and working in town, the central and three of the four provincial governments did not consider it necessary to include women within the scope of the pass laws at that stage.

The Orange Free State was thus exceptional in this regard. In the early twentieth century, the Free State pass laws net enmeshed the entire black population, male and female, African and 'Coloured'. The scope of these laws was very wide, forcing men and women to negotiate a maze of bureaucratic restrictions in the most routine aspects of their lives. Even entertainment required official sanction—and a fee. An inter-departmental committee on the Native Pass Laws, reporting in 1921, listed the following passes which black town-dwellers in the Orange Free State could be required to possess: 'stand permits, residential passes, visitors' passes, seeking work passes, employment registration certificates, permits to reside on employer's premises, work on own behalf certificates, domestic service books, washerwomen's permits and entertainment permits'.[3] Each of these cost money (5s a month to work on one's own); failure to possess the necessary papers led to arrest. In addition, according to Sol Plaatje, a leading figure in the ANC at the time, 'no native women in the Province of the Orange "Free" State [*sic*] can reside within a municipality (whether with or without her parents or her husband) unless she can produce a permit showing that she is a servant in the employ of a white person, this permit being signed by the Town Clerk'.[4] In the Free State, domestic work by black women was regarded by whites as part of the natural order of things.

To answer the question why women should have been included within these pass provisions in the Free State, when elsewhere they were excluded, requires a separate study of the State's historical development in the nineteenth and early twentieth centuries, taking in both the rural and urban areas. The Free State pass laws dated from before Union, but, according to Sol Plaatje in the account just quoted, it was only after 1910 that they came to be stringently applied against women. He offers no explanation for this. In the absence of any other in-depth study on the subject, it is impossible to offer a complete answer, but certain distinctive features of the Free State were clearly important.

Enforcement of the pass laws was left to local government, and obviously, in general terms, the revenue accruing from the issue of all these permits was an attractive prospect for the white municipalities. The fundamental purpose of the pass laws, however, has always been to control the black labour force, and this was as true of the Free State as of any of the other provinces. What distinguished the Orange Free State from the other provinces was that very little land had been set aside as African 'reserve' areas. The bulk of the rural African population were living on white-owned land, as squatters, sharecroppers, or farm labourers. Furthermore, in the towns, stable black communities with a reasonably balanced sex ratio had developed from the start. In Bloemfontein, for instance, the 1921 population census showed 9,330 African men and 8,588 African women residing there—the masculinity rate was a mere 109 compared to the Union-wide urban average of 299.[5]

As far as women are concerned, this meant that in the Free State in the early years of the century, African women were in far more direct contact with white society than in other parts of the country. This undoubtedly affected government attitudes toward them, and helps to explain the unusual degree of direct state control (as opposed to indirect and tribal) that enveloped them. Unlike the other three provinces, the Orange Free State provincial government could not bypass the question of governing African women by relegating them to the tribal authorities, since those institutions were virtually non-existent.

The burden of pass laws was widely resented, but their application to women drew special condemnation from black political organisations. The arguments they put forward have remained basic to women's struggle against pass laws since then, and are worth setting out more fully. They all attested to the special role that women performed within the home.

Both men and women were quick to argue the unique character of women, as wives and mothers, which made it particularly repugnant to apply passes to them. They stressed that nowhere else were women subject to such regulations. By imposing on women the risk of arbitrary arrest and imprisonment, passes directly threatened the well-being of the family. If mothers were taken off to gaol for falling foul of the pass laws, children would be neglected and the family would suffer. This was probably the most frequent and constantly recurring argument throughout the history of African opposition to passes for women: because of women's domestic responsibilities, they merited special treatment. At the same time, passes were also seen as endangering and insulting women's virtue. In 1914 the black newspaper *APO* printed a petition against passes for women which made this one of its main arguments. Compiled by the 'OFS Native and Coloured Women', and addressed to the Governor-General of the Union, it drew attention to two recent cases of rape, both of which it blamed on the enforcement of the pass laws. In each case an official (an African constable and a white location superintendent respectively) had stopped and then raped a young girl on the pretext of checking her pass. For women, a system 'which makes it lawful for any class of man coming under the title of policemen to interfere with them and demand a pass from them' was seen as particularly dangerous.[6]

It is very possible that there was an element of political expediency in these arguments—'women and children' as an abstract and emotive category has always been a useful slogan for politicians to brandish. Nevertheless, they were deeply felt by those on whom the burden of the laws rested. The arguments attested to the vital role that women did play in the home, as well as the strength of the ideology that kept them there.

Within a few years of Union, the bitter resentment of women against the pass laws had come to a head. For one thing, as Plaatje explained, the laws were being more vigorously enforced after 1910. For another, the African population of the country was already in a state of deep unrest because of the impending Native Land Bill. This bill, which became law in 1913, was a cornerstone in the construction of the whole edifice of cheap migrant labour in South Africa. It established the outline of the African reserves—eventually to amount to no more than 13 per cent of the total land mass in the country—and laid down that henceforth no African could own land outside these reserves. It also outlawed African squatting and sharecropping on white-owned lands.

The Land Bill threatened the very basis of an independent African subsistence on the land. It posed a particularly grave economic threat to the African population in the Free State, where the amount of African-owned land was so negligible and squatting on white farms extensive. White farmers in the Free State had always blamed the labour shortage of which they complained directly on the prevalence of African squatting and sharecropping on white-owned land. They were among the strongest champions of the bill.

The publication of the Land Bill, coming so soon after the all-white parliament had been set up in 1910, stung the tiny African elite into a new political awareness. It was largely in response to this bill that the conference was called at which the ANC was set up. Opposition to the Land Act went far beyond this tiny section of people, however. The effects of the act stirred the entire African community, creating a widespread mood of alarm and unrest, in which despondency mingled with defiance. Feelings were at their strongest in the Orange Free State, where the consequences of the new legislation were most immediately felt. As soon as the bill had become law, scores of sharecroppers and squatters were given the choice of either becoming full-time labourers for their former landlords or being thrown off their land. In mid-1913 Sol Plaatje toured the province to see for himself what the repercussions on the lives of people had been. His book, *Native Life in South Africa*, records his impressions, and documents the misery and hardship of evicted squatters and sharecroppers engaged in a fruitless search, in mid-winter, for alternative places to live.

Lobbying against the pass laws was fairly intensive in the first years after Union. Both major black political organisations of the time, the African People's Organisation [APO][7] and the ANC took up the issue in deputations, press statements, and petitions to the government. Then, from 1912, women themselves started taking an active role in the campaign.

One of the first signs of this was the establishment of an organisation called the 'Native and Coloured Women's Association', which organised the women's petition to the governor-general already mentioned. It seems likely that this association came into existence during 1912 and was involved in organising the petitions and deputations that began to appear from women in that year.

It is unfortunate—but revealing of contemporary attitudes—that it is difficult to know who the members of this association were. In the news-paper reports on their activities, the members of the association are faceless, anonymous—'the ladies', in the *APO*. Given the general position of women in the townships at the time, it is unlikely that the association ever had a particularly large following. Judging from the coverage it received in the *APO*, it appears to have had close links with both the ANC and the APO; it is very likely that it was organised by the wives of the leading figures in the local branches of those bodies.

What is interesting is that the organisation involved both African and 'Coloured' women. Overall, the 'Coloured' population of the Free State was negligible compared to the African, and their contribution to the association was probably small.[8] Certainly, 'Coloured' women do not feature in the subsequent demonstrations. Nevertheless, by involving both groups of women, the association showed clearly that, contrary to official and popular views, where people faced common difficulties ethnic differences need not be a barrier to organising a common defence.

From early on, the male-dominated APO and ANC showed a degree of ambivalence towards the women activists. While strongly supporting the campaign, they were yet alarmed by signs of too great an independence on the part of the women. In March 1912, apparently dissatisfied with the response given by the Minister of Native Affairs to a Congress deputa-tion, a group of women travelled to Cape Town to seek redress them-selves. The *APO* commented tartly:

> We think. . . the deputation might have awaited the Native Congress. It is also regrettable that the coloured women of the Orange Free State did not consult the Executive of the APO Women's Guild. We feel sure that no deputation of Coloured men of the APO would have come to Cape Town without first acquainting the Executive with the object of its mission.[9]

What the response of the women to this reproof may have been, is un-fortunately not reported.

The central government appeared cautiously sympathetic to the view that women should be leniently treated, if not actually exempted. But it was reluctant to damage its already fragile political base amongst whites in the Free State by intervening decisively, and matters were allowed to drift. The flashpoint came in mid-1913. Some Bloemfontein women, presenting a petition to the mayor, were arrested for not having passes—and the simmering opposition boiled over into open defiance. This was how the *APO* described what happened:

Friday morning, the 6th June, should and will never be forgotten in South
Africa. On that day, the Native women declared their womanhood. Six hundred
daughters of South Africa taught the arrogant whites a lesson that will never
be forgotten. Headed by the bravest of them, they marched to the magistrate,
hustled the police out of their way and kept shouting and cheering until His
Worship emerged from his office and addressed them, thence they proceeded to
the Town Hall. The women had now assumed a threatening attitude. The police
endeavoured to keep them off the steps. . . the gathering got out of control.
Sticks could be seen flourishing overhead and some came down with no gentle
thwacks across the skulls of the police, who were bold enough to stem the
onrush—'We have done with pleading, we now demand', declared the women.[10]

This incident was the beginning of a widespread campaign of passive
resistance, which spread to all the major Free State towns and involved
hundreds of women. There is no indication that the Bloemfontein protesters had worked out a careful campaign beforehand, but once the first
arrests had been made, there were definite attempts to turn a spontaneous
outburst of feeling into a more co-ordinated demonstration of popular
opposition. The women turned to the tactics of passive resistance and
civil disobedience which the South African Indian Congress [SAIC]
leader, M.K. Gandhi, had already pioneered in South Africa.

In Bloemfontein, 34 women, convicted as a result of the June demonstration, forfeited the option of a fine 'as a means of bringing their
grievances before the notice of the public'.[11] Their example was followed
in other centres, and soon there were reports of gaols being too full to
handle all the prisoners.[12] In Kroonstad, Winburg and Senekal, women
defied the pass laws and came forward for arrest. This period of unrest
coincided exactly with the period when the Native Land Act was being
enforced—the Bloemfontein anti-pass demonstration took place a week
before the act was passed.

The scale and intensity of the demonstrations made a strong impression
on observers. The *APO*, jubilant at the stand the women had taken, was
also taken aback, if not a little disconcerted, that it was women who had
taken the lead. It concluded its report on the Bloemfontein disturbances
in a more sober vein: 'In the meantime, we, the men, who are supposed
to be made of sterner stuff, may well hide our faces for shame and ponder
in some secluded spot over the heroic stand made by Africa's daughters.'[13]

Whites were forced to see black women in a new light. In 1913 a
white suffragist, I.K. Cross, considered the demonstrations sufficiently
newsworthy to be included in an article she was compiling on the women's
movement in South Africa. She used them to illustrate a general point,
that women everywhere were beginning to assert themselves, and made no
attempt to link the women's anti-pass campaign to the white suffrage
movement. The tone of Cross's comments was patronising—the Bloemfontein march was described as a 'rather amusing incident'—and revealed
the wide gulf across which she and other suffragists viewed black women.[14]
Nevertheless, probably for the first time she and her colleagues had been
forced to consider black women as political beings in their own right.

The spontaneity, enthusiasm and informal organisation of the campaign would be characteristic of many anti-pass demonstrations by women in the future. There was no overall strategy; nor did the women have the support of an organisation that could sustain and direct the campaign. Inevitably, therefore, the outburst of popular feeling had to exhaust itself after some months.

During the war the campaign subsided, but it flared up again at the war's conclusion, spreading to the Rand, where it was linked to a general anti-pass campaign led by the ANC at the time. By that time the central government had taken note of the campaign, and the enforcement of Free State pass laws against women was being relaxed. Nevertheless, as late as 1920, 62 women in Senekal were reported to have refused resident-ial permits and gone to gaol rather than pay a two pound fine.[15]

This anti-pass campaign represents the first large-scale entry of black women, operating in terms of the modern (non-tribal) political structure in South Africa, into the political arena. The issue around which they rallied to form the Bantu Women's League, that of passes, was to remain a central area of concern. The 1913 events were the first of many indica-tions of how strongly women felt against passes and what an explosive issue it could be.

While the resistance focused strongly on the particular evils seen to be inherent in applying these laws to women, the pass laws provided an area of common experience for both men and women that was exclusive to the African group. The suffragists had shown how indifferent they were to the problems and the organisations of black women; the only possible political home black women could find at that time was in the already existing black political organisations. From the beginning, then, African women's political behaviour was shaped in terms of their community of interest with African men.

The anti-pass campaign of 1913/14 had nothing to do with the women's rights movement then rocking the western world and to which white South African suffragists looked. It can in fact be argued that in defying the law as vociferously as they had, African women were looking back to a cultural tradition that had allowed women a great deal more independence and authority than western society considered either 'natural' or 'respectable' at the time.

The Bantu Women's League

The most tangible result of the 1913 campaign was the establishment of the Bantu Women's League within the ANC. Walshe, in his study on the ANC, links the formation of the league directly to the campaign against passes: 'by the second half of 1913 this Free State unrest was widespread and led directly to the formation of the Bantu Women's League'.[16] Under its first president, Charlotte Maxeke, it immediately took up the question of the pass laws. In 1918 Maxeke led a deputation of women from the league to the Prime Minister, Botha, to present the women's case. It appears to have been well received. No actual legislation was passed, but it seems the SAP government did persuade the Free State authorities to relax their enforcement of the pass laws with regard to women. Faced with a number of threats to its existence, chiefly from white labour, the government was unwilling to provide a diffused, still fairly muted black opposition with so emotive a rallying point as 'the sanctity of women'. Exemption of women from the pass laws did not seriously threaten control over the African labour force, of which women constituted a minute percentage. The Free State demonstrations had in fact introduced a new and uncertain dimension for the State with regard to the pass laws. For years, the memory of the unrest was to temper its approach to black women.

The Bantu Women's League was formed under the aegis of the ANC, to which it affiliated. However, the role of women within the ANC was to be a very limited one in the early twentieth century. In terms of the ANC constitution that was drawn up and adopted in 1919, women could not become full members, but were accorded the status of 'auxiliary member-ship' only, without voting rights.[17] With this was laid the basis of the ANC's treatment of women for the next twenty-five years, as a separate category of members outside the scope of its regular activities.

In its thinking on the position of women, the ANC was no more progressive than any of the white political parties at the time. The function of the Women's League during this period was to provide the catering and organise the entertainment at meetings and conferences—the community of interests of African men and women did not extend to the kitchen. There was, at that stage, little effort to broaden established views on women's role on the part of either the men or the women of the ANC.

Unfortunately, once the anti-pass campaign had subsided, very little material on the subsequent development of the Bantu Women's League is available. One catches a faint glimpse of ANC women at Potchefstroom in the Transvaal in 1928. There, a system of residential permits for Africans that the local municipality was enforcing sparked off a wave of unrest that involved women as well as men. The campaign and the circumstances surrounding it are poorly documented, however. There were apparently two main issues at stake, firstly, the cost of the permits, secondly, the fact that children over the age of 18 were deemed 'lodgers' and obliged to take out permits in order to continue living with their parents.[18] Apart from its intrinsic interest as an early sign of community organisation and grassroots resistance, the campaign is significant for bringing to the fore a local woman leader, Josie Palmer. She was a Potchefstroom resident who played a leading part in the campaign. She joined the Communist Party at this time and rapidly became a prominent member of it, remaining an active political campaigner in both local and national issues until she was forcibly silenced by the Nationalist government in the 1950s. For a long time she was one of the very few black women to take an active lead on political issues.

According to Palmer, women were deeply involved in the Potchef-stroom demonstrations, which emphasises once again the power of any pass-related issue in mobilising them to action. The momentum seems to have come largely from local sources, but once under way, the Communist Party became involved in organising meetings and recruiting members. These activities are looked at in more detail in the following chapter. The extent of ANC involvement is not known, but it did send a female member, a Mrs Bhola, to at least one women's meeting held in a Potchefstroom location. She travelled to the meeting in company with two women from the CPSA, Rebecca Bunting and Mary Wolton. This indicates that contact between women within these two organisations had been established by that time. Information about Mrs Bhola is scant. Simons and Simons describe her briefly as an organiser in the 'women's section of the ANC'.[19] They also mention that she was the first woman to stand trial under the notorious 'hostility clause' of the Native Administration Act of 1927, a provision which made it an offence for anybody to incite 'racial hostility' —as broad and flexible a category of misdemeanor as the authorities could desire. Simons and Simons do not say what occasioned this trial and when it took place.

Apart from these fragmentary references, the available material is silent on women in the ANC at this time. In the 1920s and 1930s the ANC was itself a weak and badly organised body, speaking to and for the tiny group of middle-class Africans in the towns. It had no mass following and no aspirations to create one. The lowly status of women within the ANC, coupled with their insignificant presence in the towns, meant that they could play almost no part in its affairs.

There was certainly no lack of issues round which women could have been organised—housing, education, the cost of living, police raids against illicit beer brewing, all basic issues that daily harassed and squeezed township women. Roux, in his history of 'the black man's struggle for freedom', *Time Longer Than Rope*, describes a wave of protests and boycotts aimed at municipal beerhalls which disturbed the Natal towns of Greytown, Weenen, and especially Durban in 1928/29. He also records an outbreak of unrest in the African location in Germiston against a lodger's tax in 1932. In a similar fashion to the residence permit in Potchefstroom, the lodger's tax imposed a levy of half-a-crown a month per 'lodger', a lodger defined as any occupant of a house over the age of eighteen and not the registered tenant or his wife. In all of these demonstrations, women featured prominently at meetings, marches and in picket lines.[20] At that stage, however, the ANC lacked both the interest and the organisational structures to take these issues up. It was left largely to individuals in other organisations, particularly in the Communist Party and some of the trade unions, to respond to these questions and use them to politicise women.

The Bantu Women's League did manage to survive this period of inactivity, and by 1935 it was still in existence. It was the only women's body specifically invited to the All African Convention [AAC] held in that year. This conference was called to register a broad-based African opposition to the 'Hertzog Bills' then being debated by parliament. These bills finally achieved what the Women's Enfranchisement Act of 1930 had only partially managed—the removal of the common roll voting rights still enjoyed by a minority of 'qualified' Africans in the Cape. They also consolidated the Native Reserve territories. Like the Land Act of 1913, these measures stimulated African political organisations to protest, and thus prodded the ANC out of its former slump.

Charlotte Mexeke, president of the Bantu Women's League, was honoured at the AAC by being invited to be one of the speakers. However, the League was obviously in a weak state, and during the course of the convention the following resolution was passed by a group of the women delegates,

> that the time has come for the establishment of an African Council of Women on lines similar to those of the National Councils of other races, in order that we may be able to do our share in the advancement of our race.[21]

This was later agreed to by the convention as a whole, and thus the National Council of African Women [NCAW] came into being.

The NCAW

According to an undated typescript, 'National Council of African Women', the foundations of the NCAW were laid, in 1933, by a group of women in Kimberley who were anxious to form an organisation 'to care for Non-European welfare'. Subsequently, other centres initiated similar councils 'quite independently'.[22] It would seem, then, that at the AAC in 1935, these groups decided to amalgamate to establish a national council. The NCAW seems to have superceded the Bantu Women's League. Charlotte Mexeke became the first national president of the NCAW, and thereafter the Bantu Women's League appears to have been totally eclipsed.

The NCAW itself does not appear to have lived up to the expectations vested in it. Like its white counterpart, the National Council of Women [NCW], with which it developed links, it did not regard itself as primarily a political organisation, but rather one involved in 'non-European welfare'. It derived its support from the tiny group of African professional women (teachers and nurses, for the most part), not from the masses of working-class and peasant women. From an early stage, it came under the influence of white liberals in the Joint Councils Movement. This was a multiracial movement that had been set up in 1921 by whites who were sympathetic to the political aspirations of moderate black organisations, and anxious to initiate dialogue between black and white leaders.

Mrs Rheinhallt-Jones, wife of the first director of the South African Institute of Race Relations and very active in the Joint Councils movement, played a particularly dominant role in the affairs of the NCAW. This becomes very clear from the NCAW correspondence of the time. Her influence did not pass unnoticed, and earned the NCAW the criticism of more radical organisations. In 1940 the then national president, Mrs M.T. Soga, writing to Mrs Rheinhallt-Jones, referred to 'the belief amongst Africans that the NCAW is being run by white people'. She added, 'I hope that you did not strengthen that belief.'[23]

In 1937 Josie Palmer, by then prominent within the Communist Party, criticised the NCAW as an ineffective body that had fallen into the wrong hands. In a fierce article that appeared in the left-wing weekly *Umsebenzi* in June, she attacked its leadership, accusing them of having 'buried' the organisation.[24] The time was long overdue, she wrote, for an effective organisation that would bring women into the general struggle against unjust laws. Her call was a sign of the restlessness among the few African women who were politically active, regarding the limitations of existing organisations and political work involving women.

From the above, it is clear that before the second world war the organisation of African women, both within and without the ANC, was in a poor state. Nevertheless, it is clear, too, that women were not entirely the passive and silent objects of history that the dearth of information about them might seem to indicate. They marched and demonstrated in the Orange Free State in 1913 in large numbers. They fought the introduction of municipal beerhalls in Natal in 1928/29, and were present when Potchefstroom and Germiston residents protested against housing policies in the townships. It is likely that they were involved in many other small local campaigns and organisations, but their presence has been overlooked by contemporary observers and later researchers.

Only three African women have received any attention from historians of black political organisations at this time: Charlotte Maxeke, president of the Bantu Women's League and later the NCAW; Josie Palmer, active in the CPSA; and Mrs Bhola, who attended the CPSA meeting in Potchefstroom in 1928. Of the three, the most prominent at this time was undoubtedly Maxeke—'the mother of African freedom in this country', as Dr Xuma, president of the ANC, described her at the All-African Convention in 1935.[25] Since something is known of her life, while that of other women political leaders and the history of the Bantu Women's League itself are so poorly documented, it seems useful to look at it in greater detail. Charlotte Maxeke was an exceptional woman, but in many ways she was typical of both her position as a member of the tiny black middle class and her times. Her life marked out the very limits of opportunity to which a black woman could aspire at the time; the dominant concerns of the Bantu Women's League were manifest in her thinking.

Charlotte Maxeke: Mother of African Freedom[26]

According to the *African Yearly Register* of 1931, Charlotte Manye (her maiden name) was born in 1874 near Beaufort West and educated at Uitenhage and Port Elizabeth. Little is known of her parents and schooling, except that she was brought up within a Christian framework and educated in mission schools. As with many of the leaders of the early ANC, Christianity remained a dominant and moderating influence throughout her life. Later she moved with her parents to Kimberley, and there was offered an opportunity that for a black South African woman at the end of the nineteenth century was virtually unheard of—to join an African choir and tour England. As a member of this same choir, she later toured Canada and the United States as well. In the United States she was offered a scholarship to attend a segregated negro college in Ohio, Wilberforce University, and she enrolled for a B.Sc. degree. Maxeke thus joined that tiny group of African students (estimated at between 100 and 400 by the beginning of the twentieth century) who were able to continue their higher education abroad.

In the US she would have come into contact with the ideas of the prominent civil rights leader Booker T. Washington, who exerted considerable moderating influence on the political philosophy of the early ANC. At this time, she also joined the African Methodist Episcopal [AME] church, the earliest and one of the largest of the African separatist churches. The separatist churches were one of the first areas where black nationalist sentiments and aspirations for a more just society could assert themselves; in involving herself in the AME church, Maxeke was, whether consciously or not, identifying herself with this process. Religion offered both a cathartic release from the pressures of a discriminatory society and a politically respectable area in which blacks could work.

In 1901, with experiences and an education that few of her contemporaries in South Africa could match, Charlotte Manye returned to South Africa to begin 'active pioneer work' for the AME church. She subsequently married Rev. M.M. Maxeke, an AME minister and another graduate of Wilberforce. Through him, she had links with the ANC from its beginnings, for he joined it at its start in 1912. These links were strengthened through the anti-pass campaign and the establishment of the Bantu Women's League.

As president of the league, Maxeke was active in pressing for the relaxation of the Free State pass laws, and in 1918 she led a deputation to put the women's case to the Prime Minister, Louis Botha. At about this time she also developed contacts with the Industrial and Commercial Workers' Union [ICU] of Clements Kadalie, a short-lived but major channel of African political aspirations in the 1920s. The extent of Maxeke's contacts with the ICU is shadowy. It seems likely she was in touch with its leaders in its early stages, before it had fully emerged as a rival to the ANC. It is interesting that in 1920 the ICU tried to initiate a women's branch in Cape Town—perhaps Maxeke had some part in this. (The attempt is discussed more fully below.)

But although politically active throughout her working life, Maxeke's major concerns were social rather than political, and centred on the church. In this she differed little from many socially active white women. The Maxekes lived in a number of different places before settling finally in Johannesburg. Here Charlotte Maxeke became 'a leader in church work and social service', and president of a missionary association.[27] Then, with the death of her husband (the date is not known), she was thrown on her own resources. At a time when hardly any black women had entered the professions, she first set up an employment bureau and was later employed as a probation officer, attached to the courts, by the Johannesburg municipality. E. Rosenthal describes her as the first African social worker in South Africa.[28]

By the 1920s her reputation had travelled beyond the confines of the ANC. In 1921, the Women's Reform Club, a white women's suffrage group in Pretoria, invited her to speak at a public meeting they were hosting to coincide with the annual conference of the WEAU. It would seem that she was the first and the last African woman thus singled out by the suffragists.

Her topic was conditions of life for African women in the towns, a subject on which her probation work made her an authority. Significantly, despite the fact that it was a meeting convened by a women's suffrage organisation, neither the suffragists nor Maxeke herself made any reference to the vote. Educated black and white women might meet in the area of social reforms, with its emphasis on charity and soup kitchens; political rights were of another order. A report on the meeting noted the indifference with which Maxeke's speech was greeted by all the white reporters present. Despite the fact that she spoke 'fluently, clearly and with dignity', and represented those 'most nearly concerned', they all sat back and stopped taking notes as soon as she began to speak.[29]

Subsequent references to Maxeke are scanty. During the 1920s she became involved in the Joint Councils Movement and thus came into contact with Mrs Rheinhallt-Jones. How significant a movement she considered it to be is unfortunately not known. Nevertheless, she was sufficiently impressed by their approach to propose, in 1930, that similarly structured 'Joint Service Councils' be established amongst white and African women. Here, too, the meeting ground between white and black was envisaged in the social rather than political sphere, since the purpose of the councils was to solve the problems faced by young black domestic workers in town. (From the available evidence it does not appear that anything materialised from these suggestions.)

In 1928 Maxeke represented the AME church at a general conference held in America. By 1930 she seems to have retired from her job, but was still in demand as a speaker, addressing a student Christian conference at Fort Hare in 1930 and the All African Convention in Bloemfontein in 1935. Presumably, she played a leading role in the establishment of the NCAW at the convention, and was subsequently elected its first President. She was then 61 years old. Four years later, in 1939, she died.[30]

While the biographical material is sketchy, it is clear that Maxeke's life experience was far removed from that of the average black woman at the time. Her career was remarkably similar to that of contemporary male leaders in the ANC. From an early stage she was exposed to the same influences that helped shape their political thinking—Christianity, negro aspirations in the USA, the Joint Councils Movement in South Africa. Both her education and her work qualified her for membership of the tiny middle class fraction of the African population from whom the bulk of the ANC leadership was drawn. Thus, while the momentum for the establishment of the Bantu Women's League had come from that broad swelling of popular agitation in the Free State anti-pass campaign, its leaders, as in the ANC itself, came from this tiny and relatively privileged fragment of the population.

Yet, at the same time, because she was a woman Maxeke did not enjoy an equal status within the ANC leadership with her male colleagues. She did not, for instance, have the vote. What she herself thought about women's suffrage in general and the South African campaign in particular, is unfortunately not known. What is clear is that even though her own life represented a radical break from the normal pattern of women's lives at the time, she did not reject conventional attitudes about women out of hand. In her speech to the Women's Reform Club in 1921, she referred to the 'unhappy consequences' of the breakdown of the old system of parental control 'under which native women had had all the virtues of noble women'.[31] She did not question the assumption that women's primary function was a domestic one. Speaking to the Students' Christian Association in 1930 she described the home as the centre of family life, women as its 'keystone'.[32] Under existing conditions in the townships, the traditional African family was being destroyed. Maxeke's chief concern was how to preserve it, not how to restructure it to allow women greater autonomy.

Maxeke's work in the Johannesburg courts brought her into daily contact with the reality of the destruction of family life. The devastating effects of the migrant labour system on the family were particularly marked on the Witwatersrand, where Maxeke worked. That area had the highest masculinity rate amongst Africans in the country, and some of the worst slums and shanty towns. Crime, prostitution and illegitimacy flourished under such conditions. These conditions reinforced Maxeke's middle-class values of the stable family, in which women played a central role, the source of both its physical and its spiritual well-being. Such values represented the standard by which the devastation of African family life could be measured, the alternative at which political and social reformers could aim.

This theme, of the sanctity of the family and the special role of women within it, was, as has been seen, a major strand in the arguments condemning pass laws for women. It dominated the ANC's thinking on women at the time and would remain strongly entrenched in later years as well. Those criticisms and re-evaluations of the primacy of women's domestic role which would surface within black women's organisations from time to time, came generally from sources other than the ANC.

Maxeke was also clear that the primary commitment of a women's organisation had to be to the common struggle of all black people against the disabilities they suffered under a white minority government. Her association with the Joint Councils Movement indicates that she was committed to a multiracial society. She believed, however, that this would be achieved by black endeavour and not simply by white patronage. In a speech to the AAC in 1935 she stressed these points. The convention, she said, represented not only the various parts of the country, but also the two sexes—and unity, she affirmed, was strength.

The Non-Europeans, while thanking their European friends for their support, had to go ahead themselves. The Natives were not a peculiar people who had to be carried on the backs of others forever. They had to be helped to help themselves.[33]

Thus, by the mid-1930s, some important lines of thought had already emerged within the women's section of the ANC. The emphasis was on women working alongside their men to overthrow those structures that oppressed them as blacks. Furthermore, women were not seeking radical change in established patterns of relationships with men and their families. There were signs, too, that individual women were becoming aware of the importance of organising women. With this went the recognition that women had particular interests and difficulties which necessitated their organising as a distinct group from men. This awareness had already led to the establishment of a separate women's organisation within the broader movement.

The scope for women in politics in the pre-war period was still very circumscribed. Yet, in the years that had elapsed since the foundation of the Bantu Women's League, there had been important shifts in the position of black women. By the mid 1930s, the inadequacies of the league in adjusting to these shifts were becoming apparent to several observers. The NCAW was one—unsuccessful—attempt to come to terms with the league's deficiencies. In the CPSA, other approaches to the problem were being tentatively tested, and these are considered in the next chapter.

African Women in the Towns in the 1930s

Fuelling these shifts in the position of women were the economic changes restructuring society, and the related process of urbanisation. While economic developments were fundamental in shaping the role of women, African women, still an insecure and marginal minority in the towns, were not being drawn into production at this time in the way that white and then 'Coloured' women were. More important for them, both as an indication of long-term structural changes in their position in society, and as a stimulus for new forms of organisation, was the fact of continued movement by rural women to town. By the 1930s, the impact of rapid urbanisation on the role of African women was beginning to show; and both the state and black political organisations were forced to pay greater attention.

By 1936 the urban population had risen to almost one-third of the total population.[34] All race groups shared in this increase. Amongst whites, the flow to the towns of the rural poor continued at a rapid rate throughout the twenties and thirties. In 1932 the Carnegie Commission noted the effects of urban life on these new immigrants: 'In the larger towns and especially in the cities a process of adaptation is taking place among the younger generation of rural immigrants, since life in the cities gives them the opportunity of becoming skilled workers.'[35] These new economic opportunities gave women a degree of independence and a status within their families that was previously unheard of—'cases are by no means rare of whole families subsisting on the earnings of working girls'.

African women formed a far smaller proportion of this townward migration than did white women but, nevertheless, the movement of African women away from the rural areas to the towns had become noticeable by the late 1930s. In 1936 the majority of African women (52.6 per cent) were still living in the 'Native Areas', but both the reserves and the 'white' countryside showed a decrease in the proportion of women living in them compared to 1921. The percentage of African women living in towns had risen by 4 per cent to just under 11 per cent of their total; the urban masculinity rate among Africans had dropped from 299 to 220.[36] Thus, although African women were still a tiny fraction of the urban population, the trend towards their increased urbanisation was unmistakeable.

This trend was not so much a response to new opportunities that the towns might hold out, as a reaction against the oppressive conditions in the reserves. There was little enough that town life offered black women in the 1930s in the way of jobs, security, or housing. But the little that could be gleaned from the towns was more than could be found in the reserves, and so the tiny population of born-and-bred townswomen was being supplemented all the time by newcomers from the countryside. Already the potentially disruptive effect on the reproductive role of the reserves that a large-scale townward migration of women would bring, had been officially noted. Speaking in parliament in 1937, the Minister of Native Affairs, Grobler, referred to the influx of Africans to the towns as

> one of the things that is undermining the morality and family life of the natives. . . It not only weakens tribal and parental control, but there is a tendency for these young men and women to become permanent town dwellers. The parents are left behind uncared for, and for the most part they never hear again of these natives.[37]

His concern was reflected in a more restrictive policy on influx control for women, as the government sought to bolster the migrant labour system. Before 1930 there were no systematic controls on African women moving to urban areas. They were not included in the terms of the 1923 Urban Areas Act, an act which has been described as containing the 'skeleton' of all subsequent urban areas legislation.[38] It laid the basis for strictly segregated 'locations' (or townships), where Africans were to be housed. It also established the basic criteria for qualifications to live in the locations. Any African who did not qualify, and stayed without official permission for longer than 72 hours, was henceforth guilty of an offence.

The fact that women were not included in the provisions of the 1923 act points to the insignificance of their presence in town at that stage. However, in 1930 and again in 1937, the first legislative attempts to stem the tide of African women entering the urban areas were made. In 1930, municipalities were empowered to prohibit African women from entering their area without their prior permission—though not if the woman's husband or father had been working there for a minimum of two years and, a damning proviso, accommodation was available. A woman's right to live in town was thus seen as dependent on her relationship to a resident male—she could have no independent claim to live there. In 1937, the legislation was tightened up still further. From then on, women wishing to travel to town were required to obtain the permission of the magistrate in their home districts in addition to that of the local urban authority.

However, since women, unlike men, were exempt from the compulsory carrying of passes, the enforcement of both acts was difficult and generally ineffective. Female migration to the towns continued to grow. A survey carried out in the Keiskammahoek district of the Ciskei estimated that at least in that one district, from about 1936, the rate of women migrating to towns was increasing faster than that of men, even though their numbers were still far less.[39]

For white immigrants to the city, the shock of adjusting to the alien conditions of urban life was cushioned to a large extent by vigorous state action aimed at combating the so-called 'poor white problem'. Jobs, often protected against competition from black workers, were created for them and attempts made to raise and protect their living standards. For blacks, no such mediation was forthcoming. For them, the transition to urban life was a particularly violent one.

The impact of township life on the structure and stability of the traditional African family was generally extremely destructive. Most of the available data refer to the post-war period, but it is clear that the developments which sociologists and anthropologists would later comment on were present in the pre-war years. Charlotte Maxeke was already expressing concern about it in 1921, at her meeting with white suffragists in Pretoria. Illegitimacy was on the rise. Marriage was becoming increasingly less stable, less binding. The effects of the migrant labour system, and the unequal sex ratios in both town and country, the acute poverty, insecurity and lack of political rights of township residents, combined to undermine the structure of the family without creating the basis on which new and viable alternatives could be built.

While many of the traditional restraints on female independence were crumbling, their status was riddled with contradiction and ambiguity. Even though the decline of the traditional family structure meant women were often *de facto* heads of households, the law continued to define them as minors. Patriarchal values were still deeply entrenched within the African community. Some twenty years later an opinion poll conducted by *Drum* found that a majority of its respondents were against equal rights for women.[40]

Women's position in town was tenuous. They had no security of tenure in housing. Because women were regarded as minors, leases were made out to men only, which put enormous accommodation problems in the way of single, divorced, widowed or deserted women. Employment opportunities for them outside of domestic service were scant. Frequently only through illicit trading in prostitution or drink, or by precarious and marginal occupations such as hawking food or some other commodity, could a woman make a living in the townships. Dora Tamana, living in Queenstown during the 1930s, used to scrape together a meagre income by fetching thatching grass from the surrounding hills to sell in the locations. One bundle which took most of the day to gather and sell, would fetch about 1/6d. During this time three of her four children died, and finally in desperation, she insisted that she join her husband in Cape Town, where he was working, before she lost her entire family.[41]

The impact of urbanisation on African women was clearly not a straightforward liberatory one. Old restraints on their independence were being eroded, but new and daunting restrictions on their mobility and their security were replacing them. The pressures on African women were enormous. The need for finding a voice to give expression to their frustrations and demands was growing more urgent, but the obstacles preventing this from taking a political direction were still considerable. Apart from the handicaps women suffered because they were women, the general level of political activism and organisation amongst Africans at the time was low. The ANC had not fully emerged from a general slump, and the ICU, which had appeared to hold the promise of a mass awakening, had collapsed. The CPSA, too, was only just beginning to pick up the pieces after a period of bitter internal strife; its numbers were in any case always very small. For many women, the only organisations available to fill this vacuum were the churches or mutual aid societies such as *'stokfels'*.[42]

Notes

1. Walshe, *The rise of African Nationalism in South Africa, the ANC 1912-1952*, p. 34.
2. Karis and Carter, *From Protest to Challenge*, vol. I, p. 53.
3. *Inter-Departmental Committee on the Native Pass Laws*, 1920, pp. 3-4.
4. S. Plaatje, *Native Life in South Africa*, p. 92.
5. *2nd Census, 1921*, Part I, UG 15-23, Table VIII, p. 64. The masculinity rate was calculated by the *Industrial Legislation Commission*, 1951, p. 14, Table 16.
6. 'Petition of the OFS Native and Coloured women', printed in *APO*, 21/3/14. The petition was addressed to the Governor General, Viscount Gladstone.
7. The APO was founded in 1902. Its membership was primarily 'Coloured' and its leader Dr Abdurahman, a member of the Cape Provincial Council.
8. In 1911, the 'Coloured' population of the Free State was 27,054, compared to 175,189 whites and 325,824 Africans. The percentage of this figure which would have been urbanised is unavailable, but in 1921, fewer than 7,000 'Coloureds' were urbanised, compared to 67,500 Africans. The 'Coloured' urban population was not therefore of great significance numerically. *Union Statistics for 50 Years:* Tables A-3, A-5, A-10.
9. *APO*, 6/4/12.
10. *APO*, 28/6/13.
11. *APO*, 23/9/13.
12. For instance, S. Plaatje, *op. cit.*, pp. 94-7.

Women and Resistance in South Africa

13. *APO,* 28/6/13.
14. I.K. Cross, 'The women's movement in South Africa and elsewhere', p. 307.
15. *International,* 26/11/20.
16. Walshe, *op. cit.,* p. 80.
17. *Ibid.,* p. 206.
18. This is based on information supplied by J. Palmer in J. Wells, *Interview with Josie Palmer.*
19. Simons and Simons, *Class and Colour in South Africa,* p. 400.
20. Roux, *Time longer than Rope,* pp. 189–92 and pp. 260–2.
21. Karis and Carter, *op. cit.,* vol. 2, Document 9, p. 39.
22. 'National Council of African Women', Rheinhallt-Jones papers.
23. Correspondence, 1/4/40, NCAW File, 1940, Rheinhallt-Jones papers.
24. *Umsebenzi,* 26/6/37.
25. Karis and Carter, *op. cit.,* vol. 2, Document 9.
26. Biographical material is sketchy. This account draws on G. Gollock, *Daughters of Africa;* T. Skota, *The African Yearly Register* (which Maxeke helped compile); E. Rosenthal, *Southern African Dictionary of National Biography,* and Karis and Carter, *op. cit.,* vol. 1, Document 51c.
27. Gollock, *op. cit.,* p. 138.
28. Rosenthal, *op. cit.*
29. *Women's Outlook,* August 1921.
30. Karis and Carter, *op. cit.,* vol. 4, biographical sketch of Maxeke. E. Rosenthal's estimate of the year of her death as 1930, in his *Southern African Dictionary of National Biography,* is incorrect.
31. *Women's Outlook,* August 1921.
32. Karis and Carter, *op. cit.,* vol. 1, Document 51c.
33. *Ibid.,* vol. 2, Document 9.
34. *Union Statistics for 50 Years,* Table A-10.
35. *Report of the Carnegie Commission,* vol. 1, p. xiii.
36. Based on figures supplied by the *Industrial Legislation Commission,* 1951, Table 9, p. 8; S. van der Horst, *op. cit.,* p. 57, *Union Statistics for 50 Years,* Table A-5; and *Industrial Legislation Commission,* 1951, Table 16, p. 14.
37. *House of Assembly Debates,* 1937, col. 4219.
38. R. Davenport, 'African Townsmen: South African Natives (Urban Areas) Legislation through the years', p. 99.
39. *Keiskammahoek Rural Survey,* vol. II, p. 29.
40. *Drum,* May 1954, see below, p. 149.
41. Interview with D. Tamana.
42. For a discussion on African women and the church, see M. Brandel, *Black Women in Search of God.* B.G.M. Sundkler, *Bantu Prophets in South Africa,* also contains some reference to the scope offered women in the independent African churches. A *stokfel* is a fund-raising party.

3

'Toiling Native Women, White Working Women . . . Wake Up!': Women and the Early Communist Party

The Communist Party of South Africa [CPSA] had a tiny membership in the 1920s and 1930s, estimated to have been about 300 in 1921, its inaugural date, rising to nearly 3,000 by the end of 1928 and then dropping drastically in the early 1930s as a result of internal dissension and turmoil.[1] Beginning with an all-white membership, it later expanded into having a predominantly black membership, although the whites within it retained an importance beyond their numbers. The CPSA was always a fringe organisation, out of the mainstream of both black and white political movements. Nevertheless, despite its smallness and the unfamiliar radicalism of its ideas, it yet exerted considerable influence on black opposition. It certainly made a significant contribution towards the development of a women's movement within the national liberation movement.

In the period between the wars, the CPSA's relationship with the two leading African political organisations, the ICU and the ANC, were far from amiable. Its radical class analysis conflicted with the more moderate, assimilationist approach of these bodies, even though its non-racial stand recommended it to Africans smarting under a system of racially oppressive laws. Thus, in 1926, the ICU expelled all its communist members, accusing them of preaching a 'doctrine of murder' and inciting 'subject races like the Natives to act unconstitutionally'.[2] Within the ANC, the CPSA enjoyed favour during the presidency of Josiah Gumede (1927–30), and several leading party members were front-rank Congress members too, eg Moses Kotane, J.B. Marks and Edwin Mofutsanyane (husband of Josie Palmer). However, after 1928, relations became more strained. In that year, under pressure from the Communist International, the CPSA adopted a programme of action that called for the establishment of an 'independent South African native republic as a stage towards a workers' and peasants' government'. This phrase, appearing as it did to envisage the total elimination of white participation in government, conflicted with the more cautious approach of the ANC. According to Walshe, for the ANC 'freedom' meant 'equality of opportunity and not African domination', and was to be achieved 'by consultation and the growth of a more enlightened public opinion rather than by African political assertion and mass action'.[3]

The fortunes of the CPSA went into a serious decline during the 1930s as the party split over this 'Native Republic' programme. It was only towards the end of the decade, when the rise of fascism had become a major issue in both international and domestic affairs, that the CPSA began to revive. It adopted the slogan 'a united front against fascism' and, in keeping with this approach, showed its willingness to co-operate with more moderate, liberal organisations. As a result, relations with the ANC improved, although tension between communist and non-communist Congress members was to remain a feature of black opposition politics right up to, and including, the period of the Congress Alliance in the 1950s.

While there are no figures available for the extent of the CPSA's female membership, certainly it was far smaller than its male membership. Yet, in the area of women's emancipation, too, the CPSA brought new perspectives to the incipient national liberation movement. It also produced important leaders. Mary Wolton, Ray Alexander, Josie Palmer, all political activists in their own right, first rose to prominence within the CPSA at this time.

The emancipation of women and their full participation in all spheres of public life has always been a feature of communist doctrine. Communists argue that capitalism oppresses women. Women workers therefore have a common interest with men in fighting for the establishment of a socialist state, and for conventions and practices that prevent women from joining the fight to be abolished. Locating the source of women's inferior status to men in their exclusion from the production process in society, the Communist International rejected (with practice frequently falling far behind theory) the bourgeois argument that women's reproductive capacity determined, and justified, their subordinate place within the home.

In 1922 a circular from the executive committee of the Communist International to all executives of national communist parties, set out the official position on women clearly. It stressed the importance of 'communist work' among proletarian women, arguing that if women were not drawn into the workers' struggle, a serious breach in proletarian unity would result. Men and women workers had common interests against the bourgeoisie: proletarian, peasant and petty bourgeois women represented 'sources of fresh, untapped fighting power'. Communist parties were urged to put all their energy into the more systematic training of women 'comrades'—'The Communist work among women is half the battle.'[4]

These were new perspectives for political parties in South Africa. While the community of interests between men and women was stressed (and working-class women's sexual exploitation by working-class men underplayed), it was delineated not on colour but on class terms. This perspective deflated the importance of 'race' and held out the prospect of a broader, non-racial alliance amongst opponents of the state. Furthermore, women were to be regarded as a central part of the political struggle, and the fact that they suffered special disabilities, requiring special attention, was recognised. The CPSA endorsed the slogan 'no discrimination on the grounds of race or sex' from the beginning. However, for the most part, the reference to sex reflected a theoretical agreement rather than a practical commitment, particularly in its early years. In attitude and behaviour towards women, most communists did not differ from their non-communist counterparts in other organisations.

When the CPSA was formed in 1921, it brought together several tiny socialist groups which had begun to establish themselves in the main urban centres at the end of the nineteenth century. Marxism was brought to South Africa by European immigrants responding to local mining and industrial developments. In South Africa they faced a very different labour situation from the one they had left behind in Europe—a racially hetero-geneous working class in which the vast mass of workers were black, most of them still rooted in a foreign, tribal culture and divided from white workers by all sorts of barriers, political, economic, legal and social. In the pre-war period, the most fundamental issue facing the party, which dominated its course of development, was what should be its attitude to the great mass of workers, the black proletariat. In the 1920s women were not members of the non-domestic labour force in any significant numbers. At the same time, the ideology of female subordination permeated all levels of society, and most of the early leaders of the CPSA upheld conventional views on the institutions of the family and marriage and the sexual division of labour within them. Among the workers they were attempting to organise, as well, patriarchal attitudes were deeply entrenched. For all of these reasons, the question of women's emancipa-tion was completely overshadowed by other party work.

The party's views on women were frequently inconsistent. On the one hand it subscribed to the official viewpoint already set out, that women suffered a particular form of exploitation under capitalism, which needed to be broken. The heroic achievements of Russian women in breaking with the past after 1917 received a fair amount of coverage and much praise in left-wing publications. South Africans who visited the USSR in the 1920s and 1930s were struck by the sexual egalitarianism they encountered, singling this out for comment in letters, articles and speeches on their visits. The two left-wing newspapers, the *International* and later *Umsebenzi*, printed a number of serious articles dealing with the problems of women's emancipation and the need to involve women more actively in the political struggle. In 1922 *International* printed the circular from the Communist International calling for national parties to pay greater attention to women. Probably in response to that, the same issue also carried an article by a local South African woman, Alice Harrison. This urged women to join the workers' movement: 'The time for sitting at home and waiting is past.'[5] Harrison's article, called 'Words to Women', was a pioneering piece in socialist circles in South Africa.

In a similar vein, in 1936 Mrs Denys Reitz, the first woman elected to parliament, was taken to task by *Umsebenzi* for suggesting that women's domestic role should be paramount.[6] A few years later, criticism of this viewpoint emerged in an even more radical form. In response to an article carried by the left-wing newspaper, the *Guardian*, on whether or not women should be paid for housework, a correspondent argued that 'socialism will be a very poor and lopsided affair if it does not involve pretty drastic changes in domestic life'.[7] Wages for wives would be a poor solution, however, as that was 'simply subsidising incompetence'. Domestic work should rather be communalised, to free housewives from its drudgery and allow them to earn their living at work in which they could take pride. 'The real fact is that ordinary domestic life fails to satisfy the material, mental and emotional needs of the housewife.'

Yet on the other hand, and despite these progressive sentiments, many of the CPSA's references to women revealed an unquestioning acceptance of stereotyped and sexist attitudes. In 1919, two years before the party had been established, women's part in the annual Mayday celebrations on the Rand was to make tea for the participants. In the words of *International*, they 'asserted working class dictatorship by arranging which tea rooms were needed open for the day'.[8] Even once the CPSA had been established, women's participation in Mayday did not show appreciable changes at first. Reports on the celebrations of 1928 indicate that black women were completely peripheral to the whole occasion. According to Douglas Wolton, who was present, 'Bantu housewives rushed from cooking the evening meal to the doors to see their menfolk celebrating the first of May just like the white workers had always done.'[9] Their exclusion from the celebrations was not even remarked upon.

Sexist jokes also found their way into the pages of the *International*, *Umsebenzi*, and, later, the *Guardian* (after 1937, the premier left-wing newspaper in the country). For example, from *International:* 'How did you vote?' the young girl was asked. 'In my brown suit and squirrel toque' came the ingenuous reply. (This appeared several years before white women were enfranchised.)[10]

Such inconsistency was not confined to the men only. In 1931 the women's department of the CPSA (which is described below) issued the following call to women on the occasion of International Women's Day, on 8th March: 'Women organise! Don't let your menfolk keep you back. To win their freedom, they need your help.'[11]

During the 1930s more attention came to be focused on the position of women as workers, yet the regular 'Women's Page' feature of the *Guardian* continued to be filled mainly with recipes, advice on nutrition and childcare, fashion and beauty hints. Thus, prevailing views on femininity and women's apolitical, domestic nature were tacitly endorsed.

Despite these inconsistencies, which are particularly striking for the reader from a more media-conscious age, the CPSA did take a lead in expanding the scope of political work to include women. Even though it always remained very much a subsidiary issue, over the years the extent and depth of the party's attention to organising women increased. Its role in establishing the women's movement within the national liberation movement was a pioneering one, and it set its imprint on that movement from an early date.

Women and the CPSA in the 1920s

Although women were active within left-wing organisations in South Africa from the start, it was on an individual basis at first. As in the Bantu Women's League, the early activists were members of the privileged middle class. They were also white. Before the CPSA was founded, the flamboyant Mary Fitzgerald, nicknamed 'Pickhandle Mary' for her skill in wielding a pickhandle against strike breakers, was probably the most prominent woman in socialist circles. Walker and Weinbren, in their book *2000 Casualties*, describe her as a 'typical Irish beauty', 'a rousing speaker', and someone who 'knew no fear and took the lead in many struggles'.[12] In the early years of the century she was actively involved in socialist organisations on the Rand, but after the war she moved away from her earlier radicalism towards a more moderate trade unionism. She thus did not follow many of her former colleagues into the CPSA. In 1921, the year the CPSA was formed, she was an official government delegate to the ILO Conference in Geneva.

During the 1920s Rebecca Bunting, Fanny Klenerman (who was married to C.F. Glass), and, later, Mary Wolton, participated actively in party work. Significantly, all were wives of leading men within the party and their contribution tended to be seen in this context. In his study of the CPSA, Johns refers to Mary Wolton as a 'fiery orator', one of the most significant recruits to the CPSA in the late 1920s, along with her husband Douglas Wolton, yet it was her husband who was elected to the posts as party secretary and newspaper editor, while her role was supportive. 'Throughout he was backed by his wife.'[13]

By the late 1920s the party had managed to shake off most of the traces of white worker chauvinism that had characterised its beginnings, and it was starting to pay attention to the recruitment of black members. At the same time, it also made its first approaches to black women. In his biography of CPSA leader S.P. Bunting, Eddie Roux (himself a member at the time) refers to a meeting organised by the CPSA outside Vereeniging location in 1928. At this meeting several hundred new members, 'including numbers of women', joined the party.[14] Roux's special mention of the women makes it apparent that this was a noteworthy occurrence. According to Simons and Simons, 63 women joined at this meeting.[15]

That same year, 1928, the CPSA also became involved in the struggle against residence permits that had been launched in Potchefstroom location. The permit question in Potchefstroom was clearly of deep concern to women. Local community issues were always the ones that women could identify with most easily; in treating these seriously, the CPSA was making an important start in popularising itself amongst black women. It was this readiness to get involved in local issues that distinguished the CPSA from the ANC at the time. Josie Palmer, who joined the party during the Potchefstroom campaign, has singled out its concern for basic domestic issues as a major reason why she chose to join the CPSA rather than the ANC.[16]

As already mentioned, the Potchefstroom campaign is poorly documented. There is only one reference to that women's meeting which was attended by both CPSA and ANC women, and it is frustratingly sketchy. It appears in a letter from S.P. Bunting to E. Roux that was written at the time. In it he mentions that 'Becky (Rebecca Bunting, his wife) went to Potchefstroom to a women's meeting with Molly (Mary Wolton) and coloured Mrs Bhola, a new chum from the African National Congress.'[17] Although Bunting does not specifically mention the purpose of the meeting, it seems more than likely that it was connected to the permit unrest. This was possibly one of the very earliest meetings where black and white women came together within a common, explicitly political framework. At that stage, the whites-only suffrage campaign was nearing its conclusion. Here, in marked contrast to the suffrage campaign, an attempt was being made to reach out to women across colour barriers and deal with issues of vital popular concern. The non-racialism inherent in the CPSA's class analysis of society was thus beginning to penetrate into the sphere of women's organisations.

New Directions in the 1930s

The first years of the 1930s saw a sudden flurry of activity amongst women within the CPSA, which coincided with the recruitment of new and energetic women members. Josie Palmer, the first black woman to play any significant role within the CPSA, joined in 1928 as a result of the Potchefstroom anti-permit campaign. Roux has described her as 'the only African woman to play any part in the Communist Movement at this time'.[18] According to Palmer herself, she was not, strictly speaking, African, but 'Coloured'.[19] This is a peculiarly South African distinction— and obsession. What is relevant is that she lived in African areas, was married to an African man, and always identified herself strongly with issues affecting blacks, African or 'Coloured'. In early newspaper reports her name is frequently spelled in an Africanised version, Mpama, instead of Palmer.

Another important recruit was Mary Wolton. For a time, in the early and middle 1930s, she and her husband, Douglas Wolton, and another member, Lazar Bach, dominated the party. They led the purge against members accused of being 'right wing, social democratic, and vacillating elements'[20] once the 'Native Republic' programme had been launched. This shattered the party structure that had so painstakingly been built up in the 1920s. There is no record of Mary Wolton ever paying particular attention to women, and if, as Roux and others maintain, the influence of the new 'Bolshevik leadership' was so damaging for the party, her contribution to the organisation of women during this time was probably negative rather than positive, overall.

Undoubtedly the most important woman to join the party at this time was Ray Alexander. She arrived in South Africa from Latvia in 1929, a young girl of 15 or 16, and became active in left-wing trade unionism almost from the moment that she first set foot in South Africa. It would be difficult to overestimate the extremely large part Alexander played in preparing the ground for the establishment of the FSAW over the next twenty five years. Dedicated and dynamic, she came to South Africa with an already developed commitment to the workers' cause that nothing could sway. She was actually sent to South Africa to escape the attentions of the secret police in Latvia. Far from being deterred by this brush with the authorities, she plunged straightaway into the mammoth task of organising unions, more or less from scratch, among the dockworkers, shopworkers, and, later, food and canning workers in and around Cape Town.

Alexander also brought with her a strong feminist consciousness that made her particularly sensitive to the position of working women. She grasped the importance of the increasing presence of women in industry and urged her colleagues to pay greater attention to them. Both within the CPSA and in various trade union organisations, she actively promoted issues concerning women—their need to organise, their poor working conditions, the difficulties for women who combined two jobs, one within the home and one within the shop or factory.

During the 1930s *Umsebenzi* and its successor, the *Guardian*, printed several articles by her on these subjects, for instance, 'Working Women and War'[21] and 'The Mother's Means Test, Inadequate Confinement Allowances'.[22] A number of other unsigned articles on related topics were probably written by her, too. At the sixth congress of the CPSA, in September 1936, she spoke on the great increase in the numbers of women employed in the clothing, textile and leather industries, where hardly any trade unions were operating; she appealed to the congress for organisational and educational work among women.[23] The greater degree of attention paid to women workers by the CPSA from this time was in large part her responsibility.

As a sign that women were beginning to be taken more seriously by the CPSA, it began to commemorate International Women's Day (March 8) fairly regularly during the 1930s. This anniversary had been established on the international communist calendar as a day designed to focus attention on the progress made and the problems faced in the emancipation of women.

By February 1931 the more active presence of women within the CPSA had led to the establishment of a separate women's department. The origins of this department are not clear. Its earliest statements showed an unselfconscious acceptance of women's supportive, rather than directly involved political, role—it was this group that in 1931 urged women to organise so that their men could win their freedom. But it soon showed signs of beginning to explore the wider possibilities of organising women as well. In June 1931 it announced that it would be convening a Women's National Conference shortly, and called on local women's departments to organise preliminary meetings to elect delegates. At these meetings, 'all questions affecting women should be discussed. . . and linked up with the men's struggles'. In August, the aims of the proposed conference were set out more fully: 'This conference is being called in order to unify and consolidate the sectional struggle of women. . . and in order to bring into existence a permanent organisation of struggle for the working women of South Africa.'[24] This was far more radical than anything envisaged by other, contemporary groups.

Once again, it was a pass-related issue that sparked off the activity, in this instance, an attempt to enforce curfew regulations on the Witwatersrand for African women. *Umsebenzi* reported the curfew as pending on 12th June 1931, and vigorous protest, harking back to the anti-pass campaign in the Free State, followed within the African community. Then, in July, garment workers on the Rand came out on strike. The strike, one of the longest and largest by women workers yet witnessed, received considerable publicity and no doubt contributed to the feeling already present that women were ripe for organising into a national body.

The CPSA seized upon the anti-curfew protests as a lever for raising the level of resistance to the state on a number of issues, as well as extending the base of resistance to include women. *Umsebenzi* urged African women that they 'must not content themselves with struggle against this incident of persecution, but. . . must fight against the whole system of Imperialist oppression, for a Native Republic, in defence of the Soviet Union'.[25] The women's department described the forthcoming conference as a fitting answer to attempts by Pirow (Minister of Justice) 'to force the women of Africa into the position of serfs by the imposition of passes'.[26]

It does not appear, however, that the conference ever took place. The meeting, originally set for late September, was postponed in the middle of the month, and thereafter no further references to it appeared in the pages of *Umsebenzi*. There were probably several reasons for this. By that time, the CPSA was in a state of confusion and disarray over the expulsion of Bunting and his supporters. But even without those difficulties, the degree of actual support the party had generated among women was far too small to sustain so ambitious a project as a national organisation of working women. In the proposal for a national conference, one can see the germ of an idea which later would re-emerge and contribute to the establishment of the FSAW in the 1950s. In the early 1930s, however, given the position of most women at the time, the proposal was premature.

The attempt to convene a conference marked a high point in practical efforts to organise women as a group within the CPSA before the war. No further attempts were publicly launched, although women members continued to argue the need for such efforts. In May 1935, an article in *Umsebenzi* complained that the party was neglecting its work among women, and 'must endeavour in the course of the next year to set up special organisations for drawing women into the struggle'.[27] Ray Alexander repeated this call at the 1936 party congress.

In 1927 Josie Palmer also called for women to 'join the struggle against oppressive laws'.[28] She was reacting to the new amendments to the Urban Areas Act which tightened up on the previously relaxed influx control measures for women. Palmer was anxious that women should realise the dangers they faced:

> Women, we can no longer remain in the background or concern ourselves only with domestic and sports affairs. The time has arrived for women to enter the political field and stand shoulder to shoulder with their men in the struggle.[29]

A few months later she wrote an article for *Umsebenzi* which also stressed the need for African women specifically to organise. This time the motivation was supplied by a recent spate of police raids against illicit beer-brewing and selling in the African townships. Domestic beer-brewing was a traditional activity of African women, but in the townships it was more than a social pastime—for many women, it was an economic necessity, one of the few areas open for self-employment. From the late 1920s many municipalities were usurping this role by opening up municipal beer-canteens, the revenue from which was intended to finance expenditure on township affairs. The municipal canteens hit women hard. Not only was their own beer-brewing prohibited, but they were now forced to watch their husbands' precious earnings drain away into municipal coffers rather than their own enterprises.

The beer laws were always a potent source of friction. Their enforcement in some towns in Natal in 1928/29 sparked off a round of boycotts and picketing of canteens by women which led to violence on several occasions.[30] In taking up this issue in 1937, Palmer attempted to broaden the focus of the angry women who were at the receiving end of the raids, to take in the whole range of discriminatory legislation they faced. She also criticised the NCAW for its ineffectiveness, and repeated the call for a separate organisation of African women—without the participation of women, no successful fight against injustice could be waged.

The CPSA was also making some overtures to 'Coloured' women in the Western Cape. The passage of the whites-only Women's Enfranchisement Act in 1930 had produced a ferment within 'Coloured' politics. 'Coloured' women, who were deliberately excluded from the terms of the act, despite earlier promises from the Prime Minister, Hertzog, that they would be considered, were indignant. Many who had paid scant attention to women's suffrage before, were now made to think about it. At the same time, by drastically reducing the effectiveness of the 'Coloured' vote, the act had a generally radicalising impact on 'Coloured' people's thinking. Their ambiguous status, halfway between the privileged whites and the grossly exploited Africans, was being more clearly defined in terms of their common 'non-whiteness' with the African majority, although recognition of this was still confined largely to a small group of intellectuals.

Cissy Gool, daughter of the veteran Dr Abdurahman (of the APO), and married into a powerful political family, achieved prominence at a huge protest meeting that packed City Hall in Cape Town, condemning the discriminatory enfranchisement act. She was unequivocal about the radicalising effect of the act on her. In the less security-conscious language of the time, she declared, 'I am afraid that I am slowly going Red', a remark that led a sympathetic white observer to comment on the tragedy of a situation that could drive such a beautiful young girl to such drastic lengths.[31]

Subsequently, Cissy Gool came to play a prominent part in radical black circles in the Cape. Her status within the CPSA is unclear—in some reports she is described as a member, while in others she is described as a

SCCCC - LIBRARY
4601 Mid Rivers Mall Drive
St. Peters, MO 63376

WITHDRAWN

non-Communist. However, she certainly liaised very closely with the CPSA once it had embarked on its 'United Front' programme in the late 1930s. In 1937 she became president of an organisation called the National Liberation League [NLL], which was established in Cape Town. According to Roux, this was largely the product of Communist-inspired ideas.[32] It drew its membership mainly from 'Coloured' intellectuals in the Western Cape. The NLL co-operated with the CPSA's United Front against fascism, which aimed to co-ordinate the NLL, the CPSA and the ANC in a broad programme of action in the form of demonstrations, boycotts and strikes.

Gool was not particularly concerned with women's rights, but she did initiate several attempts to organise 'Coloured' women, none of which appears to have survived very long. Thus, in 1938, when 'Coloured' men were still enfranchised, she presided at a meeting to establish a 'League for the Enfranchisement of Non-European Women'.[33] Its appeal was very limited, however. Women's suffrage was relevant to only the tiny section of 'Coloured' women who, if it were not for their sex, would otherwise have qualified for the vote in the Cape. Women's suffrage was not an issue with broad appeal to black women, and little more was heard of the league. At about the same time, Cissy Gool was also busy setting up a local women's organisation, the 'Salt River and Observatory Ladies Welfare Organisation', the apparent aim of which was to protest against a proposed Residential Segregation Ordinance—an early precursor of the notorious Group Areas Act of 1950.[34] The fortunes of this group have vanished into obscurity.

The easiest entrée to women was through local issues that affected the community. Ray Alexander was particularly quick to make use of this, and in 1939 encouraged the CPSA to take part in a broad-based 'Consumer Vigilance Council' in Cape Town. The council was formed to protest against the prosecution of a local baker who had been charged for selling bread below the official price. From the start, it aimed to campaign against rising food costs generally. The issue had broad appeal, particularly amongst working-class women, and its reception among black women was more promising than that afforded the Suffrage League.

This was the time of the United Front, and on the Consumer Council the CPSA joined forces with a wide range of organisations, all of which had an interest in checking the upward spiral of food costs. They included the determinedly apolitical National Council of Women (which had a white, middle-class membership), the NLL, the South African Trades and Labour Council, the South African Railway and Harbour Workers Union, the Chemical and Allied Workers Union, and the South African Socialist Party.[35] Although the council was not an exclusively female body, the issues it took up were of primary concern to women, especially house-wives, and women, including Ray Alexander and Cissy Gool, were active on it. During the war, the rising cost of living would become a particularly important issue round which the CPSA tried to organise women in Cape Town and on the Rand.

Through the 1930s the overriding concern of the CPSA in organis-ing women, whether against passes, rising food costs or discriminatory legislation, was to mobilise them for a common struggle with men against the white supremacist state. While Communists might debate the tactical precedence that they should grant the black nationalist struggle over the workers' struggle—was it to be a two-stage or a one-stage route to a workers' and peasants' republic—they never doubted that women's struggle for emancipation was subordinate to the broader general struggle of both blacks and workers. In this regard they shared the perspective of the ANC on the place of the women's movement.

Nevertheless, it was within the CPSA that the idea of organising women on a broad-based political level was most successfully nurtured during the 1930s. Individual women played a far more prominent part in it than in any other political body, and several important female political leaders of the 1940s and 1950s emerged publicly at this time. In 1938, when the party headquarters were shifted to Cape Town, Ray Alexander and Cissy Gool were elected to the new 'Political Bureau' of the CPSA. Although the number of women actually involved was very small, the influence of the CPSA was more extensive than its numbers might imply. Through the left-wing press, it managed to disseminate its ideas widely amongst other black political organisations and within the trade union movement, where it was very involved.

Frequently, as we have seen, it seemed to endorse rather than challenge conventional views on women's domestic, apolitical role. Yet, for all its inconsistencies, the CPSA was encouraging new ways of thinking about the position of women, particularly by focusing attention on working women and trying to establish contact between women of different colour groups:

> Toiling native women, white working women, realise your interests, wake up to fight for better conditions side by side with your husbands, fathers, and brothers: only by a united front can you get rid of all the exploitation which you suffer under capitalism and where you as women are the greatest sufferers.[36]

In the 1930s these were subversive words indeed.

Notes

1. S.W. Johns, *Marxism-Leninism in a Multiracial Environment*, pp. 245, 399, 577.
2. Walshe, *op. cit.*, p. 174, quoting from *The Workers' Herald*, 17/5/27.
3. Walshe, *op. cit.*, p. 178.
4. Reprinted in *International*, 10/11/22.
5. *International*, 10/11/22.
6. *Umsebenzi*, 28/11/36: 'Women's Place in the kitchen?'
7. *Guardian*, 19/5/39.
8. *International*, 2/5/19.
9. Wolton, *Whither South Africa?*, p. 73.
10. *International*, 21/7/22.
11. *Umsebenzi*, 20/2/31.
12. Walker and Weinbren, *2000 Casualties*, p. 291.

13. Johns, *op. cit.,* p. 400.
14. Roux, *S.P Bunting,* p. 79.
15. Simons and Simons, *Class and Colour in South Africa,* p. 399.
16. J. Wells, *Interview with Josie Palmer.*
17. Roux, *op. cit.,* p. 103.
18. *Ibid.,* p. 86.
19. J. Wells interview.
20. Roux, *Time Longer than Rope,* p. 256.
21. *Umsebenzi,* 22/8/36.
22. *Guardian,* 14/4/38.
23. *Umsebenzi,* 19/9/36.
24. *Umsebenzi,* 26/6/31.
25. Quoted by Johns, *op. cit.,* p. 556.
26. *Umsebenzi,* 21/8/31.
27. *Umsebenzi,* 16/5/35.
28. *Umsebenzi,* 20/1/37.
29. *Umsebenzi,* 26/6/37.
30. Roux, *op. cit.,* p. 189–192.
31. Empire Group of South Africa, *Franchise Rights and Wrongs,* gives a description
    of this meeting and Cissy Gool's speech.
32. Roux, *op. cit.,* p. 357.
33. *Guardian,* 26/8/38.
34. *Guardian,* 21/8/38.
35. *Guardian,* 31/1/39.
36. *Umsebenzi,* 10/2/32.

4

'Mayday Greetings to All Women of South Africa': Women in the Trade Unions Before 1939

The Ideological Contribution of Trade Unionism to the Women's Movement

In the 1940s and 1950s certain trade unions would play a very important part in nurturing and directing the course of the women's movement. The significance of the unions lay in the fact that they dealt with large numbers of working-class women, women who up until this time had been virtually excluded from political and other women's organisations. The trade union movement thus acted as a training ground for a new class of leader, working women who rose to leadership positions within their union and who from there were frequently drawn into a wider political involvement. Hetty McLeod, Bettie du Toit, Hetty du Preez, Frances Baard, Lily Diederichs, all of them co-sponsors of the inaugural conference of the FSAW in 1954, were trade unionists who fit this description.

The unions also introduced a far wider range of women, their general membership, to new techniques and concepts of organisation, while encouraging them to reflect more critically upon their experience as workers within society. For most women workers, generally poorly educated, without political rights, the trade union was the one area where they could come into contact with ideas and issues that stretched beyond their narrow experience within the home or factory. Certainly the more radical unions, which were prominent in the efforts to organise black workers in South Africa, included political education of their members in their programmes.

In the trade union movement, many women came into contact for the first time with ideas that challenged the dominant ideology of white supremacy and its corollary, racial exclusiveness. The non-racialism which the CPSA was espousing received much wider dissemination through trade unions, which stressed that all workers should stand together, regardless of race (and, less prominently, of sex), against exploitative bosses. This fundamental principle of international trade unionism was not, however, adopted by all South African worker movements. It was bitterly disputed by many right-wing white unions, who were anxious to protect the privileges and status of the so-called 'white labour aristocracy' at the expense of their black fellow-workers. This led to deep and crippling divisions within the trade union movement. Yet non-racial ideas did take tentative root among important sections of the working class in the pre-World War II period. In the 1940s, when trade unionism spread rapidly among African workers, they proved an important ideological influence on black political thinking.

Women workers were not exempt from the fierce disputes dividing the trade union movement. Yet the potential for women to co-operate across colour lines, as workers with perceived common interests, was probably larger in this sphere than in other areas which could be regarded as more purely 'political', for instance, that of the suffrage. Nowhere was this better illustrated than in the Garment Workers Union in the Transvaal, at that stage the largest and most militant of the unions with a predominant female membership. Despite its overwhelmingly white, Afrikaner membership during the 1930s, the Garment Workers Union took the lead as a champion of worker solidarity and multiracial trade unionism, and faced enormous pressure from Nationalist organisations within Afrikanerdom as a result.

The notion of working-class solidarity regardless of race or sex reinforced those ideas already present in the Bantu Women's League and the Communist Party that women had a common struggle to wage, with men, against a common exploitation. In the early years, when the numbers of women in industry were very small, some attempts were made to unionise women into a general union, on the basis of their sex. They did not take root. Women were drawn into the trade unions within the existing framework of industry-based unions that embraced all employees within a particular industry, for instance, the leather or steel industry. However, because of the sex-stereotyping of jobs, women tended to be concentrated in those few industries conforming most nearly to work previously done by women in the home, most importantly the clothing and food industries. The unions established in these areas developed a predominantly female membership and, to some extent, leadership. As a result, they did take a more active interest in issues relating particularly to female work conditions, for example, pregnancy leave or compulsory overtime.

However, in the period before World War II, the impact of trade unionism on the political consciousness of women was still very limited. This period should rather be seen as a preliminary to the more significant one that followed in the 1940s and 1950s, when women were far more strongly represented in industry. As already described, there were relatively few women employed in industry in the earlier period. In 1924/25 the employment figures for private industry were 154,403 men to 15,273 women.[1] The numbers of women in factory work were on the increase, but at this stage it was primarily white women who were entering industrial employment. African women were almost entirely absent—only 709 of the fifteen thousand women working in factories in 1924/25 were African.

The importance of trade union work amongst women was obviously tempered by the smallness of the female labour force. At the same time, the fact that so few African women were involved probably shifted the attention of many trade unionists away from women workers still more. The issue of whether and how the African labour force should be organised preoccupied the trade union movement.

Early Attempts to Organise a General Union of Women

As in other spheres, hardy pioneers led the way in the organisation of women workers long before society at large had accustomed itself to the idea that women were involved in factory employment. Individual women, generally from privileged backgrounds, were involved in labour organisations from an early stage. In 1911 Mary Fitzgerald organised and led a group of women to assist a tramway workers' strike in Johannesburg.[2] By sitting down on the tracks outside the tram depot, they effectively prevented scabbers from taking trams out. In 1913 Fitzgerald was again prominent in a strike by white miners on the Rand.

However, in the years before the first world war women played a very minor role in worker organisations. Women as workers had taken no part in the primary phase of South Africa's industrial development, the opening up of the mining industry. It was only once secondary industry got under way, encouraged largely by the coming of the war and the cutting of foreign import markets, that bosses began to turn to women as a new source of cheap labour. Thus, only after the war did women begin to appear in worker organisations in any numbers. According to Walker and Weinbren, the first strike in which women workers predominated took place in 1917 in the printing industry in Johannesburg.[3] Led by the newly formed Printers' Assistants Union, the workers struck for higher wages with apparent success.

By 1919, women's presence in industry was sufficiently noticeable to have prompted an attempt to organise women within a single general union, in the form of a 'Women Workers Industrial Union'.[4] The circumstances surrounding this union are obscure—and the one reference encountered does not suggest that it had a markedly progressive line on the role of women. This was the group which took part in the annual Mayday celebrations of that year as tea stewards, mentioned above.

Just how far women workers were from organising themselves on a unified basis was highlighted that same year by strike activity within the clothing industry. In Cape Town, two strikes by clothing workers ran simultaneously but totally independently. The one, conducted by 112 white clothing workers (88 of them women), was successful in achieving higher wages. The other, run by 'Coloured' women workers at a nearby factory, was unsuccessful, and all those women lost their jobs. At no stage was there any show of solidarity or attempt to link the two strikes together, although the newspaper *International* did draw attention to the anomalies of the situation.[5]

The following year, a remarkably early but premature attempt at organising black women was made by the ICU in conjunction with the APO. According to van der Ross, these two bodies arranged a meeting in Cape Town in September 1920 which was attended by about fifty women.[6] As already mentioned, Charlotte Maxeke was in touch with ICU leaders Kadalie and Msimang in the early stages of their union. Whether she had any influence in prompting this step is a matter of speculation, however. There is no available evidence that she ever visited Cape Town in this regard. Unfortunately, information on any subsequent developments of this women's group is unavailable. With the small number of African women in private industry in 1924, it is hard to know what the scope of a women's section of the ICU could have been, unless it was to help with 'shelter and entertainment' on the lines of the Bantu Women's League.

Working conditions for women were uniformly bad. At this stage the fledgling clothing industry consisted mostly of sweatshops. Small, cramped, often one-man businesses, these workshops were generally inefficiently run, with a small turnover. They offered little security for their employees. Women worked long hours for minimal pay. Pregnancy leave and maternity benefits for women were unheard of—a baby often meant the loss of a precious job. The first legislation dealing with labour relations and wage enforcements, the Industrial Conciliation Act, was only passed in 1924, and there was little attempt to see that the provisions it laid down for minimum wage levels—low as these were—were enforced. One woman recalled her first experiences of factory work thus:

> At the beginning of 1911 I arrived in Johannesburg and obtained employment through a school friend. . . she found me a job in a small workshop where she was a tailoress. I started at 10 shillings a week. The hours were from 7 am to 6 pm daily, with an hour for lunch, and 7 am to 12 noon on Saturdays. The workshop was terribly overcrowded and hot. . . Very often, we had to take work home and sit up late at night, finishing it. For this we received no pay.[7]

In 1920, *International* reported on a clothing factory where girls of 12 and 14 were working, making caps, at between five and six shillings a week.

The oppressive work conditions did not pass the CPSA unnoticed. In 1925 Fanny Klenerman, a member of the party, tried to establish another general women's union to campaign for improvements for women. 'The conditions under which the majority of working women live and work in South Africa is a disgrace to civilisation', she declared.[8] She organised a meeting, at which a committee was elected, but that was as far as it went. No further references to this committee or the union appeared in newspaper columns. In view of the tremendous problems encountered in organising the male industrial labour force, the lack of consciousness about the position of women in the major political bodies of the time, both white and black, and the small numbers of women actually involved in production, such attempts were almost bound to fail. However, as stages in the spread of trade unionist consciousness among women in South Africa, they are worth noting.

The Garment Workers Union

As the numbers of women in industry increased, they began to spill over the boundaries of any single general workers' union and become drawn into the already existing industry-based unions. From about this time, the most significant and well documented trade union work among women took place among garment workers on the Rand under the auspices of the Garment Workers Union [GWU].

In later years this union moved away from its early radicalism toward the so-called 'centre' in South African trade union politics. In so doing, it moved out of the orbit of the women's movement, and thus out of the range of this history. However, in its early years, before the aims and scope of the union were so clearly defined, it had a significant politicising effect on many of its members and the trade union movement in general. It also contributed several prominent organisers to the union movement, women who helped clear the ground in which the women's movement was taking root. Among them were the sisters Johanna and Hester Cornelius, Katy Viljoen, and Bettie du Toit (later a signatory of the invitation to the inaugural conference of the FSAW). The history of the union, particularly in its early days, is a stirring one and reveals the high degree of trade union militancy that South African women workers have, on occasion, shown. It also provides an insight into the effects of the existing colour divisions in society on black and white workers, and shows how these have been exploited by white political parties. For these reasons, it is worthwhile including a brief look at the GWU before the second world war.

The GWU grew out of an organisation of tailoring and garment workers that was formed in about 1918.[9] At first, the tailoring section dominated union affairs. This created a number of difficulties and tensions. The tailors, individual craftsmen with a long craft tradition, had little in common, in either their conditions of work or general outlook, with the flood of female factory operatives who began to enter the union as the industry switched over to mass production. These newcomers came to resent the 'paternalistic' attitudes[10] of the tailors, but only in 1934 did the union split and a purely garment workers organisation develop. 'This historic event meant that the Garment Workers Union could adopt an industrial-worker approach to trade unionism, unhindered by craft traditions.'[11]

The great majority of women in the clothing industry in the 1920s and 1930s were young, white, Afrikaner women. As already mentioned, they were part of a huge townward movement by rural Afrikaners—indigent farmers, sharecroppers, farmworkers and their families—who could no longer make a living out of agriculture. The 'poor white' problem had become a major political issue by this time. At one stage it was estimated that out of a total Afrikaner population of one million, about 300,000 were 'very poor', ie living below the poverty line, and a further 300,000 were 'poor'.[12] In their poverty, lack of education and marketable skills, as well as their reasons for migrating to towns, the 'poor whites' did not differ markedly from the thousands of blacks who were making a similar trek from country to town at that time. But as members of the ruling white group, they occupied a wholly different place in the minds of white politicians, town planners, churchmen, and welfare organisations. Their poverty, the degraded living conditions, their fraternisation with blacks in makeshift housing schemes on the edge of town, were all seen as a direct threat to white hegemony. In 1932 the Carnegie Commission, set up to investigate the poor white problem, commented:

> Although sexual intercourse between white and coloured exists to a greater degree now than in the past, it is still on the whole the exception, even among poor whites. . . Signs are however not wanting that this racial barrier is being broken down, especially where the standard of living of some Europeans is approximating more and more to that of natives.[13]

For the Carnegie Commission and many other experts, white poverty was a danger and an insult to white supremacy. Black poverty, however, was part of the order of things—there was never a concept of 'poor black' in political and sociological circles.

Once the Afrikaner-dominated National Party of General Hertzog had been elected into government in 1924, increased attention was focused on solving the 'poor white' problem. The National Party introduced a range of social and economic measures designed to eradicate the problem. These included the reservation of certain areas of skilled and unskilled employment for white workers, at skilled rates of pay (job reservation), subsidised housing schemes, special education schemes, and general relief work. It was a massive programme of social rehabilitation that proved enormously successful, and by the late 1930s the problem had been brought under control.

In the meantime, many of these newcomers to town were fair game for industrialists and employers anxious to make the most of the expanding economic opportunities available to them. An account of work conditions encountered in a Johannesburg clothing factory in the early 1930s does not differ very much from the one already quoted of conditions in 1911. Katy Viljoen, subsequently a prominent organiser in the GWU, described her first job in 1932 as follows:

> I left the house at five-thirty as I had to walk a distance of about four miles [she could not afford the tram fare on one pound per week]. . . For a month I walked to and from work every day but these long journeys became unbearable. The work was really slave driving. We started at 7 am and finished at 6 pm. I could not send anything home to my parents, as my total earnings just covered my board and lodging.[14]

Later, she found other work at one pound ten a week which she budgeted as follows,

> Rent 17s 6d per week, saving up for new clothes, 7s 6d per week, 10s a month sent my parents. The balance of 2s 6d a week had to be sufficient for food. Once a week I used to buy bread for 6d and a pound of butter at 1s 8d.

The balance was 2d per week—not even enough to join the union, whose weekly subscriptions was 6d.

The transition to urban factory employment after a childhood in the country was a brutal one. For Katy Viljoen and the thousands of other girls in a similar position, the GWU offered the only practical way out of their misery. Under its general secretary, Solly Sachs,[15] the union was building up a solid reputation of first establishing and then defending members' rights to decent work conditions and security of employment. This won for both Sachs and the union the staunch loyalty of rank and file members.

In its early years, the union used the existing industrial conciliation legislation with as much force as possible against defaulting employers. It also campaigned for membership tirelessly, organising street and factory meetings, demonstrations and rallies. In 1931 it felt sufficiently strong to challenge the bosses more openly. A deadlock between employers and the union over new wage negotiations led to a strike on the Rand. Over two thousand workers came out, and an uneasy short-term compromise with employers was reached. When discussions broke down once more in 1932, the union called for another general strike—the most ambitious yet undertaken by women workers.

The strike was noteworthy for the discipline and solidarity of its participants, as well as the rough handling meted out to strikers by policemen on several occasions. The National Party was contesting a by-election in Germiston, one of the Rand towns where the strike was at its strongest. In an attempt to break the strike, which was seen as damaging to Nationalist chances, Pirow, then Minister of Justice, encouraged strong-arm tactics by the police against strikers. He also invoked the 'hostility' clause to serve Sachs with an order that banished him from the Witwatersrand for twelve months. The strike coincided with unrest concerning lodgers' taxes in the Germiston location. The CPSA was already active in that struggle. For Pirow, the garment workers' strike and the demonstrations against the lodgers' tax were part of the same sinister plot. In the words of Sachs, Pirow exploited 'the communist bogey' in these elections to label the strike as communist-inspired, despite the fact that Sachs had been expelled from the CPSA in 1931, after the Woltons and Bach had embarked on their purification of the party.

The strike had a mixed outcome. The loyalty of the union's members withstood the enormous pressures exerted on them to turn against Sachs, and he himself managed to evade his banishment order successfully. In addition, the Nationalists failed to take the Germiston seat, despite their all-out drive against the CPSA, Sachs, and the union. But the resources of the union were depleted by the length of the strike, and it was finally forced to submit to an arbitration committee, which came out on the side of the employers. The unfavourable settlement had the effect of weakening the union, and the next few years had to be devoted to rebuilding its position.

Most of the union's members came from deeply conservative, parochial backgrounds. Their childhood had been imbued with strong notions of white *baasskap*[16] and Afrikaner exclusivism. Johanna Cornelius, who became president of the Garment Workers Union in 1934, summed up the legacy of her upbringing thus: 'It took me years to get used to the notion that even the English—let alone natives—were human beings.'[17] Even though mutual poverty could blur the harsher outlines of racism amongst those whites and blacks who were working together and often living together in rundown tenements and mixed neighbourhoods, the belief in white supremacy ran deep. For many poor whites it was their last, precious claim to dignity and status.

The GWU challenged many of these assumptions with its broader principles and more radical creed of working-class unity. It had an important educative influence on its members, who were not only learning new organisational skills—how to run a meeting or keep records—but also absorbing new ideas about how wealth was produced and controlled, who were one's allies during a strike, and what the united action of workers could achieve in the way of concessions from bosses.

During the 1930s, a number of prominent garment workers were sponsored by the CPSA on workers' delegations to the USSR. They included Johanna Cornelius and Kathleen Parker in 1933, Julia Kruger in 1936, Anna Scheepers and Sophie Venter in 1938.[18] These women were exposed to new experiences and ideological influences which enlarged their political education, sometimes very rapidly. For instance, when Johanna Cornelius went on board ship for the USSR in 1933, she had no knowledge of Lenin or the Bolshevik revolution. Basil Davidson, in his *Report on Southern Africa*, quotes her thus:

> I hadn't the slightest idea who Lenin was. And I remember on the boat that people began to talk about us as Bolshies and Katie Parker and I were worried about this and asked why they did. Then P. Farmer, the other delegate, told us about the revolution and about Lenin.

Delegates were both impressed and at times disconcerted by the economic independence and equality Russian women appeared to experience. Kathleen Parker, for instance, commented at a report-back meeting in Johannesburg on a woman she had met cleaning engines, and wondered what the effect on her nails must have been. Johanna Cornelius was struck by being addressed as 'Comrade' instead of 'Miss' or Mrs'.[19]

The effect of such experiences was, of course, too limited to produce a general reorientation in all garment workers' thinking. Nevertheless, through report-back meetings and letters home, some of the new ideas which trade unionists abroad were absorbing filtered into the general membership as well. Far more important an influence on rank and file members, however, was the success of the union in winning pay increases and general improvements in conditions of work. This demonstrated what organised workers could achieve, and won over a substantial sector of members to more liberal ideas about worker equality and unity. It also threatened the claim of the Afrikaner Nationalists to represent and lead all Afrikaners down a path of unmitigated white supremacy and Afrikaner hegemony. In 1938 Johanna Cornelius, along with two other Garment Workers Union leaders, had the following Mayday message printed in the

Guardian: '(Ons) stuur Meidag groete aan alle vrouwerkers en hoop vir eenheid vir die vrou van Suid Afrika.' ([We] send Mayday greetings to all women workers and hope for unity among the women of South Africa.)[20] She had travelled a long way from the days when 'even the English' were not fully human.

The Growing Presence of Black Women in Industry

As secondary industry continued to expand and diversify, so the demand for female labour expanded as well. In the eight years between 1924/25 and 1932/3, the female labour force in manufacturing rose from 12 per cent to 17 per cent of all workers.[21] The proportion of white women in this total rose from six per cent to 12 per cent, while the percentage of black women remained roughly the same as in the 1920s.

With the exception of the GWU, the trade union movement as a whole was slow to respond to the new opportunities that this increase in female workers offered. Individuals like Ray Alexander were urging trade unionists and the CPSA to pay greater attention to women, and were also campaigning for issues like pregnancy leave and maternity benefits, but, as in other spheres, the position of women remained a low priority on trade union agendas.

In the mid 1930s, the composition of the female labour force began to show significant changes. As the economy continued to expand, the demand for women in the clerical and administrative sector increased dramatically. Following the same pattern of ranking by colour that characterised male employment, it was white women who moved into these new posts and black women who took their place on the factory floor; at that stage, mostly 'Coloured' women, since they were less hemmed in by restrictions on their mobility and independence than African women. By 1936, the dominance of white women in the female industrial labour force had reached its peak, and from then on their importance began to decline. Already by 1939/40 their percentage of the total industrial labour force had slipped to ten per cent. In contrast, in the fifteen years between 1923 and 1938/39 their presence in the clerical field doubled from 12 per cent to roughly a quarter of all clerical workers.[22] By 1936 clerical work had become the largest single area of employment for white women.[23]

In view of the politicising potential of productive work on women, the growing numbers of black women being drawn into manufacturing was a development of major importance. It helped lay the base for the larger role women would play in the national liberation movement during and after the war. It also posed new challenges to the trade union movement, which threatened to destroy the achievements already won.

By the late 1930s the radical sentiments about worker unity and solidarity that Cornelius and others had been espousing were coming under attack from both within and without the garment industry. For one thing, the influx of black women into the industry was putting non-racial working-class principles to a practical test. For another, after 1934, agents of the Nationalist Party were engaged in a bitter struggle to gain control of those unions with a predominant or large Afrikaans membership. They aimed at smashing the influence of 'alien' (non-Afrikaner) ideologies and harnessing the unions to the political service of Afrikaner nationalism. In doing so they exploited prejudices and fears. While the Garment Workers Union resisted the attack on its leadership which focused particularly on general secretary Sachs, its commitment to an open trade unionism was blunted. Up to the outbreak of war in 1939, this process had only just begun to get under way. The war, and the tremendous expansion that it generated in manufacturing industry, hastened it on, evidenced by the establishment of a parallel branch for 'Coloured' garment workers, instead of their incorporation within the existing body, in 1940.

Before World War II, then, trade unionism was only must beginning to make headway among women workers in South Africa. Most union work was being carried out among white women, who, apart from several extremely important individuals, would not make a large contribution towards the establishment of a broader movement. Some new ideas on the need to organise women and their changing economic roles were, however, beginning to circulate in trade union circles, encouraged particularly by the CPSA. During the war and after, these would take a firmer hold amongst an expanding black female labour force.

The Position of Women in 1939

A brief review of the material covered shows that, by the time of the outbreak of war in 1939, some of the ground in which the FSAW was later to take root had been prepared. The idea that women needed to organise themselves to deal with particular problems had already surfaced in a number of ways within certain organisations. Along with it went the conviction that, to be truly effective, a women's organisation would have to commit itself to the broad political struggle, involving both men and women, for the overthrow of the structures of white supremacy. Several women who would be important in getting the FSAW established were already active—Ray Alexander, Josie Palmer, Bettie du Toit. Contact between women of different races was sparse, but the ideal of non-racialism was already present.

In the economic sphere, the pattern of 1921 still prevailed. The largest occupational category for women was still that of housewife or, in the case of women in the reserves, peasant farmer. In both instances their primary importance lay in the reproductive not productive sphere. Domestic service and agriculture were the largest areas of employment for black women, with industry trailing far behind. Notable increases in female employment were taking place in the field of manufacture, however. By 1936 the earlier dominance of white women in manufacturing was on the wane and more and more black women were being drawn into factory work. Women were still defined primarily in terms of their family and their domestic responsibilities, but the boundaries of the female world were being pushed back to incorporate other areas of activity as well.

The actual organisation of women within the ANC, the CPSA and the trade unions was at an early stage, sketchy and hesitant. For the most part, women were viewed by society and viewed themselves as apolitical and domestic beings. This was true whether they were living in the tribal reserves or the westernised towns. However, prompted by some far-reaching economic and demographic developments, women in the towns were beginning to stir. As far back as 1913, the Free State anti-pass campaign had revealed that a potential for political activism did exist amongst women—a potential on which the coming of the war in 1939 was to act as a catalyst.

Notes

1. *Union Statistics for 50 Years*, Table G-6.
2. Walker and Weinbren, *2000 Casualties*, p. 29.
3. *Ibid.*
4. *International*, 2/5/19.
5. *International*, 24/10/19.
6. Van der Ross, *A Political and Social History of the Cape Coloured People, 1880–1970*, p. 108.
7. Quoted in D. Welsh, *op. cit.*, p. 200.
8. *Forward*, 27/3/25.
9. Scheepers, 'The Garment Workers face the challenge', p. 230, states that the Union was started in 1918, according to the available records, but might possibly have got under way earlier. *International*, 5/9/19, reports on a meeting to be held 'to forward the new' Union.
10. Scheepers, *op. cit.*, p. 124.
11. *Ibid.*
12. Sachs, *Rebels' Daughters*, p. 31, quoting from the *Carnegie Commission Report*.
13. Carnegie Commission, *The Poor White Problem in South Africa*, vol. 1, p. xix.
14. Quoted in E.S. Sachs, *Rebels' Daughters*, p. 46.
15. Sachs was general secretary of the union from the early 1920s till 1952, when he was forced to resign in terms of the Suppression of Communism Act. Sachs was a member of the CPSA during the 1920s, but in 1931 he was expelled, along with S.P. Bunting and others. His book, *Rebels' Daughters*, gives an 'inside' history of the union.
16. *Baasskap:* literally 'mastership', i.e. domination, overlordship.
17. Quoted in B. Davidson, *Report on Southern Africa*, p. 179.
18. *Umsebenzi*, 7/10/33, 18/7/36, 16/12/38.
19. *Umsebenzi*, 3/2/34.
20. *Guardian*, 29/4/38.
21. S. van der Horst, 'Women as an economic force in Southern Africa', p. 56.
22. *Ibid.*
23. *Union Statistics for 50 Years*, Table G-8.

PART TWO: POLITICAL ORGANISATION AMONG WOMEN, 1939–53

5

'Today We Fight for Food, Tomorrow for the Vote, and Then Freedom for All': Grassroots Organisations Among Women During the War

The General Economic and Political Impact of the Second World War

In the political and economic history of South Africa, the second world war marks a divide between two different periods. Economically, it encouraged a shift in the structure of the South African economy away from its former dependence on the mining and agriculture sectors, toward a growing dominance by secondary industry. The numbers employed in manufacturing rose rapidly, and the proportion of black to white workers rose significantly as well. Black workers came to dominate to a still greater extent at the unskilled and semi-skilled levels, while white workers tended to move up the scale into the skilled strata or into administrative and clerical posts.

By this time, too, the ability of the reserves to continue functioning as a reproductive base for the migrant labour system had been almost completely depleted. One of the ironies inherent in the migrant labour system is its destructive impact on the very social and economic structures on which it is based, so that if these structures are to be maintained at all, a larger degree of state coercion becomes necessary. By the 1940s, any semblance of a genuine subsistence economy in the reserves had collapsed under the weight of the migrant labour system, which over the years had drained off the most able-bodied workers from the reserves to the mines, factories and farms of the modern sector. The reserves could not compete against the cheap, mass-produced goods of the towns. Deprived of their most productive labour, without any meaningful capital investment or infrastructural development, they were becoming more and more dependent on the industries of white South Africa to supply them with both their basic life support needs, and the cash with which to purchase those needs. In 1949, a survey on the Keiskammahoek District of the Ciskei commented on the economic exhaustion into which the area had sunk:

> The dependence of the villagers upon the earnings of their emigrant workers is so great that it would probably be more accurate to say that the economy of the district rests firstly upon the fact that it is a reservoir of labour for the mines and industries of the Union, and secondly upon the subsistence farming of those who remain behind.[1]

It was a comment applicable to any one of the impoverished reserve districts scattered throughout the country.

As a result of the economic developments, the pace of black urbanisation accelerated enormously. Municipal and government housing schemes could not keep up with the rapid influx of people to the towns. Despite pressures for reform in some quarters, migrant labour remained in force as the standard form of labour. Nevertheless, more and more men, and women too, were abandoning their links with the reserves and swelling the group of those who already regarded themselves as permanent town dwellers. Figures supplied by the 1936 and 1946 censuses show that in those ten years the percentage of the total African population found living in the towns increased from 18.4 per cent to 23.4 per cent. Existing townships grew increasingly overcrowded, their very rudimentary facilities even more inadequate, and huge and illegal squatter camps grew up on the fringes of all the major towns.

Though the manufacturing industry had launched upon a boom period, most workers derived no benefits in the form of higher wages or cheaper consumer goods. The severe political restrictions on the bargaining power of black workers, plus the existence of a huge reserve army of labour in the reserves, held down wages at an artificially low level. At the same time, the war unleashed an upward spiral in the cost of living that further depressed the standard of living of black workers and peasants.

Numerous different sources detail the inflationary effects of the war in South Africa. According to Walshe, the cost of staple foods rose by 91 per cent between 1939 and 1944, outstripping both cost of living allowances and increases in basic wages.[2] The following index of retail prices on all items (including food, rent, transport, clothing, etc.) between 1936 and 1948 shows that the major jump in prices occurred after 1940.

Fig. 1
Index of Retail Prices, Average for the Union
(1938 = 100)[3]

1936	1938	1940	1942	1944	1946	1948
94.3	100	103.4	117.3	128.8	134.1	147.8

The rise in prices becomes even more significant when one notes that, in the ten years between 1928 and 1938, retail prices as a whole had actually dropped, from 106.9 in 1928 to 100 in 1938.[4] The rise in food prices during the war years was even higher than that of the average on all items of consumption, moving from a base of 100 in 1938 to 156.8 in 1948. Basic foodstuffs that became more expensive between 1938 and 1947 included rice (from 2/7d to 7/9d per lb), tea (25/7d to 50/7d per lb), beef (8/2d to 11/5d per lb), eggs (21/7d to 37/-d per doz.), and jam (5/5d to 17/3d per lb).[5]

The situation was further aggravated by dislocations in the marketing and supply system, which led to periodic shortages of basic foods in the shops. Black marketeering contributed to the problems by causing artificial shortages and pushing up prices of food still further. One of the major demands of consumer bodies was for the government to introduce a system of rationing of basic foods. This was never done but in response to public pressure, the government finally introduced a system of mobile food vans which sold limited quantities of food and groceries which were in particularly short supply—rice, soap, tea, etc.—at regular places in the suburbs and townships. It would appear that these vans were operating by 1945, if not before. Later, in May 1946, the government also appointed a director of food supplies and distribution.[6]

How serious the price rises were for the average working-class family becomes clear when one considers the level of black wages at the time. Grossly inadequate to start with, they did not keep up with the cost of living. In other words, the standard of living of blacks was, overall, declining. In 1951 a cost of living study, sponsored by the South African Institute of Race Relations, compared the average income of a black urban family of five with its 'essential minimum expenditure' requirements in 1944 and 1951, in the Witwatersrand-Pretoria area.[7] It found that, with the exception of Pretoria, where the disparity between essential expenditure and actual income had remained roughly on a par, the minimum level of essential expenditure (which was greater than income to begin with) had increased more than had average wages between those years. In 1944 the gap between the two was already as follows:

Fig. 2
Average African Family Income and Essential Minimum Expenditure,
Monthly, 1944

	Income	Expenditure
Johannesburg	£9.18.1	£12.18. 6
Pretoria	£9. 6.4	£12.19. 4
Reef Towns	£9. 7.9	£11. 0.11

Such stark evidence of the extreme poverty in which urban Africans were living was not confined to the Rand only. In 1942, the Smit Committee, appointed by the government to investigate 'the social, health and economic conditions of urban natives', produced a report[8] which covered the whole country. It began by saying that what had impressed the committee 'above all' had been the poverty of the 'native community'. It referred to 'an appalling amount of malnutrition amongst urban natives both young and old', and cited a survey of African schoolchildren in Durban which found that over 40 per cent were suffering from 'clinical stages' of malnutrition.[9]

Nor was this extreme situation confined to Africans. In 1948 a government body, the Social and Economic Planning Council, produced a report[10] which looked at the degree of urban poverty for the total population. It provided statistics for Cape Town, Durban and Johannesburg on the percentage of the different race groups living below the poverty datum line [PDL] in each city. (The PDL barely covers the most basic items necessary for human existence.) In Cape Town (the figures were for 1938/39), some 55 per cent of 'Coloured' and five per cent of white households were found to be earning below the PDL. In Durban, the comparable figures in 1943/44 were 70.6 per cent of Indians, 38.2 per cent of 'Coloureds', 24.8 per cent of Africans and 5.2 per cent of white families. For Johannesburg, the report quoted from the *Non-European Bus Services Commission* of 1944 to show that, in 1940, 86.8 per cent of 'non-Europeans' were earning below the PDL.

Statistics are far easier to come by for the urban areas. Poverty and malnutrition in the rural areas go largely undocumented. But all studies agree on the desperate poverty of the black rural areas which the collapse of the subsistence economy had engendered. 'Today even an exceptionally good harvest produces food enough for only half the nutritional requirements of the people living at home', commented the rural survey for Keiskammahoek in 1949. 'In a drought year, scarcely one-twentieth of requirements are produced.' The report referred to 'such manifest poverty in the vast majority of the families'.[11] The great flow of people from the countryside to the towns confirmed the extreme extent of rural immiseration. The towns, hostile and brutal as conditions there were, yet offered the victims of rural poverty a possibility of cash earnings and held out a promise of some relief.

With poverty so acute and widespread, any increase in food prices or dislocation of the market threatened not just an abstract standard of living, but the very survival of a large percentage of black households, particularly bearing in mind that the largest slice of black wages went on food. (The 1951 cost of living survey cited above estimated that, in Johannesburg, an average of 87 per cent of black earnings was spent on food.)[12]

Economically, then, the war years saw a dangerous drop in the already inadequate living standards of blacks. Politically (and developments here must be related to the economic changes), the war ushered in a period of growing militancy among black workers and political organisations, fired by the rapid proletarianisation of blacks, the rising cost of living, the acute housing shortage in the towns, and rising black expectations in the midst of a war 'for democracy', a war 'to stamp out fascism'.

During the 1940s, the political positions of government and black opposition groups became increasingly polarised. At first, the war appeared to usher in a more liberal spirit in government circles. As manufacturing industry expanded, big business began to press demands for a labour force more skilled and stable than the migrant labour system appeared capable of providing. The United Party government under General Smuts, which held office between 1939 and 1948, was sympathetic to the interests of industrialists, and gave hints that it was prepared to consider a more flexible approach to influx control and black urbanisation. In 1942 the Smit Report recommended relaxing the pass laws, and in 1946 the Fagan Commission (Native Laws Commission) came out in favour of qualified recognition of a permanent African population in the towns.

Both reports raised hopes among blacks that there would be a gradual relaxation of some of the more oppressive laws governing their lives, but the hopes proved unfounded. The Smuts government, preoccupied with the war, did nothing to restructure existing economic and political relationships between black and white in any fundamental way. Matters were allowed to drift, and moderate black opinion became increasingly disillusioned. Then in 1948 the National Party was elected to power, in an upset victory over the United Party, and the apartheid era in South African politics was introduced. It put paid to any hopes of a gradual accommodation of black aspirations by the state. Far from moving away from discriminatory economic and political practices, the new government reinforced them. It overhauled and extended the migrant labour system, tightened up influx control, and introduced a range of measures designed to coerce and control the black labour force still more ruthlessly. One of its first actions was to introduce the Suppression of Communism Act in 1950. This outlawed the CPSA and gave the government extremely wide powers to suppress any opposition in the name of 'state security'. The election of the Nationalist government heralded an intensification of conflict between the state and the disenfranchised black majority, and launched South Africa into a decade of confrontation politics in the 1950s.

The second world war thus marked a turning-point in South African politics. During the 1940s, as the possibilities of reconciliation faded, black political organisations became more militant. In 1943 the Congress Youth League [CYL] was established, marking the emergence of a more radical group of young leaders in the ANC organisation. The CYL acted as a pressure group within the ANC, pushing for a more militant line of action and urging the cultivation of a mass membership. The previously quiescent South African Indian Congress [SAIC] also emerged as a more active and militant body, with some claim to a mass following. In 1946 it launched an ambitious campaign of passive resistance, to protest against a new law that established segregated areas of land ownership for whites and Indians in Natal towns. This campaign raised civil disobedience to a new prominence as a tactic of resistance, and was indicative of a more assertive, less conciliatory mood in black opposition groups.

The 1940s were also a time of growing militancy among black workers. As the numbers of black industrial workers swelled, and the pressures of low wages and the rising cost of living mounted, black trade unions grew rapidly. Despite the fact that strikes by Africans were illegal, the war years saw a spate of strike activity, particularly on the Rand. In August 1946 the African Mineworkers Union led a strike of major proportions in support of a demand for a minimum wage of ten shillings a day. Over seventy thousand African miners came out. The Smuts government's reaction to the strike demonstrated forcefully how very far it was from considering any fundamental change in the position of black workers. It came down unequivocally on the side of the mineowners, ordering direct police intervention, which forcibly drove miners back to work and crushed the strike, killing nine strikers in the process.

While black political organisations were becoming more active, much of the most significant political organisation of this time took place at a local community level, frequently outside the framework of established national bodies. The war years were a time of enormous social ferment and unrest, which found expression in numerous local campaigns and protests in all major cities. Much was informal and spontaneous—particular local pressures and difficulties would reach a point at which they could no longer be tolerated, and would provoke a reaction by township residents—meetings, election of local committees, boycotts, etc. Grassroots leaders emerged to direct local campaigns; sometimes other political organisations intervened to assist or direct the course of action. The CPSA was particularly aware of the importance of local issues. At times, local campaigns achieved national prominence before subsiding.

The urban housing shortage and inflation were two of the most explosive issues round which communities rallied. In 1943, residents of Alexandra Township, on the outskirts of Johannesburg, challenged an increase in the bus fare to town, by boycotting their bus service *en masse*. They succeeded in getting the increase set aside, and prompted the Smuts government to appoint a commission to investigate the black bus service on the Rand. Squatter movements proliferated in the towns. The most prominent started in Johannesburg in 1944. James Sofazonke (We shall all die) Mpanza led thousands of homeless people out of the desperately overcrowded township of Orlando, outside Johannesburg, to establish Shantytown—out of 'sticks, sacking, old tins, and maize stalks'[13] —on the open veld nearby, in open defiance of municipal and central government regulations.

Another very important area of community organisation centred on the rising cost of food and periodic shortages of basic commodities. Action took the form of protest meetings, street marches, and deputations to the authorities. Many trade unions took up this issue on behalf of their members. Protest also led to the establishment of buying clubs and consumer protection societies, notably the People's Food Council in Johannesburg and the Women's Food Committee in Cape Town.

Community bus boycotts, squatter movements, consumer organisations—these were all indicative of the growing frustration and restlessness of township residents. They fed off and into the heightened political consciousness of groups such as the ANC and the SAIC.

The 1940s and Women

To an increasing extent women were swept along by both the economic and political currents of change. The spread of manufacturing industry encouraged trends already noticeable in the 1930s. More women were entering factory employment, more and more of them black, at this stage mainly 'Coloured'. The crumbling economic and social order in the reserves was driving large numbers of African women to make the trek to town, despite legislative and social proscriptions on their townward migration, and the bleak employment prospects facing them once they arrived. As a result, for a growing number of African women, the established values and customs of tribal society, which were already under fire, became increasingly inappropriate to their lives, inadequate for the new conditions of township life. The situation confronting them in town forced them to take a more activist role than either tribal or western bourgeois ideology condoned as natural and desirable for women.

The rising cost of living and periodic food shortages, as well as the urban housing crisis, pressed particularly heavily on women, since they were most immediately involved in feeding and caring for their families with meagre resources. Because of their position as wives and mothers, as well as their general economic insecurity, township women could not afford to ignore what was happening. As the following section will show, women featured prominently in many of the grassroots movements and campaigns that centred round these home issues. It was the most important area in which women were active at the time.

Although it took time for political organisations to adjust to the new circumstances shaping women's position in society, the extent and scope of female involvement in existing political organisations expanded during the 1940s. As will be described in subsequent chapters, women became more prominent in the ANC, the CPSA, and the trade union movement. In the SAIC, which previously had paid scant attention to women, some signs of activity by female members became apparent. Contact between women in these organisations increased, and several leaders began to canvass actively for the idea of a national women's organisation that could draw the various strands together.

Grassroots Protests Among Women

The numerous protests and demonstrations over local issues which punctuated this period involved a much wider range of women than those who were already members of political parties. Given the restrictions that limited the social and economic horizons of the female world, it was obviously easier for women to get involved in politics at a local rather than provincial or national level, and the domestic nature of the issues at stake in local campaigns—housing, food prices, permits, etc.—had a far more immediate appeal and significance to them than abstract issues of national politics such as political rights or the constitution.

Once again the material is scanty, but what has been uncovered supports the conclusion about the pre-war period that what appears as the passivity of women historically is not so much that they did not take part in political movements, as that frequently their involvement has been overlooked by both contemporary observers and later researchers. It seems, more than has been generally realised, that in many townships there is a long tradition of female protest which becomes reactivated in times of crisis. So, in the 1940s, women were often very active in the grassroots campaigns. Generally they were not leaders, though now and then some remarkable women did emerge. Women, however, formed a significant part of the groundswell of discontent and resistance that rumbled through the townships.

Alexandra township is one community with a long history of female involvement in grassroots resistance movements. Women joined in when the community launched its bus boycott, first in 1943 and again in 1944. Along with the men, they walked the 9½ miles between the township and the city centre until the bus company agreed to revert to the old fare. A few years later, there were reports of women getting involved in squatter movements in and around Alexandra. In February 1947, members of a group called the Alexandra Women's Council demonstrated against the official Native Affairs Commission when it arrived to investigate squatter groups in the area.[14] Who was represented on the council and what happened to it are not known. Possibly it had links with the ANC Women's League, which was established in 1943. In the 1950s, Alexandra women would certainly be a strong force in this league, on the Rand.

Women were involved in other squatter movements as well. Urban residence rights and access to housing are areas where township women have always been particularly vulnerable. Historically, squatter movements have always involved large numbers of women and produced important leaders. The recent squatter movement in Crossroads, outside Cape Town, is a contemporary example of how women in squatter communities have organised themselves. The Crossroads Women's Committee that emerged in the 1970s was a strong and active body; it frequently pushed a far more militant and radical line than did the men of the community. Crossroads, however, is only one well-documented and publicised instance in a long history of squatter organisation among women.

The war years were an especially active time for squatter movements. In Cape Town in the early 1940s, squatters in a community called Blouvlei, near the suburb of Retreat, successfully resisted attempts by the local authorities to demolish their camp.[15] They were assisted by the CPSA, which stressed the importance of mobilising the entire community, and helped draw women into the organisation of the campaign. Dora Tamana, who by that time had settled permanently in Cape Town, was a resident of Blouvlei. She became active as an organiser of women, and as a result of the campaign joined the CPSA, thus becoming drawn into the national liberation network then developing in Cape Town.

Women were also present in large numbers when, in 1944, James Mpanza established Shantytown near Johannesburg. Later, in March 1947, women took part when squatters marched through the streets of Johannesburg, demonstrating against the housing shortage.[16] Further research will undoubtedly reveal many more instances of female participation in the squatter movement.

Dora Tamana was one women for whom agitation over the housing crisis acted as an opening to wider political involvement. Another was Julia Mpanza, wife of James Mpanza and an activist in her own right. She is reported to have led an attack on township women who were queueing up for soup from a charitable soup kitchen, a few years before the establishment of Shantytown; she argued that the women should boycott the kitchens—they needed houses, not soup.[17] Although her subsequent political career passed largely unrecorded, she was apparently a natural leader and did develop wider political contacts. On 8th March 1947 (International Women's Day), she took part in a march of 'hundreds of African, European, 'Coloured', Indian, and Chinese women through the streets of Johannesburg, demanding freedom and equality'.[18] Later, she was elected as chairperson of a new women's organisation, the Transvaal All-Women's Union, which was formed on the Rand in 1947.[19] This union, which is described below, was formed with communist backing to mobilise women on as broad a front as possible; it was an early attempt to launch a national women's movement. Whether Mpanza remained in touch with the women's movement as it took shape in the early fifties is unfortunately not known, but the fact that she featured so prominently in 1947 was indicative of the contribution the squatter movement made to the women's movement.

Another issue which roused women on the Reef was the clampdown on home-brewing of beer. This, as has already been mentioned, was always a potent source of friction between women and local authorities, since beer-brewing was a major source of income for township women. (One study undertaken in 1959 found that, in Johannesburg's Eastern Native Township, 60 per cent of women brewed and sold beer.[20]) In July 1945 unrest broke out in Springs, near Johannesburg, when local women organised a boycott of municipal beer halls, with backing from the CPSA. On 28th July 1945, the boycott erupted into violence, when police opened fire on an unarmed crowd of pickets and boycotters. As a result of the disturbances, 111 people, the majority of them women, appeared in the Springs Magistrates Court.[21]

Probably the most important issue to mobilise township women at this time, and one that undoubtedly fuelled unrest in other quarters, was the so-called 'food crisis'. Some signs of organisation round the question of rising food prices had already been seen before the war. In 1935, the newspaper *Umsebenzi* carried a single brief article on a committee that had been established in Durban to encourage 'all house-wives' to boycott firms engaged in profiteering. According to the report, 'various women's organisations' and a group calling itself the League Against Fascism and War were responsible for the committee.[22] Four years later, in Cape Town, the Consumer Vigilance Council campaigned against high food prices and the apparent indifference of the authorities. In both organisations, the influence of the CPSA was apparent. The League Against Fascism and War had been established in 1943 by 'trade unionists, communists, Labour Party members, Friends of the Soviet Union, and radical societies'.[23] The role of the CPSA and the NLL in the Consumer Vigilance Council has been described already.

During the war, as the cost of living soared, consumer protests became still more vociferous. The rising cost of living was a fundamental factor in the general unrest of the time; the organisations it encouraged were of particular significance to the political organisation of women. In response to the pressures of rising costs and erratic distribution of foodstuffs, consumer organisations emerged in Johannesburg (The People's Food

Council), and Cape Town (The Women's Food Committee), while sporadic signs of activity, apparently without a single co-ordinating body, were seen in Durban.

Black women, as mothers and those responsible for the catering for their families, could hardly ignore the 'food crisis'. Its effects were insistent and immediate. Price rises and food shortages threatened the health and stability of their families. They impinged on their daily lives in such a way as to force women to look outside the home to the wider political and economic context in which the crisis was located. As with the squatter movement, involvement in protests against the rising cost of living sprang from vital domestic concerns. Nevertheless, it could lead women to a greater interest in general political issues. Political organisations that took up the food question found a number of new recruits from amongst the women they worked with.

The People's Food Council

The first reports of organised activity around the food question during the war centre on Johannesburg. In early November 1943, a People's Food Council was formed, with communist backing, to organise consumer resistance to the rising cost of food.[24] Material on the council is very thin—it is another area calling for extensive research. Whether it was entirely the brainchild of the CPSA or not is not known, but certainly, as in Cape Town, the CPSA was closely involved in it. In late 1943 Hilda Watts, a communist candidate in the Johannesburg municipal elections, was described as being a 'prominent member' of the council.[25] It is worth noting that the council was established a few months after the 1943 Alexandra bus boycott. The boycott received much publicity, and possibly its success prompted the formation of the People's Food Council to deal with the problem of rising costs in another field.

One of the People's Food Council's first actions was to call a public conference on the food situation, in conjunction with the white National Council of Women. The conference condemned the chaotic food supply situation and unscrupulous profiteering by retailers. The conveners of the conference hailed it as a success, and a council circular reported that 'This conference resulted in increased interest in the food situation, which is the cause of the Minister of Agriculture calling for comments from the public on the Egg Control Board which is being formed.'[26]

That the NCW should participate with an organisation having such radical sponsorship is interesting. In part it was a sign of the times. After 1941, once the USSR entered the war, the CPSA swung over to a whole-hearted support for the Allied war effort. This made the communists less suspect amongst members of the white establishment. Yet the reason for co-operation went deeper than simply fraternisation between wartime allies. Opposition to rising food prices was something all women could agree on and identify with, because they were affected in a common area, that of their domestic responsibilities. They therefore had a mutual interest in seeking a solution to the food crisis. As with other home and family-related issues, the food crisis cut through class and race barriers and allowed a degree of united action by women. Thus, in 1946, Mrs A.E. McCallum, chairwoman of an organisation called the Housewives League, referred to the 'close co-operation' between women's organisations as a noticeable feature of the previous year. 'On all vital questions women are prepared to put aside pettiness and jealousy in order to work for the common good of all.'[27]

On other issues that touched black women in the 1940s, however—issues which were fundamentally linked to the maintenance of white supremacy, eg passes, and the unionisation of black workers—white women offered no solidarity. The commitment of an organisation like the NCW to greater equality for women and an improvement in the living standards of all did not go beyond its basic allegiance to the institutions of white, bourgeois South Africa. In this it differed not at all from the earlier WEAU. When the Food Council began to look at these institutions more critically, the NCW parted company with it.

In 1943/44, the Food Council involved itself in organising co-operative food clubs in working-class suburbs and townships 'to obtain vegetables at about half the ordinary retail prices'.[28] These clubs were not meant to be charitable organisations, but 'clubs which are fostering united action on the part of housewives'. By March 1944 there were eleven such clubs involving more than five hundred families. They operated in Ophirton, Fordsburg, Jeppe, Vrededorp, La Rochelle, Noordgesig, and Alexandra.[29] A circular described the council's aims as

1. To form food clubs in every working class suburb of Johannesburg.
2. To persuade the Municipal Council to carry out its promise to open suburban markets.
3. To persuade the Government to form a Ministry of Food to watch the interests of consumers.[30]

It also described the council as having the support of a number of trade unions and women's organisations (not specified) in 'this struggle to put food within the reach of every family'.

While the People's Food Council appears to have continued operating in the next few years, the vigour and scale of its operations are not known. In May 1947 the *Guardian* carried a small report showing that agitation on the Rand about the food situation had not yet died away. A deputation representing the women of Kliptown, near Johannesburg, sought an interview with the Johannesburg City Council. They demanded that foodstuffs be rationed, and complained about the way the food vans were operating. The *Guardian*'s report did not refer explicitly to the People's Food Council, but the presence of Josie Palmer in the deputation shows that the CPSA, if not the Food Council itself, was represented at the protest.[31]

Women's Food Committee

The material on the Women's Food Committee in Cape Town is more substantial. This could mean that it was a more active body than the Johannesburg group, but it could also merely reflect the fact that the *Guardian,* a major source of information on the committees, was based in Cape Town. By 1945–46, the *Guardian* was reporting numerous manifestations of discontent about the food situation among Cape Town women. In September 1945 it carried a brief reference in its 'Women's Column' to a new campaign that would be starting 'soon' to fight against the rising cost of living, but it did not elaborate.[32] In mid-January 1946, the food crisis was its main front-page story. It described the militant mood that was developing among consumers, and reported anti-government meetings, incidents of angry women raiding abbatoirs in search of meat, and threats of strikes by workers.

The following month, two women members of the CPSA led a march of black women (predominently 'Coloured') past parliament in support of their demand that the government introduce a rationing system for food. Interviewed by the *Guardian,* one of the leaders, Pauline Podbrey, stressed the need for unity between black and white women: 'European women must not be too proud to join non-European women in the general demand for rationing. . . Unity of this kind between the races is terribly important.'[33] It is not clear whether the march was organised by the Women's Food Committee. The first explicit reference to the committee comes a few months later, in April 1946, when the *Guardian* carried a feature article on it. In the article, an anonymous woman, a member of the committee, described its make-up and aims to John Morley Turner (who was a prominent member of the NLL in Cape Town). According to her, the committee had been formed by ordinary working women and housewives.

> Recognising our troubles, and facing up to them practically, we organised a Women's Food Committee. At first it was difficult due to the fact that most of us had so little experience of organisation other than running a house which in itself is an excellent training ground.[34]

As she described it, the committee had grown out of the food queues that formed at each mobile food van. Each queue elected a queue committee to maintain order and ensure 'fair deals'. This was important, since it was feared that any disorders could lead to the withdrawal of the vans. In turn, these committees elected a representative to a general committee, which represented all the food queues. At that stage, in April 1946, twelve food queues were represented on the general committee, and a chairwoman and secretary had recently been chosen. Their names are not recorded, but, in 1947, the chairwoman was a Mrs G. Anthony and the secretary Hetty McLeod, who seems to have been the more important of the two.

The Women's Food Committee was thus clearly a grassroots

organisation. In 1947 the *Guardian* described it as 'a working class organisation springing from the housewives who stood in the food queues'.[35] However, although it was certainly the product of a widespread mood of dissatisfaction among black housewives, and was also thoroughly representative of them, it is clear that there was both prompting and advice from the CPSA and the NLL, two bodies whose membership and activities frequently overlapped in Cape Town. They provided speakers at many of the committee's public meetings, and also spokesmen for the several deputations the committee arranged with various officials. The one person who seems to have been most closely involved in the committee on a day-to-day level was John Morley Turner, who wrote the initial feature article describing its establishment. According to Katie White, a member of the committee, it was largely through him, acting in conjunction with Hetty McLeod, that the committee got started.[36]

The Women's Food Committee grew rapidly till, by the end of 1947, it claimed to represent 59 queues scattered throughout the Cape Peninsula.[37] From all accounts it was a vigorous body. In March 1947 it organised a conference at which two hundred delegates, representing not only the food queues but also trade unions, the CPSA and some churches, agreed to organise a demonstration on 1st May outside parliament. The immediate issue seems to have been a threat to withdraw the food vans. The demonstration drew 'thousands' of Cape Town housewives to a meeting on the Grand Parade. Carrying banners, 'We fight for food', they marched through the streets while a small deputation, which included Sam Kahn and Joey Fourie of the CPSA, met with the Minister of Finance, J. Hofmeyr.[38] Hofmeyr agreed to meet a further deputation, and the following week twelve women, representing the Food Committee plus the Durban Housewives' League, the Food and Canning Workers Union and the Sweet Workers Union, met with him. They handed over a petition signed by seven thousand women who wanted the government to keep the food vans till an adequate system of rationing could be introduced. Hofmeyr dismissed rationing as impracticable, but did promise that the food vans would continue to operate.[39]

The Food Committee also organised so-called 'food raids' against merchants who were suspected of hoarding foodstuffs. These raids involved direct consumer action against black marketeers. Large numbers of women, with members of the committee acting as marshalls, would descend on suspect individual merchants and attempt to pressure them by numbers and the threat of reprisals into unlocking their storerooms and selling their accumulated stock. The *Guardian* carried several reports on such raids, for instance, a 'rice raid' in May 1946, involving hundreds of women. First they assembled at the Grand Parade outside the City Hall, then they marched through the streets to the premises of the suspected hoarders. Speakers included Sam Kahn of the CPSA and Cissy Gool.[40]

By encouraging such demonstrations and organisation, the food crisis of the 1940s had a definite politicising effect on many black women who would otherwise have remained uninvolved. Numbers of black women were brought into contact with the political network then being established among women in the national liberation movement. Several of these women would later become active in the FSAW and Congress Movement. One such was Katy White, a domestic worker living in the Harfield Road Station area in Cape Town. Prior to getting involved in the Women's Food Committee, her background had been completely apolitical. She was first elected to represent her food queue on the general committee and from there went on to become one of the leaders of the FSAW in Cape Town in the mid-1950s.[41] Hetty McLeod, by 1947 secretary of the committee, was another woman for whom the Food Committee was a gateway to the national liberation movement.

Already in 1946 the Food Committee in Cape Town was showing signs of shifting its focus from the food situation to wider political issues. Its motto, as quoted by the *Guardian* in June 1946, was simple and direct: 'Today we fight for food, tomorrow for the vote and then for freedom for all.'[42] By 1948, the question of the vote had moved to the forefront. Thus Mrs Anthony, chairwoman of the committee, declared in January 1948:

> The vote is a weapon we must have so that we can safeguard the future of our children. . . We women have to deal with the everyday things of life. We have to worry about managing with our husband's pay envelopes, about keeping the cost of living down, about getting enough bread for our children and seeing that they go to school. We want to put people in Parliament who understand our problems and will fight in our interests.[43]

The committee had come to see its powerlessness as an organisation of individuals who were excluded from the existing political structures. At that point, before the National Party had come to power and when 'Coloured' men had not yet been disenfranchised in the Cape, the remedy was still looked for within existing structures. Most of these women saw the political future in terms of a sharing in the institutions of white supremacy—that parliament would yet be induced to broaden its electoral base to include other race groups.

In pursuit of these goals, the Food Committee decided, in 1948, to form a Non-European Women's League 'to fight for the vote for all black women'. It described the food issue and the franchise as inseparable— 'whoever controlled the key of the food cupboard controlled the food'; for them the key to the cupboard was the vote.[44] No follow-up was reported in the *Guardian*, and it would seem that the league went the way of those earlier attempts to establish a black women's suffrage movement which Cissy Gool and the NLL had sponsored in the late 1930s. (Whether Cissy Gool had any involvement in the 1948 proposal would be interesting to know. Her name is not mentioned in the *Guardian* report, but it seems probable that she would have had some connection with it.)

As already pointed out, the enfranchisement of black women was not a political goal that could be achieved in isolation from the wider struggle of blacks for full political and social rights in South Africa. By the end of the 1940s that struggle was becoming more clearly defined as irreconcilable with the institutions of white supremacy (such as parliament). A Non-European Women's Suffrage League was too narrow a base on which to mobilise black women. In recognition of this, in the early 1950s many of the leaders of the league, and of the Food Committee as well, were absorbed into the Congress Movement and later the FSAW. Their involvement in the women's movement sprang out of their commitment to the national liberation movement rather than to women's rights as such.

By the early 1950s, the Women's Food Committee was more or less defunct. The last specific reference to it in the *Guardian* came in January 1950, in a small report that it was organising a demonstration against the 'serious shortage of meat and increasing cost of living'.[45] By 1953, when the food crisis had eased off and the food supply situation was more stable, the committee's functions had been transformed into a 'Christmas Club'—an organisation that offered its members differently priced Christmas food hampers at wholesale prices.[46]

Yet the issue of rising prices was still a potentially important one for mobilising women. In August 1953 the threat of an increase in the price of bread reactivated the Food Committee network in Cape Town. With Ray Alexander playing a leading role, a delegation of women was organised to meet with the Minister of Finance, Havenga, to protest against the price increase. At least two of the women apart from Alexander—Gladys Smith and Katy White—had been closely involved in the old Food Committee. Dora Tamana, by now active in the CPSA, was also a delegate.[47] This protest, which is described below more fully, was important in promoting the idea of a national women's organisation amongst Congress women in Cape Town, an idea that had already been raised in Port Elizabeth and was under discussion in other centres. According to Alexander, the bread issue in 1953 was significant because it vitally affected women as mothers, and made the women's movement 'imperative'.[48]

In the Women's Food Committee and the People's Food Council can be seen, the beginnings of the growth of political consciousness among previously politically isolated black housewives and women workers. The starting point was an issue that directly affected them and to which they could easily relate—increased prices and the shortage of basic foods. In organising in protest, they came up against their political impotence in society, and began to look more critically at the wider context in which both this and the food crisis itself were operating.

The demonstrations and deputations organised by the food committees in Johannesburg and Cape Town were thus politicising experiences for those women who participated in them. They also highlighted for the national liberation movement the potential for political activism that existed among women on issues directly affecting them. A similar claim could be made for the other grassroots campaigns that women were involved in at the time. Although the available material is biased toward the two major cities of Johannesburg and Cape Town—which undoubtedly were major centres of political activism—it is almost certain that further research would uncover many other instances of localised, informal organisation and resistance scattered across the country. This grassroots activity and restlessness formed part of the context in which the established political organisations worked when they took up the question of women in the 1940s. The tradition of local activism was also the base for the massive anti-pass campaign of African women in the 1950s, which fanned out over the whole country.

Notes

1. *Keiskammahoek Rural Survey,* vol II, pp. 4–5.
2. Walshe, *The Rise of African Nationalism in South Africa,* p. 302.
3. Compiled from *Union Statistics for 50 Years,* Table H-23.
4. *Ibid.*
5. *Ibid.,* Tables H-22, H-16, H-17, H-18.
6. *Guardian,* 23/5/46.
7. E. Wix, *The Cost of Living,* p. 19.
8. *Report of the Inter-Departmental Committee on the Social, Health and Economic Conditions of Urban Natives* (1942).
9. *Ibid.,* pp. 1, 5.
10. Social and Economic Planning Council, *The Economic and Social Conditions of the Racial Groups in South Africa* (UG 43-48). The report explained that the figure of Durban Africans living below the PDL was misleadingly low, since most African families in the area were not classified as living within metropolitan limits. Most Durban African workers were therefore classed as 'single workers', disguising the dependence of families on their wages.
11. *Keiskammahoek Rural Survey,* vol. II, p. 177, p. 179.
12. Wix, *op. cit.*
13. Roux, *Time Longer than Rope,* p. 323. 'Sofazonke' was the slogan of Mpanza's movement.
14. C. Kros, *Urban African Women's Organisations and Protests on the Rand from the Years 1939 to 1956,* p. 44.
15. Interview with D. Tamana.
16. Kros, *op. cit.*
17. *Ibid.*
18. *Ibid.,* quoting from *Inkululeko,* March 1947.
19. *Guardian,* 7/10/47.
20. Kros, *op. cit.,* quoting L. Longmore, *The Dispossessed: a study of the sex life of Bantu women in and around Johannesburg.*
21. Kros, *op. cit.*
22. *Umsebenzi,* 21/9/35.
23. Simons and Simons, *Class and Colour in South Africa,* p. 471.
24. People's Food Council circular, dated 11/3/44, A.B. Xuma Papers, University of Witwatersrand, Box 1, 440311.
25. *Guardian,* 18/11/43.
26. People's Food Council circular, 11/3/44.
27. *Guardian,* 21/3/46.
28. People's Food Council circular, 11/3/44.
29. *Ibid.*
30. *Ibid.*
31. *Guardian,* 29/5/47.
32. *Guardian,* 13/9/45.
33. *Guardian,* 14/2/46.

34. *Guardian,* 25/4/46.
35. *Guardian,* 2/1/47.
36. Interview with White.
37. *Guardian,* 20/11/47.
38. *Guardian,* 8/5/47.
39. *Guardian,* 15/5/47.
40. *Guardian,* 23/5/46.
41. Interview with White.
42. *Guardian,* 27/6/46.
43. *Guardian,* 20/1/48.
44. *Ibid.,* 5/8/48.
45. *Guardian,* 26/1/50.
46. *Guardian,* 18/6/53.
47. *Ibid.*
48. Interview with R. Alexander.

6

'Reviving the Women's Section': The Establishment of the ANC Women's League

The Revival of the ANC

In the 1940s the organisation and programme of the ANC underwent several significant changes. These years were a preparing ground for the decade of mass political action that followed in the 1950s. The apparent failure of its previous tactics to make any impression on the government, coupled with the growing restlessness of black urban dwellers and workers, was forcing the ANC to reassess its political orientation. As first the United Party and then the National Party rejected black political aspirations, Congress leaders came, some reluctantly, others with relief, to accept the inevitability of confrontation rather than conciliation.

Under the presidency of Dr A.B. Xuma (1940–49), the ANC over-hauled its structure and laid the basis for a mass political party. At the policy level, the CYL, established in 1943, played a leading role in pushing the ANC in a more radical direction. In 1943 the ANC committed itself to a policy of universal adult franchise for the first time—and, also for the first time, included women in the definition of 'adult'. By 1946 it was talking of a common voting roll in place of the racially segregated rolls that the Hertzog government had instituted in the Cape in 1936. Implicitly, the ANC was thus now endorsing majority rule instead of mere partner-ship with the white minority, as before. The strategy for achieving this programme was also coming under more radical scrutiny. In 1949, under pressure from the CYL, the ANC adopted a 'Programme of Action' which called for such extra-legal methods as boycotts, strikes and civil disobedience to pressurise the government into accepting change. In the programme, the ANC now defined its goal as 'national freedom', the 'right to self-government under the banner of African nationalism'.[1]

In 1952 the ANC launched a massive Defiance Campaign of civil disobedience against unjust laws. This was its first attempt to put its more radical sentiments into practice on a large scale. During the campaign, some eight and a half thousand volunteers came forward over a period of about six months to defy descriminatory legislation and court arrest. They entered whites-only post offices, rode on whites-only trains and ignored permits and regulations governing entrance to African townships.

These developments encouraged an increase in members from an estimated formal membership of just under 2,000 in 1944–45, to 5,517 in 1947.[2] (This does not take into account the informal membership—individuals who considered themselves ANC members and supporters but did not pay the annual subscription of 2/6d.) In the early 1950s, once it had adopted the 'Programme of Action', the ANC witnessed a spectacular increase in membership. Under the impact of the Defiance Campaign, its membership reached a peak of almost 100,000.[3]

The 1940s also witnessed the start of greater co-operation between the ANC and other political bodies which shared its opposition to the white supremacist state. The African identity of the ANC was always jealously guarded, but the possibility of working alliances with other groups was explored. Relationships improved between the ANC and the Indian Congress. In 1945 the SAIC was taken over by a radical leadership under Dr Naicker in Natal and Dr Dadoo in the Transvaal. In 1947 they and Dr Xuma of the ANC signed the so-called 'Doctor's Pact', which confirmed the growing measure of co-operation between the two organisations. These developments foreshadowed the implementation of the Congress Alliance in the early 1950s, when the SAIC co-operated with the ANC during the Defiance Campaign.

Relationships with the Communist Party were not as smooth. Between 1943 and 1945 the ANC co-operated with the CPSA in an anti-pass campaign that the latter had launched. Dr Xuma agreed to act as chairman of the campaign, thereby underlining the closer working relationships that the war and the CPSA's 'United Front' strategy had nurtured. Mounting state repression against all opposition did lead to a more sympathetic and accommodating attitude towards the CPSA within the ANC, but the presence of communists within ANC ranks continued to be a source of tension and conflict. For its own part, the CPSA tended to downplay ideological differences with the black nationalist movement.

The revival of the ANC during the 1940s was, however, a slow, uneven process. Internal conflicts and organisational weaknesses continued to undermine its potential strength. Dr Xuma failed to eradicate a tendency towards regionalism, and friction between the centre and provincial congresses remained a problem. Ideologically, there were significant differences between the supporters of a radical, exclusive African nationalism (found mainly within the Youth League) and the supporters of a broader, non-racial approach. Nevertheless, the post-war period saw the emergence of the ANC as a major channel of African political expression. From an organisation representative only of the tiny African elite, it was coming to assume the proportions of the national liberation movement it later claimed to be. As such, it was more readily identified as a dangerous threat by the state.

The Establishment of the ANC Women's League

Women did, to some extent, share in this process of reorganisation and revival. In its attempt to build up a mass membership, the Congress hierarchy identified women as an area for potential recruits that had previously been neglected. The new concern with women did not simply reflect a desire to attract greater numbers to the ANC. It also reflected the recognition that the position of women had undergone real changes since the first ANC constitution had been drawn up in 1919. Congress was lagging behind, and it was time to upgrade the status of women within its ranks. At the same time, it had become apparent that existing organisations, such as the NCAW, were not undertaking political work amongst the broad masses of African women. The complaints of activists such as Josie Palmer were having an effect—the ANC now conceded that a new structure, under its direct supervision, was required.

The first signs of a change of attitude came in 1941. At the annual conference of the ANC that year, delegates passed the following resolution:

> That this Conference recommends to the parent body the necessity of reviving the women's section of the Congress in terms of the provision of the Constitution. Further, that women be accorded the same status as men in the classification of membership. That the following means be made to attract the women: (a) to make the programme of the Congress as attractive as possible to the women, (b) a careful choice of leadership.[4]

The following year, women were again singled out for special mention at the annual conference, when Dr Xuma called for a mass membership drive. It should aim at the 'involvement of the chiefs, ministers of religion, women, youths, indeed "every African" '.[5]

These preliminary discussions finally bore fruit at the 1943 annual conference, at which women were granted full membership status within the ANC, with the right to vote and participate in Congress affairs at all levels.[6] At the same time, the ANC Women's League (ANCWL) was set up and Madie-Hall Xuma, wife of Dr Xuma, was elected its first president.[7]

Madie-Hall Xuma was an American from Georgia whom Xuma had met and married while on a visit to the USA in 1937–38. Like her predecessor in the Bantu Women's League, Charlotte Maxeke, she too was a graduate (MA from Columbia University) and a social worker. Walshe refers in general terms to her influence, as an American negro, on the continued identification of the ANC with the civil rights movement in the USA.[8] Josie Palmer once criticised her for being largely apolitical, but she certainly considered herself to have more advanced views than most South Africans on the question of women's place in society. In 1953 *Drum* interviewed her for an article entitled 'Is a woman's place in the home?' In her reply she criticised men who kept their wives at home all the time, and described how 'in my country' women and men work 'on a 50–50 basis'.[9] Although Walshe does not say so, she presumably played a large role in getting the ANCWL established.

The programme of action for the ANCWL drew together the different strands of thought that had already developed within Congress circles on what the contribution of women to the political struggle should be. The role of the ANCWL was, at a later date, spelled out more fully as follows:

> (a) to arouse the interest of African women in the struggle for freedom and equality and assist the widespread organisation of women;
> (b) to take up special problems and issues affecting women, and
> (c) to carry on propaganda against apartheid and discriminatory laws among African women.[10]

It was clear from the beginning that the national struggle for 'freedom and equality' took precedence over the 'special problems and issues' of women. The ANCWL was not an independent body, but a subsection of the ANC proper: 'It [the Women's League] is under the political direction and control of the Congress, and it follows the policy and programme of the Congress.' In structure, too, the ANCWL followed that of the parent body. It operated on three levels, national, provincial and branch, each of which was run by an elected committee, responsible to their general membership and, finally, the ANC national executive.

The ANCWL was set up within the ANC as a subsidiary body to which all female members automatically belonged. Like the CYL, which was set up at the same conference to cater specifically for younger people, the ANCWL had a particular audience to reach and a particular function to perform. No longer auxiliary members, women were still a special category of members with 'special additional duties and responsibilities'. By establishing a separate Women's League, the ANC recognised that women occupied a distinct and inferior position to men in society and that this posed particular organisational problems and required special attention. Yet, by directing women into a separate body, the ANC was also perpetuating the existing sexual divisions within its organisation. This tended to reinforce stereotypes about 'women's role' and 'women's work', and subtly undermined the formal equality of the sexes that had been proclaimed. As later critics of apartheid would maintain, separate is not equal. The dilemma was not unique to the ANCWL. It confronts any women's group or women's caucus within a more general movement— to what extent can women's issues be treated as a special area, without detracting from their importance as issues of general social and political concern? The question is still pertinent for the national liberation movement today.

The establishment of the ANCWL in 1943 was, in retrospect, a significant event. A body aiming to represent the interests of the majority of South African women had been set up within the premier African political organisation—the ANC had finally come to incorporate women, one half of the people it claimed to represent, into its political frame of reference. A structure was created whereby African women could be channelled into the national liberation movement on a footing that was, at least theoretically, equal to that of men. In the ANCWL, as in the Bantu Women's League before it, women were being organised specifically as African women, setting its mark on the subsequent form that the women's movement would take in the national liberation movement. In 1943 the ANC stated clearly that it was not prepared to submerge the ANCWL into a general non-racial women's movement. This standpoint dominated later discussion on what form a national women's organisation should take, when the structure of the proposed FSAW was being discussed in Congress circles in the mid-1950s. Yet in 1943 only the barest outline of the ANCWL was created. It took several years for the new organisation to get off the ground. According to an anonymous history of the league, provincial congresses were not set up until the late 1940s, and the Women's League did not get going as a 'real force' until then.[11]

For the entire period of the 1940s, material on the ANCWL is very thin. In the *Guardian*, the only reference to it was in a report of a 'Women's Anti-Pass Conference' held in Johannesburg in March 1944.[12] The main force behind the conference was the CPSA, but the ANCWL was one of the organisations represented. The conference is of interest in view of the very large role that the issue of passes would play in the rapid growth of the ANCWL after 1950. But in 1944 African women did not yet have to carry passes themselves. The focus of the conference was on the supportive role women should play in the national campaign against passes for men.

In his account of the ANC during the 1940s, Walshe too barely mentions the Women's League. The only direct reference is in connection with the ANC's constitution of 1943. His single other reference to the work of women in the ANC at the time concerns a fund-raising event organised by Madie-Hall Xuma—a 'successful stage production', the 'American Negro Revue', which contributed £216 to ANC funds.[13] It seems likely that the ANCWL was involved in the production, although Walshe does not say so.

Both the content and the skimpiness of the material on the ANCWL indicate that it was not a dynamic organisation during the 1940s. According to Josie Palmer, Madie-Hall Xuma was, for all her belief in sexual equality, a conservative woman who was not politically motivated. She was more interested in the 'Zenzele' clubs which she helped found— social, self-help societies that attracted a middle-class following and focused on sewing and social or charitable activities. With her as leader, the ANCWL of the 1940s was in much the same position as the earlier Bantu Women's League had been in relation to the ANC. Middle-class women dominated, and despite its enhanced status formally, it was not particularly active. Its work was limited to conventional 'women's work' such as fund-raising and catering.

There were many difficulties in stepping outside of these limits. It was hard enough trying to organise African men—the treatment meted out to striking miners by the Smuts government in 1946 made clear the ruthlessness with which the state would put down black demands for better living and working conditions. The difficulties were compounded in the case of women, by those additional forces relating to their particular role in society. Women in the towns were economically more vulnerable and politically less secure than men; patriarchal ideology was deeply entrenched in all strata of society. Members of Congress, both male and female, were conditioned to accept that women's role in any organisation was supportive rather than innovative, in the background rather than the forefront. In 1952, Madie-Hall Xuma herself testified to the strength of these values in inhibiting African women from a more active involvement in organisations outside the home. Referring to the Zenzele Clubs, she said,

> some women have been reluctant to join our clubs because their husbands feared they'd meet unsuitable women who might mislead them. . . You see,

the position of the women here is a little different from what it is in other parts of the world.[14]

Many male Congress members were reluctant to let their wives and daughters become more fully involved in the running of the ANC. Ten years after the ANCWL had been founded, in 1954, a woman delegate to the annual ANC conference complained that 'women have been used as tools to raise money without representation in Congress'.[15] The gap between a theoretical endorsement of equality between the sexes and daily practice was still a very large one in the ANC.

Yet, as consumer and squatter movements of the time demonstrated, working-class African women were by no means indifferent to the political campaigns of the time. There was no lack of issues round which to organise them, and the indications were there that women would respond positively to political leadership. That leadership was not forthcoming from the ANC or the ANCWL under the Xumas. Neither of them fully accepted the more aggressive and populist strategy of the CYL. For most of the 1940s, the ANCWL lacked both commitment to the issues of concern to the masses of women and initiative in confronting the problems that obstructed their large-scale involvement in politics.

By the late 1940s, however, the ANCWL was beginning to stir. By this time the CYL had succeeded in turning the ANC in a more radical direction. In 1949 the ANC adopted the 'Programme of Action', and replaced Dr Xuma with the more pliable Dr Moroka as national president. At the same time, Madie-Hall Xuma stepped down from the presidency of the ANCWL, allowing the more activist spirit of the CYL to infuse the women's organisation as well. Ida Mtwana—'Youth Leaguer, moving spirit among women, orator and heckler'[16]—took over her position.

The election of Mtwana as Women's League president initiated a new era in the history of the organisation. At about this time the structure of the ANCWL was overhauled and provincial leagues, on the pattern of the parent body, were established. This put the ANCWL in closer touch with township women throughout the country, and opened the way for a new and more dynamic leadership, with a broader representation of working-class women, to come to the fore.

The emergence of the ANCWL as a 'real force' was in part a product of the general heightening in the mood of black resistance that the 1949 'Programme of Action' both reflected and encouraged. As the ANC grew into a mass organisation, the scope of the ANCWL's work inevitably expanded as well. Women participated in large numbers in the Defiance Campaign of 1952. The ANCWL was also affected by the growth of interest in a women's movement in other Congress-linked organisations, and the greater measure of co-operation between these bodies.

But probably the single most important stimulus for the growth of the ANCWL came from a familiar source that directly touched African women—the threat of passes. In 1950, after less than two years of Nationalist rule, the issue shot into the headlines when proposed amendments to the Urban Areas Act were leaked to the press. The amendments envisaged a far tighter control over the movement of African women, a control which could only be enforced by some form of pass system for women. The news was met by a storm of protest amongst women, taking in many parts of the country, and greatly stimulating the activity of the ANCWL.

The reasons why the new government was anxious to tighten up on its control of women, as well as the response it provoked amongst women, are considered in Chapter 10. The issue directly affected women in their homes and in their communities, and yet took on a national dimension. As the question of passes had led to the establishment of the Bantu Women's League in 1913/14 so now, some thirty-five years later, it precipitated a resurgence of political activity amongst a wide cross-section of African women in different centres throughout the Union. While the ANCWL was not the only nor always the most important body involved in the demonstrations, the outburst of protest did politicise many African women, to the general benefit of the league. It also gave the ANCWL a clear focus for activity. 'Our fight is on', declared Bertha Mkize, provincial secretary of the ANCWL in Durban, in April 1950.[17] As the next ten years would show, they were prophetic words.

Notes

1. Walshe, *The Rise of African Nationalism*, p. 291.
2. *Ibid.*, pp. 19, 47.
3. *Ibid.*, p. 403.
4. Karis and Carter, *op. cit.*, vol. 2, Document 25C, 'Resolutions of ANC Annual Conference of Dec. 14-16, 1941'.
5. Walshe, *op. cit.*, p. 390, citing Xuma's presidential address to the conference.
6. Walshe, *op. cit.*, p. 380, citing the 'Constitution of the ANC 1943'.
7. *Ibid.*, p. 101.
8. *Ibid.*, p. 340.
9. *Drum*, September 1952, p. 10.
10. 'Rules and Regulations of the African National Congress Women's League', mimeo, p. 1, FSAW II H1.
11. 'The history of the ANC Women's League and the role of women', nd, carbon typescript, p. 3.
12. *Guardian*, 6/4/44.
13. Walshe, *op. cit.*, p. 396.
14. *Drum*, September 1952, p. 10.
15. *Drum*, February 1954, p. 11.
16. *Drum*, August 1953, p. 9.
17. *Guardian*, 6/4/50.

7

'A Matter of Bread and Butter Issues': The CPSA and Women, 1939–50

Like the ANC, the CPSA enjoyed a period of revival in the 1940s after its internal difficulties in the 1930s. By the time the Suppression of Communism Act forced it to disband in 1950, its membership had risen to an estimated 2,000. The great majority were Africans. Karis and Carter estimate there were only about 150 whites and 250 Indians amongst the 2,000 members.[1]

By the late 1930s, the party had abandoned its early Bolshevisation programme. It concentrated instead on the 'United Front' with liberal organisations against fascism, which it regarded as the major threat in both Europe and South Africa. The second world war encouraged this policy of co-operation with other organisations for common, short-term goals. Although the CPSA originally opposed the war as 'imperialist', when the Soviet Union entered the war on the side of the Allies in June 1941, it swung round in support of the war effort in South Africa.

The war years saw a remarkable softening of previously hostile attitudes towards the Soviet Union among the Allied powers, and to some extent this rubbed off on domestic politics. National communist parties were regarded with more tolerance after 1941. Within South Africa, communist-sponsored organisations supporting the Soviet Union were well patronised. The 'Friends of the Soviet Union', for instance, was a flourishing body in 1942, with the Minister of Justice, Colin Steyn, one of its patrons; collections for medical aid for the USSR were well supported. In her novel *A Ripple From the Storm*, Doris Lessing creates a vivid picture of wartime fraternising between liberals and communists in the neighbouring colony of Rhodesia. Conditions in South Africa, where the Communist Party was larger and more active, were analogous.

In 1941, the annual conference of the CPSA adopted a moderate programme of democratic aims. While the long-term aim was 'to organise the workers as a class to establish working class rule and a socialist republic', in order to 'prepare the way' and 'defend and promote the interests of the workers and oppressed nationalities' the party agreed to work for the abolition of imperialism, a universal adult franchise, the removal of all 'political, social and economic colour bars', wage increases, improved living conditions and a redistribution of land.[2] The conference also re-affirmed the 'United Front' approach, which allowed for continued co-operation with black resistance groups and, on selected issues, with more conservative white groups.

On the basis of this programme, the party involved itself in all the key political issues within the black community—passes, the squatter movement, bus boycotts, wages, and demonstrations against the rising cost of living. Its relations with the ANC improved as that body revived and radicalised, although, as already mentioned, ANC suspicions against the communists were never completely allayed. In accepting the chairmanship of the anti-pass campaign sponsored by the CPSA between 1943 and 1945, ANC president Dr Xuma was also accepting the closer working relations between the two organisations. Communist influence within the Indian Congress was increased when Dr Dadoo, a member of the CPSA central committee, was elected SAIC national president in 1947. In the trade unions, too, the CPSA continued to work actively, propagating a doctrine of non-racial class solidarity while concentrating on the organisation of black workers. The more moderate line of the party at the time was shown by its participation in white elections at both national and local levels. They were seen as opportunities for educating the white electorate and raising issues otherwise ignored in the sphere of white party politics.

With the ending of the war, however, official tolerance of the CPSA ended too. In January 1947, the central committee of the party was arrested and charged with sedition. The charges, which were eventually withdrawn, arose out of the CPSA's support for the African mineworkers' strike of 1946. The white establishment's hostility towards the communists was intensified once the National Party came to power in 1948. For long it had singled out 'communist agitators' as the real menace in both trade unions and black political organisations. Now in power, it turned its attention towards suppressing the menace in a far more ruthless and decisive fashion than the previous United Party government had dared.

In 1950, the Suppression of Communism Act was passed. It was the first link in a long chain of repressive legislation that the Nationalist government passed, designed to curtail democratic freedoms and strengthen the hands of the state in moving to suppress the national liberation movement. The act contained an extremely wide definition of 'statutory communism', the propagation of which was henceforth outlawed. It also vested in the executive branch of government extensive powers to ban individuals and organisations from any political activity, also widely defined. The act meant the end of the CPSA as a legal political party in South Africa. It was faced with the painful choice of either disbanding completely or going underground. After much internal debate, it chose to disband publicly in June 1950.

Its ideas and influence were not finally destroyed, however. Ex-members continued to work in the trade union movement and various Congress bodies. White ex-members found a new political home in the Congress of Democrats [COD], set up in 1953 by a mixed group of liberals and radicals. Later, the Communist Party itself regrouped, underground.

So, although the CPSA was not entirely eliminated as a presence in South African politics, after 1950 it could operate only in a clandestine way. It had to work through existing organisations which did not subscribe fully to its own aims, and became heavily dependent on personal contacts with Congress leaders. It had to abandon any ambitions of leading a mass political programme of worker organisation and education. After 1950, anybody wanting to learn about marxism and communism had to do so furtively. Books were banned, free discussion limited and, inevitably, marxist ideas became confined, almost entirely, to a tiny circle of embattled and often frustrated intellectuals.

Women within the CPSA

The CPSA was again a major influence in the political organisation of women at this time, and its influence did not disappear completely when the party disbanded in 1950. Yet, once again, women's rights were not an issue of central importance in the party programme. The party's aims, as set out in 1941, recognised sex discrimination as something to fight against— they talked of the 'extension to all adults, regardless of race, colour or sex, of the right to vote and be elected to. . . representative positions'.[3] Sex discrimination was, however, seen as a minor problem in the South African context. The CPSA had already recognised the importance of mobilising women on the political front; as in the earlier period, however, it emphasised the contribution women could make to the general struggle, as workers and as blacks, and was inclined to overlook women's issues. Thus, an editorial in the *Guardian* on the occasion of International Women's Day in 1940 described the anniversary as 'the day on which women throughout the world demonstrate their opposition to war, to oppression and injustice'. The particular forms of oppression women suffered by, as distinct from men, were not mentioned.[4]

Separate figures for male and female members are unavailable, but one can safely assume that the majority of the 2,000 members belonging to the CPSA in 1950 were men. Nevertheless, in the 1940s the number of women associated with the party at leadership level definitely increased, and there are a few indications of an increase at the rank and file level as well. Several energetic women became members during the war and soon began to feature prominently. In 1940 Hilda Watts[5] left the Labour Party to join the Communist Party in Johannesburg. By 1945 she had become important enough in the party hierarchy to be elected to the central committee. Betty Sacks (neé Radford), editor of the *Guardian* until 1948, joined the party in Cape Town in 1941. She, too, was elected to the central committee, in 1946.

Although white women were still predominant, several valuable black women were also recruited. Rahima Ally, a trade unionist and associate of Ray Alexander, was one. In 1942 Dora Tamana became a member of the CPSA in Cape Town, in the squatter community of Blouvlei. Her background was very different from that of the white recruits to the party— poor, rural and working class. Her recruitment was an indication that the CPSA was beginning to broaden its base among women.

Dora Tamana first became aware of the CPSA through its regular lunchtime meetings on the Grade Parade in central Cape Town. The Grand Parade was a major meeting-place in the city, since it adjoined both the main railway station and a bus terminus. Tamana, *en route* to catch a train or bus, or walking to the city centre, would stop and listen to the speeches and discussion. She describes the process of her political education as 'a slow awakening'.[6] Concepts and phrases she overheard would mesh with her own experience, open up new prospects, and challenge or confirm what she had already understood. From the meetings she learnt about the state-subsidised crèches and childcare facilities in the USSR, inspiring her to organise a rudimentary crèche among the women in her own community of Blouvlei. The need for adequate childcare facilities for working mothers, the importance of providing township and squatter children with decent care during the day while their parents were at work, would remain lifelong concerns of hers. With the barest minimum of facilities—a shack, cardboard boxes for the babies to sleep in, a large pot and a fire to cook on—she set about organising a scheme with local mothers.

Later, when the authorities were applying pressure on the squatters of Blouvlei to move, the CPSA became involved in the community's efforts to resist. Dora Tamana found herself taking a more and more active leadership role. She met Ray Alexander and came to take an increasing interest in affairs beyond her own small community. Through the CPSA she became involved in broader political work in Cape Town, later joining the ANCWL. She was (and at seventy nine, still is) a woman of remarkable strength and dignity. She brought to her political work a sincerity and directness of understanding that a mere intellectual analysis and grasp of the issues could never, on its own, match.

During the 1940s, women featured more prominently than they had before on committees and in executive posts within the CPSA. In 1945 two out of the fifteen members elected to the central committee were women—Ray Alexander and Hilda Watts. In 1946 Ray Alexander was re-elected, along with Betty Sacks.[7] The CPSA also put up a number of women as candidates in both municipal and national elections, a further sign that women's status within the party was improving. In 1943 Betty Sacks and Sam Kahn were elected to the Cape Town City Council.[8] That same year, in the general elections, Joey Fourie, a trade unionist, was one of three unsuccessful communist candidates. She contested the Cape Flats constituency. Two years later she was elected to the Cape Town City Council.[9] In 1944 Hilda Watts became the solitary communist member of the Johannesburg City Council, representing the Hillbrow Ward.[10] In no other political organisation of the time were women as active or as respected as in the Communist Party.

The impact of these women was not confined to the CPSA. While the organisation of women did not take priority in the party as a whole, several of the women already mentioned, notably Ray Alexander, Hilda Watts and Josie Palmer, did feel strongly on the subject. They directed much of their work towards women, and extended the CPSA's policy of co-operation with other progressive organisations to include the women. In the trade unions, the ANC and the SAIC, they fostered contact between women and encouraged steps to organise women on a larger scale. Ray Alexander, Joey Fourie and Bettie du Toit, all party members, were prominent trade unionists, with Alexander again playing a particularly large part in unionising hitherto unorganised black workers. Roux states that before and during the war the 'breaking of new ground in the Cape was largely the work of a young girl communist, Ray Alexander, who was associated with the organisation of at least a dozen new unions'.[11] Alexander did not confine her attention narrowly to women workers, but continued to pay them special attention as a particularly exploited and neglected category of workers. The union most closely linked to her name, the Food and Canning Workers Union [FCWU], established by her in 1941, had a largely female membership. It developed rapidly into a militant and cohesive body that contributed several leaders to the women's movement in later years.

The question of passes in relation to women was taken up by Josie Palmer, a member of the CPSA's Anti-Pass Campaign Committee between 1943 and 1945. In March 1944, Palmer convened a Women's Anti-Pass Conference in Johannesburg, to discuss the part that women could play in the national campaign.[12] The conference drew a number of different African women's organisations together, including the ANC Women's League. In 1950, when women themselves were being threatened with passes, the CPSA strongly identified itself with their opposition, participating in demonstrations and deputations until it had to disband.

As already described, the CPSA was alert to the significance of the wartime grassroots campaigns and protests within the townships. It was particularly active in organising around the issues of the rising cost of living and recurring shortages of basic foods. Communists appear to have played a large, possibly decisive, role in channelling the general discontent and unrest among black women about the food situation into its organisational forms in the People's Food Council in Johannesburg and the Women's Food Committee in Cape Town.

The CPSA also supported women resisting municipal attempts to stamp out private beer-brewing in the townships. In 1945, the CPSA helped women organise a protest meeting in Springs Township, on the Rand. As at Blouvlei, where Dora Tamana lived, the party worked in squatter communities too, liaising with and sometimes recruiting community leaders. By so doing, the CPSA was carrying on a tradition of involvement in local affairs that had already been established in the 1930s. Josie Palmer recalls that the CPSA was 'most active' in fighting domestic issues—'they were working for all-round improvement in the townships on all kinds of domestic issues. It was more a matter of bread and butter issues.'[13]

Once again, the material is frustratingly sketchy. Nevertheless, it seems clear that the role of CPSA women in nurturing and spreading ideas of political organisation among women was a particularly large one at the time—and that they were thus performing a major task in preparing the ground for the subsequent establishment of a national women's organisation within the liberation movement. Despite their small numbers, their leadership role in encouraging contact among women and focusing on issues of direct concern to them was a key one.

The International Women's Day meeting held in Johannesburg in

1946 provided evidence of the degree of contact between different women's organisations achieved by then. It brought together a remarkable cross-section of women's organisations, the broadest grouping yet witnessed, from the CPSA (in the person of Hilda Watts) and the SAIC (represented by Dr Goonam, of whom, more later) to the Child Welfare Association and the League of Women Voters. In addition, messages of support were received from the 'Moscow Anti-Fascist Committee', Josie Palmer, Betty Sacks and two women MPs, Margaret Ballinger and Bertha Solomon. Included in the resolutions was one that stressed the need for all women to support the removal of all legal, political and economic discrimination against black women.[14]

The idea of drawing together the different areas in which women were involved and establishing a national organisation was once again emerging among CPSA women. In 1941, the party's annual conference passed a resolution supporting the idea of an organisation which would represent working women.[15] The following year, at a women's meeting held to pay tribute to Soviet women's contribution to the war effort, the subject of women's political role was raised again: 'We look forward to the day when. . . the women of the world will play their part in the building of the future—freedom, justice and security for all mankind.'[16] Then in 1945, these hitherto vague plans for creating a national organisation of women were sharpened by international developments. In November, an international conference of socialist women established a new body to represent their interests, the Women's International Democratic Federation [WIDF].[17] This acted as a definite example to the women of the CPSA, crystallising earlier plans and stimulating more intensive work towards the goal of a national body in South Africa that could affiliate to the WIDF.

The WIDF

The WIDF was formed at a conference held in Paris which was attended by left-wing women's organisations from 31 different countries. Although it certainly saw socialism as the key to the full emancipation of women, the aims it adopted in 1945 were very loosely formulated under three general headings, without any specific reference to socialist ideology. In the aftermath of the war, peace was its first priority, followed by two very broad claims on women's behalf:

1. The organisation of peace and the destruction of fascism.
2. Equality for men and women in all domains.
3. Protection for mothers and children regardless of their legitimacy.[18]

In the next few years, the WIDF campaigned on behalf of the 'child victims' of the war, took up the case of women political prisoners in Spain, and sent commissions to Germany and South-East Asia to investigate the conditions of women living there. It also called several international conferences which appear to have been well-attended.

Then in 1953, at a third World Congress of Women, the WIDF issued a 'Declaration on the Rights of Women'. The document is worth quoting at some length, because it put in writing many of the ideas then circulating within the CPSA on the purpose of a women's organisation in South Africa. Phrases from the declaration would find an echo in resolutions and statements made by the FSAW in later years.

The declaration began with a general preamble on the position of women in the world:

> There are too many countries in which women still have no rights. They are oppressed and their dignity as human beings is continuously insulted. Millions of peasant women live under tragic conditions.
>
> In the midst of war preparations, when the economic conditions of the workers are deteriorating and the offensive against democratic rights and liberties is being intensified, women's lives are becoming still more difficult.
>
> This is why the fight for the defence of women's rights and for winning full equality is today more essential than ever.[19]

It went on to list the rights to which all women, 'irrespective of their race, nationality and position in society', were entitled. These included equal pay for equal work; equal opportunities in education, the economy and politics; equal legal status with men; state provision of crèches; maternity care and welfare clinics. Throughout, the declaration stressed the importance of ensuring that these rights were extended to peasant and rural women, as well as to urban women. It concluded with a call to solidarity:

> The World Congress calls upon the women of the whole world to cooperate closely in organised and persistent action for their rights as mothers, workers and citizens.
>
> Let us unite our efforts in the common struggle. Unity is the condition of victory.

There do not appear to have been any South African representatives at the first WIDF conrerence in 1945, but Hilda Watts was at the second WIDF conference, held in Prague in March 1947, and she drew attention to conditions in South Africa.[20]

The Transvaal All-Women's Union

While Hilda Watts was in Prague, a group of women attending the 1947 International Women's Day meeting in Johannesburg passed a resolution to establish a 'non-colour bar women's organisation', and the Transvaal All-Women's Union was formed. A cross-section of women leaders was represented at the meeting—speakers included Mrs Suriakala Patel (SAIC), Hetty du Preez (Garment Workers Union) and Josie Palmer (CPSA).[21] Although the newspaper report on the meeting is not very informative, it is explicit about the link with the WIDF: 'The committee hopes to link up with women's organisations in other provinces and so to build up an organisation capable of affiliating to the Women's International Democratic Federation.' Unfortunately, the report does not record who proposed setting up the committee, but, whether directly or indirectly, the initiative came undoubtedly from the CPSA.

Unfortunately, information on the organisation is sketchy. It did not last long enough to become sufficiently well known to leave a well-documented record behind it. Links with the CPSA were very close. Its committee in 1947 consisted of Mrs J. Mpanza (the women's leader from Shantytown) as chairman, Rhona O'Meara as vice-chairwoman, Josie Palmer as secretary, and Hilda Watts.[22] At least three of these office-bearers—O'Meara, Palmer and Watts—were members of the CPSA. As already mentioned, there is no record of whether Mpanza was a member, but she was certainly in close contact with the CPSA on the Reef.

The aims of the Union mirrored those of the WIDF—equal rights for all South African women, protective legislation for women and children, and a commitment to join with women of other nations in a struggle for world peace against fascism and racism.[23] From the beginning, it was committed to the idea of forming a national organisation. However, despite several attempts to expand its membership, it did not succeed in operating beyond the Transvaal; even there, it appeared to be confined to the Reef towns. In July 1947 the *Guardian* reported that the Union was making arrangements for a mass national conference of women in the 'near future'.[24] But while meetings were held on the Rand to popularise the proposal, it never got off the ground at this stage.

A few references to the Union in the next couple of years show that it was still functioning. It made contact with Reef food committees, and took up the question of housing conditions in Benoni with the city council.[25] In 1948 it contributed material on South Africa to an exhibition held by the WIDF in Paris on the lives and conditions of women in different parts of the world.[26] That it had not abandoned the idea of setting up a national organisation was shown in 1949, when it changed its name to the 'Union of South African Women'.[27] Dropping the 'Transvaal' label was not, however, accompanied by any actual expansion on a national scale.

Although the organisation remained small and localised, it apparently did continue to exist in some form or other into the early 1950s. Ray Alexander made contact with a women's group of this nature in Johannesburg when she was making arrangements for the inaugural conference of the FSAW in 1953.[28] In 1954, the FSAW certainly drew on the Union's leadership—Hilda Watts, Josie Palmer—and must have benefited from the work the Union had already done among women on the Rand to popularise the idea of a radical national women's body.

Not enough is known about the Union to explain why it failed in its attempts to get a national organisation established. Possibly it was hampered by the serious external difficulties then facing the CPSA. In 1947, the CPSA leadership was embroiled in the sedition trial that followed its involvement in the mineworkers' strike of 1946. The electoral victory of the National Party in 1948 pushed the CPSA into an even more insecure position. When the CPSA was forced to disband, in 1950, communication between radical women activists in the various centres was temporarily disrupted, as at that stage it was being maintained mainly by CPSA women.

In summary, by 1950 the idea of a national women's organisation had already taken on a concrete, if limited, shape under communist sponsorship, in the form of the Transvaal All-Women's Union. The contribution of the CPSA in nurturing the idea within Congress circles during the 1940s was considerable. It produced important individual leaders, women such as Ray Alexander, Josie Palmer, Hilda Watts and Dora Tamana, and was actively encouraging an emerging political consciousness amongst township women. The dissolution of the CPSA thus retarded the movement to establish a national women's organisation that had been gathering pace within left-wing organisations; it took another three years to get under way again.

The national organisation of women that finally emerged in 1954 was not a communist organisation, even though individual members might have subscribed to communist principles. It did, however, owe much, both conceptually and organisationally, to the legacy of the CPSA.

Notes

1. Karis and Carter, *op. cit.,* vol. 2, p. 107.
2. *Guardian,* 19/6/41.
3. *Ibid.*
4. *Guardian,* 8/3/40.
5. Her married name is Hilda Bernstein, but since she became prominent in the CPSA as Hilda Watts, I have chosen to continue referring to her by this name to avoid confusion. Similarly, I have used only Ray Alexander's single name, rather than her married name of Ray Simons—a practice followed by many of her colleagues in the 1940s and '50s as well.
6. Interview with D. Tamana.
7. *Guardian,* 10/1/46.
8. CPSA, *Communists in Conference.*
9. *Guardian,* 2/8/45.
10. *Guardian,* 2/11/44.
11. Roux, *Time Longer than Rope,* p. 330.
12. *Guardian,* 6/4/44.
13. J. Wells, interview, *op. cit.,* p. 4.
14. *Guardian,* 14/3/46.
15. *Guardian,* 15/5/41.
16. *Guardian,* 21/10/42.
17. *Guardian,* 20/12/45.
18. *Ibid.*
19. *Advance,* 16/7/53.
20. *Guardian,* 20/3/47.
21. *Guardian,* 24/4/47.
22. *Guardian,* 7/10/47.

23. *Guardian,* 24/4/47.
24. *Guardian,* 10/7/47.
25. *Ibid.*
26. *Guardian,* 12/2/48.
27. *Guardian,* 3/3/49.
28. Interview with R. Alexander.

8

'No Nation Can Be Free When One Half of It Is Enslaved in the Kitchen': Women and the South African Indian Congress

The SAIC Before the Second World War

Several references have been made to the SAIC but its programme with regard to women has not yet been looked at in any detail. Before the second world war the SAIC paid very little attention to women as either a source of membership or a group with particular disabilities. It was not an activist organisation at that stage. It derived its following mainly from the wealthy merchant class and was not interested in building up mass membership or support.

The only time it did adopt a more populist strategy before the war was between 1906 and 1913, under the influence of M.K. Gandhi. He inspired and led a campaign of passive resistance against a number of measures that discriminated against Indians, including a Transvaal law that made a form of pass compulsory for all Indians over the age of eight, male and female, another law that prevented Indian migration into the Transvaal, and a £3 poll tax that was levied on Indians in Natal. In addition was a Supreme Court ruling in 1913, which stated that all non-Christian religious marriage ceremonies were invalid in the eyes of the courts, thus reducing the status of Indian women married according to Moslem or Hindu rites to that of concubines. It roused a storm of protest. Not only was the ruling insulting; it also imposed additional legal disabilities on Indian women, who were sufficiently roused to join Gandhi's passive resistance campaign in large numbers, forsaking a traditional passivity and startling contemporary observers in the process.

Overall, the campaign of passive resistance was a qualified success. It eased the most irksome of the restrictions on Indian mobility and succeeded in getting the offending Supreme Court ruling overturned. In later years, the campaign served as a model of civil disobedience tactics for the SAIC and ANC. At the time, however, it did not turn the SAIC into a mass movement. Gandhi left South Africa in 1916, and for the next thirty years the SAIC devoted most of its energies to the business interests of the small Indian elite who dominated its proceedings.

Throughout this time Indian women were, as a group, particularly isolated and secluded from public affairs. Though the participation of women in the 1913 passive resistance campaign set a precedent for later years, unlike the contemporary struggle by African women against passes in the Free State, it did not lead to any attempts to organise women as a group on a more long-term basis. Once the offending measure had been withdrawn, Indian women retreated into the obscurity of their homes again. In the SAIC itself they played little, if any, role for the next thirty years.

The reasons for this must take into account the particularly lowly status occupied by women in the Indian community, a status which reinforced and compounded the obstacles put in their way, as blacks and as women, by the wider society. Culturally, Indian women could be regarded as the most subjected group of women in South Africa. Both the Hindu and Moslem religions sanctioned an extreme form of submission and passivity among women. Prejudice from within the Indian community against women participating in any form of activity outside the home was deeply rooted. Because women were acting in defence of their religion and their domestic role in 1913, their participation in that campaign was condoned, even encouraged. Even so, contemporary observers were all struck by the radical departure from accepted norms of behaviour that it represented. It was an extreme response to an extreme provocation.

The strength of such attitudes within the community is illustrated by the employment statistics for Indian women. The idea of Indian girls working, except at home or in the family business, was shocking, even within very poor families. In the 1936 census a mere 3,710 Asian women, or 7.3 per cent of those over 15 years of age, were found to be 'economically active', compared to 33 per cent of 'Coloured' and 19.4 per cent of white women.[1] Nearly two-thirds of the Indian women in wage employment were found either in service (1,263) or agriculture (1,082).[2] Unlike other sections of the population, the wartime boom did not have a noticeable effect on Indian women by drawing them into public employment. Even by the 1950s, when many of the general obstacles to female wage employment in society had considerably weakened, Indian women continued to shun wage employment. As late as 1960, only 4.9 per cent of the Asian female population (all ages) were 'economically active'.[3]

The social pressures keeping women confined to a subordinate position within the home prevented them from taking a sustained and active part in political organisation *en masse*. However, the coming of the second world war did usher in a more dynamic and radical phase in the history of the SAIC, and this in turn encouraged a small number of women to become involved in its affairs.

The Impact of the Second World War on the SAIC

Within the SAIC, the general radicalising effects of the war were reinforced by a number of developments that particularly stirred the Indian community in South Africa. On the one hand, the nationalist drive for independence in India quickened their community pride and fanned similar aspirations at home. On the other hand, and in marked contrast to what was happening in India, further acts of discrimination were pressing heavily upon them, making apparent how very far from any meaningful participation in political life they were. The most contentious issue concerned successive attempts by the government to segregate Indians into separate residential areas and check the expansion of Indian traders into 'white' areas, where they were regarded as an economic threat by their white counterparts.

These developments encouraged the growth of a radical faction within the SAIC. Radical intellectuals, with trade union experience and worker support, challenged the SAIC old guard for leadership of the Congress. While the established leaders called for a policy of negotiation and compromise with the government, and advocated a system of voluntary segregation, the radicals rejected such tacit support for segregation. They aimed, at the minimum, for full political and social rights for all blacks. In opposing the government they turned to the methods of passive resistance and civil disobedience pioneered by Gandhi.

By 1945 the SAIC had undergone a marked transformation. The struggle for leadership had resulted in victory for the radicals in both the Transvaal and Natal, the two provinces in which most Indians lived. Dr Dadoo, a member of the CPSA, assumed the presidency of, first, the Transvaal Indian Congress [TIC] and then, in 1947, the SAIC itself. The leadership struggle in Natal was more protracted. Dissidents first formed an anti-segregation committee within the Natal Indian Congress [NIC]. By 1945, under the presidency of Dr Naicker, they had taken over the provincial leadership. At the same time, and part of the reason for their success, the radicals launched a membership drive which broadened the ranks of the SAIC and drew in working-class members. Thus, between 1943 and 1945, the NIC membership rose from 17,000 to 35,000.[4]

The first opportunity for the radicals to put their leadership and their methods to the test on a national scale came in 1946, when the government passed the segregationist Asiatic Land Tenure and Representation Act. The act had two aspects. The first set up 'controlled' (ie white) and 'uncontrolled' areas within municipal boundaries in Natal. Indians were prohibited from acquiring or occupying land in the 'controlled' areas. Secondly—'to sugar the pill'[5]—the act offered the Indian community a diluted form of political representation in the central and provincial governments. It proposed that Indians should be allowed to elect two white representatives to the Senate, three to the House of Assembly, and two, who could be Indian, to the Natal Provincial Council. The offer was rejected out of hand by the SAIC as a meaningless and transparent bribe, and was never put into effect.

Feelings against the act ran high within the Indian community. Capitalising on this the NIC, with the backing of the TIC, launched a sustained campaign of passive resistance against it. Over two thousand Indian resisters went to jail for camping on 'controlled' land, or, on a smaller scale, for defying an already existing Immigration Act which prohibited Indians from crossing provincial boundaries without special permission. Although the campaign reached its peak by the end of 1946, it was not officially called off till after the Nationalists had taken office in mid-1948.

The campaign marked a high point of activism within the SAIC. In terms of forcing legislative concessions to the community, it was a failure, and thereafter both the SAIC and its provincial organs slumped, membership going into a steep decline. Nevertheless, the campaign was of great importance on a number of different levels. It showed that the Indian community was also affected by the new mood of resistance stirring black South Africans in the 1940s. It also paved the way for a greater degree of co-operation between the ANC and the SAIC, formalised by the 'Doctors' Pact' of 1947. At the popular level, there was still hostility and suspicion between the Indian and African communities, which could not easily be discounted. Race riots in Durban in 1949 served as a pointed and painful reminder of this. At the leadership level, however, the two communities were drawing closer together. Events were fostering a sense of common blackness amongst political leaders and laying the basis for the Congress Alliance of the 1950s.

The Passive Resistance Campaign also signalled a new determination for mass action on the part of black political organisations. In many ways it foreshadowed the larger and more dramatic Defiance Campaign, which was launched jointly by the ANC and SAIC in 1952. From the point of view of its effect on Indian women, too, the Passive Resistance Campaign was an important politicising event.

Mobilising Indian Women

The problems of mobilising Indian women—isolated, poorly educated, almost totally dependent on the network of their families for both social and economic support—were still very large. The impact of general developments did have some reverberations in the home, however. By the beginning of the 1940s, the first signs of political activity among a tiny, privileged segment of Indian women could be discerned, coinciding with the emergence of the radical splinter group within the SAIC. Undoubtedly the radicals supported and possibly actively encouraged a greater degree of female participation within the SAIC. Contact between the SAIC radicals and other organisations in which women were actively involved—the CPSA, the trade unions, the NLL—probably also contributed to the growth of more liberal ideas within the Indian Congress on the role of women.

In 1941, Hawa Ahmed, a member of the NLL in the Cape, addressed the Durban-based Liberal Study Group, the meeting-place for the NIC radicals. Her subject was the status of women. She concluded her talk by saying that no nation could be free when 'one half of it is enslaved in the kitchen'.[6] The following year, this study group formed a special 'Women's Class'; whether or not as a direct result of Ahmed's speech is not known, but certainly it represented support for her ideas. In opening the inaugural meeting, the president of the study group, I.C. Meer, noted that 'non-European women had not had sufficient opportunity to contribute to the struggle of their people', and expressed the hope that from the class would come 'a powerful women's organisation'.[7] The object of the women's class, according to a *Guardian* report, was to show 'the important part Indian women can play in the progress of a community'.[8] It appears to have been the first such group established among Indian women, and its inauguration marked a new era of female participation in the Indian Congress.

In the 1940s, the most prominent woman in the SAIC was Dr Goonam, one of the handful of black women doctors practising at that time—in 1946 there were five black women 'medical practitioners, physicians, surgeons, radiologists' of whom four, including Goonam, were Indian.[9] She joined the radical anti-segregation committee within the NIC in the early 1940s. Thereafter she rose quickly to prominence. In February 1944 she spoke at a meeting held in Durban in support of independence for India.[10] By 1946 she was already a vice-president of the NIC, a remarkable achievement in a community so conservative about the place of women. In March 1946 the *Guardian* described her as 'one of the few Indian women playing a leading part in the political struggle of the Indian people of this country'.[11] In an interview with that newspaper, Goonam spoke optimistically about the strides Indian women were making, citing the increasing number of university graduates and skilled workers among them as indices of change. She felt that community prejudices against women were 'rapidly disappearing'—the real obstacles impeding their progress stemmed from the government plus the widespread poverty.[12]

Dr Goonam was a privileged member of a very tiny professional class—in 1946 the total number of Indian women in the professions was only 302.[13] Both at this time and later, in the 1950s, women activists within the SAIC were drawn largely from this small core of well-off, educated women. They were in a relatively strong position to reject the traditional stereotypes that defined the lives of the great bulk of Indian women. Very few Indian women had either the economic independence or the education to challenge those structures which confined them to the home. For most of them during this time, politics was, emphatically, men's work.

Nevertheless, political developments during the middle and late 1940s were sufficiently intrusive upon the home to rouse a wider circle of women to take a keen interest in political affairs; for a short time, the base of Indian women's participation in politics was broadened. One very important development was the pressure put on Indian homes by the 'food crisis' of the war years. The impact of rising costs and erratic distribution of foodstuffs hit all women hard, and Indian women were not more shielded from its repercussions than other women. There are indications that in Durban, the home of the largest Indian community in the country, some of them organised in protest. The consumer protests amongst Indian women do not appear to have been as extensive or effective as those being organised in Cape Town and Johannesburg at the same time— partly, perhaps, because the CPSA was very weak in Natal, and partly because of the particularly suppressed position of Indian women. Nevertheless, they were indicative of an unaccustomed assertiveness.

In June 1946, just before the Passive Resistance Campaign was launched, the *Guardian* carried a report on a Mrs L. Govender, an illiterate woman and the sole supporter of five children, who was taking a leading part in organising local women against the black market in food in Durban. The *Guardian* commented:

> Mrs. Govender, who is a leader of a food squad, is symbolic of the growing political consciousness of the Indian working class women in Natal who, day after day, since the commencement of the food raids, have demonstrated in the streets of Durban, demanding the cessation of the black market and the selling and rationing of food.[14]

Furthermore, according to the report, there was a growing realisation among these women that the food struggle was only one aspect of a wider struggle against 'the oppressive laws of this country'. While the polemical aspect of the *Guardian*'s analysis must be kept in mind, and its optimism treated with some caution, it is worth noting that this same Mrs Govender appears to have been one of the first women to volunteer for inclusion in the Passive Resistance Campaign a few weeks later.

The Passive Resistance Campaign, which drew on the whole community, was very important in its impact on Indian women. It is also better documented than the food struggle. The launching of the campaign, in June 1946, initiated a new phase of political activism amongst Indian women within the SAIC. Congress leaders made active attempts to draw women in; Dr Goonam, who was closely associated with the running of the campaign, took the lead. In March 1946, when the campaign was still in its planning stages, a large meeting of 'hundreds' of Indian women was held in Durban to discuss what their role in it should be.[15] The *Guardian* described the meeting as the first of its kind among South African Indians; the size does indicate that interest in the campaign amongst women was widespread. Speakers were Dr Goonam, and newcomers Fatima Meer and Mrs N.P. Desai. The meeting pledged its support for the campaign and elected a committee to direct support along practical lines. Once the campaign was under way, women came forward as volunteers.

Six of the 17 people who initiated the campaign were women. Four of them came from the Transvaal (Zainap Asvat, Zahna Bayat, Amina Pahap and Zubeida Patel) and two from Durban in Natal (Lakshini Govender and T.M. Pather).[16] Along with their male colleagues, they crossed over from the Transvaal into Natal without the necessary permits, and were promptly arrested. Zainap Asvat gave up her university studies to take part; from then on, she was a prominent activist within the SAIC. The subsequent participation of women in the campaign received considerable publicity. In the *Guardian*'s news coverage, photographs of women participants featured prominently. In 1947, speaking at the anniversary of the launching of the campaign, Dr Goonam singled out the fact that women had marched 'side by side with the men' as 'the greatest factor in the year's resistance'.[17]

In fact, the number of women participating was not large. According to Simons and Simons, about 300 of the 2,000 passive resisters who went to jail were women.[18] Nevertheless, the fact that these women did participate, and so prominently too, had repercussions throughout the Indian community. The popular image of women as passive, docile creatures was undoubtedly dented. Within the SAIC itself, the status of women was augmented. In October 1946, three women were elected to the TIC executive committee, the first time women had ever held such senior posts. One of them was Zainap Asvat, the other two were Mrs P.K. Naidoo and Mrs Suriakala Patel.[19] In Natal, Dr Goonam was elected acting chairman of the Provincial Passive Resistance Council while Dr Naicker was temporarily absent on a tour of India. In 1947 she was again singled out and asked to stand in for A.I. Meer, general secretary of the NIC, while he was attending the United Nations General Assembly to present the case of South Africa's Indian community against the Smuts government.[20]

As individual women became more prominent within the SAIC, they began to forge links with women activists in the CPSA and ANC. Here too, Dr Goonam was in the forefront. In 1946, she appeared on the platform at the International Women's Day Meeting organised by the CPSA in Johannesburg. The following year, Suriakala Patel was a speaker at the annual Women's Day meeting and thus party to the decision to launch the Transvaal All-Women's Union. The closer co-operation that existed between the ANC and the SAIC after 1947 encouraged contact between their women members. In 1950, Dr Goonam appeared on the platform at an African women's anti-pass meeting in Durban, and pledged the support of Indian women in the fight against passes.[21] Her presence at the meeting as well as her speech indicated that by that time women in the national liberation movement were aware of the importance of solidarity.

Thus, during the 1940s some Indian women began to cross barriers that previously had barred them from political work. A number of active women appeared in the Indian Congress, reaching out from there to liaise with other politically active women. There were also signs that Indian women in general were more aware of political issues than previously. But the weight of tradition still dragged, and Indian women in politics were the exception, never the rule. The slump experienced by the SAIC in the wake of the Passive Resistance Campaign made it even more difficult to organise Indian women on a large scale.

In 1950 Amina Cachalia, sister of Zainap Asvat and one of the most prominent Indian women within the FSAW after 1954, tried to establish a self-help society among Indian women in Johannesburg. There was nothing overtly political about the organisation. Nevertheless, the organisers encountered enormous problems getting it off the ground, indicating how resistant the Indian community still was to anything that challenged the supremacy of home, family and filial duty for Indian women. This society, the Progressive Women's Union, set itself up to teach young Indian girls marketable skills such as typing, dressmaking and literacy, with the idea of helping them to achieve greater social and economic independence. It did not envisage any radical rearrangement of male and female roles, but did challenge the assumption that women's place was only in the home.

Her experience with the union confirmed for Cachalia the value of the work it was trying to do. Her dominant impression of the girls who took part in its classes was their extreme isolation from events in the world outside of their homes—they were 'living in a rut'.[22] The establishment of such an organisation at that time was both an indication of the new horizons opening up, and an acknowledgement of the enormous social and economic barriers that yet existed to block the emancipation of Indian women and their full entry into political life.

Notes

1. *Union Statistics for 50 Years,* Table G-2.
2. *Ibid.,* Table A-32.
3. van der Horst, 'Women as an economic force in South Africa', p. 51.
4. Johnson, *Indians and Apartheid in South Africa,* p. 66.
5. Simons and Simons, *Class and Colour in South Africa,* p. 550.
6. *Guardian,* 16/1/41.
7. *Guardian,* 23/4/42.
8. *Guardian,* 26/3/42.
9. *Population Census,* 1946, UG 41-1954.
10. *Guardian,* 3/2/44.
11. *Guardian,* 21/3/46.
12. *Ibid.*
13. *Union Statistics for 50 Years,* Table A-32.
14. *Guardian,* 6/6/46.
15. *Guardian,* 28/3/46.
16. *Guardian,* 20/6/46.
17. *Guardian,* 10/6/47.
18. Simons and Simons, *op. cit.,* p. 552.
19. *Guardian,* 24/10/46.
20. *Guardian,* 4/9/47.
21. *Guardian,* 6/4/50.
22. Interview with A. Cachalia.

9

'Many Veterans Scheduled to Move Some of the Most Progressive Resolutions': Women in the Trade Unions after 1939

The early years of the war were a heyday for black trade unions. The conditions for trade unions to spread among black workers were very favourable. Manufacturing industry was expanding and the numbers of black workers growing rapidly. Such wage increases as were won failed to keep up with the rising cost of living. According to one study, in 1939 there were 25 African unions, with a total membership of about 37,000; by the end of the war membership had tripled, and more than 100,000 African workers were estimated to be union members.[1] In 1944 the Transvaal Council of Non-European Trade Unions was established to act as a centre body for black unions. Later it dropped its provincial delimitation and operated on a national basis. Increased trade union activity in the early years of the war led to a spate of strikes involving 'sweet workers, coal miners, dockers, dairy workers, brick workers, labourers and municipal employees',[2] amongst others. The peak of African trade union activity during the 1940s was undoubtedly the massive mineworkers strike in August 1946, in which over 70,000 miners came out on strike for higher wages, under the leadership of the African Mineworkers Union.

Black trade unionism, threatening as it did the entire system of cheap black labour on which the South African economy was based, was regarded as a real economic and political danger by the state. As a result, numerous obstacles were put in the way of the African trade unions. From the start, the most damaging of these was the exclusion of all male African workers from the definition of 'worker' under the Industrial Conciliation Act of 1924. While their trade unions were not declared illegal outright, they could not be registered, and were forced to operate outside the existing conciliation machinery. The wave of strikes during the war resulted in further state control of worker organisation. In 1942, the government promulgated War Measure 145, which declared all strikes by African workers to be illegal. This measure was put to immediate use by the government. In 1946, in the wake of the mineworkers strike, over fifty leaders within the trade union movement and the CPSA were arrested and charged with conspiracy and infringement of the measure.

During the 1940s, the trade union movement was under attack from both the state and right-wing elements within the movement. The vicious ideological infighting between left-wing and right-wing unions, that had surfaced during the 1930s, was intensified during the war, to the detriment of the trade union movement as a whole. Right-wing Nationalist-inspired organisations kept up their attack on non-racial unions. Finally, in the late 1940s, several anti-black unions hived off from the national organisation, the Trades and Labour Council [TLC], to establish 'Die Ko-ordinerende

Raad van Suid-Afrikaanse Vakvereniginge' (The Co-ordinating Council of South African Trade Unions), which pushed a militant pro-Afrikaner and anti-black line. It brought enormous pressure to bear on unions with a predominant or large Afrikaans membership to force them to conform to its programme. The Garment Workers Union in particular was the target of a sustained attack throughout the 1940s. Though the garment workers continued to resist the more extreme manifestation of Afrikaner nationalism, there was a definite shift to the right within the union.

After 1948 the Nationalist government intensified the attack on the radical strand in the South African trade union movement. The Suppression of Communism Act was used not only against the CPSA itself, but also against black and non-racial trade unions. 'Listed' communists were debarred from trade union work while the banning powers conferred on the Minister of Justice were used extensively to silence and isolate many liberal and radical trade unionists, whether or not they were communists. In 1952, Solly Sachs of the Garment Workers Union was the first trade unionist to be banned in terms of the act—despite the fact that he had been expelled from the CPSA years before, during the purges of the 1930s. He was soon followed by many others. They included important organisers of women: Ray Alexander, Bettie du Toit, Hilda Watts, Joey Fourie in the early 1950s, and many more since—the list of banned trade unionists has not yet been closed.

The Suppression of Communism Act was followed by two further pieces of legislation which finally destroyed the framework of a non-racial unionism. The Native Labour (Settlement of Disputes) Act of 1953 set up separate conciliation machinery for all African employees. The Industrial Conciliation Act, first debated in 1954 but only enacted in 1956, introduced compulsory segregation of unions with a common white and 'Coloured' membership into separate white and 'Coloured' branches. Henceforth no union could organise all workers within one industry into a single body. Those unions which already had African members had to set up 'parallel' African unions alongside the registered parent body.

Within the Trades and Labour Council itself, differences of strategy in the face of the government attack, and of commitment to the non-racial principle, divided the conservatives from the radicals. The conflict was finally brought to a head in 1954, when the announcement of the impending Industrial Conciliation legislation caused the TLC to split. The majority of its affiliates regrouped to form the Trade Union Council, which was prepared to work within the new framework. Those unions which opposed this surrender of principle came together with the Council of Non-European Trades Unions to form the South African Congress of Trade Unions [SACTU], within the ambit of the Congress Alliance.

By the 1950s, after an initial upsurge of activity during and shortly after the war, the trade union movement in South Africa was in considerable disarray. It is in this general context that trade unionism among women during the period must be viewed.

Women in Industrial Employment in the 1940s

While the 1940s marked a definite upswing in activity amongst women workers compared to the 1930s, the scope was still restricted, both by the general obstacles that hampered the trade union movement as a whole and by the relatively small numbers of women in industry.

By 1951, the year of the fifth general census, economic opportunities open to women had become more varied when compared to the situation in 1921, but the great majority of women were still occupied with domestic responsibilities. Only 23.7 per cent of all women (this time the figure includes Africans) were described as 'economically active', compared to 91.9 per cent of the same sample of men.[3] Furthermore, the largest single group of African women was still to be found living in the reserves, although they no longer formed a majority of all African women.

Women's reproductive role was still paramount. Nevertheless, women could no longer be defined so exclusively in terms of their domestic occupations and, in comparison with before the war, they were now entering the public sector of employment in increasing numbers. Since the 1951 'economically active' figure of 23.7 per cent included African women, it is clear that the proportion of women in wage employment had increased since 1921, when approximately 23 per cent of white, 'Coloured' and Asian women, but only 10 per cent of African women, were economically active. White and African women had experienced the biggest increase of women in wage employment. The percentage of white women economically active increased from 19.2 per cent in 1921 to 23.6 per cent in 1951. That of African women moved from 12.9 per cent of all those ten years and older in 1936, to 13.5 per cent of those 15 years and older in 1951. 'Coloured' women remained the largest group of 'economically active' women, but their percentage had shown little change, being 37.4 per cent in 1921 and 37.5 per cent in 1951. (Asian women showed an actual decrease, from 12.6 per cent to 7.3 per cent in the same period.)[4]

The diversity in jobs for women was greatest for white women. The trend of their upward job mobility was continuing—increasingly, white women were being drawn into clerical and sales posts. By 1960, clerical work was by far the largest area of white female employment, while sales work had outstripped industry to rank third after the 'professional and technical' category. For black women, the largest area of employment was still overwhelmingly in the service sector, primarily in private domestic work, where the difficulties of organising, either politically or as workers, were immense.

During the 1940s, developments already noted in the composition of the female industrial labour force in the pre-war period became more clearly marked. The proportion of white women to black in the female industrial labour force was continuing to decline. In 1939/40 there were still more than twice as many white women as black in private industry. By 1951/52 this predominance had declined to the point where black women just outnumbered white.[5] Interestingly, the total female labour force in private industry remained more or less constant between these two periods, at approximately 14 per cent. The proportionate increase of black women in private industry was still being counteracted by the proportionate decrease of white female workers. Only during the 1950s did the percentage of women in the total manufacturing labour force begin to rise again, with an accelerating influx of African women into industrial employment.

The growing numbers of African women in industrial employment was an important development, with far-reaching implications for their position in society and the attitude of the state towards them. In the 1940s, however, the trend was only just beginning to become apparent. Statistics show that the increase in general employment was actually occurring at a more rapid rate among black women than black men. Within private industry the rate of increase of African women was faster than that of 'Coloured' women, while both categories outstripped the rate of increase of the labour force as a whole. But in terms of actual numbers employed, men far exceeded women. Between 1939/40 and 1944/45 the percentage of African men in the total industrial labour force increased from 45.7 per cent to 51.3 per cent, while that of African women increased from 0.4 per cent to 0.8 per cent—still a miniscule amount, but nevertheless a doubling of the percentage of women employed. 'Coloured' men showed an actual percentage decrease, from 9.2 per cent to 8.8 per cent, while 'Coloured' women increased from 4 per cent to 5 per cent of the total labour force.[6]

In the 1940s, then, the bulk of black women in industry belonged overwhelmingly to the 'Coloured' group as they had in the 1930s. Although the number of African women in industry was increasing at a faster rate than 'Coloured', they still formed a minute fraction of the manufacturing labour force. In the period 1939/40-1951/52, the number of 'Coloured' women in private industry rose from 11,263 to 34,372, that of African women from a mere 1,254 to 7,810.[7] (Asian women in this category, numbering only 1,474 in 1951/52, remained an insignificant force.) The real take-off of African women entering manufacturing only began during the 1950s, picking up momentum in the 1960s. During the 1940s they were, in the main, of scant importance as a source of labour for industrialists. Their economic significance was still, overwhelmingly, in the reproductive sphere. The growing numbers of African women in the towns looked to either domestic service or the informal sector for employment.

A further feature of the pattern of female employment in industry during these years was the continued sex-stereotyping of jobs. The influx of women workers was still directed primarily into those areas of manufacturing which corresponded broadly to traditional female domestic occupations. The clothing and textiles and, to a lesser extent, food industries dominated. In the clothing and textiles industry, the total female labour force increased from 17,293 in 1937/38 to 43,527 in 1952.[8] The 1952 figures represented a very large slice of the total female workforce in private industry—roughly 50 per cent of the total of 87,049 women in industrial occupations.

The Trade Unions and Women

The composition of the industrial labour force had important implications for trade union work amongst black women. 'Coloured' women were clearly a more important area for organisation than African women in the war years. Since the bulk of the 'Coloured' population lived in the Western Cape, this was the major area of union activity amongst women workers. Although the Rand and Port Elizabeth were important centres as well, it was in the Western Cape that the role of the trade unions as politicising agents amongst women was most marked.

As the numbers of women in industry grew, so women became more prominent in the trade union movement at both the leadership and the general membership level. The *Guardian*'s coverage of successive Trades and Labour Council annual conferences during the 1940s indicates that the number of women working as trade union organisers was on the increase. Old stalwarts, such as Ray Alexander, Bettie du Toit and the Cornelius sisters, were being joined by other women, several of whom were CPSA members, eg Hilda Watts, Pauline Podbrey, Joey Fourie. The influx of black women into the industrial labour force meant that black women too were beginning to be recruited as organisers, particularly in the garment and food industries, the major growth points of black female employment. Hetty du Preez and Lucy Mvubelo in the garment industry on the Rand, and Frances Baard in the food canning industry in Port Elizabeth, were three important black organisers recruited at this time.

The recruitment of black women into the trade union movement was an event of major importance. For the women themselves, it opened up new opportunities for political training. For the trade union movement as a whole, the influx of black women into industry opened up a potentially very large area for organisation. It also precipitated a crisis in unions with a large white membership. White workers were being asked to accommodate black workers in their organisations—and many resisted fiercely. The Garment Workers Union, in particular, was confronted with major ideological choices. It came under increased pressure, from both the left and the right, to take a clear stand on where it stood in the battle between open and segregated unions.

The history of the GWU during the 1940s was tense and troubled. As more and more 'Coloured' women flooded the industry, its previous stand on non-racialism in worker organisations was put to a severe test. It was clear to the union leadership that black newcomers to the industry had to be unionised, in the interests of all workers. Because of pressure from the right, however, they were hesitant about organising black women within the existing structures. Race prejudice amongst the union's membership had been considerably diluted—even, for some members, contained— during the 1930s; it had not, however, been eliminated entirely. In 1940, bowing to the pressure it exerted, the GWU established a separate branch for 'Coloured' workers, the No. 2 branch. It was organised as a parallel to the parent union, which remained exclusively white.

Although it formed a major area of activity amongst black women workers, the establishment of a No. 2 branch represented a clear breach in the tradition of non-racialism within the GWU. It was also the first concrete sign of a shift to the right within the union. The union continued to resist successfully the Nationalist attack on its leaders during the 1950s, but the establishment of the No. 2 branch had made clear that it would no longer take the lead as the champion of an unqualified open trade unionism. Nevertheless, the increase in 'Coloured' women in this sphere of industry was spectacular during this period, and the No. 2 branch, with Hetty du Preez as organising secretary, expanded rapidly into a busy organisation.

The flare-up of trouble in the Germiston branch in 1944 illustrates the kind of difficulties the union experienced. Two white garment workers, members of the Nationalist Party, succeeded in launching a spontaneous strike when the firm took on nine 'Coloured' women. The strike was in open defiance of the policy of the union, which thereupon expelled the two instigators. Immediately there was an uproar from Nationalist organisations and press, who launched a nationwide campaign in support of the two expelled members, using the slogan 'white civilisation in danger'. They even raised the matter in parliament, attacking the union as an agent of communists and the enemy of white workers. The union responded to the attack with vigour. It organised a mass meeting in Johannesburg which was attended by about five thousand members. Feelings at the meeting ran high. When about fifty young supporters of the Nationalist Party tried to disrupt proceedings, they were forcibly ejected by shop stewards. The meeting then went on to pass an overwhelming vote of confidence in the GWU and its policies.[9] The episode encapsulates the history of the GWU at that time.

The history of the other major area of union activity among women workers, the Food and Canning Workers Union [FCWU], was quite different. White women played no part in production in the food industry, and the particular problems of the GWU, on the frontier between white and black workers, passed it by. The FCWU was established by Ray Alexander, with encouragement from Bettie du Toit, in 1941. Alexander first started organising in the fruit-growing district of the Western Cape. Conditions were uniformly bad. Work in the canning factories was seasonal, poorly paid, with long and irregular hours. When Liz Abrahams, later general secretary of the union, started work in a canning factory in Paarl, in 1950, at the age of fourteen, she earned 2½d for every tray of fruit she sorted. One tray took on average a quarter of an hour to sort into the three grades of fruit. The work was tiring since it involved standing all day, and at the height of the season overtime became compulsory. When fruit was coming in and had to be cleared, one could work until eleven, twelve or even one o'clock at night with only an hour's break for supper. Nevertheless, conditions had improved substantially from the days when Abrahams' mother was working in the same factory, in the 1930s and '40s. When friends or neighbours would caution Abrahams' mother about her daughter's political involvement, she would reply in her daughter's defence: 'I worked for two pennies, and since this union started I can see what I earn now.'[10]

After an uncertain start, the FCWU established itself as an active, well-supported body with workers' interests at heart. Ray Alexander was elected its first general secretary. She concentrated her considerable energies on fighting for workers' rights and exposing the extremely poor conditions under which they worked and lived. As the union demonstrated its willingness to press for improved conditions, it won strong support from workers in the industry. Later it expanded its activities to take in the fishing industry on the west coast, as well as the food processing industries in the Eastern Cape and on the Rand.

Though its membership was not exclusively female, women workers predominated in the food canning industry and soon came to play a leading role in the management of the union. In the Western Cape the FCWU was an active politicising agent among black female workers in the food industry. It identified with the tradition of radical, non-racial workers' organisations that in 1955 led to the establishment of SACTU, and, under the influence of Alexander, forged close links with women's organisations and groups within the national liberation movement. Several leaders of the FSAW in the Cape—Liz Abrahams, Elizabeth Mafeking, Frances Baard—rose to political prominence through the union.

The career of Liz Abrahams illustrates clearly the FCWU's role as a recruiting and training ground for political leaders. When Abrahams started work in the Paarl factories, she had gone as far as the sixth year in school. She was obliged to start work because her father had died and the family needed another breadwinner. At first her outlook was apolitical—she preferred to spend her lunch break knitting with friends, rather than attending union meetings. Then, in 1955, the union's president, Frank Marquard, was banned and forced to resign his post. The event shocked her into a greater awareness of and interest in the union's role in factory affairs. She became active in the local branch, and thereafter rose quickly to prominence within the national organisation. In 1956 she was elected general secretary (the position that Ray Alexander had held until she was banned in 1953). Through the FCWU Abrahams came into contact with a wide circle of people opposed to the political order in South Africa. She also learnt some fundamental political lessons about organisation, discipline and perseverance. She was drawn into other spheres of political work and subsequently became an executive member of both SACPO and the Western Cape regional committee of the FSAW.[11]

Another working-class woman who was drawn into a position of leadership within her community through the FCWU was Elizabeth Mafeking, an African woman also from Paarl. Reflecting on this process, she once commented:

> I used to think that education was the only thing required to change working conditions in the factory, but today I now know that education is not everything. When I was elected Vice-President of the Union in 1947, I explained my educational standard, because I thought I could not lead workers without education and I could not get education when I was a child. The workers replied that they did not want [my] education but they needed [my] leadership. I

accepted the leadership because I saw that my nation was starving and poverty-stricken.[12]

The establishment of the GWU's No. 2 branch and the FCWU both heralded an increase in union activity among 'Coloured' women workers. In 1944, the trade union movement achieved what looked like a major breakthrough with regard to the unionisation of African women. Before that date, it had always been assumed that African women were affected equally with African men by the 1924 Industrial Conciliation Act, which forbade African membership of registered unions. The GWU decided to challenge this assumption. In an historic court case—Christina Okolo vs the Industrial Council for the Clothing Industry, Transvaal—it succeeded in establishing African women's right to belong to registered unions by proving that they did not fall within the definition of 'pass-bearing' worker as laid down in the Industrial Conciliation Act.[13] In other words, they were eligible for all the benefits of union membership and industrial legislation that non-African workers enjoyed.

This judgement meant that African women qualified to be treated in the same way as other union members with regard to wages and general work conditions. Both the GWU and the FCWU were free to recruit African women along with other employees in their respective industries. Undoubtedly, this facilitated union work amongst African women and held out the prospects of developing a broad and non-racial trade unionism among women workers. However, since the numbers of African women in industry were still so small, the significance of the Supreme Court's ruling was limited, both amongst women and for the status of African workers in South Africa generally.

During the war, female membership of trade unions grew steadily. White women still predominated, but the presence of black women was making itself felt. By 1948 the female trade union membership in South Africa stood at 59,155 (compared to 278,740 for men).[14] Roughly two-thirds of this membership was white (39,921). At the eighteenth annual conference of the TLC in that year, the *Guardian* pointed out, with a note of pride, that of the two hundred delegates about twenty-five were women—'Among them are many veteran trade unionists who. . . were scheduled to move some of the most progressive resolutions.'[15] Obviously women were still a long way from approaching anything like parity with men, in either the trade union movement or industrial employment itself. Nevertheless, at that stage, the future of trade unionism as a politicising force among South Africa's growing number of black women workers looked promising.

It was a promise that was not realised. A few months after the 1948 TLC conference, the Nationalist Party came to power. Its onslaught against the trade union movement in general undermined the progress already made among women workers. Their most prominent and active leaders were quickly singled out for 'listing' and banning, or both. As new organisers stepped forward to take their places, they too became targets for repressive government action. The GWU and the FCWU soon felt the effects. Bettie du Toit and Solly Sachs were banned in 1952, Ray Alexander, Hilda Watts and Joey Fourie in 1953. Although banning could not completely silence individuals like Bettie du Toit and Ray Alexander, they were forced to retire from open, public work in their unions. Continuity within the unions was broken, workers intimidated.

The industrial legislation that followed shortly afterwards further emasculated worker organisations. In 1953 the loophole through which African women had squeezed into the registered unions was closed by the passage of the Native Labour (Settlement of Dispute) Act. This redefined 'employee' in the Industrial Conciliation Act to exclude all Africans, male and female. The FCWU was compelled, reluctantly, to organise African members into a parallel organisation, the African Food and Canning Workers' Union. Although it worked as closely as possible with the parent body, and the union leadership impressed on members that the split was one of expediency, not principle, nevertheless, the existence of two organisations drove a wedge between African and 'Coloured' members and weakened their commitment to non-racial organisations.

The banning of important leaders, coupled with the exclusion of African women from the registered unions after 1953, deflected the course of trade union work among women into weakened and segregated unions. While female industrial employment and trade union membership continued to grow during the 1950s—in 1961 the total female membership of registered unions was 86,126[16]—the potential of the unions as an area of mass political organisation among black women had been sharply cut back.

The attack on their leaders did not pass without fierce resistance on the part of the more militant workers. In 1952, the government's enforced removal of Solly Sachs from his position as general secretary of the GWU led to a huge show of support for Sachs from garment workers, both black and white. Thousands of workers from all over the Rand gathered at an enormous public protest meeting held outside the Johannesburg City Hall, to hear Sachs defy his banning order by addressing the meeting. Sachs himself estimated the crowd at 27,000. The meeting and Sachs' stand were in open defiance of the government, which was not slow to demonstrate its willingness to suppress opposition with force. Police moved in on the meeting in large numbers. Sachs was arrested at the start of his speech, and the meeting collapsed amid scenes of violent confrontation between workers and police. Many women landed in hospital as a result. Both observers and participants at the meeting were shocked by the rough handling the women received from the police. The treatment served as an ominous warning that henceforth women should not expect leniency on the grounds that they were female, if they chose to defy the state. For many women the violence came as a rude awakening.

This demonstration, coming shortly before the launching of the Defiance Campaign, added to the mood of crisis and confrontation that was prevailing in the national liberation movement by then. It also came on top of an upswing in political activity among African women in response to the threat of passes, and helped galvanise the desire for a strong national women's organisation that certain women within the Congress Alliance felt. Several women who would play a leading role within the FSAW in later years were present at the meeting and experienced the rough handling of the police first-hand. These included the future president of the ANCWL, Lilian Ngoyi, the future secretary of the FSAW, Helen Joseph, and a future leading member of SACPO on the East Rand, Mary Moodley.

By the early 1950s, the South African trade union movement was in retreat. Yet despite the difficulties the unions were facing, several had already played a significant part in developing a wider political consciousness among their members. The tradition of a radical, non-racial workers' consciousness was under siege, but had not been defeated. This tradition would continue to inform important sections of the South African working class as well as their organisations during the 1950s and later. The trade union movement had also contributed both leadership and direction to the incipient women's movement. Individual women within the post-war trade union movement built up a network of contacts that were invaluable when it came to promoting the idea of a national women's organisation in 1953/54. They reinforced the links already being forged within Congress circles.

The years of work put in by Ray Alexander proved especially useful. In organising the inaugural conference of the FSAW, she relied on these contacts to popularise the idea of a national women's organisation and recruit delegates from among a broader spectrum of women than those already active within the various Congress organisations. Without the trade unions, many working-class women would never have found the means to participate in the women's movement of the 1950s.

Notes

1. I. Davies, *African Trade Unions*, p. 62.
2. Roux, *Time Longer than Rope*, p. 331.
3. *Union Statistics for 50 Years*, Table G-2.
4. *Ibid.*
5. *Ibid.*, Table G-6.
6. *Ibid.*
7. *Ibid.*
8. *Census of Industrial Establishments*, 1937–38, Table 2 and *Industrial Census*, 1951–52, Special Report No. 206, Table 5. The 1952 figure includes footwear workers as well.
9. Sachs, *Rebels' Daughters*, p. 151.
10. Interview with L. Abrahams.
11. *Ibid.*
12. Anonymous: 'Elizabeth Mafeking', FSAW F(1).
13. Sachs, *op. cit.*, p. 116.
14. Calculated from *Union Statistics for 50 Years*, Table G-18.
15. *Guardian*, 1/4/48.
16. M. Horrell, *South African Trade Unionism*, p. 91.

10

'Too Many Blacks Who Have Turned Their Backs on Tribal Customs': The Nationalist Government and Passes for Women after 1948

It is impossible to understand the women's movement after 1948 without taking into account the place that African women occupied in the theory and practice of apartheid, the political programme of the Nationalist government. This determined the legislation that affected women and shaped both the content of their organisation and the context in which the women's movement of the 1950s unfolded.

The system of apartheid can be summed up in one word—control: economic control of the work force, political control of opposition to the state. Both the state bureaucracy and its repressive machinery (the police, army etc.) were vastly extended after 1948. More and more aspects of daily life were brought under the direction and close surveillance of the central government. African women, previously largely exempt from direct state control, soon felt the pressure of these developments.

Apartheid in 1948

The Nationalists came to power in 1948 with support from white farmers and workers. Their apartheid policy rested on the fundamental principle of white supremacy, which they sought to maintain by a system of rigid social, political and residential segregation between the four official 'races' in the country. They justified their programme in terms of 'race purity' or, when pushed, white survival. Even at its purest, in the hands of ideologues and academics, apartheid was never more than an exalted form of racism. Far from being an archaic, backward-looking policy, however, (as many liberal opponents of apartheid have described it) apartheid proved to be a flexible and increasingly sophisticated mechanism for sustained economic growth and modernisation. It gave to the state a far greater degree of centralised control over the reproduction and distribution of the black labour force, and served to buttress the system of cheap black labour in a changing economic climate. It also helped to consolidate the Nationalists' hold on power, by redirecting black political aspirations into the reserves. The reserves were gradually revamped as 'Bantustans', with some measure of local self-government, always within the limits set by the central government.

The apartheid policy was not a ready-made package when the Nationalists came to power in 1948. It grew and developed during the course of the 1950s, due as much to external events as to its own internal logic. Nevertheless, certain economic and political considerations were basic to its conception from the start. Of fundamental importance was the resolve to maintain the system of cheap migrant labour, even though the reserves could no longer contribute significantly to the subsistence of the migrant worker and his family, and certain sectors of the economy were wanting to adopt a more flexible approach to their labour requirements. As already mentioned, during the 1940s large-scale manufacturing industry began to favour policies that would create a more stable and highly skilled black work-force in the urban areas. They accepted that this would involve recognising at least a section of the African population as permanent residents of the towns, allowed to have their families with them. The most progressive of industrialists even conceded that such a group would be entitled to some hazy form of political rights.

The Nationalist government's electoral victory put paid to such ideas. They drew their support from sectors in the economy which either did not have the resources (or the inclination) to abandon the cheap labour system which migrant labour ensured, as in the case of white farmers, or else feared the competition that a more highly skilled black labour force would provide, as in the case of white workers. Accordingly, the Nationalist government set its face against any policy that would legitimise the African population's claim to permanent residence in the towns.

Another important concern of the new government, which meshed in with the above, was the redirection of a portion of the black labour force away from the towns and into the white countryside. Wages in the towns, poor as they were, were relatively attractive when compared to those offered in the white farmlands. White farmers had always complained bitterly about an inadequate labour supply. Rather than raise wages to make farm labour more competitive, they looked instead to the state to intervene on their behalf, through revised pass laws, stricter influx control and a centralised regulation of the labour flow—all measures which were written into the statute books in the early 1950s.

There was a clear political dimension to this programme. The decision to channel black workers into white agriculture represented not only a response to the labour needs of the agricultural sector, but also a political choice, satisfying the demands of a significant sector of the white electorate. Similarly, the Bantustan policy had an important political component to it. The reserves were still envisaged as a labour reservoir and dumping ground for those blacks not required to service capitalism's immediate needs. The list of those falling within this category has become a litany of the dispossessed for liberal and radical South Africans: women and children, the old and the young, the sick, the disabled and the un-employed. Starting in the 1950s the reserves, first restyled 'Bantustans', later 'Homelands', were also restructured to serve a crucial political control function. Successive legislative acts were passed which were designed to channel African political initiatives out of the cities, where they posed the most serious threat to white hegemony, and into ethnically based, de-centralised regional authorities in the various reserves. It was a classic case of divide and rule.

The Bantustan policy as it developed later, in the 1960s and 1970s, was certainly not part of the 1948 programme. Originally there was no intention of granting Africans 'separate freedoms' in supposedly independent 'Homelands' or 'Black States'. The content of the policy took shape slowly. Between the passage of the Bantu Authorities Act in 1951, which set up the first tribal regional authorities with very limited powers of local government, and the Promotion of Bantu Self-Government Act of 1959, which conceded that homeland self-government could, eventually, lead to political independence, it underwent a series of adjustments and enlarged its scope. This was largely in response to external political pressures confronting the government. The most important pressure group was the national liberation movement, more recalcitrant, less conciliatory in its demands as the decade wore on. In an attempt to diffuse and displace their attack, the government tacked an increasingly elaborate and topheavy superstructure of local government on to the shaky foundations of tribal government.

The ideological function of the reserves also increased in importance after 1948. The official explanations of later years stated that apartheid as separate development did not deprive Africans of political rights, since they all had the opportunity of exercising such rights in their own 'homelands'; South Africa was not one but several nations—a white nation, living in the whites' historical homeland (the 87 per cent reserved for white ownership in 1913 and again in 1936), and a number of African nations, Xhosa, Zulu, Tswana, Venda etc., living in their historical homelands. In 1948, however, *'baasskap'* and 'white supremacy' were not the politically embarrassing terms they would later become.

The Nationalists' victory was a shock to many whites who had assumed that General Smuts would retain his parliamentary majority. It was even more of a shock to blacks, and sent waves of apprehension rippling through their political organisations. In later years the term 'apartheid' would become a byword throughout the world for virulent racism and exploitation. Yet few in 1948 could foresee to what lengths the Nationalists would go to retain their grip on power, or imagine the scale of the conflict thus engendered. However, for a later generation to imagine that only after 1948 were blacks in South Africa exploited, political opposition forcibly silenced and racism elevated to a principle of government would be to make a gross mistake. There were many points of continuity between the pre-1948 and post-1948 state.

As the previous chapters have indicated, the apartheid era had profound repercussions on the position of women and political organisations amongst them. Apartheid as control was most forcibly felt by African women in the form of influx control and the pass laws. Stepped-up influx control and the threat of passes shook African women into a keener awareness of their oppression, as blacks and as women, and launched a decade of militant and sustained protest amongst them. The 1950s were a turbulent period politically. They saw an upsurge of mass political action by blacks on an unprecedented scale. Nowhere was this better demonstrated than amongst African women. Their anti-pass campaign was one of the most vociferous and effective protest campaigns of any at the time.

Passes for Women after 1948

Influx control and passes had long been crucial mechanisms of state control over the African population. When the Nationalist government came to power, these mechanisms were further modified and refined to suit the Nationalists' concerns. In 1952, after several hints and in spite of repeated denials that the government intended to extend the pass laws to women, two very important pieces of legislation passed through parliament representing an overhaul of the entire pass system.

The first, the Native Laws Amendment Act, *inter alia* amended the Urban Areas Act and greatly strengthened the existing influx control measures. Henceforth, it would be an offence for any African, women included, to remain for longer than 72 hours in any urban area without special permission, unless he or she fell within a limited range of exempted categories. In order to be exempted, an African had to prove either that he/she had lived in the area continuously since birth, or had worked continuously for one employer for a minimum of ten years; or had lived there continuously and lawfully for a minimum of 15 years prior to the act; or was the wife, unmarried son or daughter under 18 years of age of a man who qualified for urban residence in terms of the above. The second act, the so-called Natives (Abolition of Passes and Co-ordination of Documents) Act, far from abolishing passes, extended them under the new euphemism of 'reference books' to the entire African adult population. Despite repeated assurances to the contrary, women were now in line for the compulsory carrying of passes.

The reasons why the state was anxious to extend its control over women is an area of study that has been largely ignored by historians and other researchers. The whole subject of women's place within the pass laws system, and the changes it has undergone, is a fascinating one that deserves far greater attention than it has yet received. Thorough investigation of the topic would not only throw light on the place of women within the political economy of South Africa, it would also provide fresh insights into the workings of and rationale behind the pass laws system itself. Here I do no more than suggest an approach.

Some theorists, notably H. Wolpe, have analysed the new influx control measures (and indeed, the establishment of the apartheid state) largely in terms of the collapse of the reserve subsistence economies.[1] In the face of this collapse, which meant the collapse of the subsistence base of migrant labour, the government was forced to extend its coercive powers in order to maintain the supply of cheap labour. Critics of this thesis have argued that Wolpe concentrates too much on the reserves, and overlooks developments in both the white countryside and the urban areas. M. Morris, for instance, argues that the pass legislation of 1952 was concerned not with labour supply, but rather with labour allocation—control of the distribution of African labour through the different sectors of the economy. In particular, the main purpose of the legislation was to ensure an adequate supply of labour to the agricultural sector.[2]

However, despite the usefulness of both arguments, they are

inadequate explanations of the extension of pass laws to African women. Any analysis of why they were incorporated into the pass laws system has to take account of the specific place of African women in society, as well as the changes it had undergone by the time the Nationalists came to power. One cannot look at African women as if they were on a par with African men.

The available evidence suggests that, in the eyes of the state, the primary function of African women in 1952 still lay in the reproductive, not the productive sphere. The state was not interested in controlling their mobility as workers as it was with African men. In 1946, and again in 1951, African women accounted for a mere one per cent of the industrial labour force. Only during the 1960s did their numbers in industry begin to rise significantly. By 1960 they accounted for two per cent. Thereafter, their presence in industrial work grew rapidly and, by 1970, they accounted for seven per cent, on a par with 'Coloured' women.[3] Clearly, the expanding role of African women in production had important repercussions on later state policy. In the early 1950s, however, they were too insignificant a part of the industrial labour force to carry much weight in state planning. Influx control in the 1950s, and in the 1970s and 1980s, cannot be interpreted in exactly the same terms—although, because African women's productive role is still limited today, many of the earlier considerations with regard to women still prevail.

The relative unimportance of women in industry applied to the agricultural sector as well. Although there were many more women working on farms than in manufacture, they were not that important a source of labour in agriculture either. In 1954, according to calculations based on available census figures, black women accounted for only some 13 per cent of the total number of farm employees.[4] Morris quotes numerous farm labour reports and agricultural congress reports to support his argument that pressure from the farming community for greater controls on the mobility of farm labour lay behind the revised pass laws of 1952. None of these sources refers specifically to women, however, either as a source of labour or as contributing significantly to the migration of workers that they were anxious to stem. The odd reference to women made in the reports takes the form of a very different kind of complaint: that the farms were the holding ground for unproductive women and children, while the men went to town to look for more lucrative employment.[5] The most progressive farmers wanted to replace the existing labour tenant system with one that established a permanent and full-time labour force within agriculture. Controls were certainly needed to achieve this, but if farmers did want to keep women on their farms, it was as reproducers of the labour force, rather than as full-time workers in their own right. (Women could, however, be used for part-time and seasonal work as the demand arose.)

Official statements and reports, as well as parliamentary debates, indicate that what concerned the state most about African women in this early period of apartheid was their presence in the urban areas, and the growing permanency of the urban African community that it revealed.

The mounting rate of urbanisation amongst African women was one indication of the pre-capitalist subsistence sector's collapse. By 1951, the percentage of African women living in the urban areas had increased to 21.57 per cent, more than three times the 1921 figure.[6] The half-hearted official attempts of the thirties and forties to curb the flow to the towns had not been particularly successful, and the urban female population had been increasing at a more rapid rate than the male. In 1946 the average masculinity rate for the urban areas of the Union as a whole was 186, that of the Rand 275, Durban 271 and Cape Town 223. By 1951, the average masculinity rate had dropped to 157.5, although the Rand, Durban and Cape Town continued to have a larger excess of males over females than the average.[7]

The government-appointed *Industrial Legislation Commission* described the declining masculinity rate amongst urban Africans as 'a clear indication that the native population in urban areas is, to an increasing measure, beginning to assume a normal family structure which is indisputable proof of a growing tendency towards permanent urbanisation'.[8] Increased urbanisation of African women thus had important economic and political implications, which the upholders of apartheid could not countenance. If the government were serious about maintaining the migrant labour system and presenting the reserves as the true homelands of the African population, it could no longer allow women's previous relatively uncontrolled access to the towns. For the planners of apartheid, the logical corollary of 'women's place in the home' was 'women's place in the homelands'. Since the traditional tribal institutions in the reserves were no longer capable of exercising sufficient control over the mobility of women, the direct surveillance of the pass laws had become necessary. In 1950 the Minister of Native Affairs made the point clearly:

> It is constantly being said that the natives in the cities deteriorate. The undesirable conditions are largely caused by the presence of women who in many cases leave their homes contrary to the wishes of their fathers or guardians and contrary to tribal custom. To my mind there are already too many urbanised blacks who have turned their backs on the tribal customs and I do not intend to assist the process.[9]

However, it should be pointed out that at no stage did the government intend to eliminate women from the townships completely. The 1952 legislation provided for wives and unmarried daughters of the tiny group of men who qualified for permanent residence to stay with them. In this way, these women were incorporated within the capitalist mode of production, again not as workers but as reproducers of the already existing urbanised work-force.

From then on, the position of African women in the urban areas became even less secure, as the government sought to enforce the system of migrant labour and eliminate all Africans other than productive workers from the towns. Coming on top of the already heavy pressures squeezing African women, in both town and country, the impact was severe. The reaction against the new passes, particularly in the towns, was explosive.

The Anti-Pass Campaign 1950–53

Although it was not till 1952 that the revised pass system was enacted, clearly the new government envisaged greater control over women from the beginning. The threat of passes for women first emerged publicly in early 1950, when proposed amendments to the Urban Areas Act were leaked to the press. The proposals suggested tightening up control of the movement of African women to town, registration of their service contracts, and a compulsory medical examination for all African women town-dwellers.[10] The African response was immediate, vociferously and unequivocally hostile. For several weeks the demonstrations, deputations and meetings organised in protest were front-page news in the *Guardian:* 'We will not carry any passes: African women indignant', 'African women up in arms, mounting opposition to passes for women', 'Campaign against passes for women gathers force'.[11] The protests spanned the country.

Durban was a particularly strong centre of protest. In March 1950, a meeting of over six hundred men and women denounced the new proposals.[12] In April hundreds of women marched through the streets to the Durban City Hall.[13] A key figure in these protests was Bertha Mkize, provincial secretary of the ANCWL and chairwoman of a women's society called the Durban African Women's Organisation. In an interview with the *Guardian,* she was extremely outspoken in her views, particularly about the proposed medical examination: 'African women will not tolerate a move which is most disgusting and which should outrage the conscience of all democrats. Our fight is on.'[14]

Other demonstrations were reported by the *Guardian* in Langa (26.3.50, 6.4.50), Uitenhage (2.4.50), East London (6.4.50), Kensington and Elsies River in Cape Town (6.4.50), Phomolong (13.4.50) and Pietermaritzburg (13.4.50). In Cape Town an action committee was formed, representing the Langa Advisory Board, the CPSA (soon to be banned), the Ministers' Wives Association, women's sections of township vigilance associations, and the African Students Association. Together with Sam Kahn and Fred Carneson (communist members of parliament and the Cape Provincial Council respectively), the action committee sought an interview with the Minister of Native Affairs, to press its opposition to the proposed passes.[15]

These demonstrations revealed that popular feeling against passes for women was as strong as in 1913. In the far more polarised political situation of 1950, the pass laws were a powerful rallying point for a much more militant African opposition. The government's response indicates that it was unprepared for the extent and vigour of the outcry. Still consolidating its grasp on power after the 1948 elections, it was obliged to move warily on so emotive an issue. In parliament, the Minister of Native Affairs, Jansen, hastened to describe 'the whole uproar' as 'premature', as the contents of the Urban Areas Bill were yet to be finalised.[16] Finally, in April, the Department of Native Affairs issued a statement denying, in tortuous language, that new control measures were to be introduced for women:

> It appears. . . that practically no local authority had asked for permission to apply in its area the control measures in regard to Native females which are already available under existing laws. It appears therefore to be unnecessary to make provision in legislation concerned for stricter measures regarding matters in connection with which not even the existing control measures are being used.[17]

As a result of these assurances, the popular outcry died down temporarily.

However, the idea of passes for women was not abandoned by the government, merely shelved. Its determination to push ahead with the measure was revealed again in 1952, when the Native Laws Amendment Bill was first published. It was apparent that tighter influx control against women could not be administered without a system of passes. 'Slave Labour Bill means passes for African women', the *Guardian* headlined in response to the bill.[18] Once again, the government was anxious to discredit such views. Thus, Dr Verwoerd, then Minister of Native Affairs, said to Sam Kahn in the course of the debate on the new bill:

> I repeat that notwithstanding the fact that these provisions are applicable to Native women, it is not our intention to proceed with its practical application at the moment because we do not think the time is ripe for that. Now I do hope the Honourable member will stop his agitation of telling Native women that we are introducing a law by which we are going to force them to carry passes because that is not true.[19]

Despite such promises, the Natives (Abolition of Passes and Co-ordination of Documents) Bill was enacted shortly thereafter, and it became clear that women could be issued with the new reference books at any time.

Thus, by 1952, the basis for the state's extended control over women had been laid. The central government still felt it expedient to move cautiously in putting the control to the test. It was not till 1956 that it made the first moves to issue African women with reference books. Its low-key approach and deliberate downplaying of the new legislation's coercive aspects with regard to women, testified to its awareness of the strength of popular feeling on the subject. However, from 1952, local municipalities themselves began enforcing Section 10 of the new Urban Areas Act, issuing their own urban residence permits to both men and women. Although not reference books and hence outside a national system of control, these permits were still a form of pass, controlling entry to individual towns. They were certainly identified as such by those who had to carry them.

Passes for women remained a constant source of unrest throughout the early 1950s, periodically erupting in local demonstrations and protests. Newspaper reports on the protests kept the issue alive for a wider audience than those women immediately affected. The *Clarion*, successor to the *Guardian* (which was banned in May 1952), carried several reports. In June 1952, an announcement that all women residents in the Odendaalsrus district would have to be registered led to riots in which one

African man was killed, a woman wounded, and 71 people arrested. Forty-seven of these were brought to court, 44 of them women.[20] In early 1953, the municipalities of Cape Town, Port Elizabeth, Oudtshoorn and Stellenbosch announced that they would start enforcing influx control measures against women, precipitating protests by local ANC branches in all four centres.[21]

The Port Elizabeth protests were of special importance. It was there, a few months after the municipality had announced that it would introduce influx control measures, that women decided to establish a strong, national organisation of women to fight for their rights. The meeting at which this decision was made, and the circumstances surrounding it, are looked at in the following chapter. It was the beginning of a fresh and ultimately successful initiative to launch the women's movement within the national liberation movement.

Most of the anti-pass protests of the early 1950s, localised and sporadic, do not compare in intensity and impact with the campaign that developed after 1956, when the actual distribution of reference books to women was begun. However, they certainly encouraged many African women to adopt a more aggressive, critical attitude to their standing in South Africa. Undoubtedly, the question of passes was the major issue round which the ANCWL rallied in the early 1950s, and formed an important element in its subsequent willingness to work towards establishing the FSAW.

The issue of passes also played an important part in drawing African women into a far more active role within the national liberation movement than before. Previously, black women's involvement in politics had been mainly at the local level. Now a national dimension was becoming more evident. It could be seen in the Defiance Campaign, which followed the anti-pass campaign by a few months. The extensive participation of women in this campaign gave an added boost to their rising status within the national liberation movement, and stimulated further discussion on the role of a women's movement within the broader movement.

The Defiance Campaign and the Revival of the ANCWL

The Defiance Campaign, launched jointly by the ANC and the SAIC in June 1952, marked the first large-scale implementation of the more radical pressure tactics envisaged in the ANC's 1949 'Programme of Action'. Over a period of some months, some 8,500 Congress volunteers demonstrated their opposition to selected targets of racial discrimination, by publicly defying them. The politicising impact of the anti-pass campaign helped encourage a large turnout of women in the Defiance Campaign. According to one study, in one sample group of defiers in the Eastern Cape, 1,067 out of a total of 2,529 were women. In another sample in the Transvaal, 173 out of 488 defiers were women.[22] Several ANCWL members played leading roles in the campaign. One of the most important was Florence Matomela, at that stage president of the ANCWL in the Eastern

Cape. During the Defiance Campaign she was one of the 35 leaders arrested and charged by the state under the Suppression of Communism Act.

The Defiance Campaign was an important stimulus for the ANCWL in key areas on the Rand and in the Eastern Cape, and helped create the climate in which the FSAW took shape. A number of new recruits to the Women's League entered politics via the campaign, for example, Lilian Ngoyi, later national president of both the ANCWL and the FSAW. Before the Defiance Campaign her background was largely apolitical. Her family's answer to the hardships and inequalities they experienced was to seek comfort and hope in religion. Increasingly this failed to satisfy Ngoyi and, for her, the Defiance Campaign offered a dynamic, political alternative to religious quietism.[23] Her rise to prominence within the ANC was rapid after 1952.

With passes as a galvanising issue, the ANCWL of the early 1950s was in a much stronger position than it had been in the 1940s. Little is known about its day-to-day organisation, which probably was not particularly efficient or extensive, judging by reports on the later period. Nevertheless, the league was showing itself capable of rallying women on particular issues on a greater scale than ever before. Membership was evidently increasing, although here, too, actual figures are unavailable. At the same time, the ANCWL was expanding its scope of activities beyond 'tea and typing'. In 1953, apparently for the first time, the Transvaal Women's League celebrated International Women's Day.[24] In doing so it took over a function formerly sponsored by the CPSA before its dissolution in 1950, and signalled its willingness to take a more active lead in organising women to promote a greater awareness of their position within society.

While passes were the immediate spur to action and the focus of protest, the attention of African women participating in the protests was being directed as well to the wider political-economic context in which the pass laws operated. In February 1952, for example, the Transvaal section of the ANCWL announced it would hold several women's conferences to register opposition to the Native Laws Amendment Bill then before parliament. In its announcement, passes were regarded as just one link in the chain of exploitation. What right, the statement demanded, did the government have

> to force us off the land and then to seek cheap labour for the farmers? To divide us into racial groups so as to rule us even better? To starve us and expose us to tuberculosis? To have jailed our men day in and day out and now to come and say: You women must carry passes too?[25]

By the beginning of 1953, with the Congress Alliance established, the way was clear for activists to transform the network of contacts that women had already developed, linking the various Congress organisations loosely together, into a tighter organisational structure. The national women's movement, long a dream cherished by a few, had finally become feasible. The various strands—opposition to influx control, the Defiance Campaign, a more activist national liberation movement and a stronger

ANCWL—were knitted together at the women's meeting in Port Elizabeth from which the FSAW grew.

Notes

1. H. Wolpe, 'Capitalism and cheap labour power in South Africa; from segregation to apartheid'.
2. M. Morris, 'Apartheid, agriculture and the state: the farm labour question'.
3. *Population Census,* 1946, vol. 5; and S. Van der Horst, 'Women as an economic force in Southern Africa'.
4. This is based on figures supplied by *Union Statistics for 50 Years,* Table G-3.
5. See, especially, the *Report of the Native Farm Labour Committee,* 1937–39.
6. Calculated from figures supplied by the *Population Census,* 1951, vol. 1, Table 11(a), pp. 94–5.
7. *Industrial Legislation Commission,* 1951, p. 14.
8. *Ibid.,* p. 13.
9. *House of Assembly Debates,* 1950, Col. 3766.
10. *Guardian,* 9/3/50.
11. *Guardian,* 9/3/50, 30/3/50, 13/4/50.
12. *Guardian,* 30/3/50.
13. *Guardian,* 6/4/50.
14. *Ibid.*
15. *Guardian,* 13/4/50.
16. *House of Assembly Debates,* 1950, Col. 3765.
17. Quoted by S. Kahn, *House of Assembly Debates,* 1952, Col. 737.
18. *Guardian,* 14/2/52.
19. *House of Assembly Debates,* 1952, Col. 2955.
20. *Clarion,* 26/6/52, 31/7/52.
21. *Advance,* 1/1/53, 8/1/53, 22/1/53, 26/2/53.
22. D. Carter, 'The Defiance Campaign—a comparative analysis of the organisation, leadership and participation in the Eastern Cape and the Transvaal'.
23. Interview with L. Ngoyi.
24. *Advance,* 5/5/53.
25. *Guardian,* 6/3/52.

11

'So Much Enthusiasm for It': Planning the Inaugural Conference of the Federation of South African Women

Port Elizabeth, April 1953

In April 1953 the city of Port Elizabeth was simmering with political unrest. The Defiance Campaign, which had reached its peak in the Eastern Cape, was only recently past; influx control was a major political issue. For Florence Matomela, provincial president of the ANCWL, Frances Baard, local organiser in the AFCWU, and Ray Alexander, who was attending a trade union conference in the city, it was an opportune time to call a meeting of women. They wanted to focus attention on the part that women could play in the struggle for liberation. All three women had worked closely together for a number of years—according to Alexander, they had discussed the importance of establishing a national women's organisation on several occasions in the past.[1]

Unfortunately, it appears that the meeting which ensued was not documented; the following account of its proceedings is based on an interview with Alexander. It was an informal affair, organised at short notice. Alexander's presence in the area probably provided the immediate incentive for holding it at that time. Notice of the meeting was spread by word of mouth during the day, and the meeting took place that same evening. An evening meeting was essential if working women were to attend, yet also made it very difficult for women with family commitments to attend—meals had to be cooked, small children put to bed. Nevertheless, a gratifying number of women were present, some forty to fifty in all.

Most of the women who attended were African, but in addition to herself, Alexander recalls at least three other non-African women—a Mrs Pillay, a Miss Damons and a trade unionist, Gus Coe. All the women who attended were there in their personal capacities rather than as representatives of any organisations. However, all were drawn from within the ambit of the Congress Alliance, and their overriding loyalty was to that political grouping.

Alexander brought to the meeting the internationalist perspective of the disbanded CPSA and also of the WIDF. She opened the proceedings with a short talk on the position of women in the world: women's subordination and oppression were worldwide and not unique to South Africa, women elsewhere had made significant contributions to the struggle for liberation within their own countries. Thereafter, discussion was opened to the floor.

The focus shifted from a general overview of women's position to the particular situation in which black women found themselves in South Africa and, even more insistently, in Port Elizabeth. Very few, if any, of the local women present would have travelled beyond the Eastern Cape. They were concerned about basic daily issues—influx control, passes, rising food and transport costs. But in the highly politicised environment of Port Elizabeth in 1953, these local concerns had taken on a clear national dimension. For those present, it was not enough to meet to discuss their problems in isolation from women in other parts of the country. They realised that their problems were not simply local, nor unique to Port Elizabeth. Women across the country—throughout the world, was Alexander's message—shared their problems and their concerns.

What the women required was a national strategy to fight for the improvements they wished to see; and only a national organisation, with a national perspective, could hope to achieve it. According to Alexander, the proposal to hold a conference where such an organisation could be established, came from the floor. The rest of the women present enthusiastically adopted the proposal, and subsequently entrusted to Alexander the responsibility of putting their decision into effect.

From a general perspective, this meeting was a product of that lengthy process of political awakening amongst women which has already been described. Both the ANC and trade union movement were particularly strong in Port Elizabeth, and it was women in those two organisations who had taken the lead in organising the meeting. Clearly Alexander's personal influence, as general secretary of the FCWU and long-time campaigner on behalf of women, was important—she also brought to the meeting the experience and perspective of the banned CPSA. But it was local concerns which provided the immediate impetus for the meeting, and local political developments which gave it its context.

The national liberation movement's strength in Port Elizabeth contributed directly to the readiness of women leaders to take the initiative in organising the conference. There was a variety of reasons why the African community in Port Elizabeth was so highly politicised. Leo Kuper, in his book *Passive Resistance in South Africa*, lists the following reasons for

> the greater strength of resistance in the Eastern Province. . . the longer period of contact with Europeans, the extent of conversion to Christianity, the strength of the trade unions, the relatively more liberal policies and hence the sharper reaction to the deprivations of apartheid, political training acquired in the exercise of a limited franchise, the greater stability of family life and the more homogeneous character of the African population.[2]

Many of these factors, all bound up with the 'more liberal policies' of local government in the Eastern Cape, had a particular bearing on women in the townships, and made them receptive to political organisation. Prior to 1953, Port Elizabeth was one of the few large cities where the entry of Africans was not restricted by influx control measures. In addition, the local government pursued a housing policy in its African townships that concentrated on family housing, rather than single accommodation for migrant (and hence mainly male) workers. As a result, a reasonably stable and sexually balanced African community was allowed to develop, in strong contrast to the other major cities of Johannesburg, Cape Town and Durban. In 1946 the African population of Port Elizabeth was 47,056, of whom 23,728 were males and 23,328 females.[3] The masculinity rate was a mere 102. This compared very favourably with the Union-wide average of 186, and even more favourably with the Witwatersrand average of 275.[4]

Compared with women in other areas, African women in Port Elizabeth thus enjoyed considerable security of residence and freedom of movement before 1953. This undoubtedly made it easier for them to organise politically, and contributed to the greater political maturity they displayed. Trade union organisation among women workers was strong. According to Alexander, laundry and textile workers' organisations, both with large female memberships, were active.[5] The FCWU, under Alexander, had established a vigorous Port Elizabeth branch in the 1940s. It produced several important local leaders, including Frances Baard, co-organiser of the April meeting—a large, quietly-spoken woman, who started her political career as a union organiser in the late 1940s.

The ANCWL was also an active body, its own vigour complemented and enhanced by the vigour of the ANC itself. Eastern Cape women participated in the Defiance Campaign in significant numbers. Florence Matomela, provincial president of the ANCWL, was one of those who launched the campaign nationally on 26th June 1952, by defying the curfew regulations and entering locations without permits. Later that year, in September, she was one of the thirty-five ANC leaders arrested and charged under the Suppression of Communism Act as the government moved to crush the campaign.[6]

The Defiance Campaign indicated clearly the strength of the ANC in the Eastern Cape, centred on Port Elizabeth. Out of a national total of 8,557 defiers, fully 5,719 came from the Eastern Cape.[7] The relative success of the campaign in Port Elizabeth boosted popular support for the ANC still further. In October 1952, the local ANC branch called for a one-day general strike among residents of Port Elizabeth's African townships. It was spectacularly successful: about 90 per cent of the people stayed away from work and in their homes.[8] By the end of 1952, the political atmosphere in Port Elizabeth was highly charged. The mood of resistance was buoyant and militant.

Then, in early 1953, the Port Elizabeth municipality announced that, for the first time, influx control measures would be enforced against Africans living within its boundaries. This was a product of more rigorous influx control measures that the Native Laws Amendment Act had introduced for the whole country. The enforcement of influx control in Port Elizabeth was a direct attack on the stability and cohesion of the African community. Its announcement provoked a storm of protest which boosted general ANC support still further—a huge protest meeting organised by the ANC in January 1953 drew, according to the newspaper *Advance*, some 20,000 people.[9] The implementation of influx control measures (in terms of the newly amended Urban Areas Act) affected women even more directly than had the Defiance Campaign, and served to push their leaders into action. The relative security of residence and freedom of movement that they had enjoyed before 1953 had undoubtedly made it easier for them to organise politically. Conversely, the threat that influx control posed to their security after January 1953 provided women with compelling reasons for wishing to organise still more effectively. The implications of the new measures were particularly disturbing for them, since relatively few women, compared to men, qualified for legal residence in terms of the amended Urban Areas Act.

At the April women's meeting, women's issues fused with general ones, local concerns encouraged a national perspective. Acting within the context of the national liberation movement, and with the specific example of its campaigns before them, politically involved women had come to the realisation that if women were going to make any impression on those who wielded power, they would have to organise around the issues that particularly affected them, but on a national scale.

It was not a new idea. As long ago as 1931, the CPSA had tried to launch a women's department, with aims that were not very different from those put forward in 1953. By 1953, however, the conditions in which they could be put into practice were far more favourable than before. Long-term changes in the general position of women, coupled with the rise of the national liberation movement, had combined to make a national women's movement a feasibility. Local developments in Port Elizabeth provided the spark that set the process in motion. The energy that Port Elizabeth provided, in 1953, in getting a women's organisation off the ground, continued to characterise the women's movement there. In the years to come it would remain a strong ANCWL and FSAW centre.

Planning the Conference

After the meeting in Port Elizabeth, the impetus toward the proposed national conference of women shifted with Ray Alexander, to her home base in Cape Town. Thereafter Cape Town and Johannesburg came to the fore as the main centres of organisation, Cape Town largely because of Alexander, and Johannesburg because it was the natural headquarters of the Congress Alliance. Alexander assumed the primary responsibility for implementing the Port Elizabeth women's decision, by enlisting the support of other women leaders across the country. Energetic, enthusiastic, she was an ideal person for such a task. Her commitment to women's emancipation stretched back over many years, to her earliest days in South African politics in the 1930s. In the trade union movement and the CPSA she had been a tireless campaigner for women's rights, the importance of organising women, and the need to treat their disabilities as serious political issues. Over the years she had built up an extensive network of contacts amongst women in all the main urban areas, and many of the smaller towns as well. These ranged from highly politicised members of the ANC or CPSA to ordinary factory workers and housewives. In the next few months her contribution towards getting the FSAW off the ground was a major one.

In Cape Town there were already loose links among radical women activists from the Food Committee days. These had been reactivated by the recent anti-pass protests. In July 1953, a threatened increase in the price of bread provoked further food protests along lines similar to those of the 1940s, and stimulated local interest in a national women's organisation. Alexander used the issue to popularise the idea of the women's conference. In August she led a deputation of six women to protest against the price rise to Havenga, Minister of Finance. Included in the deputation were Gladys Smith (Cape Housewives' League), Katie White (Women's Food Committee) and Dora Tamana (ANCWL and CPSA), all of whom had been involved in women's organisations in the 1940s.[10] This group, with two additional ANC Women's Leaguers, Annie Silinga and Mrs Thaele, appears to have formed the nucleus of the planning group for the women's conference in Cape Town. By February 1954, Alexander was describing it as the 'Women's Committee'. It was meeting regularly, under her chairpersonship, to discuss the shape the conference should take.[11]

In Johannesburg, Alexander turned to Hilda Watts, a colleague from the former CPSA days, to take responsibility for the conference at that end. Watts, too, had a lengthy record of activity in various left-wing organisations on the Rand. Her own interest in women's emancipation had already led to her involvement in the Transvaal All-Women's Union in the late 1940s. When Alexander visited Johannesburg, in August 1953, for a TLC conference (to discuss the council's stand on the impending Native Labour (Settlement of Disputes) Bill), she took the opportunity to meet with Watts and discuss plans for the conference.

Whether a 'Women's Committee' on similar lines to the Cape Town group existed in Johannesburg is not known. It is clear from the invitation to the conference that ANC Women's Leaguers, trade unionists, members of the Transvaal All-Women's Union, the Congress of Democrats and the SAIC were all drawn in at the planning stage. Women who signed the invitation included Ida Mtwana (national president of the ANCWL), Josie Palmer (ex-CPSA and Transvaal All-Women's Union), Helen Joseph (COD), Mrs M. Cachalia, Mrs M. Naidoo (SAIC), Bettie du Toit, Lucy Mvubelo, and Hetty du Preez (trade unionists).[12]

Yet, while both Watts and Alexander were working in co-operation with other politically involved women, it seems that their personal influence in shaping the final form of the conference was considerable. The frequent correspondence that passed between the two women indicates that the main weight of organising the conference rested on them. By March 1954, Alexander was writing to Watts on an average of once every three or four days. They were responsible for relaying information and progress reports across the 1,500 kilometres that separated Cape Town from Johannesburg, as well as enlisting the support of other women. All final decisions concerning the agenda appear to have been made by them. In this regard, Alexander showed a stubborn, hard-headed streak. Writing to Watts on a disagreement about the agenda that had risen with women in Durban—who were opposed to including a talk by Walter Sisulu of the ANC on 'Women in China'—she declared emphatically, 'We are not giving in on this.'[13]

In September 1953, both women were served with banning orders which curtailed their public involvement in various organisations. The main thrust of the bannings was against their trade union work, however, and their work for the forthcoming women's conference was not impeded. At that stage, banning orders were not as comprehensive in their restrictions as they would later become.

As communists, they brought to the conference ideas which many in the national liberation movement did not fully share, in particular their analysis of society in terms of class rather than colour as the crucial determinant. Their stand on feminist issues was also more explicit than that of many of their colleagues—both women were committed to the abolition of sex discrimination in all its forms. In 1953/54 however, these differences were not at issue. In the political climate of the time they appeared differences of degree rather than of kind. Both Alexander and Watts, along with other CPSA members, saw the national liberation movement as a vital stage along the road to the socialist state they wished to see. They endorsed its general democratic aims wholeheartedly. 'Justice', 'equality', 'a fair distribution of wealth'—nobody disagreed with any of these general concepts. They were broad statements of principle that at that stage, when political power was held so firmly by the common enemy, nobody within the national liberation movement needed to define more rigorously.

With the main axis of activity lying between Alexander in Cape Town and Watts in Johannesburg, other areas became drawn into the planning stages of the conference too. In mid-1953, Alexander made contact with individual women in Durban, who responded favourably to the idea of the proposed conference. In early 1954 she visited Durban and strengthened these contacts.[14] Women involved there included Dr K. Goonam, Fatima Meer and Fatima Seedat, all of the SAIC, and Bertha Mkize and Henrietta Ostrich of the ANC. The last four were all involved in the FSAW subsequently. Dr Goonam, however, despite her impressive career within the SAIC, did not maintain her links with the FSAW after 1954. The reason is not clear, though, from the gossip column in *Drum* magazine, it appears she had come into conflict with the SAIC hierarchy by November 1952.[15]

After January 1954, the idea of the conference was taken to a larger audience than the one already existing within the Congress network, when Alexander was nominated to stand in a parliamentary by-election for Native Representative in the Cape Western Division. (After 1936, when the Cape African franchise had finally been destroyed, qualified African voters were limited to electing three native representatives for the House of Assembly plus one for the senate, all of whom had to be white.) The 1954 by-election was necessitated by the expulsion from the House of Assembly of the sitting representative, Brian Bunting, in terms of the Suppression of Communism Act. Exploiting a loophole that was closed too late to prevent her nomination from going through, Alexander launched upon an extensive election campaign, under the slogan 'Vote for Alexander. Vote for Afrika.'

Her campaign gave her a prominent platform from which to promote the women's conference. She based her election manifesto on the abolition of the colour bar in all spheres—political, economic, social—and on full support for 'all progressive organisations. . . in the struggle for liberation from unjust laws'.[16] She stressed the need to strive for full equality between men and women, and used every opportunity to canvass the idea of the women's conference. Her election tours took her, *inter alia*, to Durban, East London, Port Elizabeth, Beaufort West, and De Aar. Frequently she followed general political meetings with special women's meetings, where she discussed the conference and made arrangements for local delegates to attend. 'Am having meetings with women all over and they are electing delegates, undertaking to raise the money for fares', she reported to Watts from Beaufort West in March 1954.[17] An enthusiast herself, she was impressed by the enthusiasm and interest displayed by the women she met. 'The interest and enthusiasm for the conference is beyond expectations', she wrote on 30th March.[18]

Alexander's personal prestige among the bulk of her electorate was very high—even hostile observers conceded that hers would be a runaway victory. On 28th January 1954, when her campaign had just begun, *Advance* quoted the following extract from an editorial in the Nationalist daily, *Die Burger:* 'It is now too late to prevent her from participating in the election and I think I can just as well say that it's too late to prevent her from winning the election.' The following month, *Advance* printed a praise-poem, honouring Alexander, which indicated the strength of the support she had awakened. The poem had been written in Xhosa originally by an African worker at a hotel in Hermanus, a seaside resort about fifty miles from Cape Town.

We congratulate her for beauty—it is her deeds which are beautiful;
We congratulate her for beauty—it is the head of cattle we receive with her
    which pleases us;
We congratulate her for beauty—it is her humanity which is beautiful.[19]

Alexander's campaign enjoyed wide publicity. She eventually won the seat by an overwhelming majority. It had been made clear from the start that the Nationalist government would never allow her to take her seat. They closed the loophole she had exploited before election day, and, thus armed, declared the elections to be invalid as soon as the returns were in. Determined to press her point, Alexander attempted to take her seat on 27th April 1954, but was forcibly prevented from entering parliament by a large police contingent.[20] Although thwarted from final victory, the campaign had succeeded as a political demonstration. It had forced many contentious issues into the public limelight—workers' rights, women's rights, universal suffrage—and had also exposed, beyond debate, the sham of so-called 'native representation'.

From the point of view of the women's conference organisers, the election campaign had been beautifully timed. Polling day was only a few days before the conference itself took place. Alexander made women a special target of the campaign, and, through it, drew several women from outlying areas into the conference planning. In mid-March, *Advance* reported that African women in Beaufort West were to send delegates to the conference.[21] Even though their delegates did not, as it turned out, make it to the conference, the attempt to broaden the base of the conference was an important and necessary one. No women's organisation could ever consider itself truly national if it ignored those women who were living outside the larger urban centres.

On 16th March 1954, a formal invitation to the conference 'to promote women's rights' was sent out. It went to a wide range of potentially interested organisations—women's organisations, trade unions, township vigilance associations, the different Congress bodies and their branches. It was an open invitation. Women 'of all organisations' were called upon to attend or send delegates to the conference—'any group of women, from factories or areas, can get together and send a delegate to this historical conference'—and there seems in fact to have been no tight quota system for choosing delegates. The invitation appealed to women in very general terms as 'mothers of the nation—a half of the whole population'.[22]

Despite the invitation's openness, its political orientation was clearly slanted towards the policies of the Congress Alliance. The sixty-three women who signed the invitation were all prominently associated with the Congress movement, and the content of their appeal ranged far beyond the question of equal rights for women.

> We women, like men, want to be free to move about in the country of our birth, to live where we like, to buy land freely. We want an end to the migrant labour system. . . We claim for ourselves and our daughters, as well as for men, the right to education and employment in all occupations and professions. While our main struggle is with men against racialism and the colour bar, to make our national struggle more effective, we ask that men support us in our fight for equality.[23]

From the beginning then, the intention was to establish a political body involved in the national liberation movement. Not surprisingly, the only white organisation to respond to the invitation was the tiny Congress of Democrats. Several black women's organisations, too, looked askance at its politically activist stance. The NCAW, for instance, did not attend the conference as an organisation, though its national president, M.T. Soga, did attend a preliminary meeting held by Alexander in East London in February 1954,[24] and individual members may well have been at the national conference in their personal capacities. Within the Congress Alliance itself, the organisers of the conference appear to have had general support. Certainly in the Cape, the ANC leadership undertook to publicise the conference to all its branches. On 19th March, Alexander reported to Watts that she was working in Cape Town and Port Elizabeth 'with full support of ANC'.[25] Material on the other provinces is unavailable. In the Transvaal, the main link between the conference organisers and the ANC appears to have been Walter Sisulu. He was a leading member of the ANC executive, who saw that a national women's organisation could play an important role in the liberation struggle.

Yet, if the organisation of women was accepted as a useful project by most activists within the Congress Alliance, it was certainly not something they paid much attention to in 1954. *Advance* gave the conference scanty preliminary coverage, indicating that it did not regard it as an event of major importance on the calendar. It first mentioned the conference in passing, on 18th March 1954, when it reported on an election meeting that Alexander had held in Beaufort West.[27] Thereafter it published one further, very small report that announced the forthcoming conference in a phrase borrowed from the conference invitation, as intended 'to promote women's rights'.[28] Its coverage of the actual meeting was very skimpy as well. The conference was held on the weekend of 17th April, but *Advance*, a weekly, did not bring out a report till two weeks later, on 29th April.[29]

Perhaps the men of the Congress Alliance were more apprehensive about a conference to promote women's rights than they were prepared to admit. To what extent the conference could disrupt existing relationships between men and women within the national liberation movement was not apparent in 1954—and few delegates would have seen that as their main purpose. It was apparent, however, that women were wanting to make their presence more strongly felt in the Congress Alliance and in its campaigns. Implicit in this was a rejection of the assumptions of male superiority and female dependence that were still strongly entrenched in the organisation. For the two chief organisers of the conference, Alexander and Watts, that rejection was quite explicit. In March 1954 Watts wrote to Alexander suggesting that all the catering at the conference be done by men. Alexander received her suggestion with enthusiasm: 'am enjoying your arrangement that the men are to do the catering—excellent idea— and a taste of real emancipation for both men and women'.[30]

The conference held out the prospects of a stronger female voice within the Congress Alliance. Many male members were ambivalent, adopting a low-key response. The organisers of the conference felt no such restraint, however. For the women who had been working to get the project off the ground, it was an event of major importance. Expectations of the conference were high. In March 1954 Alexander summed up the mood of optimism that preceded it when she wrote: 'It is truly going to be a fine conference. So much enthusiasm for it.'[31]

Notes

1. Interview with R. Alexander.
2. L. Kuper, *Passive Resistance in South Africa*, p. 124.
3. *Report of the Native Laws Commission*, 1948, p. 10.
4. *Industrial Legislation Commission*, 1951, p. 14, Table 16.
5. Interview with R. Alexander.
6. Benson, *The Struggle for a Birthright*, p. 148.

7. L. Kuper, *op. cit.*, p. 123.
8. Benson, *op. cit.*, p. 151.
9. *Advance*, 22/1/53.
10. *Advance*, 6/8/53. The other two members of the deputation were Hilda Lotz and Katie Altman, two trade unionists.
11. FSAW correspondence, 20/2/54 and 11/3/54, FSAW BII.
12. 'Conference to Promote Women's Rights, to be held in the Trades Hall, Kerk Street, Johannesburg, on Saturday, 17th April, 1954.' FSAW A I. Hereafter referred to as 'Conference to promote Women's Rights'.
13. FSAW correspondence, 2/3/54, FSAW BII.
14. FSAW correspondence, 8/2/54, FSAW BII.
15. 'Durban Diary', *Drum*, November 1952.
16. *Advance*, 8/4/54.
17. FSAW correspondence, 11/3/54, FSAW BII.
18. *Ibid.*, 30/3/54.
19. *Advance*, 25/2/54.
20. *Advance*, 29/4/54.
21. *Advance*, 18/3/54.
22. 'Conference to Promote Women's Rights', *op. cit.*, p. 1.
23. *Ibid.*
24. FSAW correspondence, 8/2/54, FSAW BII.
25. *Ibid.*, 19/3/54.
26. FSAW circular, 20/2/54, FSAW BII.
27. *Advance*, 18/3/54.
28. *Advance*, 1/4/54.
29. *Advance*, 29/4/54.
30. FSAW correspondence, 5/4/54, FSAW BII.
31. FSAW correspondence, 19/3/54, FSAW BII.

12

'Courtesy But No Rights': The Position of Women in the 1950s

By early 1954, then, efforts to convene a national conference for the purpose of establishing a strong organisation of women within the national liberation movement had finally triumphed. Part Three will detail the history of the organisation that was thus set up. Before doing so, however, it is important to consider briefly how women in South Africa were living in the early 1950s, and how they themselves viewed their position. The momentum to establish the FSAW came from a small number of politicised women in the main urban centres. Although anxious to mobilise women on a larger scale, they were not typical of most women in either their attitudes or their work. In order to understand the scope of the task that the organisers of the national conference of women had set themselves, it is necessary to consider how unified, as well as how ready to embrace the new national body, the majority of women in fact were.

Earlier chapters have indicated the dimensions of the changes that had shaped the position of women by the middle of the twentieth century. The greater economic independence and mobility enjoyed by white women in particular, were calling into question those institutions which continued to define them as minors, in the custody of male relatives. In 1946, after many years of representation from various white women's organisations (the National Council of Women, Die Vroue Federasie, the University Women's Association, Women's Christian Temperance Union), parliament finally appointed a commission of enquiry into the legal disabilities suffered by women under common law. (African customary law was excluded from the scope of the enquiry.)

The struggle to reform the common law provisions with regard to the legal status of women was, in many ways, a continuation of the earlier women's rights campaign conducted by the suffragists in the WEAU. Once their political disabilities had been overcome, these women focused attention on their legal disabilities. The enfranchisement of white women made it possible to wage the campaign from within parliament itself. Bertha Solomon, one of three women members of parliament at the time, played a leading role—so much so, that the subsequent Matrimonial Affairs Act was popularly known as 'Bertha's Bill' in the press and in parliament.[1] It was finally passed in 1953, after much delay and prevarication by the male-dominated parliament. It relieved married women of the worst disabilities that their legal status as minors under the guardianship of their husbands had imposed upon them. To quote Solomon:

> No longer would a man be able to claim his wife's earnings as a right. Nor sell her tools of trade or seize her damages. . . It would be possible now for an

innocent wife in divorce to ask for, and get, alimony at the discretion of the courts. The courts could even grant her guardianship as well as custody of her children in a suitable case.[2]

However, and significantly, the act did not touch the status of African women under customary law, which, as has been already described, made women far worse off than they were under common law. This was no accident. Despite the degree to which African women were involved in the changes restructuring women's place in society, the state refused to lift the controls exercised over them under customary law. Rather, the move after 1948 was towards greater, not less, control.

By the middle of the twentieth century, the economic and demographic developments of the previous fifty years had profoundly affected the position of women within society. Woman's place was still within the home, but she was no longer content to confine her attention solely to domestic responsibilities. Nor was her reproductive role within the family her sole contribution to the growth and development of the economy. For white women, the developments since Union had, overall, been positive. Although still falling short of equality with men, the social and economic horizons of their world had expanded. For black women, however, the effects had not been so straightforward. All women experienced some tension and contradiction between their dominant reproductive role and the new economic demands and opportunities confronting them. For black women, the contradictions were particularly marked, placing an enormous strain on institutions such as the family and marriage. Nowhere were the ambiguities and inadequacies of women's position more apparent than in the reserves.

Women in the Reserves

By the 1950s, African women's reproductive function within the reserves was strained and stretched to near breaking-point. By then it had become manifestly clear that the reserves were no longer functioning as viable subsistence bases for migrant workers. Overpopulated, but with an unnatural preponderance of the young, the old and women, overstocked, eroded, and neglected by the state, the reserves were economically exhausted, and sunk in acute poverty.

The *Keiskammahoek Rural Survey* of 1949 painted a grim picture of what life was like for the 46 per cent of the African female population still living in these areas in the early 1950s.

By the time a woman has passed the reproductive years she has borne, on the average, 7 children which means that at any given time, 1 in 5 of the youngest and strongest of the female workers is pregnant, and as many have suckling infants. Before the normal housekeeping tasks of cooking, washing and cleaning even begin, the women have usually long distances to go to fetch water in buckets from the rivers; wood is collected and carried in large bundles from the forest; and then the mealies must be stamped and ground, preparatory to their cooking. The trading stations are sometimes miles away. . . and the women must walk the distances bringing back the small quantities of tea, coffee, sugar and groceries which their available cash enables them to afford. The huts in which they live are sometimes poorly constructed and always require a certain amount of unkeep.[3]

The survey calculated that, on an average, women and girls spent one quarter of a 56-hour week on 'the wastefully uneconomic tasks of fetching water and wood and stamping and grinding mealies'.[4] For women 'burdened with childbearing and household tasks', their work as peasant farmers amounted to the 'bare minimum'—on an average over the year, only about ten per cent of a woman's time was spent on the cultivation and harvesting of crops.[5] Yet women were, more than ever, the mainstay of the reserve agriculture. The 1953/54 annual report of the Department of Native Affairs put the number of African 'small farmers' at 2,073,356, of whom over two-thirds (1,528,617) were women.[6] *The Keiskammahoek Rural Survey* calculated that, in that one district of the Ciskei, per square mile there were approximately 53 children and aged to 28 adult workers, of whom only nine were male.[7]

The economic decay of the reserves was most brutally illustrated in the infant mortality figures. The same survey estimated that the infant mortality rate within that district was 453 per 1,000 births; 40 per cent of all children in the area died before they reached the age of ten.[8] This was by no means atypical of the reserves in general, although detailed data on other areas is not available. In 1940, a survey in the Lovedale district had found that 70 per cent of all babies between 7 and 12 months old and 92 per cent of all children between 8 and 11 years were underweight.[9]

Despite the appearance of unhurried calm and picturesque, tradition-bound life that the reserves presented to casual travellers, reserve society had become increasingly unstable. The migrant labour system involved a constant turnover of the members of a family resident in the reserves. The family itself was in disarray. Marriage was being undermined—many men abandoned their reserve families on moving to town, leaving their wives and children to cope as best they could. Illegitimacy was on the increase. The Keiskammahoek survey found that roughly a quarter of all children born in the district were illegitimate; nearly half the mothers interviewed had borne one or more illegitimate children.[10] While the rate of female migration was on the increase, the preponderance of adult women over men was enormous. In the 25–29 age group in Keiskammahoek in 1946, the masculinity rate was a mere 36.1.[11] Furthermore, as more women moved to town, the burden of childcare on those women left behind in the reserves was on the increase as well. Migrant women frequently left their children in the care of older female relatives; sometimes even older children had to bear the responsibility when both parents were away. In Keiskammahoek in 1936 there were 119.3 children under nine years of age for every hundred women of childbearing age (15–44 years). By 1946, the ratio of children to women had increased to 135.1:100.[12]

This, then, was the condition of life for nearly a third (31.09 per cent) of all South African women in 1951. Life was a daily struggle for existence at its most basic level. Nothing could be taken for granted—neither food, nor water, nor fuel, nor shelter. The secure framework of tribal society, and the institutions of marriage and the family that it had supported, had collapsed, but little had arisen to take its place. The fund of accumulated frustration, bitterness and despair amongst rural women was enormous. Although large-scale political organisation in the reserves was extremely difficult—they were too isolated, and dominated still by their outmoded tribal institutions—the potential for rural people to break out in spontaneous outbursts of anger against particular institutions and manifestations of their oppressed living conditions was always there. At times, only a small spark was needed to ignite a violent response. As pressure on the reserves increased during the 1950s under the apartheid government, several such outbursts occurred. Women, those most severely affected by the deteriorating conditions in the reserves, were prominently involved upon occasion, as revealed in demonstrations in the Zeerust district of the Transvaal in 1957 against passes and in Natal, in 1959, against cattle-dipping stations.

Women in the Towns

As discussed in Chapter 10, one indication of the precapitalist subsistence sector's collapse was the mounting rate of urbanisation among African women. The resulting decline in the masculinity rate amongst urban Africans was seen by the government as indicating the development of a 'normal family structure' amongst them.[15] However, a normal family structure depends on far more than a mere overall improvement in the balance of a population's sex ratio. The available material suggests that the urban African family, like its rural counterpart, had become far less stable, not more so, by the 1950s.

In the late 1950s, a survey of Africans living in East London revealed marriage amongst them to be in 'an uncertain and insecure condition'.[16] While it remained the ideal, it was becoming far less binding and permanent, with the number of couples living in extra-legal unions on the increase. Illegitimacy in the towns was even more marked than in the reserves. In the East London survey, more than 40 per cent of the children belonging to the women in the sample were illegitimate.[17] Such a figure was by no means unusually high for the African townships. According to Simons, in his study on the legal status of African women, in Durban the illegitimacy rate amongst African births between 1955 and 1961 fluctuated between 59 and 64 per 100 births. In Pietermartizburg in 1960, the comparable figure was 67.[18] In other large towns, the illegitimacy rate per 100 births during the late 1950s and early 1960s was as follows: King-williamstown, 1955-60, 40-58; Pretoria, 1962, 42; Port Elizabeth, 1960-63, 37-33; Bloemfontein, 1962, 42; and Cape Town, 1962, 32. Because the register of African births was incomplete, the figures are not reliable, but, argues Simons, 'there is no reason to believe that they are an exaggeration. It is more likely women would conceal illegitimate, rather than legitimate, births.'[19]

The rise in illegitimacy and increased instability of marriages was leading to the emergence of a new form of household, the matrifocal or female-headed household. Thus the East London survey already cited found that two-fifths of its sample households were headed by women.[20] In a study of social conditions in the township of Langa in Cape Town (which appeared in 1963), Wilson and Mafeje described female heads of houeholds as 'common'.[21] A further index of the declining importance of men in the urban family was the low masculinity rate. The East London survey found only 81 males per 100 females in its sample of households; when only household members fifteen years and older were taken into account, the masculinity rate dropped still further, to 63.[22] Yet, in town as a whole, men greatly outnumbered women. This survey noted that families showed 'a strong tendency to lose the father at a relatively early stage'.[23] At the same time, there was a tendency for households to extend in a multigenerational form on the matriline—a woman, her daughters (legitimate or illegitimate) and their daughters.

In the state of flux and uncertainty that surrounded the urban family, the position of women was often contradictory, their status confused. On the one hand, women tended to gain in independence and authority. In many cases they were playing the strongest part in holding their families together, an important factor in explaining why the opposition of African women to the pass laws was always so deeply felt. On the other hand, women's new position was not sanctioned by society. In the eyes of the law they were still subordinate to men, while their right of residence in town was increasingly insecure, especially after 1952, when the tighter influx control measures were introduced. Furthermore, within their own community, patriarchal attitudes and values were still deeply entrenched: '[I]n spite of structural conditions working towards a matrifocal family structure, traditional values relating to patriarchy and patrilineal kinship ties are still strongly in evidence, even among urban Bantu.'[24]

In 1954, the magazine *Drum* put the question 'Should women have equal rights with men?' to the vote of its readership. Out of 159 replies, 101 readers answered no. The winner of the prize for the best letter said: 'Let us give them courtesy but no rights. They should continue to carry no passes for they are harmlessly inferior; put on their bonnets everywhere, for it is a shame for a woman to go bareheaded.'[25] *Drum* was itself a mirror of sexist attitudes. Though it carried many serious feature articles, and provides a valuable record of the 1950s on both a cultural and a political level, its treatment of women was generally frivolous, stereotyping women as beauty queens, cover girls and social ornaments.

In the pages of *Drum* across the years, one can trace the growth of a township culture far removed from the traditional, tribal culture that apartheid attempted to sell as the 'true' African way of life—a culture brash and vigorous, as its chroniclers have described it, but which was also, for all its apparent permissiveness, in many ways more oppressive than tribalism, not less, in its treatment of women. In the 1950s, township women were becoming the victims of the new stereotypes that define women under mature capitalism—women as sex objects, women as consumers. The cover girls that flaunted their increasingly westernised figures and fashions across the pages of *Drum* in the 1950s represented the most impossible of dreams for the vast majority of the magazine's readership. Nevertheless, despite the enormous gap between the myth of consumer ease, pleasure and sophistication surrounding the cover girls and the reality of poverty and violence in which most township women lived, the cover girl was becoming a powerful, popular model for women to aspire to and be judged by. This was a new dimension to the already complex tangle of old and new, traditional and western, progressive and reactionary forces shaping their place in society.

For women themselves, their own perceptions of their position were often ambivalent. The East London survey mentioned above recorded the following conversation with a 64-year-old woman, head of a three-generation household:

Q: When a mother lives with her children as you do here in town, what is the custom. Who is taken as head?
A: The son, Makhwenkwe, is the head here.
But, later,
Q: Who really rules all the people in this house?
A: I do, all these things are mine and he (Makhwenkwe) is also mine.[26]

These ambiguities in the role of women and the ambivalent attitudes would colour the FSAW's assessment of the position of women as well. At the same time, the crisis of the urban family would be an area of major concern for it after 1954.

By the early 1950s, the position of women was in a state of flux compared to the early twentieth century. The economic changes that the country had experienced had loosened many of the constraints on women's position that operated in Schreiner's day. With their greater economic mobility and independence, more women were in a position to organise themselves politically than ever before. At the same time, the contradictions and pressures they faced in adjusting to these new conditions were mounting as well, raising the need for further and more radical adjustments in their position. This was especially the case for black women. Yet the scope for political activity amongst women in the early 1950s was still severely restricted. Apart from the general restrictions operating against black political activity, patriarchal ideology, though under pressure from various quarters, was deeply entrenched amongst both men and women. This tended to counteract the more radicalising effects of the changes described above on women's perceptions of themselves and on the degree of independence and mobility they enjoyed. Furthermore, the bulk of women were still absorbed by domestic concerns, their time, energy and skills directed towards this sphere rather than the public-political one. In addition, as the above survey must make abundantly clear, women had not been uniformly affected by the process of change. In many ways, the gulf separating black women from white had increased over the years, as witnessed by occupational stratification along colour lines and discriminatory legislation, eg the Women's Enfranchisement Act, and the Matrimonial Affairs Act.

This gulf extended to the political sphere as well. While white women could, for the most part, look to the white state for the protection of their interests and for reforms in areas where they still felt themselves to be discriminated against as women, black women stood in a fundamentally different relation to the state. For them, reforms in their subordinate status as women required radical changes in the very nature of the state itself. For this reason, political organisation amongst them did not, historically, develop along separate, feminist lines but always within the broader framework of black political resistance movements. Such was the tradition that the FSAW inherited in 1954.

Notes

1. B. Solomon, *Time Remembered.*
2. *Ibid.,* p. 261.
3. *Keiskammahoek Rural Survey,* vol. II, p. 140.
4. *Ibid.,* p. 140–1.
5. *Ibid.,* p. 182.
6. *Report of the Native Affairs Department,* 1953/54, p. 10.
7. *Keiskammahoek Rural Survey, op. cit.,* p. 139.
8. *Ibid.,* pp. 45, 182.
9. P. Walshe, *The Rise of African Nationalism in South Africa,* p. 301.
10. *Keiskammahoek Rural Survey, op. cit.,* p. 111.
11. *Ibid.,* p. 36.
12. *Ibid.,* p. 40, Table 16.
13. Calculated from figures supplied by the *Population Census,* 1951, vol. 1, Table 11(a), pp. 94–5.
14. *Industrial Legislation Commission,* 1951, p. 14.
15. *Ibid.,* p. 13.
16. Pauw: *The Second Generation,* p. 130.
17. *Ibid.,* p. 137.
18. Simons, *The Legal Status of African Women,* p. 221.
19. *Ibid.*
20. Pauw, *op. cit.,* p. 146.
21. M. Wilson and A. Mafeje, *Langa,* p. 79.
22. Pauw, *op. cit.,* p. 150.
23. *Ibid.,* p. 149.
24. *Ibid.,* p. 161.
25. *Drum,* May 1954.
26. Pauw, *op. cit.,* p. 71.

PART THREE: THE FEDERATION OF SOUTH AFRICAN WOMEN, 1954–1963

13

'We Have Come to Break These Problems': The First National Conference of Women, April 1954

The spirit of optimism and eagerness that had characterised the planning of the inaugural conference of the FSAW imbued the meeting itself. This was finally held, a year after the Port Elizabeth meeting, on the weekend of 17th April 1954, in the Trades Hall, Johannesburg. Here—'with joyful enthusiasm'[1]—the skeletal framework of a national organisation of women was created, a Women's Charter setting out the philosophy behind the new organisation adopted and its broad aims established: 'This organisation is formed for the purpose of uniting all women in common action for the removal of all political, legal, economic and social disabilities.'[2] At that stage there was no name for the new organisation and the conference was known simply as the 'First National Conference of Women'.

Alexander and Watts, as co-organisers of the conference, retained a large measure of control over the shape of the conference and its formal proceedings. It is likely that they drafted the various resolutions adopted by the gathering and probably the 'Women's Charter' as well. It seems that the final report on the conference, which contained the 'Charter', the aims of the new organisation and a summary of the speeches, was drafted by Watts. Certainly much of the behind-the-scenes planning and decision-making was vested in their hands. The two women organised a planning meeting the night before the conference began, which was attended by 'Helen' (presumably Helen Joseph, of the Johannesburg Congress of Democrats) and 'Gladys' (Gladys Smith, a colleague of Alexander's from Cape Town) as well. At this meeting they discussed what the name of the organisation should be and the programme for the weekend.

Nevertheless, the organisers were unable to achieve all they had hoped at the inaugural conference. Only the barest outline of a national organisation was created in April 1954. Much of the administrative groundwork necessary for running an efficient organisation—the constitution, on what basis membership was to be allowed, even the name[3]—was not decided. The finalisation of these matters took many months and, as well as being a source of frustration, diverted energy away from the important tasks of recruiting members and proceeding with a programme of action. It was not until 1956, at the second national conference, when a constitution was finally adopted, that this preliminary process of defining the structure of the organisation was completed.

At the inaugural conference most of the time was spent on speeches and general discussion, rather than administrative details. From all reports, the conference was a spirited, festive occasion. Singing and dancing would always be features of FSAW meetings. The township women brought an

energy and exuberance to their meetings that lifted them out of the realm
of mere business and turned them into vibrant social gatherings as well.
At times the business of the meeting was swamped by the party mood that
kept bursting through the restraints of the formal proceedings. Writing to
Watts after the conference was over, Alexander commented wryly on
this—the time was overdue for 'serious discussion and no songs!'[4]

Yet despite its shortcomings on the business side, all who attended
the conference considered it a huge success, a landmark in the history of
women's organisation in South Africa. Attending and participating in the
proceedings was in itself a politicising experience for delegates. For most
non-Johannesburg women it was their first visit to the Rand, for some
their first long journey away from home. The conference provided a real
break from their daily, pressured lives as workers and township housewives. It was also the first opportunity many women had had for meetings
and discussion with women activists from different centres. New contacts
were established; a national dimension was introduced into the delegates'
thinking. In this way the meeting fostered a fresh sense of women's
political relevance. At the opening session, Ida Mtwana, ANCWL national
president, declared:

> We know that as women we have many problems which hold us back from
> taking part fully in the struggle [for 'freedom'] and it is for precisely that
> purpose that we have come to break down these problems.[5]

The organisers took up Watts's suggestion to allocate all the catering
responsibilities to male volunteers, thus leaving the women free to concentrate on the business of the conference. This was a startling lesson in role-
reversal for all concerned, both men and women. Newspaper reports on
the conference commented on it in approving, if surprised, tones. For
Advance, it was 'something that will always be remembered about this
conference'.[6] The COD periodical, *Fighting Talk,* felt it warranted its own
report—'And the men took their place in the kitchen. . .'[7] It was a provocative sight, expressive of the new consciousness being shaped by the
conference. In the speech already quoted, Ida Mtwana made the point
explicit: 'Gone are the days when the place of women was in the kitchen
and looking after the children. Today, they are marching side by side with
men in the road to freedom.'[8]

The National Executive Committee

What the inaugural conference did achieve was the election of a national
executive committee [NEC]. Ida Mtwana, already national president for
the ANCWL, was elected the first national president of the new organisation. She does not appear to have played a dominant role in convening the
conference, but she enjoyed considerable prestige, particularly in the
Transvaal, as Women's League president and a former ANC Youth Leaguer.
Her election established clearly the leading role the ANC would play in

the affairs of the FSAW.

The pivotal position of national secretary went to Ray Alexander, in recognition of the central part she had played in getting the conference off the ground. At this stage, she was undoubtedly the most influential person within the new movement. Hetty McLeod of SACPO (at one time secretary of the Women's Food Committee) was elected treasurer. The remaining officers were four vice-presidents, one for each of the four geographical regions into which the organisation was divided: Lilian Ngoyi, Transvaal; Gladys Smith, Cape Western; Florence Matomela, Cape Eastern; and Bertha Mkize, Natal. These women were to head regional women's committees, which had still to be elected at regional conferences. In addition to these office-bearers, a further nineteen committee members were elected to complete the executive. The full committee was as follows:[9]

President:	Ida Mtwana
Vice Presidents:	Gladys Smith
	Lilian Ngoyi
	Bertha Mkize
	Florence Matomela
Secretary:	Ray Alexander
Treasurer:	Hetty McLeod
Committee:	Elizabeth Mafeking, Dora Tamana, Katie White, Freda van Rheede, Annie Silinga, Louisa Mtwana, Cecilia Rosier, Winifred Siqwana, K. Egelhof (Cape Town), Hilda Watts, Hetty du Preez, Albertina Sisulu, Helen Joseph (Rand), Frances Baard, Miss Njonwe, Chrissie Jasson (Port Elizabeth), Fatima Meer (Durban), Miss M.F. Thompson (Kimberley).

The national executive was thus comprised of women living in widely dispersed areas. To solve the problem of running the organisation on a day-to-day basis, a working committee was established from within the national executive. This was to consist of all members living in the immediate vicinity of the head office. In 1954 the head office was located in Cape Town, presumably because this was Alexander's home; the Cape Western area thus received a larger quota of committee members than other areas. In addition to Smith, Alexander and McLeod, a further eight committee members came from Cape Town and vicinity. The remainder were distributed between the main centres as follows: the Rand, four; Port Elizabeth, three; and Durban and Kimberley, one committee member each.

The newly elected national executive included several women who were already well known in Congress circles—Ida Mtwana, Ray Alexander, Bertha Mkize, Hilda Watts, Florence Matomela and Hetty McLeod. This appeared to promise a certain amount of continuity with the work that had already been done amongst women within the national liberation movement. There were also several more recent recruits, whose rise to prominence within the Congress Alliance would be rapid after 1954; the two most significant were Lilian Ngoyi and Helen Joseph who, after 1956, would take over as national president and secretary respectively.

The 'Women's Charter'

The other major concrete achievements of the conference were the adoption of the 'Women's Charter' and the setting out of the aims of the new organisation. The charter was a two and a half page document which formed a manifesto of the ideas that had gone into the calling of the inaugural conference. In it can be traced the imprint of many earlier debates on the role of a women's movement in South Africa. The influence of Alexander and Watts and the disbanded CPSA was clearly visible, particularly in the strong feminist streak that was woven through the charter. The call for women's rights was tempered, however, by the recognition that the national liberation movement took first priority in the struggle for equality.

The charter began by affirming emphatically the overriding community of interests that women shared with men.

> We women do not form a society separate from men. There is only one society and it is made up of both women and men. As women we share the problems and anxieties of our men and join hands with them to remove social evils and obstacles to progress.[10]

At the same time, however, it recognised that women were discriminated against on the basis of their sex, and committed the new organisation to working for the removal of all 'the laws and practices that discriminate against women'. Throughout the charter, as in the invitation that had preceded the inaugural conference, the dual nature of women's struggle for equality was stressed.

> As members of the National Liberation movements and Trades Unions. . . we march forward with our men in the struggle for liberation and the defence of the working people. . . As women there rests upon us also the burden of removing from our society all the social differences developed in past times between men and women which have the effect of keeping our sex in a position of inferiority and subordination.

The charter thus identified the women's movement completely with the national liberation movement, as represented by the Congress Alliance group, in its struggle to overthrow the white supremacist government in South Africa. Since roughly 80 per cent of all South African women were black, it regarded the removal of the political, economic and social inequalities suffered by blacks as of overriding concern for any broad women's political movement. But it was also explicit on the need for change in the position of women within society. It dealt gently with the 'ancient and revered traditions' by which the continued subordination of African women, in particular, was justified, conceding that 'no doubt' these had once served 'purposes of great value'. Nevertheless, it declared, those days were past.

The tribal and kinship society to which they belonged had been destroyed as a result of the loss of tribal lands, migration of men away from their tribal home, the growth of towns and industries and the rise of a great body of wage-earners on the farms and in the urban areas.

It went on to add that women had shared in these developments—large numbers of women were in fact the sole bread-winners for their families—but despite these changes, the law 'has lagged behind. . . it no longer corresponds to the actual social and economic position of women'.

Nor, emphasised the charter, had the national liberation movement kept up with the changes that had restructured the position of women; many of its attitudes mirrored the very prejudices that women had to combat in the wider society. In the words of the charter, a 'large section of our menfolk' were responsible for helping to perpetuate women's subordinate position by refusing to 'concede to us women the rights and privileges which they demand for themselves'. The charter recognised, however, that not only the men were to blame. 'Many women themselves continue to be bound by traditional practices and conventions, and fail to realise that these have become obsolete and a brake on progress.'

In its conclusion, the charter asserted that an 'intimate relationship' existed between women's inferior status and the inferior status assigned to people by 'discriminatory laws and colour prejudices'. It did not develop the nature of this relationship in any detail; nevertheless, it made it clear that the struggle to emancipate women from discriminatory laws and conventions formed an intrinsic part of any general liberatory struggle: 'freedom cannot be won for any one section or for the people as a whole as long as we women are in bondage.' Since patriarchal ideology was still so deeply-rooted and largely unquestioned amongst many Congress supporters, contained within this standpoint lay the seeds of potential conflict between the new women's movement and the male-dominated Congress Alliance.

The 'Women's Charter' was the first comprehensive statement of principles by the new women's movement and, as such, is an important document. Like Schreiner's writings of half a century before and more, it has an unexpectedly contemporary flavour—and, like those earlier writings, it stands as a landmark in the evolution of an analysis of their position in society by South African women. The charter drew together the experience of women within the national liberation movement over the previous forty years and mapped out the direction the leaders of the conference hoped the new organisation would take. As with any political manifesto, it was a more coherent and sophisticated statement of position than many who endorsed it would have made themselves. In particular, its commitment to the emancipation of women from their 'bondage' as women was probably in advance of the thinking of many delegates. Nevertheless, the charter spoke to the women present at the conference. They echoed many of its sentiments in their own speeches from the floor and proceeded to adopt it enthusiastically.

The women who came together in April 1954 all shared a broad allegiance to the Congress Alliance and its basic political assumptions. They were committed to the liberation of the black majority in South Africa from white minority rule, by a process of extra-parliamentary but peaceful change. Individual women may well have differed on their long-term political objectives—for instance, whether or not they envisaged a socialist future. In 1954, however, faced with the immediate and daunting task of the national struggle, this was not an issue. Delegates also recognised that women, as a distinct group, needed to make a larger contribution to the national struggle than they had made before. Again, individual views on what that contribution should be, and how best it could be realised, varied considerably, and a wide and not always strictly consistent cross-section of views on women's position prevailed.

Impatience with practices which tied women exclusively to the home was general. This extended to criticism of many of the men in the Congress Alliance who were blamed for upholding the status quo in this regard. Lilian Ngoyi was applauded by the conference when she said that had it not been for 'the husbands, who kept back many of the women', there would have been many more delegates present—'the husbands talked of democracy but did not practice it'. Yet, at the same time, most delegates accepted without question that women's primary identification would be with the home and issues related to that. They did not come into fundamental conflict with established ideas on the role of women within the family, as wives and mothers. The theme of fighting for their children's rights and future was a major one that ran throughout the conference proceedings. In her opening speech, Ray Alexander referred to 'the right of our children to be brought up in decent homes, schools and with opportunities for a full life' as one of the issues 'which mean so much to women'.[11] These sentiments were echoed by Ida Mtwana, Hilda Watts and numerous speakers from the floor, as well as being taken up in the 'Women's Charter'. They would dominate in the subsequent history of the FSAW as well.

Delegates to the conference nevertheless made it clear that they did not intend to accept a passive and subordinate role within the Congress Alliance. They did not view the new organisation as a mere auxiliary to the existing male-dominated structure of the Alliance; the women's organisation was not there simply to mobilise women to work for the Alliance's existing programme. Rather, the women assembled at the Trades Hall in April 1954 wanted to expand the scope of women's work within the national liberation movement. They also wanted to broaden the liberation movement's programme so that it would pay more attention to areas of special concern to women—childcare, rising food costs, housing etc. It would be anachronistic to identify the 'Women's Charter' and the women who endorsed it with the women's liberation movement of the late 1960s and 1970s. That movement belonged to a different period and, certainly initially, a different group of women, middle class and infinitely more privileged than the majority of women gathered at the Trades Hall in 1954. But the charter was a remarkably progressive document, far in advance of popular thinking about women and their place in society at that time. It staked a claim for full equality between the sexes and began the search for answers to the questions about how best that could be achieved in a society where gross racial discrimination obscured all other forms of oppression and exploitation.

In addition to the charter, the conference adopted eight specific aims for the new organisation. These were set out as follows:

(1) The right to vote and to be elected to all state bodies, without restriction or discrimination (ie universal suffrage);

(2) The right to full opportunities for employment with equal pay and possibilities of promotion in all spheres of work;

(3) Equal rights with men in relation to property, marriage and children, and for the removal of all laws and customs that deny women such equal rights;

(4) For the development of every child through free compulsory education for all; for the protection of mother and child through maternity homes, welfare clinics, creches and nursery schools, in countryside and towns; through proper homes for all, and through the provision of water, light, transport, sanitation and the amenities of modern civilisation;

(5) For the removal of all laws that restrict free movement, that prevent or hinder the right of free association, and activity in democratic organisations, and the right to participate in the work of these organisations;

(6) To build and strengthen women's sections in the National Liberatory Movements, the organisation of women in the trade unions, and through the people's varied organisations;

(7) To co-operate with all other organisations that have similar aims in South Africa and throughout the world;

(8) To strive for permanent peace throughout the world.[12]

This was a comprehensive and ambitious programme, far more sweeping in its proposals than any put forward by other contemporary women's organisations. It could best be described as a liberal, democratic programme, although traces of Communist Party ideology were clearly present in some of the terminology and objectives. The concept of equal rights and opportunities—for men and women, black and white—was dominant. The FSAW was heir to a long tradition of political thinking that still sought inclusion in the existing political and economic institutions of society, even though by 1954 faith in the ability of these institutions to accommodate black aspirations was beginning to waver. In thinking about women, the FSAW adopted the tone and terms of the national liberation movement in whose shadow it had taken shape.

In April 1954, the direction the FSAW would take in translating its aims into action was not clearly defined. No strategy for achieving these aims was spelled out, other than a vague reference to a 'nation-wide programme of education' in the 'Women's Charter'. At the inaugural conference women were just beginning to articulate their experiences, and for many it was their first opportunity for reflecting critically upon them. Despite the polished and confident phrases of the charter, they were still groping for a way of expressing these ideas in practice.

The Delegates

The 'Women's Charter' referred to the gathering in very general terms as 'we, the women of South Africa, wives and mothers, working women and housewives, Africans, Indians, European and Coloured'.[13] Certainly a wide cross-section of South African women were present—far wider than that achieved by other contemporary women's organisations—and no group of women were deliberately excluded. However, the conference was by no means representative of all South African women, nor, considering the definite political allegiance of its sponsors to the Congress Alliance and its programme, could this have been expected.

It is not easy to piece together a comprehensive picture of the women who attended the conference. Information is sketchy—even the available figures for the final number of delegates present do not agree. The official 'Report on the first National Conference of Women' mentioned 'nearly 150 women' in attendance,[14] while an earlier draft of the report referred to 146 delegates, representing 223,500 women.[15] A letter from Alexander to Watts after the conference corrected both figures, putting the final number of delegates at 137, plus 'a few representatives from some other ANC branches', whose exact numbers were not known.[16] Less than a quarter of the delegates have been positively identified; the rest are conjectural figures. Nevertheless, it is possible to draw some general conclusions about the women and who they represented from the available biographical material.

They were drawn, entirely it would seem, from organisations already within the ambit of the Alliance—the ANC, SAIC, COD, SACPO, left-wing trade unions. Other political groups which subscribed in general terms to the aims of 'national liberation' for blacks in South Africa, but which did not belong to the Congress Alliance (for instance, the Non-European Unity Movement [NEUM] in Cape Town), were not represented; nor were any of the already established national women's organisations, eg the NCW, NCAW, nor any of the white political parties other than COD.

How extensively women supported the Congress Alliance in 1954 is extremely difficult to gauge with any precision. The FSAW's draft report on the conference stated that 223,500 women were represented at the conference, but where these figures were derived from is not clear. None of the organisations involved kept accurate membership lists. Certainly at the end of the Defiance Campaign the ANC could accurately describe itself as a mass movement, but what percentage of its membership was female is not known. The SAIC's membership had gone into a decline after the Passive Resistance Campaign in 1946, while SACPO and COD were both tiny organisations with a membership that could be counted in tens rather than hundreds. Perhaps the most accurate assessment of the inaugural conference would be to describe it as a gathering of prominent individuals speaking for, rather than on behalf of, the masses of women in South Africa. In 1954 a mass base of support for the women's movement had still to be built.

The majority of delegates were African, with a sprinkling of other black and white women. This reflected the preponderance both of the ANC within the Congress Alliance and, of course, of Africans in the wider society. Yet even though the number of white women present was small, the fact that it was a racially mixed gathering was an important feature of the conference for participants and observers alike. In a society where segregation, race purity and white *baasskap* were all key elements in the official apartheid ideology, the mingling of black and white women at the Trades Hall was a radical departure from prevailing norms and a clear political statement. The report on the conference commented, with a note of pride, that 'while there are in South Africa many different women's organisations. . . there was (previously) no organisation of women that brought the many sections of women together'.[17] The Congress Alliance was avowedly multi-racial; this would be a major feature of the FSAW too.

On the available information it is impossible to establish a median age for the delegates, but most of the women present were probably in their 30s or 40s, and several would have been even older. Amina Cachalia, at 24, was one of the youngest; Bertha Mkize, at 64, probably one of the oldest; Ray Alexander, Helen Joseph, Lilian Ngoyi, Florence Matomela, were all in their 40s; Dora Tamana was already 53. This was not, overall, a meeting of young women. As a consequence, most delegates were married, with children, and thus issues relating to the home and childcare received much attention.

The educational qualifications of those delegates known to have attended varied considerably. The spectrum ranged from a smattering of university educated women (Helen Joseph, Fatima Meer) through to women who had had very little formal education. Dora Tamana, for instance, had left school in Standard Four, as had Katie White; Lilian Ngoyi had gone as far as Standard Six. It seems probable that most of the black women present would not have advanced far into high school, if they had made it that far at all—in 1955 the total number of African girls in Standard Nine and Ten throughout the country was only 432.[18]

Of the thirty-three women known to have attended the conference, over a third (although this figure could well have been much higher) were definitely in employment; of these, many came from a background of trade union work, either as full-time organisers or as factory workers involved in union affairs. They included Ray Alexander, Lilian Ngoyi, Hilda Watts, Hetty McLeod, Elizabeth Mafeking, Hetty du Preez, Rahima Moosa, Hilda Lotz, Freda van Rheede, Mabel Jones, Betty Kearns and Martha Ngxesha. This list makes clear how important the trade union movement was as a politicising agent among women. The meagre biographical data available suggests that the proportion of working women at the conference could well have been higher than that of the 1951 national average of 23.7 per cent of all women fifteen years and older. However, while it has been argued that, in general, the entry of women wage employment in the twentieth century was a very important factor in encouraging their more active involvement in politics, there was never a simple correlation between wage employment and political work amongst women. The FSAW provides many examples of women who never had regular employment, yet were politically active; Dora Tamana, for instance, was such a woman.

Another important feature of the conference was that all the delegates were urban women. There were no delegates from the scattered small country towns; not even, as originally anticipated, from Beaufort West and De Aar. Nor were there any from the reserves or 'white' farmlands. According to a letter of Alexander's, fully two-thirds of the delegates— 103 women—came from the Rand.[19] Considering the expense and time involved in getting to Johannesburg from other centres, this preponderance was inevitable, but it also reflected the political weight carried by the Rand in national politics. The next largest delegation, totalling nineteen women, came from the Cape Peninsula and area. This included a delegate from Worcester and two from Paarl, all of them members of the Food and Canning Workers' Union. Six women came from Durban, four from East London, three from Queenstown and one delegate each from Kimberley and Cradock. Strangely, Alexander does not give figures for Port Elizabeth. Certainly Florence Matomela was present at the conference and addressed the meeting from the floor. Perhaps the unknown number of representatives from those 'few ANC branches' to which Alexander referred in her list of delegates, included more women from that city.

The FSAW was to keep its urban identity throughout its years of active work; the countryside remained a huge untapped area for it. It is not hard to understand why this was the case. The conference was the product of processes which were most pronounced in the cities and large towns, where social and economic changes in the position of women were most marked and the national liberation movement was at its strongest. While, as described above, profound changes were restructuring the fabric of society in the reserves, and rural women were not completely divorced from the momentum of political events, there were not the same opportunities or incentives for them to organise politically. They were more isolated, more rigidly bound by traditional patriarchal restraints than their urban counterparts, and the practical problems of establishing and maintaining an organisation were far larger. When the conference was being organised in 1953/54, there was no existing network of women's organisations in the countryside for its convenors to approach. The towns were the natural focus of sustained political organisation, although, as events during the course of the 1950s were to show, rural women could be mobilised to action over particular issues upon occasion.

But despite certain consistencies in the composition of the conference delegates, they also brought with them a strikingly rich variety in experience and background. Between them they spoke five different languages—Zulu, Xhosa, Sesotho, English and Afrikaans. Ray Alexander had been born in Latvia, Dora Tamana in the Transkei. Helen Joseph had been born and brought up in England and worked as a governess in India before settling in South Africa. Only gradually, from a position of privilege, did she move to the realisation that the privileges she took for granted as a white in South Africa rested on the exploitation of black labour, the suppression of black liberties. Lilian Ngoyi, the daughter of a washer-woman, moved in the opposite direction, from a position of poverty and rightlessness, to come to a similar conclusion. At the conference these many diverse strands met and mingled together; much of the excitement of the occasion lay in the density of it, the interplay of the familiar with the unfamiliar. It was a pooling of many different resources and strengths.

It was not a gathering of an 'elite' among women in South Africa; most of the women were drawn from the turbulent world of the black townships. Their outlook was shaped by their lives there as married women with family responsibilities in a general situation of poverty, insecurity and rightlessness. Middle class women, black and white, were present, but did not predominate, although they brought educational and organisational skills to the conference which allowed them to exert an influence on its shape and decisions that was larger than their numbers might suggest. Nevertheless, unlike the earlier women's movement repre-sented by the suffrage organisation, the WEAU, the overall commitment of the conference was to the broad masses of South African women. In 1954 it would have been premature to describe the fledgling organisation as enjoying a mass support, but its attention was focused most sharply on the proletarianised women of the townships, from whom the bulk of the conference delegates were drawn. As political leaders, the delegates were exceptional women, but their experience and outlook did not differ substantially from that of their township neighbours.

In the 'Women's Charter', the organisers had attempted to describe the harsh conditions under which most South African women lived:

> As wives and mothers it falls upon us to make small wages stretch a long way. It is we who feel the cries of our children when they are hungry and sick. It is our lot to keep and care for homes that are too small, broken and dirty.[20]

It was in the speeches made by delegates from the floor during the course of the conference that these phrases took on their substance and meaning. Women spoke in simple, graphic terms about the poverty and hardship they suffered:

> In the Cape, the Council had brought passes to women in a crooked way. No husband could bring his wife to town without a pass. . . The mothers and children are hungry because there was not enough money to buy food. Mothers had to go to work and leave their children in the care of other children not much older.

> When it is reaping time for oranges, we work with the men under the same

conditions, from six in the morning until six at night, for which we receive only 2 shillings per head per day.

Delegates also brought to the conference their own vivid understanding of the relationships of power and of wealth that divided black from white: 'The Union Buildings came from the work of our husbands who toil in the mines—with their lamps and hammers. The gold is dug by the black hand, but it goes to the white.'[21]

The women at this first conference sketched the rough outline of an organisation that they hoped would take up these issues. Few underestimated the vast task that lay before them, but when they went home at the end of the weekend, they left filled with a sense of satisfaction and promise. The lengthy process of growth towards an organisation that would represent the interests of the majority of South African women, which had started as far back as 1913 in the Orange Free State, appeared finally to have borne fruit.

Notes

1. FSAW: 'Report of the First National Conference of Women' (hereinafter 'Report'), p. 1.
2. *Ibid.*, p. 16, quoting from 'Our Aims'.
3. The first time the name 'Federation of South African Women' was used in correspondence was in late 1954.
4. FSAW correspondence, 17.5.54, FSAW B II.
5. FSAW: 'Report', p. 4.
6. *Advance*, 29.4.54.
7. *Fighting Talk*, May 1954.
8. FSAW: 'Report', p. 4.
9. FSAW correspondence, 12.5.54, FSAW BII.
10. 'Women's Charter' in FSAW: 'Report', p. 14. All other quotations in this section refer to the 'Charter' unless otherwise specified. For a full replication of the 'Charter', see Appendix A.
11. FSAW: 'Report', p. 2.
12. 'Our Aims', in FSAW: 'Report', p. 16.
13. FSAW: 'Report', p. 14. For a list of known delegates, see Appendix B.
14. FSAW: 'Report', p. 1.
15. Unheaded typescript, p. 5, FSAW AI.
16. FSAW correspondence, 22.5.54, FSAW BII.
17. FSAW: 'Report', p. 1.
18. *Union Statistics for 50 Years*, Tables E-21, E-22.
19. FSAW correspondence, 22.5.54, FSAW BII.
20. FSAW: 'Report', p. 14.
21. FSAW: 'Report', pp. 8, 12, 9.

14

'Hard Work, But the Results are Excellent in Many Ways': Putting the FSAW on Its Feet, 1954–55

The FSAW was formed less than two years after the Defiance Campaign had foundered to a halt in December 1952. At the end of that campaign, despite its shortcomings, the national liberation movement still appeared in a relatively strong position *vis-à-vis* the government. The ANC membership had increased to an estimated 100,000; the establishment of the Congress Alliance, in 1952/53, held out the possibility of a unified and strengthened national liberation movement, operating on a larger scale than before. In addition, the Nationalist government took a few years to consolidate its position after the elections of 1948; the substantial mining and industrial sectors of the economy still had to be convinced that the apartheid policy was practicable and in their own interests, while the National Party only gained absolute majority of the seats in parliament in 1953. The extreme caution with which the government approached the inflammatory question of passes for women in 1950 and again in 1952 was one indication of its restraint in dealing with the national liberation movement in this early period.

In the short space of time that separated the ending of the Defiance Campaign and the founding of the FSAW, however, the initiative had come to be grasped more firmly by the government. By the mid-1950s the state was, to borrow a phrase from a paper written by D. Lewis, on the 'offensive',[1] while the Congress Alliance was being thrust increasingly into a defensive position. Beginning with the Suppression of Communism Act in 1950, and continuing with the Criminal Laws Amendment Act and the Public Safety Act, both of 1953, the government relentlessly extended the range of coercive powers already at its disposal—the CPSA and many prominent political leaders were banned; freedom of association and the right to organise protests and meetings were restricted; penalties for the infringement of any laws in protest against other laws increased. At the same time, the government began a far-reaching process of constitutional restructuring. The Bantu Authorities Act in 1951 established a local government structure in the African reserves—the first cautious step along a path that would eventually, in the 1970s, lead to the creation of several puppet states in these areas, states that were independent in name but politically and economically completely dependent on the South African government for their continued survival. The Separate Representation of Voters Act, finally passed in 1956 after a long constitutional wrangle, removed the last traces of the old Cape Franchise from the South African Constitution by removing 'Coloured' voters in the Cape from the common voters' roll. These acts entrenched the position of the white minority government and began the process of deflecting black political aspirations into apartheid institutions.

The Congress Alliance, in its turn, failed to generate an effective strategy with which to meet the challenge of an increasingly totalitarian state. For a long time it continued to rely on its earlier tactics of mass, non-violent demonstrations, rallies and moral appeals to the conscience of its opponents, even while the scope for such political activities was being ever more drastically curtailed. In addition, and partly as a result of the pressures it was facing, the Alliance was weakened by internal differences. A strongly nationalist 'Africanist' faction emerged within the Transvaal ANC in late 1955. This group was hostile to the multi-racial composition of the Congress Alliance and vociferously critical of its leadership and performance. Much time and energy were spent on internal quarrels and politics, to the detriment of the external political fight.

The history of the FSAW, an organisation formed within the shadow of the Congress Alliance, and operating largely within its framework, was, finally, dominated by these developments. It did not take long before it felt the pressure of repressive state action itself; within a few months of the inaugural conference Ray Alexander, national secretary, and Hetty McLeod, national treasurer, were both banned, and were thus forced to sever all legal ties with the organisation.[2] These two women were the first in a long list of FSAW leaders thus restricted. Their bannings were a clear indication that the women of the FSAW could not expect to remain unaffected by the government's rapidly accelerating drive against the Congress Alliance.

But in 1954 the problem of increased police surveillance and harrassment was only one of many problems facing the new organisation—and, in many ways, compared to the immediate problems of establishing a administrative structure and developing a membership, it appeared of secondary importance. The task that had been set, that of organising 'the most oppressed, suffering and down-trodden of our people—the women of South Africa',[3] was an immense one. Apart from the growing shadow of a repressive state hovering over the Congress Alliance, there were a number of problems facing the women's movement specifically. The general level of political organisation amongst women was pitifully low. In the face of ignorance, indifference and even hostility, this had to be built up with minimal resources. Communication between the far-flung regions represented at the inaugural conference was a problem, and finances were non-existent. As a 1956 report by the FSAW was to point out, its programme was directed to the lowest income group in the country, that of black women.[4]

The first priority facing the FSAW was thus to build a solid organisational base. Regional committees had to be established, members recruited, a constitution agreed upon, relations with the rest of the Congress Alliance clarified and a start made in developing an administrative machinery. In the next year or two much attention and energy was devoted to these matters. It took time for the new organisation to get off the ground and the slow start frustrated and exasperated its promoters. As late as February 1956, Alexander was complaining: 'I just feel that it is high time to put our house in order. We have a following and if we will neglect it much longer it will dwindle away'.[5]

Problems within the NEC

Considerable difficulties were experienced in this early period in establishing an effective national executive committee [NEC]. The forced removal of Alexander from the key position of national secretary, so soon after the inaugural conference, was a great loss to the new organisation. Her role in establishing it had, as we have seen, been a central one, and her organisational experience, energy and wide-ranging political contacts were sorely needed.

She was not the sort of woman to accept her enforced retirement from politics obediently and she continued to play an important behind-the-scenes role. But her links with the NEC and other Congress leaders had to be clandestine from then on, and this inevitably hampered her effectiveness. All her correspondence with other political leaders had to be anonymous. Often she resorted to a clumsy kind of code to disguise both her identity and the subject matter of her correspondence. Any meetings she had with the remaining members of the NEC in Cape Town had to be in secret and kept small. It was a cumbersome way of operating and it soon became apparent that her banning had left a vacuum which would be difficult to fill in Cape Town.

Part of the reason for this lay in the extremely precarious position of African women—the backbone of the FSAW—in Cape Town after 1955. This was because the Western Cape had been selected by the ideologues of apartheid as the easiest and therefore the first area where the African presence in the urban areas of the country could be visibly reduced and the grand theory of apartheid—geographical separation of white and black—vindicated. The African population in Cape Town was always a relatively small one, numbering just under 50,000 in 1951, out of a total population of 577,648. 'Coloureds', numbering 272,314 people in that census year, formed the largest single 'race' group.[6] In 1955 the government announced that it intended eventually to remove the entire African population out of the Western Cape since this was the 'natural home' of the 'Coloured' people. As a start, the Western Cape was declared a 'Coloured preferential area'. This meant that employers had to give preference to 'Coloured' workers over African in their businesses and industries. Muriel Horrell's handbook, *Legislation and Race Relations*, describes the general terms of this declaration thus:

> The Government planned, as a first stage, to remove foreign Africans, to 'freeze' the existing position as regards families, to send back to the reserves all women and children who did not qualify to remain, and to allow only the controlled entry of migratory workers.[7]

As a result, influx control measures were vigorously enforced and pass raids and arrests in the Cape Town area stepped up.

The announcement of this policy plunged African residents of the area into a nightmarish situation where nobody could feel completely secure in their houses or their jobs, not even those who previously had qualified for permanent residence. Living and working in Cape Town—even if one had been born there—was henceforth to be regarded as a concession and not a right, a concession dependent on some bureaucrat in an office with a rubber stamp. The whole community suffered because of the closing off of job and housing opportunities, the enforced removal of the 'unqualified' to remote rural areas in the Transkei and Ciskei. Women were particularly hard-hit because of their peripheral position in the labour market and the fact that very few met the requirements for permission to stay in town.

The authorities made use of this opportunity not only to remove economically redundant or superfluous women, but also to harrass individuals who were politically active. *New Age* carried several reports on their efforts to deport ANCWL activists from Cape Town on the grounds that they did not qualify to be there.[8] Thus, in late 1955, Annie Silinga, ANCWL and FSAW activist, was convicted of illegal residence in Cape Town, although she claimed she had been resident there since 1937. She was deported to the Transkei under police escort in February 1956, but returned to fight, ultimately successfully, all subsequent attempts to evict her. Annie Silinga was a woman of enormous courage and irrepressible conviction; but hers was an individual fight against bureaucracy and intimidation. Inspiring though it was, she could not challenge the structures of coercion single-handed. After 1955 African women in the Western Cape were a vulnerable, threatened group. Many of them were 'unqualified' and lived illegally in townships and squatter communities. They risked their entire future in the area if they became politically active. In this way the 1955 ruling inhibited the emergence of a strong and sizeable core of African women leaders in the Cape Town area and undermined the effectiveness of both the ANCWL and the FSAW.

As a temporary measure, until the next conference could elect a new executive, Dora Tamana of the ANCWL in Cape Town took over the position of acting secretary from Ray Alexander. Cecilia Rosier, a member of COD, took over as acting treasurer from Hetty McLeod, who had been banned at the same time as Alexander. Neither temporary appointments proved satisfactory; Rosier's work was hampered by ill-health, while for several months of 1955 Dora Tamana was overseas with Lilian Ngoyi on a tour sponsored by the WIDF. For both women, this tour—first to an international congress of women in Lausanne, Switzerland, and then to East Germany, China, the USSR and England—was an unforgettable experience. It meant, however, that the FSAW was without a full-time secretary at an important time once again.

Then, in March 1955, the NEC was further damaged when Ida Mtwana resigned her position as national president. The reasons for this are obscure. Personality clashes seem to have played a part, and, according to one informant, some members of the ANC felt that Mtwana should not be national president of both the ANCWL and the FSAW at the same time—that in some way there was a clash between these roles. However, after 1956 Ngoyi was able to combine both positions quite happily, so this explanation is not an entirely adequate one.[9] In place of Mtwana, Gladys Smith, vice-president of the FSAW for the Cape region, took over as acting president. She had neither the dynamism nor the following to prove an effective head. Not long after this, in October 1955, Dora Tamana, acting secretary, was herself banned, and for the next ten months the double responsibility of president and secretary fell on Smith.

An inexperienced and insecure NEC exacerbated the problems of maintaining communications between the centre and the distant regional committees. From the very beginning, in 1954/5, the NEC was complaining of inadequate or non-existent communications with Natal, the Eastern Cape and Kimberley: 'It is sickening how these people never acknowledge letters or report on anything', grumbled a Cape Town correspondent in mid-1955.[10] Poor communications and instability within the NEC hindered the establishment of strong, centralised identity and control within the FSAW. In a report made to the WIDF in early 1956, the Transvaal region of the FSAW commented that it had become 'to some extent an autonomous body, acting frequently on its own initiative in response to prevailing national and regional situations and pressures', although it did maintain links 'as closely as possible under the circumstances' with the head office in Cape Town.[11]

The weaknesses of the NEC proved damaging to the organisation. A few weeks after Alexander's banning, she described the general position as 'serious'.[12] In May 1955, she expressed her private misgivings about the NEC in an unaddressed letter to a Transvaal member of the FSAW: 'Am very unhappy about the NEC. . . they do not show enough responsibility'.[13] At that stage she was already urging the transfer of the head office to Johannesburg as a remedy. By mid-1955 it had become clear to others that Cape Town was not a suitable venue for the head office, and the idea to shift it to Johannesburg, the Congress heartland and political storm-centre of the country, began to gain support.

Organisational shortcomings were not confined to the NEC. Lack of funds meant that nowhere could the FSAW employ a full-time organiser. During 1955 there was discussion on employing Lilian Ngoyi to do this job, but lack of funds meant that the idea had to be shelved. All regions depended heavily on the work of a few dedicated volunteers to keep their day-to-day affairs in order. Many women did not have the necessary education or experience to keep an organisation running smoothly, and this increased the load on the women that did.

Some of the difficulties that the FSAW experienced related directly to the fact that it was an organisation of women. Members' family and household responsibilities frequently interfered with their political commitments. Some husbands resented their wives spending time at meetings and made it difficult or impossible for them to attend. Few black women could afford babysitters, and FSAW women who had small or sick children to care for found it awkward to get away from home. In April 1955, for instance, Josie Palmer missed two Transvaal committee meetings, the first because her daughter was ill, the second because her babysitter arrived too late for her to catch the train.[14] Women also faced problems with transport; private cars were a luxury in the black townships, while public transport was inadequate and often dangerous, particularly for women travelling alone at night. Helen Joseph was one of the few women in the FSAW to have a car of her own—an asset that added greatly to her efficiency, and one she donated gladly to Congress business.

This over-dependence on a few key women hampered the work of the organisation. The Transvaal region, for instance, struggled to cope in early 1955 when its secretary, Helen Joseph, was out of the country on an overseas tour for a few months. In February it failed to keep an appointment with the Johannesburg city council to discuss the issue of rents. Several days later, on the 15th February, a council official wrote to the FSAW to enquire why the appointment had not been kept—but not till the 18th April, over two months later, did the FSAW post off its reply, making apologies and requesting a further appointment. Its excuse for its failure to communicate with the council promptly was that its secretary had been overseas and postal arrangements in her absence had been 'unsatisfactory'.[15]

The Membership Issue

A further and major stumbling block in this early period arose over the question of membership. There were two alternatives. Either the FSAW could seek its own mass membership or it could base itself on a federal form, acquiring its members indirectly through each of its affiliated member organisations. The matter was not settled at the inaugural conference. A draft constitution proposing the first alternative—a mass, individual membership—was circulated but failed to win overall approval. Ray Alexander, and later the NEC based in Cape Town, supported this constitution, but Ida Mtwana and, it would seem, the ANCWL in the Transvaal, wanted a federal structure. The debate over this issue was a protracted one that was not easily resolved. Both sides fought stubbornly for their viewpoint to prevail.

In September 1954 Alexander wrote to Mtwana to set out the reasons why she felt an individual membership was preferable. Her biggest concern was that if the FSAW were to be based on affiliated groups only, it would exclude many women who were not members of existing organisations or for whom no such organisations existed. Here Alexander referred specifically to Indian women in Natal, many of whom were not members of the Indian Congress, and to 'Coloured' women who were without a separate organisation of their own. A further consideration—and one which her own banning had already highlighted—was that individuals banned from affiliated organisations would thereby be banned from the FSAW as well.[16] (A point which she did not raise but which became pertinent later on, was that if an affiliated organisation were to be banned, the FSAW would be deprived of a large number of members at one blow.)

In opposing Alexander, Mtwana spoke on behalf of the Transvaal ANCWL, acting, apparently, on the instructions of the provincial ANC. Their main fear was that if the FSAW were constituted on the basis of an individual membership, it would compete against the ANCWL to the detriment of the latter. In taking this position, the ANC revealed a degree of ambivalence towards the FSAW that it would never entirely overcome. While supporting and welcoming the entry of women into the national liberation movement, it was anxious to retain control over their activities— a control it could exercise effectively over the Women's League but not so successfully over an independent FSAW.

At the heart of the debate between these two alternatives there thus lay a matter of central importance—the relationship between the FSAW and ANC; the relationship between the women's movement and the senior partner in the national liberation movement. The ANC was adamant on this issue and finally, reluctantly, the individual membership group yielded towards the end of 1954. They conceded not because they had been convinced by the other group's arguments but because they realised that without the support of the ANC, the women's movement would be isolated from the Congress Alliance. This would be detrimental to the women's movement and also, in the long run, to the general liberation struggle itself. Writing to the Transvaal region of the Federation in November 1954, Dora Tamana, by then acting secretary in the place of the banned Alexander, stated:

> We believe that this opposition to individual membership is due to a fear that if our organisation becomes a mass organisation, it will draw women away from the ANC and perhaps lead to divided loyalties. We do not think there is any justification for this fear, but we might not be able to dispel it easily or quickly. It is only through our work that we shall be able to prove that we have no wish to compete with other organisations. . . We have therefore decided to make this special concession and exception for the Transvaal.[17]

In a report to the WIDF in early 1956, the FSAW made it clear why it was prepared to accept ANC seniority and work within the structures it laid down: 'The African women as the overwhelmingly largest racial group must always form the main basis of a multi-racial women's organisation.' Furthermore, 'Any women's organisation that stands outside this (the national liberation) struggle must stand apart from the mass of women.'[18]

In this issue the superior weight of the ANC within the Congress Alliance prevailed. By insisting on a federal structure for the women's movement, the ANC effectively stamped that movement with the multiracial structure of the Congress Alliance. The FSAW was never, strictly speaking, a non-racial organisation, although in practice, colour consciousness played very little part in its affairs. This was because it was made up of the ethnically based bodies of the Congress Alliance—the African National Congress, the Indian Congress, the white Congress of Democrats and so on. Each of these retained their identity upon affiliating to the

FSAW. In a truly non-racial organisation, colour, 'race', ethnicity would have played no part in determining membership. After 1955 the Africanists within the ANC denounced this multiracialism of the Congress Alliance as another form of apartheid, since colour was still a dominant criterion. On the available material, it does not appear that an ideological debate between multi- or non-racialism was at issue in the FSAW in 1954/55. The major concern of the supporters of an individual membership was simply to ensure that the FSAW did not lose out on potential members.

On several occasions in subsequent years, the FSAW pointed to its federal structure to allay fears within the ANC that it wished to rival the ANCWL, fears which never subsided completely. Thus Marcelle Goldberg, Transvaal president of the FSAW in 1959, wrote: 'I would like to remind you that the Federation. . . is not an organisation set up in opposition to those already existing organisations. . . whilst the ANC Women's League struggles specifically for the rights of African women, the Federation by its very nature and composition. . . strives to bring all women together.'[19] On these occasions it appeared to argue that the affiliation-only measure had been adopted by design specifically to prevent competition with other organisations. This line overlooked the very vigorous opposition to a federal structure that existed within the organisation in 1954/5. Even once the principle had been conceded in November 1954, the Cape Town region continued to query it. The matter was not finally resolved until the second national conference in August 1956. There a constitution was adopted which made it clear that the FSAW was a 'federation. . . open to organisations or groups of females above the age of 18 years'.[20]

Even once the membership question had been settled, the actual affiliation of organisations to the FSAW proceeded very slowly. Like the ANC itself, the FSAW experienced difficulty in turning general sentiments of support into formal membership. COD was the first of the Congresses to affiliate formally, in June 1955, more than a year after the inaugural conference.[21] Towards the end of 1955 the FSAW sent out a reminder notice to the other Congresses. Despite this, by June 1956 none of them had joined up officially and the FSAW was obliged to send out yet another circular, urging them to attend to the matter. Later that year the Food and Canning Workers Union complied, but it was not till April 1957 that the FSAW could report that all the Congress groups had finally paid their affiliation fees of £1. 1s.[22]

It does not seem that there was outright opposition to affiliating to the FSAW within the Congress Alliance, although certain factions, mainly within the Transvaal ANC, were critical of the organisation and the role it was coming to play. More important in explaining the delay was the fact that member organisations were either too poorly organised to deal with the administrative detail of their formal affiliation promptly, or else, as suggested earlier, did not see the new women's organisation as a particular priority. However, even though the members of the Congress Alliance were slack about affiliation, this did not prevent the FSAW from acting on the assumption of Congress membership from the start. It was always included in Congress activities and its own demonstrations were seen as part and parcel of the national liberation struggle by the Alliance.

Interestingly, however, the FSAW was not granted official representation on the national consultative committee [NCC] of the Alliance. This committee was the highest policy-making body within the Alliance, and all member organisations were represented on it. The reason given for the exclusion of the FSAW was that it already had representation through each of its member organisations; to give it a separate representative of its own would be duplication. This reason overlooked the fact that the FSAW had been formed specifically to represent the interests of women because it was felt that these were not being adequately met in the already existing structures. The exclusion of the FSAW from the NCC pointed to a certain unease about the organisation, a prejudice against women becoming too prominent rather than a deliberate policy of excluding them. However, Helen Joseph was already a member of the NCC, representing COD, and thus could act as spokeswoman for the FSAW; and, in practice, the FSAW liaised closely with the NCC on many campaigns.

Relations with the Black Sash

Outside of the Congress Alliance, the FSAW failed to elicit any positive response from other women's organisations during this period. Its open association with the national liberation movement and its commitment to the overthrow of white minority rule alienated it from apolitical women's groups (church organisations, the NCW and NCAW for instance) as well as non-Congress political groups. Black political organisations which were not linked to the Congress Alliance would have nothing to do with it. The most significant of these was probably the NEUM, which had a firm hold amongst 'Coloured' activists within the Western Cape. Liberal white organisations also shied away from too open an association with the Alliance.

In 1955 a small group of predominantly English-speaking, middle-class white women formed a new political organisation which the FSAW hoped would ally itself with them. This was the 'Women's Defence of the Constitution League', later the Black Sash. It was a tiny action group formed specifically to protest against the machievellian tactics that the government had adopted to force its 'Separate Representation of Voters Bill' through a parliament it did not yet totally dominate. In order to amend the South African constitution so as to eliminate common roll voting rights for 'Coloureds' in the Cape, the government needed a two-thirds majority of both houses of parliament sitting together. The principle was the same as in 1936, when African voters in the Cape had lost the franchise. A significant section of the white electorate had far greater sympathy for qualified 'Coloured' voters in 1956 than they had had for qualified African voters in 1936, however, and supporters of the Cape franchise, both black and white, put up a strong rearguard fight.

This was one of the major political issues within the white community at the time. Failing to acquire the necessary majority in parliament or, subsequently, gain judicial approval for its proposed constitutional amendments, the government turned to constitutional bulldozing. It increased the number of government-appointed judges in the appeal court, packed the upper house, the senate, with additional nominated senators for the duration of the constitutional wrangle, and finally placed the sovereignty of parliament above that of the judiciary.

The women who joined the 'Defence of the Constitution League' were shocked by this display of power politics—less by the actual attack on the franchise rights of the 'Coloureds', however, than by the attack on the constitution itself. They aimed to focus public attention on what was happening and demonstrate their disapproval; and, considering their small numbers, they succeeded admirably in both. They quickly developed a characteristic style of demonstration—silent, orderly stands and all-night vigils by women outside public buildings in the main urban centres. To drive home their point that the integrity and dignity of the constitution were being destroyed, the women wore black mourning sashes draped across one shoulder—hence the nickname, the Black Sash. This title soon came to replace the more cumbersome 'Women's Defence of the Constitution League' as their official name. The sight of white, middle-class women—well-dressed, well-spoken, well-behaved—demonstrating against the government outraged many of its supporters. Frequently the women were exposed to verbal abuse and threats of violence. Not only were they defying the government, they were also defying a set of unwritten rules about what was seemly and proper conduct for women. And, as their dress and manner made clear, these were women who ought to have known better.

Many supporters of the Congress Alliance, particularly the whites, were cheered by this public display of opposition to the government amongst whites. The FSAW had high hopes initially that it would draw the Black Sash into its organisation. White members of the FSAW developed links with the Black Sash and attended several of its demonstrations. All attempts to strengthen and formalise these links failed, however. Most members of the Black Sash looked askance at the Congress Alliance as a radical and potentially subversive organisation. As originally conceived, the Black Sash was essentially a conservative organisation. It was formed to protect the constitution, not to seek radical change; its members were anti-Nationalist but certainly not pro-majority rule.

After 1956, once its original purpose had been defeated with the passage of the Separate Representation of Voters Act, the Black Sash faced a crisis of identity. This split the organisation and paved the way for closer consultation with the FSAW. A small, more liberal core of women came to the fore, women who wanted the Black Sash to continue as a watchdog organisation that would protest against further inroads in civil liberties. Those women who had been attracted to the organisation over the constitutional issue only disagreed; they felt that there was no further purpose for the Black Sash and it should disband. When they failed to bring this about, they withdrew from the organisation.

The Black Sash, an even smaller but more cohesive body than before, survived this exodus of members. It continued to protest against legislation and government actions that infringed the rule of law and individual rights—bannings, detentions, inroads on press freedom etc. Over the years it shifted to a more genuinely liberal position; its preoccupation throughout the 1950s, however, was with white politics—white public opinion, white political parties and, essentially, white solutions to the political conflict in South Africa. Although it became more amenable towards the FSAW after 1956, it was still chary of too close an identification with the Congress Alliance. For its own part, despite these early rebuffs, the FSAW continued to cultivate contact with the Black Sash. It felt that it was important to try and broaden its support amongst white women. This was in keeping with its goal of an open, multi-racial organisation embracing all South African women.

Early Campaigns—Rents, Sophiatown, Bantu Education

Repressive action against important leaders, organisational shortcomings, the problems of organising women—these were major difficulties which always plagued the FSAW. Yet from the start it showed a remarkable ability to circumvent them and, with minimal resources, get involved in a programme of action.

In 1954/5 the FSAW saw its most important task as establishing regional committees and building up a local following. It recognised that the most effective way of building up support was to take up issues that affected women directly, and in 1954 it chose to make the question of rising rents in local council housing its chief campaign. Both the Cape Town and Johannesburg regions held rentals conferences during November and the NEC urged other regions to make this a national campaign: 'In this work we can establish a united campaign with other women's organisations, as the women feel bitter about these rent increases.'[23]

The rentals campaign does not appear to have been a marked success, perhaps because the FSAW was still finding its feet. By that stage only the Transvaal and Cape Western regions had functioning committees; the Cape Eastern and Natal committees took longer to establish themselves. Furthermore, rising rentals was not an issue that was taken up by the Congress Alliance in general. More important as politicising issues among women at that time were three campaigns being run concurrently under the auspices of the ANC and the Alliance. Two of these, against the Group Areas Act and the Bantu Education Act, held a particular appeal for women, since they related directly to their homes and their children. The third campaign was a major event in the Congress calendar for 1955. This was to organise a 'Congress of the People' in June 1955, a mass gathering of Congress delegates from all over the country—a kind of 'People's Parliament'. At this gathering, the manifesto of the Congress Alliance, the 'Freedom Charter', was first presented to the public for scrutiny and debate. The involvement of the FSAW in the first two campaigns will be considered in this chapter; their contribution to the Congress of the People in the next.

Both the Group Areas Act of 1950 and the Bantu Education Act of 1953 were key supports in the edifice of racial segregation that the Nationalist government was constructing. The Group Areas Act went far beyond earlier measures aimed at achieving residential segregation between the various 'races'. In terms of this act, municipal areas were to be divided into different 'group areas' for whites, Asiatics, 'Coloureds' and Africans, the four official 'races' of apartheid theory. The Minister of the Interior was empowered to proclaim any area for the exclusive occupation of one particular group—and once such an area had been proclaimed, all people who did not qualify to remain there had to move out.

Inevitably, very few whites were affected by the act. The burden fell most heavily on 'Coloured' communities in the Western Cape and Indian communities in Natal and on the Rand (Africans were, for the most part, already confined to segregated residential areas in terms of the Urban Areas Act of 1923). The act brought misery and financial loss to hundreds and thousands of people who were forced to give up their homes and properties in 'proclaimed' areas and move to bleak, raw townships on the edges of town. Thousands of people were left homeless because government and municipal housing schemes could not keep pace with the huge demand for housing that the forced removals created. These people were pushed into increasingly overcrowded lodgings or driven to become squatters in self-erected 'shantytowns' on vacant land. Settled communities were torn apart, areas that were under threat of removal were neglected by city councils, landlords and tenants and degenerated into slums. Cape Town, where an intricate pattern of 'Coloured', white and mixed areas had woven itself together over a period of three hundred years, was one of the cities hardest hit by the Group Areas Act, and entire neighbourhoods were destroyed.

The act was implemented in a piecemeal fashion over many years. The Congress Alliance found it difficult to co-ordinate and sustain resistance to it, even though it singled it out as an important issue to fight. During the 1950s, one of the most notorious and passionately opposed removals scheme under this act was the so-called 'Western Areas Removals Scheme', centred on Sophiatown on the Rand. Sophiatown, the black area to be cleared for white development, was an ANC stronghold. It was a rough, tough area, but it had a vitality and community spirit that set it apart from government-planned and controlled townships. Furthermore, many residents held freehold title to their properties, title they would lose in the new townships to which they were to be moved. When it was announced that the area would be cleared, starting in February 1955, residents vowed they would fight rather than move. The ANC declared its support for them and the stage appeared set for a major confrontation with the government.

On the eve of the move, popular speculation as to the form resistance would take ran wild. To counteract this, the authorities produced an enormous showing of force that completely overpowered any attempts by the people to challenge the removals. The anticipated leadership from the ANC never materialised and popular defiance fizzled out miserably.

It took many years before Sophiatown was finally destroyed—and the new white suburb of Triomf (Triumph) installed in its place—but the first round of removals broke the unity of the community and shackled its spirit of opposition. Thereafter further resistance was easily smothered.

For the ANC it was a humiliating and demoralising defeat. However, although this was a setback for the Congress Alliance as a whole, the ANCWL and the FSAW benefited from the campaign. The public meetings and angry discussion which preceded the removals had a politicising effect on local women, who saw their families' lives disrupted, their homes threatened. Many women joined the ANCWL in Sophiatown as a result. This branch remained a strong and active one throughout the 1950s. In March 1955, the magazine *Drum* commented on one effect of the Sophiatown evictions: 'African women too are appearing more and more at Congress meetings, particularly in Sophiatown where the present move to Meadowlands has aroused great interest.'[24]

The Congress campaign against Bantu Education was, in the short term, more successful. Yet ultimately here too the Alliance failed to produce a strategy that could harness the strong popular discontent into a coherent and effective method of resisting the new measures. The Bantu Education Act of 1953 transferred control over African education from the provinces and private (mainly church) organisations to the central government. Henceforth all facets of African education fell under the control of the Department of Native Affairs and were brought in line with the apartheid system. 'Education must train and teach people in accordance with their opportunities in life, according to the sphere in which they live', said Dr H.E. Verwoerd, then Minister of Native Affairs, when he introduced the bill in parliament.[25] Blacks rejected the act as a blatant attempt to impose an inferior educational system on them, one designed to perpetuate their role as the suppliers of cheap labour for white prosperity. Black women, concerned about the opportunities open to their children, felt particularly strongly about it. In a memorable phrase, Lilian Ngoyi likened black mothers to hens that laid eggs, only to see them taken away from them for others to use. In exactly the same way, the Bantu Education Act would take away and destroy their children.

In response to the act, the ANC launched a boycott of Bantu Education schools. This achieved good results initially, particularly on the Rand and in the Eastern Cape. It proved difficult to sustain over any length of time, however. The main difficulty lay in supplying parents and children with an acceptable alternative to Bantu Education—and since no African school was legal unless it was registered with the Department of Native Affairs, the ANC could not merely set up private schools. It made serious attempts, with the support of the Alliance, including the FSAW, to devise an alternative educational movement in the form of 'Cultural Clubs' for the children who had withdrawn from Bantu Education schools. These clubs were probably at their most effective in the Eastern Cape, where it was reported in 1956 that over 4,000 children were still boycotting classes.[26]

Club leaders were ingenious about devising ways of teaching children

without any of the trappings of education that would label their classes
as schools and hence illegal—books, paper, blackboards, pencils. Helen
Joseph helped organise conferences on the Rand and in the Eastern Cape
where techniques could be passed on—'arithmetic by look-and-see. . .
with pebbles and sand-writing. . . multiplication tables. . . translated into
African songs'.[27] Teachers and parents were enthusiastic at first but the
limitations of the clubs as viable educational alternatives in the long term
soon became clear. This, coupled with intimidation of leaders and harrassment of the clubs by the police, finally destroyed the campaign. Bantu
Education remained a potentially expiosive issue, deeply despised and
resented, but by 1957 the first round of protests against its implementation had petered out.

The failure of these campaigns was damaging to ANC morale. It also
fuelled the criticisms of the Africanist faction within the Congress. Yet
despite the defeat of these campaigns, they undoubtedly contributed to
a growth in political consciousness and militancy amongst black women.
In the same way that the rising cost of living and the housing shortage
during the second world war had drawn women into political organisations, the Bantu Education Act and the Group Areas Act forced women
to take stock of the wider political situation in which their daily lives
were located. Both acts impinged directly on black women in their homes
where they could not be ignored or overlooked.

These campaigns coincided with the preparations for the Congress
of the People. The beneficial effects of this activity could be seen in an
escalation in interest in the FSAW. In March 1955 the Cape Town region
reported encouragingly on a recruitment drive it had launched locally,
that it had been 'hard work, but the results are excellent in many ways'.[28]
In May Ray Alexander wrote to the Transvaal Regional Committee that
she was 'glad to hear that your end is livening up, so is our end too'.[29] The
NEC was still experiencing difficulties with the other regions. Earlier, in
1955, the NEC had complained that the Eastern Cape and Natal regions
appeared to be dormant. The Congress of the People, held on the 25th
adn 26th June, provided the FSAW with the focus of activity it needed
to rally women in those areas and revive their interest in a broad women's
movement. It gave women an opportunity to articulate the demands that
they felt should be included in the 'Freedom Charter'. It also established
the credentials of the FSAW within the Congress Alliance more securely.

Notes

1. D. Lewis, *African Trade Unions and the South African State, 1947–1953*.
2. FSAW circular No. 6, FSAW A2.
3. FSAW, *Strijdom, you have struck a rock*, p. 1.
4. 'Report of the Transvaal region of the Federation of South African Women to
    the Bureau of the Women's International Democratic Federation' (hereinafter
    'Report to the WIDF'), FSAW E.
5. FSAW correspondence, 18.2.56, FSAW BII.
6. *Population Census*, 1951, vol. I, pp. 46, 47, UG 42-1955.

7. M. Horrell, *Legislation and Race Relations*, p. 29.
8. See *New Age*, 24.3.55, 21.8.55, 1.3.56, 7.6.56.
9. Interview with V. Mngomo.
10. FSAW correspondence, 19.8.55, FSAW BII.
11. 'Report to the WIDF', p. 1, FSAW E.
12. FSAW correspondence, 15.10.54, FSAW BII.
13. *Ibid.*, 12.5.55.
14. FSAW correspondence, 4/55, FSAW BII.
15. FSAW correspondence with Johannesburg city council, 5.2.55, 15.2.55, 18.4.55, FSAW A2.
16. FSAW correspondence, 2.9.54, Ray Alexander to Ida Mtwana, FSAW BII.
17. FSAW correspondence, 6.11.54, FSAW BII.
18. 'Report to the WIDF', p. 1, FSAW E.
19. From 'President's Report to the Provincial Conference of the Tvl. FSAW', 27.1.59, FSAW A13.
20. This is taken from the second 'Draft Constitution' found among the FSAW papers (FSAW A7) and the one apparently adopted in Johannesburg in August 1956.
21. 'Statement for the Information of COD Members', p. 1, FSAW A7.
22. See *The Work of the Federation of South African Women*, pamphlet, April 1957, FSAW E.
23. NEC circular, 21.9.54, FSAW A2.
24. *Drum*, March 1955: 'New Faces in Congress', p. 24.
25. M. Horrell, *op. cit.*, p. 65.
26. 'Report on a tour of the major centres of the Union, submitted to the National Consultative Committee for Discussion', p. 3, FSAW BII.
27. H. Joseph, *Tomorrow's Sun*, p. 76.
28. FSAW correspondence, 24.3.55, FSAW BII.
29. FSAW correspondence, 26.5.55, FSAW BII.

15

'We Have Decided to Join Battle with Verwoerd': The Congress of the People and the First Gathering at Pretoria in 1955

The FSAW and the Congress of the People

The FSAW was first approached by the NCC to assist with the Congress of the People in August 1954. It accepted the opportunity eagerly:

> It is our responsibility to gather the women of South Africa to acquaint them with our aims, to acquaint them with the Congress of the People so that they, too, the women, can play their part in the struggle for freedom.[1]

The organisers of the congress intended it to serve a dual function—to act as a demonstration of mass popular support for the Alliance and its policies, and to provide local organisers with a focus round which to mobilise Congress branches and recruit new members.

The FSAW saw the potential of the congress in much the same terms, as a means of mobilising women specifically. It was concerned that its role at the congress should not be the one generally assigned to women at such functions, in the kitchen and behind the scenes—'bottlewashers', as one woman put it when discussing this concern.[2] Nevertheless, when requested by the NCC to assist with the accommodation of delegates—which many Congress men clearly saw as the most appropriate area for the women to work in—it agreed. It did so because it felt that this would make its organisation known among the township women who were approached to accommodate the delegates. It was a very large undertaking. Space was needed for over 2000 delegates: 'It was never a question of a "spare room", for there were no spare rooms in the tiny African township homes', recalls Helen Joseph. 'We looked for houses where room could be found to spread a mattress on the floor; delegates would bring their own blankets.'[3] The Federation felt satisfied with the results of its undertaking. According to a report made by the Transvaal FSAW afterwards, 'this work brought the Federation to large numbers of African women and won for it the high status which it did not previously possess.'[4] Subsequently at all major Congress conferences—the National Workers' Conference in 1958, the Anti-Pass Conference in 1959—the FSAW, with the ANCWL, took responsibility for the accommodation of delegates.

In mobilising women for the congress, the FSAW urged its regions to hold house meetings and local conferences at which the idea could be popularised, women's delegates elected and the demands of women for incorporation within the proposed 'Freedom Charter' formulated. One of the best documented of these meetings took place in Johannesburg, in the Trades Hall, on the 29th May 1955. Over 200 women attended, with Josie Palmer, by then president of the FSAW in the Transvaal, in the chair. The main business of the meeting was to discuss and approve a draft pamphlet entitled 'What Women Demand', a list of demands that the FSAW wished to submit to the convenors of the congress for incorporation within the 'Freedom Charter'.

'What Women Demand' was revealing about FSAW thinking on several important issues. It was a more detailed exposition of ideas already contained in the 'Women's Charter' and the FSAW's 'Aims'. It focused mainly on issues relating to health care, education, housing, social services and food, discussing its demands concerning these in some detail. For instance, the paragraph setting out demands on housing conditions specified controlled rents; indoor sanitation; water supply; street and domestic lighting; adequate roads; storm water drainage; 'the right to live where we choose'; the right to ownership of property; provision of parks, recreation facilities, public conveniences and adequate public transport.[5] That it was felt necessary to list so many basic amenities was testament enough to the grossly inadequate living conditions that women had to deal with in the townships. The document did not neglect the emancipation of women. In the second last paragraph a strong demand was made for full equality for women with men in all spheres—political, legal, economic and marital. In conclusion, the document asserted: 'We demand. . . that there shall be PEACE AND FREEDOM FOR OUR CHILDREN.'

'What Women Demand' provoked far more discussion within Congress circles than the 'Women's Charter' had done. Two aspects were particularly controversial. One was a paragraph dealing with the question of a fair distribution of land amongst all the people of South Africa. The claim for such a redistribution, as well as for 'improved farming methods' and 'sufficient food for all people' were quite straightforward and provoked no comment. So too was the demand for an end to the migrant labour system 'which destroys our family life'. What did provoke strong criticism was a call for the provision of medical, educational and shopping facilities in the reserves. A group of Congress supporters saw that implicit in this demand, whether intentional or not, was an acceptance of the notion of separate reserves for African and the political and economic discrimination and impoverishment that went with that. They criticised the women strongly for their failure to think the issue through clearly.

Subsequently, in a letter to *New Age* in July 1955, the FSAW accepted their criticisms and retracted this demand.[6] In looking at the reserves, the FSAW was stepping on risky ideological ground: it had certainly not worked through all the implications of its appeal for improved facilities in those areas, nor come to grips with the significance of the homeland policy of the Nationalist government. Nevertheless, in retracting its position so quickly, the FSAW was being unnecessarily humble. The reserves presented the Congress Alliance with a complex and contradictory set of political and strategic problems with no simple solutions. It was what made the 'Bantustan' policy of apartheid so diabolically clever. Merely ignoring those areas because they formed part of an unacceptable policy did not solve the problems of basic survival confronting the people living there. Nor did it assist those people to develop their own strategies for resisting the very policies which kept them in an impoverished and dependent position. It was much easier to criticise the FSAW than it was to offer viable alternatives for the millions of people living—trapped—in the reserve areas.

The second controversial aspect of 'What Women Demand' was a call for birth control clinics. Sex and sexuality were not socially sanctioned topics for public discussion, and, in raising this issue at a public meeting, the FSAW was breaking new ground. More than propriety was involved, however. For many, possibly most, Congress supporters, both male and female, female sexuality was totally bound up with the notion of childbearing and male hegemony. The idea of a woman being able to control whether and when she would have children challenged such deepseated attitudes and provoked a flurry of discussion both within and without the FSAW.

It is clear that the call for birth control clinics was formulated by the organisers of the meeting and did not come from the floor. Its inclusion in the list of women's demands sparked off a lively discussion which touched upon many fundamental issues relating to the position of women in the family. The response from the floor was mixed. Attitudes ranged from approval—'Once you have children every day it is ruining your life,' . . . 'We should instruct children in this. All the children we have today are children from school children and. . . from our daughters'—to a fear that birth control would disrupt established patterns of sexual relationships: 'We cannot do it if our husbands want children,' said one anxious delegate. Josie Palmer, in the chair, was anxious to avoid any impression that 'this very delicate matter' was being forced upon anybody: 'Those who accept it, OK! Those who feel it is against their conscience, very well.'[7] The controversy was not confined to the women's meeting. Virginia Mngomo, an ANCWL activist from Alexandra township outside Johannesburg, recalls how some of the men in the ANC reacted with derision when they heard that birth control had been included in the women's list of demands. They could not see the question of contraception as a serious political issue—or perhaps they saw it as too serious an issue.[8]

Although women were thus drawn into the planning of the Congress of the People, their participation at the actual meeting was limited. Close on three thousand delegates assembled at the congress, held at Kliptown near Johannesburg on June 25th and 26th, 1955. Of these delegates, approximately one quarter were women (721 out of a total of 2,848).[9] Women made few speeches from the floor, and the only female speaker on the platform was Helen Joseph, who was then Transvaal secretary for the FSAW and a member of the national executive for COD. She was given the task of proposing the clause on 'houses, security and comfort' in the 'Freedom Charter'.[10] The convenors of the congress clearly regarded this as pre-eminently a women's concern, a view that the FSAW's own formulation of 'What Women Demand' endorsed.

The 'Freedom Charter' itself was a document for liberal, democratic reform. It stated in general terms the principle of equal rights for all, without discrimination on the grounds of 'colour, race, sex or belief'.[11] For the delegates at Kliptown, the most significant of these categories was race, and it was with the resolution of this that the charter was mainly concerned: 'South Africa belongs to all who live in it, black and white.' Sex discrimination was dwarfed by these concerns and the congress did not pay particular attention to the position of women in society. Significantly, the demand for birth control was not articulated within the 'Freedom Charter'. The closest that it was approached was in the clause dealing with 'houses, security and comfort' which Joseph had proposed. This called for free medical treatment 'with special care for mothers and young children'.[12]

Nevertheless, the existence of the FSAW ensured that women were not totally excluded or overlooked at the congress. Their participation, though limited, was not insignificant, and in the organisation of the event they had been singled out as a necessary and important area for preliminary work.

The First Gathering of Women at Pretoria, October 1955

By the second half of 1955 the Federation was asserting itself with far more confidence, particularly in the Johannesburg region. It had weathered the worst of its initial organisational problems and had established itself as a going concern within the Congress Alliance. Involvement of women in politics, in the ANC in particular, was on the upswing. In September 1955 the organisation received a further boost when the Eastern Cape region finally established a FSAW committee, at a meeting held to report back to Congress women on the Congress of the People.

Until this time, most of the momentum for FSAW activities had come from the leaders at the top. Now rank and file members began pushing for a more assertive stand. This first appeared publicly in the Transvaal at a report-back meeting on the Congress of the People, held in August 1955. The women present were looking for some way of dramatising their opposition to Bantu Education, the Group Areas Act and several other contentious issues. Shortly before, the Black Sash had organised an all-night vigil by members outside the Union Buildings in Pretoria, the executive seat of government. This had been in protest against the Separate Representation of Voters Bill and related issues. Taking her cue from this protest, a woman at the FSAW report-back meeting suggested they do the same—organise a mass rally of women to go to Pretoria and present their complaints to the government directly. There would, however, be one crucial difference between their rally and that of the Black Sash: whereas that of the Black Sash had been for white women only, theirs would be open to all women to join.[13]

The motion was enthusiastically adopted by the meeting. To many of those in leadership positions, both within the FSAW and the ANC, it appeared overly ambitious. The task of organising such a demonstration was a formidable one. There were fears that the women would not respond in sufficient numbers to make a convincing impact. Previously, similar demonstrations organised by the FSAW and ANCWL had been to Native Commissioners' offices or local municipal authorities; what was being proposed here was a confrontation with the central government itself. Originally the women planned to protest against five issues—Bantu Education, the Group Areas Act, so-called site-and-service housing schemes (whereby the authorities provided housing applicants with a piece of land and minimal services and residents were expected to construct their own shelter), the erosion of civil liberties and the Population Registration Act. This last act stipulated that everybody had to be officially classified and registered as a member of one of the four statutory 'races'. The act underpinned the entire administrative basis of apartheid, and had been the cause of much individual suffering as well. Many people who had lived among 'Coloured' communities all their lives were reclassified as African, with all the extra restrictions on personal mobility, residential and job opportunities and social status that that implied. There were numerous instances of families being torn apart by bureaucratic decree—some members classified 'Coloured', others, even full-blooded relations, classified African.

Then, in September 1955, the potent issue of passes for women burst to the fore again with the announcement that the government intended to start issuing women with reference books from January 1956. With that the scale of the demonstration enlarged dramatically as the women seized upon the impending threat of passes and made it the central issue of their demonstration. Over three years had passed since the Abolition of Passes Act, when the government had been at such pains to deny that it would extend the provision of the act to women. As critics had pointed out at the time, however, this had been a stalling tactic only. In 1952, faced with a volatile and uncertain political situation, with the memory of the anti-pass campaign of 1950/51 and the Defiance Campaign still fresh, the government felt it expedient to tread warily on the question of passes for women. By the end of 1955, however, it no longer felt the same constraints. Its position in parliament and with the white electorate was far more secure. It had some tough new powers with which to counter protest, while the most recent performance of the ANC during the Sophiatown removals and in the campaign against Bantu Education had not been deeply threatening. It is also likely that despite the earlier lessons to the contrary, the deeply chauvinist Nationalist government did not take the prospect of female opposition to passes too seriously. For all these reasons, the government felt itself in a strong position to proceed with the implementation of its pass policy for women.

If the government did expect women to acquiesce relatively quietly to passes after 1956, it made a serious miscalculation; the announcement that reference books would be issued to women set the stage for an unprecedented outburst of popular resistance among them. More than any other issue, the threat of passes stirred an enormous response amongst women and raised their active involvement in politics to new levels. The anti-pass campaign that followed was the most militant and sustained of any of the campaigns waged by the Congress Alliance during the 1950s. Its peak period stretched from late 1955 to 1959 but even in the early 1960s there were still sporadic signs of resistance. The campaign drew on thousands upon thousands of women scattered over the entire country, though concentrated most heavily in the large urban centres.

For the planners of the Pretoria demonstration, the announcement of passes could not have been better timed; it overshadowed the earlier issues and acted as a spur to women to join the demonstration. With this added impetus, Congress doubts about whether the women would be able to pull off such a major demonstration proved completely unfounded. The demonstration that followed on the 27th October 1955 was a resounding success, a landmark in the emergence of the FSAW as a political organisation to be taken seriously. In the face of enormous organisational obstacles, police intimidation and harrassment—including the banning of Josie Palmer a week before the demonstration was due[14]—the FSAW managed to assemble a crowd of between one and two thousand women in the grounds of the Union Building. Most of the women were African, but white, 'Coloured' and Indian women were there in sufficient numbers to make it a more broadly representative gathering. This had special significance for the FSAW. It described the demonstration as 'of historical importance, for it is the first time that women of all races have joined together in such a protest'.[15]

The scale of the protest was doubly impressive in view of all the obstacles the authorities put in the way of the women. In a letter written to the *Pretoria News* the day after the demonstration, Helen Joseph described what the women had had to contend with. In the first place, all the cabinet ministers the FSAW approached for interviews refused to have any dealings with the women. Then the town clerk of Pretoria refused permission for the FSAW to hold a public meeting outside the Union Buildings or organise a procession through Pretoria, on the grounds that it would create a public disturbance and provoke 'feelings of hostility between different races'.[16] Finally, on the day of the demonstration, police and public transport officials combined forces to make it as difficult as possible for the women to reach the Union Buildings. Natalspruit women were refused a license to hire public transport and obliged to walk the eight miles to Germiston before proceeding to Pretoria; Alexandra women travelling on public transport were delayed by police; many women trying to buy railway tickets to Pretoria were refused by the ticket officials; private cars travelling to Pretoria were stopped and the occupants questioned by police; the railways refused to supply extra coaches, while bus companies refused to supply extra buses and transport the women from Pretoria Station to the Union Buildings, a distance of some miles.[17] Yet despite all these counter-measures, well over a thousand women managed to reach Pretoria undeterred by the obstructionist tactics of the authorities. Driving to Pretoria with Ngoyi on the morning of the demonstration, Joseph passed a train heading for that city: '. . . it was filled with African women leaning out of the window and singing in triumph. I couldn't hold back my tears, but they were tears of joy and pride.'[18]

The gathering itself was orderly, the general mood dignified and confident. Joseph described it thus:

> There they were: two thousand women, sitting calmly and quietly in a huge semi-circle on the stone stops of the ampitheatre. It was a hot day, and umbrellas were up against the sun. Babies were unstrapped from their mothers' backs; some were at their mothers' breasts. . . I realised that they had been better than their leaders. They had done what we had not ventured to suggest; they had occupied the ampitheatre, had indeed peacefully stormed the Bastille of the privileged whites. For the Union Buildings were regarded as sacrosanct; not even 'Whites Only' notices were placed there, because in all these years the non-whites had never gathered there, had never thought of doing so. [19]

Since the women were denied access to the cabinet ministers responsible for the various laws they were protesting against, they handed hundreds of individually signed protests to the four leaders of the demonstration— Lilian Ngoyi, Helen Joseph and two other FSAW leaders in the Transvaal, Rahima Moosa and Sophie Williams. These women ducked through the guards at the doors and deposited their armfuls of protests outside each of the ministers' doors.

The impact of the demonstration was considerable. The national press gave it good coverage; for many readers, it was the first time they had heard of the FSAW. Newspaper reporters found something unusual and provocative in the sight of this large, multiracial gathering of women, come together with a common political purpose. Many whites found it impossible to conceive of such a demonstration except as the result of incitement by 'Europeans'. Thus, *Die Vaderland,* a pro-government daily in Pretoria, focused its report on the presence of white women amongst the black crowd, presenting them as the co-ordinators and planners of the demonstration: 'Blanke vroue. . . was doenig met die reelings. . . veral bedrywig om toe te sien dat alles stil en vlot verloop' ('White women. . . were involved in the organisation. . . particularly concerned with seeing that everything went peacefully and smoothly').[20] Prime Minister Strijdom described the demonstration to a women's branch of the Nasionale Jeugbond as 'scandalous because it was incited by Europeans'.[21]

Within the Congress Alliance, at that stage experiencing a slump in the wake of the Congress of the People, the demonstration directed attention to its female membership, and enhanced the prestige of their organisations. One fairly direct result came in December 1955 at the annual national conference of the ANC, when Lilian Ngoyi was elected to the national executive. It was the first time a woman had been elected to such a high position.

For the FSAW, the demonstration was a breakthrough and a major morale-booster that firmly established its credentials as a serious political organisation. In congratulating the Transvaal region on its achievement, the Cape Town branch commented that 'The 27th affair will make many organisations who in the past ignored our letter to reconsider their attitude.'[22] By late 1955, with this achievement behind it, the FSAW and ANCWL were both in a bouyant mood. They were preparing to tackle the anti-pass campaign with vigour and optimism. At a Women's League conference in November, Lilian Ngoyi declared confidently: 'We have decided to join battle with Verwoerd on this issue and we say without the slighest hesitation that we shall defeat the government.'[23]

Notes

1. FSAW circular letter no. 3, 25.8.54, FSAW BII.
2. FSAW correspondence, 1.4.55, FSAW BII.
3. H. Joseph, *Tomorrow's Sun,* p. 59.
4. 'Report to the WIDF', p. 2, FSAW E.
5. FSAW: 'What Women Demand', FSAW IIA. See Appendix C for a copy of the pamphlet.
6. FSAW Letter to the Editor, *New Age,* 9.7.55, FSAW IIA.
7. 'Women's Meeting: Held in the Trades Hall, 30 Kerk Street, Johannesburg, on the 29th May, 1955', pp. 2, 4, 5; Treason Trial exhibit, G771. This document is a police transcript of the proceedings at the meeting.
8. Interview with V. Mngomo.
9. Extract from 'Report of Credentials Committee, Congress of the People', FSAW II A 13.
10. 'Agenda for the Congress of the People', FSAW IIA 8.
11. 'Freedom Charter', FSAW IIA 12.
12. *Ibid.*
13. Evidence of Helen Joseph, *Treason Trial Record,* vol. 66, pp. 14165–66.
14. FSAW correspondence, FSAW C.1.2.
15. FSAW leaflet, FSAW CI 2.
16. FSAW correspondence, FSAW C.1.2.
17. Helen Joseph, letter to the *Pretoria News,* 28.10.55.
18. Helen Joseph, *Tomorrow's Sun,* p. 71.
19. *Ibid.*
20. *Die Vaderland,* 28.10.55.
21. This is mentioned in a letter from L. Ngoyi to the *Rand Daily Mail,* 2.11.55 which dismisses the allegations as 'absolutely unfounded', FSAW CI 2.
22. FSAW correspondence, 17.1.55, FSAW BII.
23. *New Age,* 24.11.55.

16

'You Have Tampered with the Women, You Have Struck a Rock': Anti-Pass Protests in 1956

On this note of militant optimism, a new phase in the history of the FSAW opened. Previously, the FSAW had still been feeling its way. The announcement of reference books for women gave it a focus of action; the anti-pass campaign that followed, an identity. From late 1955, passes for African women dominated all other issues. For the next four to five years most of the FSAW's energies were directed into the anti-pass campaign. The demands of the campaign were such that there was little time for sustained activity in other spheres, and inevitably many of the FSAW's more general aims for improving the position of women in South Africa were neglected. Nevertheless, as the FSAW realised, this was the major issue confronting the majority of South African women and, as such, it took precedence.

The ANC and the Anti-Pass Campaign

The Congress Alliance had always identified passes as a key structure in the political economy of the apartheid state: 'There is nothing in the country that makes an African a prisoner. . . more than the operation of pass laws,' declared a memorandum drawn up by the national consultative committee of the Alliance in October 1956.[1] The FSAW shared this perspective. In organising against passes it was acting on the belief that not till the apartheid state had been dismantled could women begin to emancipate themselves. For this reason, while passes had become an issue of major concern to African women, the fight against them was not a sectarian one; it was a struggle that embraced the whole liberation movement: 'The struggle against the pass laws is not a matter for African women alone; it is not a matter for the African people alone. It is part and parcel of the struggle for liberation.'[2]

The exact demarcation of authority between the FSAW and ANC in the organisation and coordination of the anti-pass campaign was never clear. From the beginning, the ANC regarded itself as ultimately responsible for the campaign, but it was divided on the best tactics to adopt and failed to initiate a well worked-out plan of action. It recognised the importance of broadening the women's anti-pass campaign into a general campaign involving men as well. It also showed some understanding of the political potential in the outspoken rejection of passes that women across the country were displaying. In 1956 the NCC reported:

Clearly the women are in the front rank of the battle now opening. But the

189

struggle is not one for women alone. . . By themselves the women can perhaps resist the latest attacks. But their resistance would be stronger and lead more surely to victory if the menfolk fight with them. . . This must be a joint campaign of men and women, whose aim is to end the pass system and the government which upholds it.[3]

Yet the details of the ANC campaign were not immediately forthcoming. At the annual ANC conference held in December 1955, the ANC postponed making an immediate decision on what line of action it should pursue against reference books. Passes dominated the discussion, but instead of taking steps to capitalise on the mood of resistance sweeping the country, the conference finally avoided the problem. It delegated responsibility for working out a strategy of resistance to a working committee, and postponed all decisions till that committee could report back to a special national conference on passes, scheduled for the Easter weekend of 1956. The failure of the ANC to take the lead straight away was condemned vociferously by the Africanists. They emerged publicly as a dissident faction at this conference. According to *Drum,* 'hot-heads' were urging that resistance to passes should take the form of destroying them, 'but the official ANC line is to work out a careful campaign'.[4]

The FSAW, in contrast, though it never had a clearly worked out long-term strategy, launched immediately upon an extensive campaign of conferences, meetings, demonstrations and local protests as soon as it was announced that passes would be introduced for women. Ultimately it conceded that final authority on the campaign rested with the ANC; in the absence of a clear lead from the men, however, it assumed a large measure of independence, an independence it became increasingly reluctant to yield.

The Anti-Pass Campaign Gets Under Way

From the beginning, the women's opposition to passes kept spilling over the limits laid down by Congress leaders, whether in the ANC or the FSAW. The anti-pass campaign was never a highly centralised political campaign, conceived and managed by a small core of people. It was carried along on the huge groundswell of popular feeling against passes among women, a current that frequently swept the women's leaders along faster than they themselves intended to go.

The announcement in September 1955 that passes were soon to be issued to women precipitated a flurry of activity. The pages of *New Age* in late 1955 and early 1956 were filled with news reports, letters and editorial comment on the gathering momentum of the anti-pass campaigh. 'Will our Women Carry Passes?' asked *Drum* in January 1956—this, it said, was 'the very big question of the year'.[5] In February 1956 it described the impact of the announcement of reference books for women thus:

On the political plane too women have come to the fore. . . For the laws of this country have now started pots and pans rattling in the kitchen and a number of things are on the boil. Passes for the women, for instance, and the schooling of their children under Bantu Education are on their minds.[6]

Women's meetings across the country drew enormous crowds. In Bloemfontein, in November 1955, some 600 people attended an anti-pass meeting. *New Age* described it as the largest meeting ever held there.[7] Elsewhere in the Orange Free State there was a spate of meetings organised by the ANC. These meetings were spirited, optimism high. M. Rantekane, of the ANC Youth League in the small farming town of Bethlehem, reported to *New Age* on an anti-pass meeting they had organised in their community: 'This Sunday seemed as if it was the Day of Freedom. Everybody was shouting Afrika Mayibuye.'[8] In January 1956 Lilian Ngoyi addressed a huge anti-pass meeting in Port Elizabeth. *New Age* estimated the crowd at some 6,000 men and women.[9] In Johannesburg a series of meetings at this time culminated in one organised by the FSAW in March 1956 to commemorate International Women's Day. About 1,000 women were expected, but the final attendance was closer to 2,000 women.[10] The meeting was considered an enormous success, with passes forming the major topic of discussion. In Durban, East London, Cape Town and Germiston there were similar, if smaller, protests and meetings in anticipation of the issuing of passes as well.

The mood amongst women at these meetings was militant. In 1955 Annie Silinga of the ANCWL in Cape Town declared that 'intimidation does not frighten us and we women are prepared to fight these passes until victory is ours.'[11] A pamphlet put out by the Transvaal FSAW to advertise its meeting in March 1956 proclaimed: 'Women do NOT want Pass Laws! We are not prepared to submit to the humiliations and sufferings that Pass Laws bring.'[12] Once again, as in earlier anti-pass campaigns, the threat the pass laws posed to the home was their dominant concern. Alice Kunene, a delegate to an anti-pass conference held on the East Rand in March 1957, spoke for all women when she declared: 'The Pass Laws means the death of our children. The oppression of the Pass Laws is going to bring destruction to our homes.'[13]

The government's response to this show of opposition was to threaten reprisals against any organisation that tried to stop it from issuing passes to women. It did not spell out what it intended to do, merely warned that the 'necessary steps' would be taken.[14] The looming shadow of state intervention had an inhibitory effect on some of the planners within the ANC and helps account for their cautious approach to the question of resistance. It also impelled some FSAW leaders to urge caution. In early 1956, Ray Alexander warned a Transvaal committee member:

Re passes for African women—note I was careful about it not only from the repercussions point of view, but also what it will entail to the African women. We must have greater discussion and appraise the situation carefully.[15]

Pass-Burnings in Winburg

Despite its threat of strong action, the government chose to adopt a very low profile when it first started issuing reference books to women. It deliberately avoided the larger towns, where opposition was most organised, and concentrated instead on the smaller towns and remote country districts of the 'white' countryside. Many women in these areas were ignorant about the implications of the new book that magistrates or employers instructed them to receive. Women on white farms were often gathered up by their boss-cum-landlord and driven into town to be issued with their books by the lorryload—for them to refuse to take a book was particularly difficult because of their dependence on the goodwill of their employers.

The first target in the reference book drive was the small farming town of Winburg in the Orange Free State, a town where, some forty years before, women had demonstrated strenuously against the old Free State pass laws. Mobile vans—the so-called 'Reference Book Units'—entered the district in March 1956 and started issuing books to women in the town and on the farms. At first it seemed as if the strategy of concentrating on the country districts would pay off; officials met with no resistance, and by the 22nd March they had issued 1,429 women with books.[16]

The apparent ease with which this had been achieved was a source of consternation within the Congress Alliance. At the beginning of April, the ANC's special national conference on passes took place in Johannesburg. It was decided then that steps had to be taken to counter the developments at Winburg. At least one ANCWL member from Winburg was present at the conference. The meeting made a deep impression on her. She confessed later to her colleagues back at home, 'Ek het. . . eintlik skaam toe hulle my se julle Winburg vrouens het die stam doodgemaak cor julle die paste gevat het.'[17] ('I was. . . ashamed when they said that you Winburg women had destroyed the tribe by taking passes.')

As a first step, the conference agreed to send senior Congress representatives to Winburg to make contact with the women locally. The following week Lilian Ngoyi and a couple of ANC men arrived quietly in the district. On the 8th April the local ANCWL organised a meeting which Ngoyi attended. Their delegate to the national conference in Johannesburg reported back on that meeting and then the discussion was opened to the floor. Spurred on by the presence of their national leader and more mindful of the national dimension of the pass question, the women were in a militant mood. They decided that only a strong stand could succeed in counteracting the steady progress of the reference book unit through the district—passes already issued would have to be burnt. At the end of the meeting, they collected together their newly-issued reference books and the next day marched with them to the magistrate's office and there publicly burnt them. With this act, the opposition to passes that was simmering throughout the country had burst into open defiance.[18]

The decision to burn the passes was a spontaneous one, coming from the Winburg women themselves. When the ANC representatives left

Johannesburg they were under instructions to avoid any 'rash action'.[19] Once in Winburg, however, they found the mood amongst the women so strong that they decided to go along with it. Nevertheless, the ANC had clearly played a part in bringing the women of Winburg to the point of defiance, by inviting them to send delegates to the national anti-pass conference and sending as important and charismatic a leader as Lilian Ngoyi to assess the situation locally.

The impact of the Winburg pass-burnings was considerable. For the Congress Alliance it came as a great boost to morale after the gloom the initial success of the reference book units had caused—even though the Winburg women had overstepped ANC instructions. The authorities took the defiance very seriously. Numerous women were arrested in Winburg and charged with 'common theft'; in several cases bail was refused.[20] In May 1956 *New Age* reported that women in Winburg were being refused their monthly old-age pension cheques unless they could produce their reference books, the first report of a pressure tactic that later would be widely used.[21]

Following on from Winburg, a huge wave of protests swept the country. In the first seven months of 1956 alone, the FSAW estimated that approximately 50,000 women took part in 38 demonstrations against the pass laws, in 30 different centres.[22] These included Klerksdorp (400 women), Brakpan (2,000 women), Bethlehem (400 women), Johannesburg, Pretoria, Evaton, Ermelo, Port Elizabeth, Kimberley, Durban, Uitenhage.[23] In the smaller towns, these were organised mainly by the local ANC or ANCWL, while the FSAW was active in the major towns. The format of these protests was generally the same. Either the women held mass meetings at which they adopted resolutions condemning and rejecting passes, or they organised mass deputations to the authorities, generally the local Native Commissioner. In addition women boycotted the reference book units as they appeared in their districts. The emphasis was on peaceful demonstrations of opposition and in this early period they met with little counterforce.

Figures put out by the South African Institute of Race Relations at the end of 1956 made it clear that these protests were not succeeding in stopping the reference book units from their work, only in slowing them down. By September 1956 the units had visited 37 small country towns and issued some 23,000 reference books to women—an average of just under 4,000 a month.[24] Seen in an overall context, these figures were a depressing indication that the government machine was moving forward, ponderously but relentlessly. At the time, however, when no reference book unit had dared to show itself in major ANC strongholds, and women all over the country were on the march, 23,000 seemed a pitiful figure compared to the total adult population of African women.

The extent of resistance throughout the country generated considerable optimism within the FSAW; as a mark of its confidence and in memory of the successful demonstration to Pretoria in October 1955, it launched upon an even more ambitious undertaking. It decided to go once again to Pretoria. This time, however, it aimed to gather together not simply women from the Rand, as in 1955, but women from all over the country and as many different organisations as possible. This would be a national protest by women, to drive home to Prime Minister Strijdom their unequivocal opposition to the pass laws.

'Women's Day', August 9th 1956

The proposal to go once again to Pretoria was made in March 1956 at the meeting called by the Transvaal regional committee to celebrate International Women's Day. It was also agreed that the long overdue second national conference would take place in Johannesburg immediately afterwards, to make the long trip to the Rand as worthwhile as possible for the women. By the middle of the year plans for the demonstration were well under way. In July the FSAW sent off a letter to the Prime Minister requesting an interview. Their request was bluntly refused, but the FSAW went ahead with its plans anyway.

In June/July, the NCC sponsored a tour of the main urban centres by four Congress leaders. Helen Joseph and a women by the name of Bertha Mashaba, increasingly prominent in both the FSAW and the ANCWL on the Rand, were asked to go, along with Robert Resha of the ANC and Norman Levy of the Congress of Democrats. Maintaining communication between the widely separated regions of the Congress Alliance was always a problem and the tour was invaluable as a means of bringing a stronger sense of national purpose to the different centres. It also greatly facilitated the planning of the women's demonstration, by then scheduled for August 9th. Joseph and Mashaba used this opportunity to consult with other women in the various centres they visited and to make arrangements to send delegates to the mass gathering.

On the whole, the two women were encouraged by the enthusiasm of the women they met and the signs of activity in the different centres. The weakest of the four FSAW regions they found to be in Durban, where cooperation between the ANC and NIC was described as 'excellent', but COD was extremely weak.[25] Joseph was particularly impressed with the women of the Eastern Cape. She described the 'high standard of ANC organisation' in Port Elizabeth as 'deeply impressive and unequalled in any other area'.[26] The women won her lasting admiration for the lengths to which they were prepared to go to make the demonstration in Pretoria a success. When sceptical ANC men asked them how they intended finding the money to cover the cost of the long journey to the capital, they replied firmly, 'We'll sell our furniture.'[27] With that kind of commitment, the FSAW leaders felt they need not fear the outcome of the demonstration.

Their confidence was not misplaced. The gathering of women at the Union Buildings on the 9th August 1956 was a spectacular success. The FSAW more than reached its goal; vast numbers of women, estimated variously at between six and twenty thousand, managed to make their way to Pretoria and the Union Buildings. Estimates of the number of women present varied according to the reporters degree of sympathy with the demonstration. *Die Vaderland,* an Afrikaans daily, said that estimates varied between 6,000 and 10,000. The *Cape Times,* a more liberal English daily, put the number at 10,000.[28] The FSAW estimated that 20,000 women were present, and this figure has passed into Congress histories of the time.[29] All agreed, however, that it was a gathering of unprecedented size. The *Cape Times* described it as one of the largest crowds ever to assemble at the Union Buildings—'and probably the largest mass gathering of women in the country's history'.[30] The women had come from all over the country. The Reef areas were best represented, but substantial numbers of women came from as far afield as Cape Town, Bloemfontein and Port Elizabeth, travelling by train and chartered bus.

As sheer spectacle, it was an impressive and moving sight. The huge crowd of women filled the amphitheatre before the Union Buildings and overflowed down the steps. Many of the African women wore traditional dress, others wore the Congress colours, green, black and gold; Indian women were clothed in white saris. Many women had babies on their backs, and some domestic workers brought their white employers' children along with them. Throughout the demonstration, the huge crowd displayed a discipline and a dignity that was deeply impressive. Once again, there was nobody from the government to receive the women. For the women gathered outside the office of the Prime Minister, this was a confirmation of their own strength:

> He refused to see us. . . he just ran away, away from us. . . We were proud that we went there, although disappointed not to see him. Still, the message was there. We left our message there. He knew by that. . . we were a lot of people.[31]

To drive home their point, the women left masses of individually signed protests against the pass laws outside Strijdom's office—later, during the Treason Trial, it emerged that the security police removed all these papers before the Prime Minister had even looked at them.[32] After all the protests had been delivered, the women stood in perfect silence for half an hour, before breaking into a triumphant rendition of the ANC anthem, 'Nkosi sikeleli Afrika': 'God bless Africa'.

For many who participated in the demonstration, it formed the emotional highpoint of their political careers, a yardstick by which all other meetings of that nature would be measured. It was 'marvellous , recalls Amina Cachalia, who was there, 'the greatest demonstration either the FSAW or the Congress Alliance generally ever staged'.[33] In a booklet printed shortly afterwards, the FSAW described the protest in glowing terms as a 'monumental achievement'.[34] A protest song composed in honour of the occasion asserted boldly: 'Strijdom, you have tampered with the women, You have struck a rock.' (And when Strijdom did die, shortly after this, many women who had been present at the demonstration saw it as a direct consequence of their protests.)

The significance of the protest lay deeper than mere spectacle. The fact that it was women who had organised and carried out so impressive a demonstration challenged stereotyped assumptions about women and their lack of political initiative. For the white press there was something remarkable about the sight of 'blanket-clad Native women', to quote from the *Cape Times*, confronting the central government.[35] Once again, as in 1955, *Die Vaderland* could only conceive of the demonstration as the work of white women. It accompanied its report with a photograph of some white women talking to some black women. Underneath, the caption read: 'Hier word gehelp dat die nie-blanke vroue die vorms. . . kan onderteken' ('Here the non-white women are being helped to sign the forms'). It also included two photographs of black domestic workers with white children in their care, captioning them accusingly: 'Weet hul ouers waar hulle is?' ('Do their parents know where they are?').[36]

Undoubtedly, the unqualified success of the demonstration enhanced the prestige of the FSAW within the Congress Alliance. The Alliance acknowledged the women's achievement by deciding to commemorate August 9th henceforth as 'Women's Day'—it is still celebrated as such today. The FSAW had demonstrated to itself, to the Congress Alliance and the authorities that it was capable of staging a demonstration of major proportions and could reasonably claim to be taken seriously as a political organisation. Yet at the same time this very success heightened some of the ambivalent feelings already present within the Congress Alliance towards the women's movement. Earlier in the year, the FSAW had singled out the 'backward attitude of the men' towards women's political activity as a brake on its progress.

> Many men who are politically active and progressive in outlook still follow the tradition that women should take no part in politics and a great resentment exists towards women who seek independent activities or even express independent opinions. This prejudice is so strong that even when many of those in leading positions in the ANC appear to be co-operating with the Federation, it is sometimes difficult to avoid the conclusion that they would prefer to hinder the work of the Federation and to withdraw their own womenfolk from activities.[37]

Success, and the growing confidence of the FSAW which that encouraged, fed these resentments on the part of some male members of Congress even while winning for the FSAW the genuine respect of its allies. For many Congress men, particularly, it seems, in the Transvaal ANC, the women's achievement conflicted with their deeply-rooted views on the junior position women should occupy in society at large and within the national liberation movement in particular. For many African men their chief reason for opposing passes for women was that the government was thereby usurping their own authority: 'The government cannot give your woman pass if you do not want to, because the woman she is under the control of a man,' asserted one male speaker at an ANC anti-pass meeting.[38]

Higher up in the hierarchy such sentiments were never expressed so baldly, but there, too, there were signs of unease at the growing independence of the women's organisations. It was the same unease that in 1954/55 had led the ANC to insist on a federal structure for the FSAW. Though generous in its praises of the women's achievement at Pretoria, the Transvaal consultative committee [TCC] of the Congress Alliance was anxious to re-assert its ultimate authority in the planning of the anti-pass campaign. Accordingly, it requested the FSAW to submit a written report on the Pretoria demonstration to it. The FSAW, however, rejected this approach— 'no further purpose can be served by the preparation of a written report'— though it reassured them that it would continue to maintain their 'valuable liaison'.[39] Further signs of tension came to the surface in September 1956 with the publication of an article in the ANC bulletin, *Sechaba*, entitled 'Don't stifle the work of the Women's Federation'.[40] This reaffirmed the valuable and necessary work being done by the FSAW and ANCWL and pleaded for a greater tolerance and respect for their initiative within the ANC.

These contradictory attitudes towards the women were inevitable in a society as strongly patriarchal as South Africa. Yet although men might grow uneasy at the implications for their own lifestyle if women were acknowledged as equal partners in the political struggle, they could not fail to be impressed by what had been achieved at Pretoria on August 9th. Menw orking in the city on that day showed their respect spontaneously, in their own way:

> At the bus ranks there were many men waiting for transport home after the day's work, for it was late. But when they saw the women they fell back, saying 'Let the women go first.' It was yet another tribute.[41]

The Second National Conference

The Pretoria demonstration provided the FSAW with a large injection of energy. The second national conference, held immediately afterwards in Johannesburg and attended by some 500 delegates, was a resounding success. Here much of the organisational work of the past two years was consolidated and the Federation put on a firmer footing.

A new and more vigorous national executive took over from the caretaker executive in Cape Town. The conference approved the suggestion to transfer the Head Office from Cape Town to Johannesburg, thus formally confirming what the Pretoria demonstration had clearly established, that the Transvaal region was the strongest in the FSAW. The conference also went on to demonstrate its faith in the existing Transvaal leadership by electing Lilian Ngoyi as national president and Helen Joseph as national secretary. These elections meant that the NEC and the Transvaal regional executive overlapped considerably; in practice, the distinction between the two would frequently be blurred in the years to follow.

Ngoyi and Joseph together offered the FSAW a strong and dynamic leadership. Ngoyi had already proved herself to be a charismatic figure

amongst the women, a fine public speaker with a highly developed sense
of the dramatic. She had a strong personal following in the ANCWL.
In March 1956, *Drum* described her as 'the most talked-of woman in
politics', 'a brilliant orator'; 'She can toss an audience on her little finger,
get men grunting with shame. . . and infuse everyone with renewed
courage. . . She is not much of a political thinker but she gets down to a
job in a manner that shames many a political theorist. For this woman has
bundles and bundles of energy.'[42] Joseph brought to the FSAW the
administrative expertise that the organisation badly needed. Highly efficient
and capable, she had joined the national liberation movement relatively
late in her life and brought to her work all the enthusiasm and dedication
of the convert. As secretary she was in a key post, since on her fell much
of the responsibility for implementing and following up decisions taken
by the National and Transvaal executives. Concern was soon expressed
that too much responsibility was being concentrated on her at the expense
of training other women to perform these tasks. Alexander, in Cape Town,
stressed this point when she wrote to Joseph shortly after the conference.
Not without a trace of paternalism, she commented on the elections:
'. . . in our country we have to strain every nerve of ours to train Non-
European leaders, rather slow and painstaking at first, but in the longterm
policy will yield better results.'[43] For this reason, a joint-secretaryship was
instituted in the Transvaal region shortly afterwards and Bertha Mashaba
appointed to work with Joseph.

The other major achievement of the conference was to adopt a
constitution for the FSAW. This formally resolved the membership dispute
that had continued to flicker on and off even after the Cape Town group
had conceded the principle of a federal organisation to the Transvaal
ANC. Federalism satisfied several political criteria concerning relationships
between the women's movement and the national liberation movement,
but also imposed a structural clumsiness on the FSAW that led to complications upon occasion. The main problem was that member organisations of
the FSAW were responsible in two different directions at the same time,
both to the FSAW itself and to their own parent bodies. The procedures
for deciding which organisation took precedence in which situations
were not clear.

This clumsiness was highlighted almost immediately by a dispute
which arose between the FSAW and COD over the way in which the
constitution had been adopted at the conference. The COD NEC argued
that before the FSAW could adopt a constitution, each of the FSAW
affiliates (ANC, COD, etc.) should approve and ratify the document first,
at their own national conferences; following on from this, they then
accused the FSAW leadership of pushing through the constitution in a
'high-handed manner'.[44] The FSAW responded by vigorously defending
the independent authority of its national conference. It pointed out that
the conference consisted entirely of delegates from the affiliated Congress
groups and that these delegates had voted, by 291 votes to 79, in favour
of adopting the constitution in August 1956 without further delay.
Moreover, the draft of the constitution had been circulated to all member

organisations in 1955, more than a year before the FSAW conference:

> If these organisations had failed to discuss the Constitution or circulate it, this must be laid at the door of these organisations. This, however, should not be allowed to hold up the development of the Federation of South African Women.[45]

If member groups were dissatisfied with the constitution as adopted, there was provision for amendments to be introduced at the next conference. Meanwhile, 'The Federation is young and must be flexible but at the same time it needs a framework within which to function, a foundation on which to build.'[46]

In late 1956 the FSAW felt confident that it had weathered its initial difficulties and knew where its direction lay. In a buoyant mood, the conference adopted an ambitious programme for 1957. It was agreed to focus on two issues—passes for women and the Group Areas Act. By taking up this latter issue, which affected Indian and 'Coloured' women most severely, the FSAW was making a real effort to make itself relevant to as broad a section of women as possible. The plan of action called for a mass signature drive—half a million individual 'pledges' by women to fight against passes and 100,000 signatures for a petition against the Group Areas Act. The sponsors of these motions hoped that canvassing individual women in this way would serve a dual purpose. On the one hand, it would bring the FSAW into close contact with women in a wide-reaching educational campaign; on the other, it would expose to the world the depth of women's opposition to both measures. The FSAW had few doubts about the strength of the mood of resistance amongst women:

> Women are not afraid of suffering for the sake of their children and their homes. Women have an answer to the threats to their families and their future. Women will not face a future imprisoned in the pass laws. Women will fight for the right to live and move freely as human beings.[47]

In the euphoria of August 1956 it seemed as if these sentiments would indeed carry the day. Yet already the more severe countermeasures the police were adopting against pass protests were sounding a warning. In late 1956 the first major violent clash over passes for women took place. In Lichtenburg, in November, a large crowd of about 1,000 women and some men who were protesting the arrival of the reference book units were baton-charged by the police. The crowd resorted to stoning, the police opened fire and two Africans were shot dead. Six police and two other Africans were wounded in the confrontation.[48]

Then, in December 1956, the entire Congress Alliance received a serious blow when 156 front-rank leaders were rounded up and detained in a nation-wide police swoop. This was the beginning of the notorious 'Treason Trial' which would drag on for the next four and a half years. After lengthy preliminary investigations and manoeuverings, the state finally brought thirty of the original detainees to trial on a charge of high treason—plotting to overthrow the government by subversive and violent means. It never managed to prove its case and finally, in March 1961, all thirty were acquitted. Acquittal was a hollow victory for the Congress Alliance. In the intervening years, most of the leading figures in the Congress Alliance were embroiled in lengthy and expensive litigation, their mobility restricted by bail conditions, their time and energy drained away from their political work into the protracted legal battle. The Treason Trial was a serious, ineradicable blight on the work of the Congress Alliance throughout the 1950s.

The FSAW suffered along with all the other Congress organisations. Many women were arrested in the first round of detentions in December 1956—they included Lilian Ngoyi, Helen Joseph, Frances Baard and Annie Silinga amongst others. Lilian Ngoyi and Helen Joseph were among the thirty people finally brought to trial on the charge of treason. They were the only women thus singled out—their performance as leaders in the Transvaal had not escaped the attention of the authorities either.

Notes

1. NCC, 'Memorandum on the Anti-Pass Campaign', p. 1, FSAW IIB.
2. From an article by Helen Joseph in *Fighting Talk*, Jan. 1956, quoted in evidence heard during the Treason Trial. *Treason Trial Record*, vol. 67, p. 14234.
3. NCC, 'Memorandum on Anti-Pass Campaign', 25.10.56, p. 2, FSAW IIB.
4. *Drum*, Jan. 1956, 'Will our Women Carry Passes?', p. 19.
5. *Ibid.*, p. 17.
6. *Drum*, Feb. 1956, 'The All-in Congress', p. 20.
7. *New Age*, 24.11.55.
8. Letter from M. Rantekane, Bethlehem ANC Youth League, *New Age*, 26.1.56.
9. *New Age*, 19.1.56.
10. FSAW correspondence, 5.4.56, FSAW (Tvl) to Indian Youth Congress, FSAW A5.
11. *New Age*, 27.11.55.
12. 'Transvaal Women's Day' pamphlet, March 1956, FSAW A5.
13. From a verbatim report on the conference, FSAW A9.
14. Quoted in *New Age*, 6.1.56.
15. FSAW correspondence, 18.2.56, FSAW BII.
16. *New Age*, 22.3.56.
17. Typescript police report on a woman's meeting in Winburg location, 8.4.56, headed 'Sondag 8.4.56', Treason Trial exhibit G900.
18. This account is pieced together from reports in *New Age*, in April 1956; *Drum*, May 1956, 'Winburg: Target for Women's Passes'; Police report on the meeting of Winburg women headed 'Sondag 8.4.56', Treason Trial exhibit G900; interview with L. Ngoyi.
19. Interview with L. Ngoyi.
20. *New Age*, 19.4.55.
21. *New Age*, 17.5.56.
22. From evidence submitted by Liebenberg (for the State) in the Treason Trial, *Treason Trial Record*, vol. 70, p. 14818.
23. From untitled typescript on resistance to passes in 1955–56, FSAW CI 1.

24. South African Institute of Race Relations: *Survey of Race Relations, 1955–56,* p. 82.
25. 'Report on a tour of the Major Centres of the Union submitted to the NCC, for discussion', p. 4, FSAW IIB.
26. *Ibid.,* p. 4.
27. Joseph, *Tomorrow's Sun,* p. 80.
28. *Cape Times,* 9.8.56 and *Die Vaderland,* 10.8.56.
29. FSAW untitled typescript, FSAW CI 1.
30. *Cape Times,* 10.8.56.
31. Interview with F. Baard.
32. *Drum,* Sept. 1957, 'Treason: End of Round One', p. 25.
33. Interview with A. Cachalia.
34. FSAW, *Strijdom. . . You have struck a rock,* p. 1.
35. *Cape Times,* 10.8.56.
36. *Die Vaderland,* 10.8.56.
37. 'Report to the WIDF', p. 3, FSAW 6.
38. 'Copy of notes taken by N.D. Const. John Patose at meeting of ANCWL, Sophiatown, 12.8.56', p. 3; Treason Trial exhibit G854.
39. FSAW correspondence with TCC, August 1956, FSAW CI 4.
40. 'Don't stifle the work of the Women's Federation', reprinted as pamphlet from *Sechaba,* Bulletin of the ANC, Sept. 1956, FSAW E.
41. Joseph, *op. cit.,* p. 85.
42. *Drum,* March 1956, 'Masterpiece in Bronze'.
43. FSAW correspondence, 4.9.56, FSAW BII.
44. Extract from letter from unidentified COD member in Cape Town, 17.9.56, amongst notes on COD NEC meetings, FSAW A7.
45. 'Statement for the Information of COD Members', p. 1, FSAW A7.
46. *Ibid.,* p. 2.
47. FSAW: 'Women in Chains', p. 12.
48. C. Hooper: *Brief Authority,* p. 143.

17

'The Women of Africa Are on the March': Anti-Pass Protests in 1957

Throughout 1957 and into 1958, the women's anti-pass campaign continued to generate an enormous response. It would be impossible to conduct a full survey of all the demonstrations with which the FSAW was associated in this time, they chequered the period with such frequency. A FSAW fact-sheet listing the women's demonstrations for 1957 and 1958 ran to seven closely typed pages.[1] These sporadic mass demonstrations proved capable of rallying considerable support. Much less successful, however, were the two campaigns to collect individual signatures. Both the anti-pass pledge campaign and the Group Areas campaign fell far short of their mark: a reflection on the organisational weaknesses of the FSAW at the grassroots level. Too few local women came forward to take responsibility for collecting signatures in their areas. In an undated letter to 'Rose', Helen Joseph complained about the 'ridiculous figure' for pledges received on the Rand, and asserted 'the target is possible if the women organise correctly'.[2]

Joseph's remarks pointed to a serious structural weakness in the FSAW that those who had wanted an individual membership had foreseen: it did not command an effective network of local branches and grassroots organisations. As a Federation, it was only as strong at the grassroots level as its member organisations. It was also dependent on member organisations to mobilise local support. The ANCWL and the Food and Canning Workers' Union were the only two member organisations with local branches outside the four main urban centres of Johannesburg, Cape Town, Durban and Port Elizabeth. The Women's League had by far the most extensive network of branches and in organising the anti-pass pledge campaign, the FSAW had to rely heavily on these contacts. In doing so, however, it was stepping into that murky area of overlapping responsibilities and poorly defined procedures of decision-making that existed between the FSAW and member organisations. The allocation of responsibilities between the FSAW and ANCWL in this campaign was not clearly demarcated, and conflict developed between the two organisations in the Transvaal as a result.

In March 1957, the ANCWL Transvaal executive expressed dissatisfaction with the manner in which the FSAW was organising the Anti-Pass Pledge and Group Areas campaigns. It complained that it was not being kept properly informed by the FSAW which was 'side-stepping' its offices and dealing directly with Women's League Branches.

> We are not told of anything, you can imagine your office being side-stepped, e.g. Pledges, straight from the Federation to the Women's League Branches. I

mean this is not healthy, we are interested to know what the Federation is
doing and have to be together.[3]

In reply, the FSAW maintained that the participation of the ANCWL 'at
all levels' had been 'full'—'As far as the Working Committee of the Federation is concerned, its very composition ensured close co-operation and full
liaison with your Executive Committee.'[4]

This was true in that there was considerable overlap between the
FSAW and ANCWL executives, starting with the posts of national president
in each organisation—both held by Lilian Ngoyi after 1956—and continuing through the regional committees and sub-committees. In the
Transvaal, for instance, Bertha Mashaba, Ruth Matseoane, Kate Mxkato
were amongst those who served on both FSAW and ANCWL committees
at the same time. In many situations this overlap between the two organisations facilitated speedy decisions and encouraged a closeness and informality that benefited the work of both organisations—both working for the
same goals in any case. But there was a distinction between the two
organisations, which the ANC in particular was anxious to maintain;
the ANCWL was its female wing and the constitution of the league made
it clear that its primary allegiance had, ultimately, to be to the ANC.[5] It
was a situation demanding skillful handling and considerable tact. Recognising this, the FSAW adopted a conciliatory tone in its response to the
ANCWL's complaints. It concluded its reply to the ANCWL's criticisms
with a plea for unity in the face of the external threats facing the Congress
Alliance.

> The whole Congress movement is threatened today as never before. . . We plead
> that now is the time for us to demonstrate our unity as women and to resist all
> efforts to divide us. We must close our ranks and not divide them.[6]

While the signature-collecting campaign proceeded sluggishly, other
demonstrations were more successful. 'Women's Day' in August 1957 was
celebrated on a nationwide scale, with large meetings and deputations to
Native Commissioners' offices across the country. The Port Elizabeth
gathering was described as a 'huge success', while the Johannesburg meeting drew over 2,000 women.[7] Both Ngoyi and Joseph were prevented
from taking part because they were sitting through the preparatory
examinations of the Treason Trial in Pretoria. In response, ANCWL and
FSAW branches flooded them with telegrams at the court hearing, to
inform them of local protests and express their solidarity with them.

The following month, in Cape Town, the FSAW achieved its first
breakthrough with white women outside of COD. At a large multiracial
gathering of women on the Grand Parade, representatives from the FSAW,
ANCWL, the Black Sash, the NCW and the Anglican Mothers' Union
agreed to establish a broad 'Cape Association to Abolish Passes for African
Women'.[8] How active this association was, and how close the co-operation
between its members might have been, is not documented. It did continue
to function as a loose co-ordinating body for several years, however,

encouraging FSAW hopes for building a united, progressive women's movement that would enjoy substantial white support. But only in Cape Town, where there was already a long tradition of co-operation between various women's organisations, did it make any significant progress towards this end. Elsewhere, white women were important on an individual basis only.

The Zeerust Disturbances

Up to this stage, anti-pass demonstrations had been confined to the urban areas of the country or else to small towns in the 'white' countryside. During 1957 the anti-pass campaign took a new turn when, for the first time, rural women, living in the Zeerust area of the Western Transvaal, became involved in resistance to reference books as well. The FSAW was not directly involved in these disturbances, but in the history of the women's anti-pass campaign they are significant. They showed that rural women, too, could be roused to political action and hinted at the enormous pressures squeezing women in the reserves to this point of defiance. The Zeerust disturbances, which dragged on for many months, also marked an escalation in violence in the conduct of the campaign, on the part of both protesters and authorities.

The causes of the Zeerust anti-pass disturbances are complex. More than simply opposition to passes was involved. Rather, the attempt to issue women in the district with reference books was the catalyst which brought many long-simmering tensions to a head. Opposition to passes fused with opposition to the Bantu Authorities Act which was being implemented in the district—this act incorporated the office of chief of the tribe into the hierarchy of government controlled by Pretoria. In addition, a severe drought had exacerbated the problems of subsistence—survival—in the area.

Resistance to passes among the Bafurutse (the name of the tribe) began passively. Many women simply failed to appear for reference books on the date that they were summoned. Women with migrant husbands felt that they could not take out a reference book without his consent; at least one of the local chiefs was opposed to passes for women too. The Department of Native Affairs held this chief responsible for the poor turnout and summarily and promptly deposed him, using the powers conferred on them by the Bantu Authorities Act. The forced removal of their chief shocked his people and enflamed their resistance to passes. Overnight, passive resistance turned to direct confrontation. Women who had already taken out reference books burnt them; those who were unwilling to do such a drastic thing had theirs taken from them forcibly and burnt. Those women who had not yet taken books swore that nothing would induce them to do so after that.

The government's action in deposing the chief split the tribe. The ease with which it did so points to the very brittle structure that existed in 1957. Supporters of the chief demanded his reinstatement. Frustrations against intolerable conditions in the reserves were turned inwards and directed against 'betrayers', and collaborators—those suspected of informing on the ex-chief to the police, those who supported the newly installed government chief, as well as other pro-government chiefs and their supporters in the area. The resisters set up popular tribunals to try suspects and deal out summary justice. The pro-government faction armed themselves and turned to the authorities for help.

Drum ran several stories on the disturbances in early 1958, once news of what was happening in the Zeerust district had leaked out. The following quotation illustrates clearly the process of tribal disintegration and fragmentation that was taking place.

> When government started to try issuing passes for women. . . it first tried to operate through the chiefs. But some of the chiefs. . . were deadset against passes for women. So these chiefs were removed by the authorities and more 'cooperative' chiefs were recognised. This set people against the chiefs as well as against passes for women. The whole tribal structure broke down. . . The police were called in, batons cracked on bones and stones were flung. The government-appointed chiefs had tribal guards, who helped the police. Faction fighting took place, houses were burned down. The land and the cattle were neglected.[9]

From mid April 1957, the authorities launched a vicious counter-attack, designed to wipe out all forms of resistance, bolster the power of the pro-government faction and punish the protesters. They established a special police unit, with very wide powers of search and arrest, to patrol the area; it was virtually a law unto itself. They also clamped down on the movement of people in and out of the area. This effectively suppressed details of what was happening from reaching a wider audience. Such stories as did begin to leak out, however, indicated that the unrest was being put down with a maximum of force and intimidation.

In March 1958, *Drum* printed the following extract from what it described as a 'typical affidavit' made by a local woman to a Johannesburg lawyer:

> I was sleeping in the house with my mother and sister and three children. . . We were woken at three in the morning by men banging on the door and shouting for us to open. When I asked them who they were, they did not answer; they broke the door down. They came in and we saw that they were 5 white policemen and 6 Africans. They shouted: 'Where are your passes?' and pulled us by the front of our nightclothes. When I said that we were not men and we had no passes they hit us and kicked us and we fell to the floor.[10]

The authorities also resorted to less overtly violent forms of coercion. Large numbers of people, including many women, were arrested. The jail at Zeerust was crammed with twice as many prisoners as it was designed to hold. The local school and post office were closed down and the local bus, the one link with the outside world, suspended from operation. In addition, women old age pensioners and widows applying for payment of their pensions were refused unless they could first produce reference books—even though no law had yet been gazetted to make reference books compulsory for women.[11]

The resistance was not easily crushed. Hundreds of people crossed the border into the neighbouring British protectorate of Bechuanaland, rather than submit to the authorities. In May 1958 *Drum* reported that there were about 1,000 refugees living in two camps in Bechuanaland. It quoted one woman as saying, 'I have had to hide in the fields and hills many times like an animal. We decided to flee the Union rather than have passes.'[12] The strong spirit of opposition among many women was conveyed by a song they composed which mocked the authorities defiantly:

> Behold us joyful
> The women of Africa
> In the presence of our baas;
> The great one
> Who conquers Lefurutse
> With his knobkierie
> And his assegaai
> And his gun.[13]

The Zeerust anti-pass disturbances of 1957 were largely a grassroots reaction to oppressive local conditions on the part of the people. The FSAW was not directly involved, although the ANCWL did make contact with the region once the unrest had broken out. The role of the ANC was exaggerated, both by officials, keen to blame the unrest on outside 'agitators', and the ANC itself, anxious to boost its sagging performance. However, it did undoubtedly have some links with the area. Many of the male migrant workers from the area were members of the ANC on the Reef. Through them news of earlier anti-pass activity on the Rand and elsewhere would have been relayed back to the people living at home. In this way, Zeerust women did have some precedents that they could draw on when the reference book units reached them. Once the unrest had erupted, the ANC made attempts to increase contact with the area. According to Lilian Ngoyi, she visited the area secretly during the unrest and addressed a meeting of local women.[14] The FSAW's own direct contribution was confined to financial assistance towards bail funds and legal defence for the scores of people rounded up and arrested during the disturbances. The attorney in charge, Shulamith Muller, appears to have been a member of COD and was thus affiliated to the FSAW.

For the most part, opposition to passes was bound up with a conservative defence of traditional institutions—chieftainship, the patriarchal family, established sex roles. The women who defied the reference book units were not demonstrating consciously for freedom or equality; one of the strongest reasons why women were opposed to passes was that they were seen as a direct threat to the family. They related directly to the maintenance of migrant labour, as instruments of influx control—shutting women off from the larger economic opportunities of the towns and preventing them from joining their husbands who were working there. The women were also aware of what passes for men had meant—arrests, fines and harrassment by the police. In saying no to all these things, Zeerust women were fighting for their homes and families. Conservative attitudes were even more marked among the men. Male migrant workers were disturbed by reports that pro-government chiefs were trying to persuade their wives to take out reference books in their absence—'How could a woman take a book without her husband's consent?'[15] 'If my wife no more belongs to me, let the government pay me back my lobola and have her,' declared one Zeerust man in an interview with *Drum*.[16] Charles Hooper, an Anglican priest working in the district at the time, described the general sentiments thus: 'As the women were concerned with the effect of pass-carrying on their roles as mothers, so now were the men concerned with the effect of this book on their relationships with their wives.'[17]

Yet, as was true of protests in the urban areas as well, the effects of the anti-pass protests in Zeerust on the women involved were politicising and radicalising. In organising to resist passes, women were learning new political skills. One woman summed up her period in jail thus:

> That jail is a good school. When we went in we knew nothing. Now we have been able to talk all day to our people from Johannesburg and to the women of other villages. We got organised in jail. We agree about these books. We know now what they are for and we agree to refuse them. The jail has given us a better education than these Bantu Education schools.[18]

The women were forced to discard traditional patterns of behaviour that did not suit the harsh conditions with which they were struggling. In the absence of their husbands who were away working on the Reef, many women were forced to make their own decisions about whether to resist passes or not, whether to flee or not. At the same time, the government's contemptuous manipulation of tribal institutions to suit its own ends seriously damaged the status of those institutions in the local people's eyes. By arbitrarily deposing a traditional chief and replacing him with a more pliant nominee of its own, the government was devaluing the very tribal structures it wished to retain. The effects rippled through the entire social structure, calling into question previously entrenched values and social norms. *Drum* interviewed one young girl who made the point very clearly. She said:

> What war is this that fights women? What law is this when our chief who is not our chief and his beat-up men have no more respect for the huts of their fellow-men, beat up their women? It must be a difficult law that cannot be explained by sticks and stones and our men cannot come from the kgotla (the tribal council) feeling our customs still work. I know, I know because my uncle often came home at night and all he could say was that the times are tarnished.[19]

This pushed women into re-evaluating their own attitudes towards themselves and encouraged a feeling of greater assertiveness and solidarity with other women. The lawyer in charge of the people's defence was, as already mentioned, a woman. Hooper once commented in some surprise that a woman should be handling their cases. He was promptly reproved by local women for his bias—'The women of Africa are on the march,' said one.[20] Yet the women lacked the resources to wage their struggle indefinitely. The unrest dragged on into 1958, but ultimately it was crushed. Eventually, after pressure was exerted upon it, the government appointed a commission of enquiry into the disturbances. The attitude of the one-man commission to the local people was distinctly unsympathetic and the results of the enquiry were never published.

For the FSAW and the anti-pass campaign generally, the events in the Zeerust district during the course of 1957 signalled that the government was determined to impose passes on women at all costs. Despite the impressive scale and inspirational value of the anti-pass demonstrations of 1956/57, they had not stopped the drive to issue passes to women. The FSAW had proved it could rally significant numbers of women to it on specific occasions; it had not proved that its tactics were capable of deflecting government policy in the long-term. Mere demonstrations of popular feeling were not enough. The government was in no way responsible to the disenfranchised black majority, and with the might of an impressive police force and army behind it, an ever-increasing range of coercive legislation and the overwhelming support of the white electorate, it could afford to ignore popular discontent or, as in the case of Zeerust, move ruthlessly to contain it.

As women emerged as a stronger force in the national liberation movement, the repressive machinery of the state was increasingly turned against them. During this time, surveillance of women's meetings was stepped up so that security became a much more urgent consideration than before. At the same time, women leaders were being harried more and more. Influx control measures were used to endorse out of town African women who took the lead in organising local protests. Women who could not be dealt with in this way faced bannings and restrictions on their mobility. In April 1957, Helen Joseph was banned and confined to the district of Johannesburg.[21] The only exception to her restriction order was the permission to travel to Pretoria daily for the Treason Trial hearings. Although the terms of her banning order did not compel her to sever ties with the FSAW, as had been the case with Alexander in 1954, her mobility and efficiency as secretary were thereby curtailed.

Joseph's banning brought into sharp focus the problem of staff that had hampered the development of the FSAW from the start. Without a full-time organiser and not having an individual membership, the FSAW relied very largely on its executive committees—both national and regional —to see that its identity, as an organisation distinct from that of its affiliated members groups, was maintained. Without an active committee, there could be no FSAW. The successive bannings of its leaders by the government was thus particularly devastating for it. In 1957 the ANCWL in Bloemfontein wrote to the FSAW head office its work:

Progress is very slow here, many women slackened in their activities and mostly lack of money as the other branches are not co-operating in our Region. The reason is that they do not understand as yet and would like to be visited now and then if it was possible, we asked them to call on us if they can afford transport but they have not done so.[22]

The letter highlighted the need for a fulltime, paid organiser who could maintain regular contact with local branches and expand the FSAW's work.

During this time the glow of optimism generated by the Pretoria demonstration in August 1956 began to fade. The 1950s had seen a steady consolidation of power in the hands of the government and by 1957 it was moving with mounting confidence against the national liberation movement. The Congress Alliance was fighting with its back to the wall. The Treason Trial preliminaries dragged on, effectively crippling the political work of the accused and draining enormous amounts of money and energy inside the national liberation movement into their defence. There was one encouraging show of strength during 1957 when the township of Alexandra launched a massive, ultimately successful boycott of buses once again, to force down the rising fares. On the whole, however, the mood within Congress circles was sombre. 'Will Congress be banned?' asked the COD periodical, *Fighting Talk*, in May 1957. It was a succinct comment on the insecurity and sense of siege which was beginning to prevail.[23]

By this time, too, the rifts within the Congress Alliance had become serious. The Africanists, having emerged as a definite faction within the ANC at its conference in December 1955, were highly critical of what they saw as the ineffectual leadership and overcautious strategy of the ANC. Their major criticism, however, was directed at the constitution of the Congress Alliance itself. They held that by sharing decision-making in it on an equal basis with the other Congress groups, the ANC had effectively renounced its vanguard position as leader of the African majority in the national liberation movement. They also viewed the multiracial composition of the Alliance with suspicion, arguing that its ethnic composition was a legitimation of apartheid. There was also a strong streak of anti-white feeling amongst the Africanists. They were particularly hostile to the white Congress of Democrats which they regarded as a communist-dominated body, with an influence on the Congress Alliance out of all proportion to its tiny membership.

Although the FSAW did not suffer from the same cleavage within its ranks—to a surprising extent the Africanist split seems to have passed it by—it was nevertheless too dependent on the Congress Alliance not to feel the ill effects. The women's campaign against passes could not prove successful on its own, as the FSAW realised very well. What was needed was for it to link up with a general campaign involving the men of the Alliance as well. As already pointed out, the ANC and Congress Alliance agreed with this in principle; FSAW attempts to translate it into practice during 1957 and 1958 were not successful, however. In June 1957 it proposed to the TCC that the Congress Alliance should organise a further mass demonstration outside the Union Buildings, one that would involve both men and women in a common demonstration of opposition to passes. The TCC accepted the proposal but thereafter nothing more was heard about it. Some eighteen months later the FSAW was still complaining that men had not made an 'active entry' into the anti-pass campaign.[24] At a time when it was looking around for allies to sustain and develop its campaign, they were preoccupied with damaging internecine quarrels.

Notes

1. 'Resistance of women to Passes during 1957', FSAW CI 5, and 'Resistance of women to Passes during 1958', FSAW CI 6.
2. FSAW correspondence, FSAW CI 1.
3. FSAW correspondence, ANCWL (Tvl) to FSAW (Tvl), 31.3.57, FSAW CI 5.
4. Letter from FSAW (Tvl) to the ANCWL (Tvl), 5.4.57, p. 4, FSAW CI 5.
5. 'Draft; Rules and Regulations of the African National Congress Women's League', p. 1, FSAW II H1.
6. Letter from FSAW (Tvl) to the ANCWL (Tvl), 5.4.57, p. 4, FSAW CI 5.
7. Telegrams to Joseph and Ngoyi on 9.8.57, FSAW CI 5.
8. *Drum,* Oct. 1957, 'Multi-Race Protest'.
9. *Drum,* May 1958, 'Zeerust: the women's battle'.
10. *Drum,* March 1958, 'People flee from their homes'.
11. Fairbairn: 'Zeerust: a profile of resistance', *Africa South,* vol. 2, no. 3, April-June 1958.
12. *Drum,* May 1958, 'Zeerust: the women's battle'.
13. Hooper: *Brief Authority,* p. 264.
14. Interview.
15. Hooper, *op. cit.,* p. 181.
16. *Drum,* May 1958, 'Zeerust: the women's battle'.
17. Hooper, *op. cit.,* p. 128.
18. Hooper, *op. cit.,* p. 181.
19. *Drum,* May 1958, 'Zeerust: the women's battle'.
20. Hooper, *op. cit.,* p. 234.
21. FSAW Press statement, 26.4.57, FSAW B II.
22. FSAW correspondence, Jane Motshabi to FSAW secretary, nd, FSAW CI 6.
23. *Fighting Talk,* May 1957.
24. 'Report by the Federation of South African Women on the anti-pass campaign', p. 6, FSAW CI 6.

18

'No Nannies Today': Anti-Pass Protests, 1958

1958 was a sombre year for the Congress Alliance. Government pressures against it were mounting; the ANC's freedom to organise was being seriously limited. In March 1958 the government imposed a ban on the ANC in several rural areas (including Zeerust), where peasant unrest was manifesting itself. The Congress Alliance suffered another serious setback the following month, when an attempt to launch a nationwide stay-away from work failed. This stay-away had been timed to coincide with the white parliamentary elections. Overall, the response was poor and, some argued, merely served to stampede white voters into the arms of the Nationalist party against 'die swart gevaar' ('the black danger'). The failure of the stay-away was damaging to the prestige of the Alliance and the ANC in particular, and fuelled further disaffection amongst the Africanists.

Despite this failure, the government still viewed the ANC as its major political enemy. In April 1958 it slapped a four and a half month ban on all meetings of Africans (other than those of a purely social or religious nature). This imposed a further damaging limitation to the organisation's ability to rally support. Congress supporters were increasingly pessimistic about their chances of bringing about a significant shift in attitude within the government, and amongst whites in general, with the tactics that they had adopted in 1949. The possibility that the ANC would be banned outright was already being discussed within Congress. In May 1958, Govan Mbeki, a prominent ANC official, predicted that a blanket ban on the ANC was inevitable 'as soon as the ANC shows greater organisational efficiency'.[1] This was a revealing statement, both about the point reached by the state in relation to the national liberation movement, and about the internal weaknesses plaguing that movement.

In the FSAW, too, signs of strain were coming to the fore. In January 1958 the national secretary, Helen Joseph, was obliged to report to the NEC that 'owing to the extreme pressure of work', she had not been able to carry out all the instructions from the last meeting.[2] Commemoration of Women's Day in August 1958, a major event in the FSAW calendar, was hampered by the ban on all meetings of Africans. In Johannesburg, the FSAW arranged an open-air meeting for non-African women, taking great care to ensure that African women did not infringe the banning order by attending.[3] This was not a great success. The lack of support from non-African women indicated clearly that the dynamism of the FSAW, certainly on the Rand, came from African women.

The anti-pass campaign too was being steadily driven back onto the defensive. In the first two years of their work, the reference book units issued some half million passes;[4] between January and November of

1958 this figure doubled to over a million books.[5] During the course of 1958 these units finally began operations in the larger towns—a sign of increased confidence on their part, and a signal for the opening of the last phase in the anti-pass campaign. The first advances on the large towns by the reference book units were oblique. In December 1957 the South African Council of Nurses announced that in future all nurses would have to produce identity numbers before they could be registered for the midwifery course. This announcement made no mention of reference books, but, as everyone quickly realised, African nurses would only be able to acquire identity numbers with these books. It was a clever ploy, similar to the pressure tactics that were already being tried in the Zeerust area where pensions, medical care, even schooling for children and postal facilities had all been made dependent on women producing reference books. The nurses represented a very different category of women from the peasant women of Zeerust, however. They were urban, educated women, whose standing in their community was high. They already had their own professional organisation to represent them. Any protest that they launched would be assured of extensive press coverage and wide public support within the black community.

In fact, black nurses were already in an uproar. In late 1957, the government passed the Nursing Act, which introduced segregation into all aspects of the profession: training, registration, administration. This provoked a storm of protest among nurses, who accused the government and the Nursing Council of degrading black nursing standards and devaluing their profession. The announcement about identity numbers enflamed their resentment still more. The FSAW associated itself with the nurses from the start. It denounced the Nursing Act as a 'further attack' upon the non-white women of South Africa, one which amounted to 'an attack on the health of the nation'.[6] In November 1957 it assisted in convening a national conference of nurses to discuss the implications of the Nursing Act.[7] When the announcement about identity numbers was made, the NEC of the FSAW agreed to make the campaign against them 'the major campaign of the Federation in 1958'.[8]

Apart from a genuine support for the issues involved, the FSAW had sound tactical reasons for doing this. It was always anxious to broaden its appeal to as wide a range of women's organisations as possible. Black nurses represented a particularly influential segment of women, since nursing was one of the few occupations open to black women that carried high status within the community. Thus, in January 1958, referring to the national conference of nurses in 1957, the NEC affirmed the importance of using 'such national non-Congress multiracial conferences. . . for making fresh contacts with women delegates to stimulate interest in the Federation'.[9] In addition, from the point of view of the anti-pass campaign, the attempt to enforce reference books on African nurses posed a dangerous threat. The FSAW regarded it as the 'thin edge of the wedge' for the pass units in the cities: 'an attempt to insinuate passes for women into the cities and large towns where until now Verwoerd has not dared to send his pass units'.[10]

In preparation for the campaign, the NEC drew up a detailed programme of action. It relied on familiar tactics: liaison with the nurses' organisations; leafletting the public; mass demonstrations to the hospital authorities, the South African Nursing Council and the Minister of Health; attempts to involve other liberal women's organisations; publicising the government's proposals internationally. The whole campaign was conducted with a maximum of newspaper publicity. It culminated in a mass demonstration of women outside Baragwanath Hospital, the major black hospital in Johannesburg, on the 22nd March 1958.

In itself this demonstration was a failure. In the build-up to the demonstration the FSAW sought and achieved extensive newspaper exposure for the proposed gathering. One result was an enormous showing of force by the police on the day of the demonstration, which effectively prevented the mass turn-out the FSAW had hoped for. Little more than 300 women managed to circumvent the tight police cordon that was thrown round the hospital. One report described the demonstration as a 'comic opera. . . with a large cast'. Police, heavily armed, outnumbered demonstrators, while inside the hospital a siege mentality prevailed— 'Rumour has it that gas masks were held in readiness at the casualty station.'[11] The FSAW found the police reaction less amusing. It described the display of armed force as 'unprecedented and outrageous' in view of its own repeatedly stated commitment to peaceful methods of protest.[12]

The authorities had made themselves clear: no more Pretorias would be tolerated. Yet the nurses' campaign as a whole succeeded in winning a respite. Shortly thereafter, the South African Nursing Council announced that identity numbers for African women would not be enforced at that stage—a victory for the nurses and for the FSAW too.[13] It was a temporary respite, however, for in August 1958 a similar measure was reintroduced, although no time limit for submission of identity numbers was set. Moreover, such success benefited only a small number of relatively privileged women; it did not deflect the reference book machine from its course. From mid-1958, passes started being issued to women in Durban, Cape Town, Port Elizabeth and the East Rand. In none of these places did the authorities meet with serious resistance. In Daveytown, the township outside Benoni on the East Rand, women were reported to be 'scurrying' to take out reference books. 'About the only Reef township where there has been big-scale acceptance', commented *Drum*.[14] In other centres women were clearly unhappy about the new books and many individuals refused to present themselves to the reference book units to receive theirs. In Veeplaats, near Port Elizabeth, about 250 women refused to take reference books in February. Such resistance, however, was isolated and fragmented, a personal stand rather than part of any concerted programme of action by political organisations.

In October 1958, the reference book units finally approached Johannesburg. Commenting on the lack of resistance in Cape Town and Durban, an article in *Drum* concluded: 'Now everyone is asking: when will the passes come to Johannesburg and how will the women in that big city react to them?'[15]

The relative ease with which reference books were issued to women in the other major centres had prompted a sense of grim urgency in the FSAW and the ANCWL. They were aware that the response to the women in Johannesburg was going to be crucial in determining whether the anti-pass campaign could be sustained for much longer. Bertha Mashaba and Lily Naidoo, at that stage joint secretaries of the Transvaal region of the FSAW, captured the gravity of the situation in a letter they wrote to the ANCWL in early October to arrange a joint planning session, where a strategy for resistance could be worked out. In it the two women referred to the 'hour of crisis' that had approached, and appealed to the ANCWL to respond promptly: 'Please, Dear Sisters, treat this matter as urgent.'[16] On one level, Mashaba and Naidoo need not have worried. The reaction of women in Johannesburg showed that resistance to passes had not been completely smothered by that stage. But at the same time, the course of events in Johannesburg during October and November highlighted the limitations of the anti-pass campaign, as then conceived, as a lever for change.

The Johannesburg Anti-Pass Demonstrations, 1958

Adopting a strategy similar to that already used with the nurses in early 1958, the reference book units moved cautiously and obliquely in Johannesburg at first. They singled out as their first targets a group of black women who were particularly isolated politically and vulnerable economically, the huge but fragmented army of domestic workers in the white suburbs. In mid-October, white households in Johannesburg received a circular from the Native Commissioner, instructing them to send their 'Native female servants' to his offices 'in order that she may be registered for the Native Population Register and issued with a reference book'.[17]

The circular made it appear as if this was a mere routine task. It did not point out that it was not yet illegal for women to be without a reference book, and, on receiving it, most householders dutifully dispatched their employees off to the pass offices. The government had chosen its target well. Domestic workers were in a vulnerable position, their bargaining powers weak. Few had the resources with which to resist their own employers, even if they were aware of the implications of reference books, which many were not. The FSAW described their position graphically:

> Living in the servants' quarters in the backyards, African women from the country, the farms, the small reserves, women far from their homes, forbidden by trespass regulations to have their husbands or even their tiny children with them, to lead a family life, isolated and unaware, dependent upon the 'madam' for the roof over their heads.[18]

With this approach it seemed at first as if in Johannesburg, too, reference books would be issued to African women without incident. But within a week the picture had changed dramatically. Beginning on the 21st October, local branches of the ANCWL organised a counter-offensive which rapidly snowballed into an exuberant campaign of civil disobedience. The extent and vigour of the demonstrations took the authorities and Congress leaders alike by surprise. It was precipitated by the still dynamic ANCWL branch at Sophiatown—the Group Areas Act might have been bleeding Sophiatown slowly to death, but the women that remained retained a fierce political awareness. They could not sit back quietly while other women all around them were receiving what they regarded as a badge of slavery.

On October 21st, Sophiatown women marched on the Native Commissioner's offices to stop domestic workers from taking out passes. Police intercepted the march and arrested the women, 249 of them, for holding an illegal procession. News of the arrests spread rapidly and soon, from all the Johannesburg townships, women began flocking to the pass offices to demonstrate their solidarity with those arrested and court arrest themselves. On the first day a total of 584 women were arrested. By the end of the week this figure had risen to 934. The following Monday a further 900 women were added to those already crowding the jails and police cells in central Johannesburg.[19] The prisons and police stations of Johannesburg were in an uproar, their facilities stretched to breaking point with the enormous intake of women. From all accounts, the mood amongst the women was defiant but high-spirited. Commented *Drum:*

> You would not have guessed this was the serious business of arrest for some breach of the law. It looked like a great festival. The women sang, and danced and pranced, flailing their arms and poking out that defiant thumb.[20]

The arrests were splashed across the newspapers. There were numerous photographs of women in dramatic, challenging poses, being arrested, filling the police vans and being driven off to jail. Once again, the fact that it was women involved in the demonstration brought a special slant to the manner in which the news was presented. *The Star,* Johannesburg's English language afternoon paper, bluntly headlined its report on the first round of arrests 'No nannies today'—a crisp statement of how most white South Africans viewed African women.[21] The FSAW itself tried to capitalise on this aspect in a circular it issued to white women urging them not to let their servants take out passes. If they did, it argued, their children would suffer when their 'nannies' were arrested for not having the correct documents.[22]

This display of passive resistance was a vigorous demonstration of grassroots opposition to passes among women. What it revealed was that in its preparations for resistance, the official Congress leadership was lagging behind its own rank and file on the highly politicised Rand. Although the ANCWL and FSAW executives had been active in mobilising opinion before the arrests with meetings and pamphlets, they had not entertained any ideas of mass civil disobedience. Only once the demonstrations had begun did they step forward to direct the campaign. An ANC report stated: 'There was no definite plan for courting imprisonment but after the arrest of the first demonstrators from Sophiatown other areas were organised by leaflets and visits to express their solidarity.'[23] *Drum* described the demonstrations as 'the biggest, best-organised resistance' since the Alexandra bus boycott of the previous year, and referred to the manifestation of a 'ghost organisation' amongst the women similar to that seen in the 1957 boycotts.[24] Virginia Mngomo recalls how, in Alexandra, the decision to march on the Native Commissioner's office was spread throughout the township by local ANCWL members walking round the streets and talking to people. On the morning of the march, the leaders were at the bus stops very early to dissuade women from going to work; the response from local residents was very good. She herself was desperately eager to join her colleagues in jail, but was persuaded to avoid arrest by senior Congress leaders. It was felt that it was important for some leaders to remain out of jail to take care of the campaign from the outside.[25]

Once the period of civil disobedience had begun, the leaders in the FSAW and ANCWL showed wholehearted support for the women. They were anxious to keep the momentum of the demonstration going. Impressed by both the militancy and the discipline of the women, they wanted to adopt a policy of 'no bail and no fines' for those already in jail and keep up the demonstrations to the pass office for 'as long as the support of the women could be maintained'.[26] They felt confident that this support could be maintained long enough to strain the resources of the jails and push police on the Reef to breaking point, and demonstrate convincingly that women did not want passes: the women had shown the way and Congress should follow.

In adopting this perspective, however, the FSAW outstripped the readiness of the ANC to take on a programme of mass confrontation along these lines, and its proposals quickly ran into opposition. The ANC's own assessment of the situation was far more cautious. ANC leaders in the Transvaal argued that more arrests would place an impossibly heavy financial burden on the Congress group which had undertaken responsibility for legal costs. They also felt that the FSAW's reading of the situation, that women were prepared to remain in jail, 'was not borne out by the facts'.[27] The FSAW countered this last argument by pointing out, with some justification, that it was not the arrested women who were anxious to be bailed out; rather, it was their husbands who were unilaterally bailing them out because they could not cope at home. It was the men, not the women, who were undermining the demonstration.

The mass arrests had undoubtedly turned many homes upside down and brought hardship to both husbands and children. In some cases, hardship turned to tragedy. In its report on the mass arrests of women in Johannesburg, *Drum* included the following story:

But at home life is bleak. Mrs. Elmah Mtshazo of 29 Gibson Street, Sophiatown, went to jail with her 18-year-old daughter. She returned to find that her 9-year-old daughter was critically ill. The little girl died next day.[28]

There was a bitter irony in the fact that the situation described by *Drum*—that of a child dying because its mother was in jail—formed one of the strongest arguments used by the FSAW and ANCWL in opposing the pass laws for women: what would happen to their children if women were subjected to arbitrary arrest for infringing or being suspected of infringing the pass laws?

In this debate about whether the women should continue to court arrest or not, more was at stake than just a disagreement about tactics. During the course of the debate, a further difference of opinion arose as to where the final authority in the Congress Alliance lay: whether with the ANC or the TCC. In this dispute the FSAW sided with the TCC which had supported its stand. The exact demarcation of authority within the Congress Alliance as well as the ranking of the women's movement in relation to the ANC were two issues that were always a potential source of friction in the Alliance throughout the 1950s. The same problem had manifested itself in 1954/55 when the FSAW's membership was being debated.

To what extent these differences developed into open confrontation is not clear. What is clear is that, in the words of an ANC report, 'unpleasantness' arose when 'certain decisions' were made by the ANC 'without other organisations within the Congress movement, especially in relation to the TCC and the Women's Federation'.[29] The ANC made its own position quite clear: it was not obliged to consult with these bodies on 'each and every aspect'. It stated emphatically what the 'real policy' of the Congress Alliance was: '. . . namely, that the ANC was responsible for the anti-pass campaign and that the NCC, TCC or any other body would be concerned with the question of coordination of the aspects which may be taken up by the allies.'[30]

On this issue the Transvaal ANC was determined to assert its seniority and dominance with regard to both the FSAW and the TCC: male authority and ANC hegemony had become fused into a single issue. In this it was successful, and by the third week of the protests the initiative had passed to the ANC. The civil disobedience phase was called off and a new 'phase' in the resistance launched—organising a mass multiracial demonstration to the mayor of Johannesburg in late November. This proposal was made by the FSAW and ANCWL once it had become clear to them that the ANC would not support a continuation of the arrests. In pressing their own point of view earlier, the FSAW had put up a strong fight, and in yielding to the ANC, it diplomatically but unambiguously expressed its own regrets at the turn of events:

> The role of the TCC at this time became obscure, as information was received that the newly elected Transvaal Provincial Executive of the ANC was entirely responsible for the anti-pass campaign. The co-ordinating machinery of the TCC, through which until then the Federation had worked and from whom

such wholehearted cooperation had been received, was therefore no longer fully available, although contact was maintained.[31]

As on the membership issue, the women in both the FSAW and the ANCWL accepted that ultimately the authority of the ANC within the Congress Alliance was superior. Without its support, the women could not sustain and certainly could not expand their campaign to take in the whole Congress movement.

In the first rush of enthusiasm that the mass arrests had generated, the FSAW put forward an extremely ambitious target of 20,000 women for the demonstration to the mayor. This was soon scaled down to more sober and realistic proportions.[32] In organising the demonstration, the FSAW experienced intense pressure from the authorities to call the event off. Originally it had hoped to stage a mass rally of women on the steps of the City Hall in Johannesburg; after a similar rally organised by the Black Sash was banned, and in the face of repeated police warnings that 'lawlessness would not be allowed',[33] the FSAW revised its plan. In place of the mass rally, it arranged for a small poster parade on the City Hall steps. The rest of the women were instructed to file past the parade one at a time, so that there could be no charge of obstruction, and deposit individual signed forms protesting against the pass laws with the demonstration leaders.

The FSAW was anxious that the protest should not consist of African women only, and made strenuous attempts to involve other women as well. It experienced difficulty with this, however:

> Organisation of the Indian women presented great difficulties, arising from there being no specific women's organisation through which to work and the loose organisation of the TIC (Transvaal Indian Congress). All work has really to be done at the last moment by three or four Indian women and such work lacks the organisational value of the intensive work done through the ANC branches in the women's campaigns. COD women responded well. . . but their small numbers cannot be denied. On this occasion no response was forthcoming from the Black Sash or the Liberal Party. Coloured women proved impossible to organise in Johannesburg, for lack of an organisation, although Benoni women of SACPO sent in a good number of Coloured women to the protest.[34]

Its comments can be taken as a summary of its standing among the women of the Reef and within the Congress Alliance in general. Four years after the organisation had been established, it had still not managed to achieve that broad support of South African women from different backgrounds that it had hoped for in 1954.

An intensive programme of visits to the Reef townships by FSAW and ANCWL organisers drew a response of between three and four thousand women to the City Hall steps, on the 27th November 1958. Critics of the women within the Congress Alliance were disparaging about the turnout in view of the initial target of 20,000 women, but the FSAW insisted that the demonstration should be regarded as a success: it had upheld the right to peaceful public protest despite intimidation; the discipline of the women protestors had, once again, been commendable; and furthermore, their numbers were not insignificant, especially when the pressures that had been ranged against the women were taken into account. It was a solemn gathering at the City Hall. All the fire and the drama of the earlier protests outside the pass offices had gone. Then, in the rush and passion of the moment, women had dared to believe that they could indeed block the government's pass machine through sheer weight of numbers and conviction. Nobody who came to the City Hall steps on the 27th November believed that their being there would be enough to deflect the issuing of reference books on the Rand. The FSAW's claim that the meeting should be seen as a success was vindicated to some extent when, the following day, the mayor and city council of Johannesburg granted them an interview to discuss the implementation of the pass laws in the city. The city council was not the central government, however; it had no power to alter or withdraw pass legislation, it could only soften the manner in which it was implemented. The parade past the City Hall steps had been presented as an alternative to the earlier period of mass arrest. It was, however, simply another mass demonstration—a statement of opposition, not a tactic that exerted any undue pressure on the government. Once it was over, once all the womem had lodged their protests, the period of widescale resistance to passes in Johannesburg was over as well. The momentum of the campaign had been lost.

Whether the civil disobedience phase of the demonstrations could have been maintained for a significant length of time is difficult to say. The FSAW and ANCWL executives had thought so at the time:

> The Joint Executives of the Federation and the ANC Women's League met and considered the ANC's decision that the first phase had ended. . . Regret at the decision was expressed for there had been encouraging signs that had a lead been given for further demonstrations at the Pass Office, it would have been followed. Nevertheless, the authority of the ANC was regarded as supreme.[35]

In later years, with the benefit of hindsight, one of the women most actively involved in the organisation of the 1958 campaign, Helen Joseph, was more inclined to agree with the ANC's assessment, that the civil disobedience could not have been maintained for much longer, and it was better to call it off at its height rather than allow it to fizzle out.[36] If, as the Transvaal ANC maintained, the women's campaign was simply part of the wider anti-pass struggle of the Congress Alliance, and the ANC in particular, then it would be reasonable to see it as only one phase that for tactical reasons could be called off when certain objectives had been achieved—grassroots organisations activated and strengthened, participants educated and politicised by their involvement, the government confronted with a show of strength and the threat of more to come. For any of this to hold, however, it was essential for the ANC to follow up on the women's campaign. Having submitted to the ANC's authority, the women were entitled to expect that the participation of the men in the rest of the campaign would be active. In this they were disappointed. The FSAW's report on the Johannesburg campaign concluded by describing women's 'impatience' as they waited for the 'active entry' of men into the campaign:

> The Federation awaits direction from the ANC as to the course which the anti-pass campaign will follow and requests that this direction may be given in the very near future. . . Women await with impatience the active entry of the men into the anti-pass campaign.[37]

During 1959, their call was repeated with greater insistence. Although the ANC took it up at national congresses, urging supporters to make 1959 the 'greatest anti-pass year of all', it failed to mobilise men on a large scale, as the following chapter will show.

By the end of 1958, the limitations of the anti-pass campaign as then constituted were clear. It had not succeeded in preventing the imposition of passes on women, only in delaying it. At the end of the year the government announced that over 1,300,000 reference books had thus far been issued to women.[38] The response of the FSAW to this announcement was doggedly optimistic: 'More than a million, but this is still little more than half of the total number of African women in the country. There is still a long way to go and much may yet happen.'[39] Strong arm tactics by the government in pressurising women to take out passes were having their effect, however. The methods of fighting which the FSAW had adopted were proving less and less effective under the harsh conditions in a state that was moving towards totalitarianism.

In January 1959, new Native Labour Regulations were published. These drew African women still more deeply into the system of labour control that the pass laws were designed to buttress. Amongst other provisions, they extended the control of the countrywide network of labour bureaus over African women. Previously, all African men had had to register at these bureaus, which were set up to control the allocation and distribution of the African labour force through all branches of industry throughout the country. Now all African women who were in employment were obliged to register with the bureaus as well. The requirements for women were not as stringent as for men—unemployed women were still exempt from registering. Nevertheless, the regulations marked an important shift in official attitudes towards African women working in town. This had important implications for future state planning concerning African women and their role in the economy.

During the 1950s, as already mentioned, the percentage of African women as a component of the total labour force in manufacturing had doubled, from one per cent in 1951 to two per cent in 1960. The 1960s witnessed a further, dramatic increase in the percentage of African women in the manufacturing labour force, so that by 1970 this figure stood at seven per cent. The primary role of African women was still, overwhelmingly, in the reproductive sphere, but as the economy continued to expand, industrialists were beginning to see them as a potential source of super-cheap labour. The 1959 Labour Regulations meant that henceforth the state intended to control the entry of African women into the labour market more effectively and regulate it to its own advantage. The regulations also meant that the pass laws net was being drawn more tightly around African women. Reference books were still not compulsory but, as Muriel Horrell's handbook, *Legislation and Race Relations*, points out: 'It became necessary for all women in towns to obtain written proof of their authority to be there in order to safeguard themselves against arrest.'[40]

Tactics in the Anti-Pass Campaign

With the ending of the Johannesburg demonstrations, the anti-pass campaign of the FSAW itself came to a virtual stop. 1959 would see further outbreaks of unrest amongst women in Natal but the role of the FSAW in organising these was peripheral. By the end of 1958, the government had shown that it could afford to ignore mere demonstrations of popular opposition, particularly by women, who formed such an insignificant section of the labour force. The FSAW leaders were aware that the momentum of the earlier demonstrations and protests could not be maintained indefinitely without a new infusion of energy and a reformulation of tactics. The problem they faced was in devising alternatives that were acceptable to their members and would draw in the active participation of the men.

The FSAW had ruled out the possibility of violence from the start. In the early 1950s, the Congress Alliance as a whole was committed to peaceful methods of change. By the late 50s, having suffered one setback after another, the Alliance had adopted a more aggressive approach, calling for boycotts and strike action that yet fell short of direct, violent confrontation with the authorities. The FSAW supported it whole-heartedly in this stand. Throughout its career, it stressed that non-violence was a key aspect of its methods of protest and resistance. During the course of being cross-examined by the Public Prosecutor in the Treason Trial, Helen Joseph was emphatic on this point: 'We would never laud any acts of violence whatsoever.'[41] She elaborated upon this in a description of the FSAW that reflected conventional views on women's inherently peace-loving nature: 'We are an organisation of women. As women we want to create life, want to preserve it, not destroy it.'[42]

Such a response would not be unexpected in a political trial where the charge was one of High Treason against the state. Nevertheless, the FSAW's entire history was a testament to Joseph's remark. Violence as a method of resistance was inconceivable to the women who planned the FSAW campaigns. Violence as a result of resistance, as at Zeerust in 1957, could be explained and even, given the provocation the people were experiencing, condoned; it was never initiated by the FSAW. Apart from it being impractical for women to launch such a programme at a time when all peaceful methods of protest had not yet been foreclosed and its organisations were still legal and above ground, the idea of violence was repugnant to the women of the FSAW. They had not been socialised to accept violence easily as a means of redressing their problems. Many of the Federation women were active churchgoers who took seriously the teachings of reconciliation and peace put out by the churches. Most of them lived in areas where violence was endemic; murder, rape, assault and armed robbery were common in the overcrowded, poorly served townships. The women saw what violence did to their children and their families and they feared and rejected it.

Although it was opposed to violence, the FSAW was not opposed to the methods of civil disobedience, as its wholehearted support of the women who went to jail in October 1958 made clear. In all its campaigns, however, one of the FSAW's major concerns was to prevent unnecessary recriminations against it and its participants. In the case of the City Hall demonstration, it referred to 'the tremendous responsibility for the safety of the women'[43] that rested upon it. Along with this, it was also concerned to uphold 'the very right to peaceful legal protest' which it saw to be at stake.[44]

The FSAW envisaged some far-reaching changes in the political sphere, aimed at achieving a broadly democratic society, but it lacked any comprehensive overall strategy and blueprint for how the changes it desired to see could best be brought about. Its campaigns were related to the eradication of specific abuses, rather than forming part of a coherent, long-term strategy for political change. During the Treason Trial, Helen Joseph was cross-examined by the Public Prosecutor about the object of FSAW campaigns. Her reply summed up this ordering of priorities which prevailed within the FSAW:

> The object. . . was to campaign against a specific evil as we saw it, to endeavour to get that evil removed and at the same time to do an amount of educational work amongst European people, to highlight the particular grievance against which the campaign was directed, and to focus attention generally upon the conditions in this country in which the majority of the population live.[45]

The Federation was not so naive as to imagine that these evils and grievances could be done away with without a major restructuring of the political institutions in South Africa. In further evidence during the course of the Treason Trial, Joseph made this clear too:

> It is correct that the Congress linked these campaigns with the general struggle for the end of apartheid, because one and all the evils against which those campaigns were directed had their roots in the system of apartheid.[46]

Nevertheless, what the 'general struggle' entailed was left at the level of rhetoric rather than strategy.

In the case of the anti-pass campaign, the pass laws were recognised as a crucial component of the migrant labour system, 'maintained in order to preserve a supply of cheap labour to the farms and to the mines. . . and also because they. . . are a means of suppressing the movement of the

African people towards obtaining their freedom'.[47] In mobilising women against passes, the FSAW recognised that it was attacking a key structure in the apartheid state. In 1957 it declared that:

> In this vast, unmeasured and as yet inadequately organised potential of the resistance of women to passes lies one of the strongest weapons against the present government, against apartheid itself.[48]

Yet the main thrust of its own anti-pass campaign was on a local rather than national scale, and reactive rather than innovative. The FSAW was an activist body, responding vigorously to political issues as they arose. In many ways this was the source of its strength and its appeal as a political pressure group in the 1950s; its protests and campaigns were among the most extensive and best organised of any mounted by the Congress Alliance. At the level of political theory and overall strategy, however, it was weak. Partly because of the pressures on its leaders and resources, the FSAW struggled to provide the ongoing educational and organisational programme necessary to sustain a campaign of resistance. In the long term, it underestimated the strength of the political forces it was opposing and failed to adjust its tactics to the increasingly totalitarian environment in which it found itself operating.

Notes

1. G. Mbeki: 'Bans and Banishment', in *Fighting Talk*, May 1958.
2. 'Minutes of the Meeting of the NEC of the FSAW', 18.1.58, p. 1, FSAW BI.
3. FSAW circular, July 1958, and pamphlet advertising meeting, both FSAW CI 5.
4. South African Institute of Race Relations: *Survey of Race Relations, 1956–57*, p. 66.
5. *Ibid.*, 1957–58, p. 51.
6. Joint FSAW/ANCWL Statement, 8.5.57, FSAW CII.
7. Organising Committee of the National Conference of Nurses, Circular no. 2, 7.9.57, FSAW CII.
8. 'Minutes of the meeting of the NEC', 18.1.58, p. 3, FSAW BI.
9. 'Minutes of the meeting of the NEC', 18.1.58, p. 2, FSAW BI.
10. FSAW correspondence, 3.2.58, FSAW to ANC, FSAW CII.
11. Jarrett-Kerr, *op. cit.*, pp. 36, 37.
12. FSAW letter to *New Age*, 29.3.58.
13. Jarrett-Kerr, *op. cit.*, p. 37.
14. *Drum*, Nov. 1958, 'Why women don't want passes'.
15. *Ibid.*, p. 33.
16. FSAW correspondence, 14.10.58, FSAW CI 6.
17. Untitled typescript on the Johannesburg anti-pass protests, no author, (hereinafter 'typescript'), p. 4, quoting the circular in full, FSAW CI.
18. *Ibid.*, p. 2.
19. *Ibid.*, pp. 4, 5, 6, FSAW CI 1.
20. *Drum*, December 1958, 'The Battle of the Women', p. 20.
21. *The Star*, 22.10.58.
22. FSAW pamphlet, FSAW CI 6.

23. *Drum*, December 1958, 'The Battle of the Women', p. 21.
24. 'An ANC Report on the Anti-Pass Campaign', p. 1, FSAW II GII.
25. Interview.
26. 'Report by the Federation of South African Women on the Anti-Pass Campaign', p. 2, FSAW CI 6.
27. 'An ANC Report on the Anti-Pass Campaign', pp. 1, 2, FSAW II G11.
28. *Drum*, December 1958, 'The Battle of the Women', p. 22.
29. 'An ANC Report on the Anti-Pass Campaign', p. 2, FSAW II G11.
30. *Ibid.*, p. 3.
31. 'Report by the Federation of South African Women on the Anti-Pass Campaign', p. 4, FSAW CI 6.
32. 'Report by the Federation of South African Women on the Anti-Pass Campaign', and 'typescript', FSAW CII, describe the planning and execution of this protest.
33. 'Report by the Federation of South African Women on the Anti-Pass Campaign', p. 5.
34. *Ibid.*, p. 6.
35. *Ibid.*, p. 4.
36. Interview with H. Joseph.
37. 'Report by the Federation of South African Women on the Anti-Pass Campaign', p. 6.
38. 'Typescript', p. 9, FSAW CI 1.
39. *Ibid.*
40. M. Horrell: *Legislation and Race Relations*, p. 37.
41. *Treason Trial Record*, vol. 66, p. 13951.
42. *Ibid.*
43. 'Report by the Federation of South African Women on the Anti-Pass Campaign', p. 5.
44. *Ibid.*
45. *Treason Trial Record*, vol. 66, p. 14060.
46. *Ibid.*
47. *Treason Trial Record*, vol. 68, p. 14420.
48. Anonymous typescript, 'Women and Passes', October 1957, FSAW CI 1.

19

'Because of These Things We Are Dying': The Natal Disturbances, 1959

A remarkable feature of the FSAW was its ability to stage well-supported and enthusiastic conferences, despite its skimpy resources. Although it could not boast of a formal mass membership, it invariably rallied large numbers of women to its functions. Inspired by the demonstrations in October 1958, in January 1959 the FSAW held a very successful regional conference in Johannesburg. Despite the pouring rain (which earned the conference the nickname 'Operation Umbrella'), over one thousand delegates packed the conference hall. The women came from all over the Reef—it was one of the most representative conferences the FSAW ever held.[1]

Before the conference, a committee member, S. Sibeko, travelled to Potchefstroom, Klerksdorp and several towns in the Western Transvaal, to advertise the forthcoming provincial conference. She travelled by local bus, relying on contacts in the areas she visited for accommodation and addresses for further contacts. Organising at this level was slow, time-consuming and unpredictable. The contrast between the politically sophisticated townships of the Rand and the small, isolated locations of the country towns was a marked one. In her report on her trip, some of the difficulties Sibeko encountered come through.

> I had no address for Klerksdorp and was advised at Potch not to go because I must enter there with my Pass book and to get a permit that will have the name and address of where I am going to. . .
> *Bethal* no contact the man to be seen was on the farms, tried to get in touch with him but failed. . .
> *Ermelo* got there by Bus as there was no train going there. . . got to his (her contact's) home after all the buses had gone. . . so I put up at his home for the night. . . A meeting was called 14 women and 8 men came spoke to them. It was not too free with the women because they had already taken pass books.[2]

Despite the difficulties, the response she encountered overall was encouraging. She recruited several delegates to the conference and made contact with a number of potential activists. It was this kind of demanding, time-consuming spadework that was essential if the FSAW were ever to expand into the rural areas: limited resources and staff meant no sustained work was ever undertaken in these areas, however. Sibeko's own conclusion was pertinent—'A full-time organiser is really *needed*.'[3]

Even in the cities and larger towns, the FSAW was still struggling to maintain an adequate level of administrative efficiency. The difficulties that plagued the NEC in its early years were described in an earlier chapter.

Even after the head office had been shifted to Johannesburg, matters did not greatly improve. NEC meetings were infrequent. In the period between October 1956 and March 1959 only six meetings in all were held;[4] the constitution laid down two meetings a year as a minimum. Attendance at the 1958 and 1959 meetings (the only ones for which minutes survive) was poor, with 8 women present at the 1958 meeting and only 7 at the one in 1959. At this last meeting 'great disappointment was expressed by the members present at the absence of so many of the Johannesburg members as this was the first meeting of the Executive after fourteen months'.[5] In introducing her report to the 1959 meeting, the secretary, Helen Joseph, admitted that 'the national work of the Federation had not received sufficient attention during the year since the last meeting'. She attributed the reason for this to 'the pressing demands of the Transvaal region'. Later that year, when seeking a six month leave of absence from her job as regional secretary, partly so that she could concentrate on the national work of the FSAW, she was critical of the degree to which the organisation had come to rely on her: 'This state of affairs cannot go on and the Federation come to a standstill just because I am unable to cope with the work of Regional Secretary.'[6]

During 1959 the restrictive hold of the police on FSAW activities tightened. At times the Security Branch were quite open about their presence. In January 1959, at the provincial conference of the FSAW (Tvl) they 'pushed their way in, armed with warrants to remain at the conference, while uniformed police remained outside in a car for the whole day'.[7] It was becoming increasingly difficult to organise as a multi-racial organisation. In early 1959 a ban was proclaimed on all meetings of Africans outside the townships. A further ban on mixed social gatherings was threatened as well. Marcelle Goldberg, at that stage president of the FSAW in the Transvaal, described the implications to a regional conference of the FSAW thus: 'The Federation of South African Women is a multiracial organisation and thus directly in the line of these attacks. Our very existence is threatened.'[8]

The heavy reliance of the FSAW on a few key individuals made it particularly vulnerable to restrictions and bannings placed on its leaders. During 1959 these continued to take their toll on the organisation. Just two months after her speech to the Transvaal provincial conference, Marcelle Goldberg was banned and restricted to the district of Johannesburg for five years.[9] Then in November Elizabeth Mafeking, a leading activist of the FSAW in the Western Cape and president of the African Food and Canning Workers Union, was served with a banishment order from her home in Paarl and driven into exile in Lesotho. Her banishment order and the arrival of the police to take her to the train in Paarl precipitated a violent confrontation between police and several thousand workers who had turned out to demonstrate their solidarity with their leader.

Mafeking was the first FSAW member forced to abandon her home and find political refuge outside the country. She had played a leading role in building up the Food and Canning Workers' Union in the Western

Cape, having been involved in the union from its very start in 1941. In 1953 she was appointed full-time secretary of the African Food and Canning Workers' Union, after losing her job at the canning factory because of her political activities.[10] At the time of her banishment, she was 42 years old, the mother of 11 children. She had lived in Paarl with her husband and family for over 20 years. Her banishment order condemned her to move to a remote town in the Northern Cape called Vryburg. Rather than accept the radical restrictions on her mobility, contact with other people and work opportunities that banishment would impose, Mafeking chose instead to cross secretly into the neighbouring British protectorate of Basutoland. She escaped from Paarl several hours before the police arrived to escort her to the train that would take her to Vryburg, and managed to cross the border into Basutoland without mishap. There after several tense, uncertain days, she was offered political asylum. She is still in Lesotho today, waiting for the time when she will be able to return to her home in South Africa.

The Anti-Pass Campaign in 1959

In late 1958 the ANC's Planning Council optimistically designated 1959 'the greatest anti-pass year'.[11] It outlined a plan of demonstrations and protests for itself and its allies in the Congress Alliance for the next eighteen months, culminating in a nationwide protest against passes scheduled for the 31st March 1960. The FSAW gladly accepted the framework thus provided by the ANC. In mid-1959 the Transvaal executive noted that it was 'agreed that the participation by the Federation should be to call upon women in all the organisations to participate fully in the demonstrations and activities planned for March 31st.'[12] The women were disappointed, however, in the poor response from Congress supporters to the ANC's plan. The ANCWL shared the FSAW's reservations about the way that the anti-pass campaign was being conducted. In November 1959 the Transvaal executive of the ANCWL pointed out critically to its provincial conference: 'It seems that the campaign against passes is being ignored because very little has been done to intensify the campaigns.'[13]

In the aftermath of the anti-pass demonstrations in Johannesburg in late 1958, the women were showing signs of impatience at the failure of the ANC to provide them with strong and dynamic leadership. Nevertheless, they never seriously questioned the ultimate authority of the Congress. Thus Lilian Ngoyi in late 1959 said: 'It is important to understand that the struggle against passes is controlled direct by the African National Congress. The struggle of the women is merely part of the general struggle of the African people.'[14] But there was a hint of tension between the women and some of the men of the ANC when she went on to say in the same speech:

> Naturally nothing must be done to curb the initiative of the women; at the
> same time, women must discuss each stage of the campaign of [sic] the mother

body. The impression seems to be gaining ground that the women are courageous and militant whilst the men are frightened and timid, this idea is harmful
to the internal disputes and harmony [which] now should exist.

If the anti-pass protests had been more or less contained by 1959, the
widespread mood of resistance amongst African women had not yet been
broken. They actively supported a potato boycott initiated by the ANC
to spotlight the extremely exploitative labour conditions on the potato
farms of the Eastern Transvaal. Then, during the second half of 1959,
massive unrest erupted amongst African women in Natal over a very wide
range of grievances; an estimated 20,000 women or more were involved
in the disturbances, which fanned out over the whole province, bringing
new life to a sluggish Congress network and striking fear and alarm in
the white farming communities in Natal.

The Natal Disturbances

There were many points of similarity between the Zeerust disturbances
of 1957 and the unrest that erupted in Natal in 1959. In Natal too, resistance to passes was bound up with opposition to and a reaction against
many features of the oppressive conditions burdening rural women. The
disturbances were not part of a carefully formulated and directed campaign of resistance. They were spontaneous and localised, the women
taking inspiration from events in neighbouring communities but focusing
their attention on particular manifestations of hardship in their own
situation. Unlike the Zeerust protests, in Natal the resisters were almost
entirely women.

The disturbances began with unrest in the sprawling squatter community of Cato Manor in Durban, in June 1959. Cato Manor was a huge,
turbulent community on the edge of the city. It had sprung up in the years
of acute housing shortage for blacks during and after the second world
war. Municipal and government officials regarded it as an ideological
eyesore, a hotbed of crime, home of thousands of 'illegals' who were
pressing into Durban from the surrounding countryside in search of work,
without official sanction and papers.

> Cato Manor was unplanned, and as a result of its spontaneous creation far less
> controlled and policed than any of the townships set up as a result of govern-
> ment planning. Because of this freedom Cato Manor was a haven for all those
> who were illegally in the urban areas, or whose livelihood contravened the
> multitude of rules and regulations governing the lives of Africans. . . The sense
> of freedom so characteristic of it meant that at weekends and holidays it was a
> central meeting-place; over weekends the population of Cato Manor almost
> doubled, many visitors being rural dwellers.[15]

Beginning in 1958, the authorities began a concerted drive to eradicate
Cato Manor from the map. Residents who qualified to be in the Durban

municipal area were to be resettled in a new municipal township called Kwa Mashu, further out from the city centre. The thousands of people who did not qualify for urban housing were to be sent back to the rural districts from which they supposedly came. The whole community, both qualified and unqualified, felt threatened by these steps. Cato Manor was a slum. It was overcrowded, unhealthy and crime-infested. Yet, in a way that was reminiscent of the doomed Sophiatown near Johannesburg, it had many attractions too. Rents were cheap. It was close to the city centre. It had its own sense of identity and community spirit. Above all, the people living there were relatively free of the constant surveillance by police and authorities that existed in the planned locations.

Women formed a large percentage of the 'illegal' population who were threatened by the removals. Few women in Cato Manor had legal employment or official permission to be in the urban area of Durban. They had come to town to escape intolerable conditions in the reserves, to be reunited with their husbands and families, to find some source of income. Many had been there for a long time. Many too had turned to illicit beer-brewing to make a living; the shebeens and shebeen queens of Cato Manor were famous. As in other locations and at other times, beer-brewing was often the only source of income women could find. They resented fiercely the laws which made this illegal, as well as the municipal beerhalls which took away their customers, their income and their husbands' pay packets.

Tension in Cato Manor built up throughout 1958 and into 1959, as the authorities stepped up the pressure on its inhabitants. Yet nobody was prepared for the outburst when it came; they were less prepared for the huge wave of unrest and demonstrations it set off throughout the province. Police raids on illicit beer-brewing and shebeens in Cato Manor provided the spark. Because of fears of a threatened typhoid epidemic in June 1959, the Durban Corporation launched a drive to eliminate all illegal stills in the community. This sudden and extreme blow to their means of livelihood, coming on top of the other pressures squeezing them, infuriated local beer-brewers and shebeen queens. On 17th June 1959, a large group of these women stormed the nearest municipal beerhall, chased out its customers and destroyed the beer. Their example inspired other women to follow suit. In the course of the next few weeks, beerhalls throughout Durban, and as far afield as Verulam and Umbumbulu, were attacked by groups of women. Beer was destroyed, and buildings damaged. The women also launched a successful boycott of the beerhalls and established picket lines to ensure that no men broke it.

Florence Mkhize, ANCWL activist and organiser in Natal, explains the attack on the beerhalls thus:

> There were hundreds of women, pouring from every part of the Cato Manor, from Chesterville. . . They went down to the beerhall to try to boycott the beerhall. They were trying to tell their husbands not to patronise them because of starvation and influx control. . . The husbands used to earn very little money. . . They would spend the last money they had in the beerhalls so the women decided not to patronise them, to protect their homes.[16]

At first the demonstrations were entirely an urban affair. But in late July and the early part of August, large areas of rural Natal suddenly erupted into violence as well. Rural women took their cue from their urban counterparts and began demonstrating before magistrates, Bantu Commissioners and agricultural extension officers against laws and practices that they experienced as particularly onerous. On several occasions, demonstrations spilled over into violence as the women attacked government property—cattle dipping tanks, government buildings, newly issued reference books. In the first week of August, 112 women were arrested at Indudutu for smashing dipping tanks in protest against the fact that they were expected to maintain them without pay. Later 350 women at a place called Dweshula demanded to see the local magistrate and the agricultural officer to complain about the lack of payment for the forest breaks they had cleared. Shortly afterwards, 1,000 women at Mehlomyami demonstrated against the same thing. Demonstrations by women followed in numerous other areas—Umzinto, Harding, New Hanover, Highflats, Pietermaritzburg. The scale of the rural disturbances was very large. *Drum* estimated that some 20,000 women took part in all. The total amount of fines imposed on them by magisterial courts across the province amounted to almost £20,000. Dipping tanks formed a major target of attack—in late August it was estimated that about 75 per cent of all the tanks in the Natal inland police division had been destroyed.[17]

The women focused on several different targets of attack, all of which related to the economic stress under which they were living. Among them were a wide range of issues connected to the introduction of so-called 'betterment schemes' in rural areas. Betterment schemes were originally intended to control land use and soil management in the reserves, to prevent soil erosion and boost agricultural yields. They were, however, enforced by government extension officers with minimal consultation with and involvement of local people; they also ran contrary to already existing social and economic structures within the community, particularly those relating to land tenure and stock ownership. Many women lost field rights when land proclaimed part of a betterment scheme was re-zoned; frequently officials in charge of the re-allocation of land only considered male household heads eligible for fields. Another explosive issue connected to betterment schemes was the enforced culling of cattle. This was implemented at government dipping tanks. Women were already resentful of the dipping tanks because they were expected to keep them filled with water but were not paid for their services. Cattle culling focused their attention on these tanks, which quickly came to be seen as the material representation of an alien, perverse but all-powerful officialdom.

Other points of grievance were more familiar to urban women. Reference books were being issued to women on a large scale in Natal at the time. Women saw the link between these books and influx control, which shut off the towns to them and penned them in the reserves. There were reports of women stoning the reference book units or simply refusing to take books out. Another grievance which women aired in memoranda and talks was an increase in the taxation levied on rural people in 1959.

The women made it clear that they felt pushed to the limits of their endurance by this combination of measures:

> We do not get enough food. Our husbands pay more than £2 in taxes. The employers do not pay them anything. Our husbands are stuck at home. If husbands come home from Durban because of the sickness they cannot go back to Durban. Because of these things we are dying.

> We dont want to see this tank. We pay money for cattle. Because of dipping, cattle have died. We cannot start ploughing. There is a tractor we can hire but it costs us lots of money. Our husbands get little money. Our husbands cannot go to Durban to earn money. We have not enough fields to plough.[18]

Cato Manor was clearly the catalyst and provided rural women with a model for their own demonstrations and protests. The ease and speed with which the unrest was spread was facilitated by the geographical situation in Natal, where town and reserves are in close contact, the reserves fragmented and scattered throughout the province. As in Zeerust, however, the protests were spontaneous responses to Cato Manor, organised initially at a grassroots level. They showed how volatile reserve society had become by 1959—one spark and it burst into flame.

Once the protests were underway and spreading, the ANC and ANCWL did become involved far more actively than they had done in Zeerust. The ANCWL had established a branch in Cato Manor which was active as far back as 1955/56, while many women of Cato Manor would have been aware of the anti-pass demonstrations of the ANCWL and FSAW in other centres over the previous three years.[19] The ANC also helped indirectly to spread the unrest from Cato Manor by organising a mammoth Freedom Day rally in Durban on the 27th June. About 50,000 people attended, a far larger crowd than usual, and of these a substantial number were women. It played no part in fomenting or initiating the rural unrest, however. The ANCWL's organisation in the rural areas was, as already pointed out, poor. Only once the women had shown the way, did it rally to their support. Thereafter ANC women organisers became involved, organising further demonstrations and articulating grievances. They thus introduced a wider political dimension to the protests, linking them to other protests that had gone before. The government of course stressed the 'agitator' theory, but, as a *Drum* article pointed out:

> Government laws produce hundreds of 'agitators' each month. Under laws dealing with slum clearance alone, a regular convoy of urban dwellers are sent back into the rural areas from the towns because there are no longer homes for them.[20]

The ANC also did everything in its power to stem the violence that erupted at times; they stressed that they were a peaceful organisation and urged women to beware of individuals who advocated violence. In August 1959,

ANC President Lutuli issued a statement condemning the violence, which was distributed throughout the villages of Natal by volunteers.[21]

Although the ANC was not involved directly in initiating the demonstrations and disturbances in Natal, it certainly benefited from them. During 1959 the ANC in Natal experienced a sudden and marked revival. Its membership increased remarkably; it was the only ANC region to meet a projected recruitment total (of 15,000) in 1959.[22] The regional committee of the FSAW, too, benefited, showing signs of much greater activity in the early 1960s than at any time during the 1950s.

For the most part, as in Zeerust, the Natal women were acting conservatively, in defence of an eroded way of life. Betterment schemes destroyed traditional patterns of settlement and threatened women's already tenuous access to land. Cattle culling too was an attack on more than an economic asset. Cattle had a social function and a symbolic value that could not be quantified in money terms alone; reduce a household's herd and you reduced a vital component in its social standing and relationships with other kin and neighbouring groups. There were many traditional elements incorporated in the style of protest too—dress, dancing, the segregation of women from men. One frequently articulated complaint against passes was that the teams issuing reference books told women to remove their headscarves so that their photographs could be taken. Traditionally, only the husband was allowed to do so.

Yet more was involved than respect for tradition and convention. As in Zeerust, the act of organising and protesting was in itself a politicising and radicalising experience for the women who took part. Referring to the photograph requirements of the reference book units, one woman said: 'They forced us to take off our headdoeks. It was against our custom but we had to do it. . . The light got to our brains. We woke up and saw the light. And women have been demonstrating ever since.'[23] Threaded through their actions, in a way that was reminiscent of the women in Zeerust in 1957, was a new sense of their political relevance and an unaccustomed assertiveness. Kuper, in his book *An African Bourgeoisie*, has described the movement as 'remarkable for the dominant role of traditionally subordinate Zulu women'.[24] A comment made to *Drum* magazine by one participant in the disturbances captured something of the militancy of the women as well as the novelty of their behaviour: 'Said an irate mother, when reproached that African women should now be carrying sticks: "It is true that African women never carried sticks before. But then they never carried passes before, either!" '[25]

In her paper on the Natal riots, Yawitch points out the contradictory aspects of the women's behaviour. On the one hand, they were fighting to defend a way of life that was being destroyed by government policies; on the other hand, by resisting passes, they were resisting influx control and a system that denied them access to the towns and the new economic and social order that prevailed there. For women in the reserves were in fact caught in the pincers of a policy whose aims and results were in themselves contradictory. By trying to maintain the traditional, tribal political and economic structures but manipulate them to their own ends, the government was undermining them. Women's position in the resulting system was ambiguous, their status and self-image ambivalent—subordinate, junior, yet burdened with responsibilities and a *de facto* authority not sanctioned by society.

The outburst of resistance by women in both Zeerust in 1957/58 and Natal in 1959 were symptomatic of the strain this situation imposed on women. They were a reaction against intolerable conditions. They showed the potential that existed amongst rural women for resistance over specific issues but, equally, they also showed the limitations of political organisation amongst rural women at that stage.

Notes

1. 'Operation Umbrella: an "outside" impression of a great conference', anonymous article, FSAW A13.
2. S. Sibeko: 'Report for the Western Transvaal', pp. 1, 2, FSAW A13.
3. *Ibid.*, p. 3.
4. This is calculated from a variety of sources, including available minutes of meetings and correspondence. See FSAW correspondence, 6.6.57, FSAW CI 5; FSAW circular 26.5.57, FSAW BI; FSAW NEC minutes, FSAW BI.
5. 'Minutes of the meeting of the NEC', 2.3.59, p. 2, FSAW BI.
6. FSAW correspondence, 30.10.59, Helen Joseph to Marcelle Goldberg, FSAW DI.
7. 'Operation Umbrella: an "outside" impression of a great conference', anonymous article, FSAW A13.
8. 'President's report to the Provincial Conference of the FSAW (Tvl)', p. 6, FSAW A13.
9. Newspaper cutting from *The Star*, 14.4.59, FSAW FII.
10. 'Elizabeth Mafeking', biographical sketch, FSAW FI.
11. ANC: 'Make 1959 the Greatest Anti-Pass Year', FSAW B13.
12. 'Notes from Regional Executive—Transvaal Executive Committee', nd, FSAW BI.
13. 'Executive Report presented at 7th annual Conference of ANCWL Transvaal', November 1959, p. 2 (Reel 8, Hoover Institute Microfilm Collection).
14. 'Presidential Address', p. 2 in 'Annual Conference of the African National Congress Women's League held at the Communal Hall, Orlando', FSAW II B7.
15. J. Yawitch: 'Natal 1959—The Women's Protests', p. 1.
16. Interview with F. Mkhize.
17. *Drum*, October 1959, 'Trouble in Natal'.
18. *Ibid.*
19. There is material in the Treason Trial Record ('ANC Women's Association Two Stick's Branch', 10.3.56, Treason Trial Exhibit G 183), as well as in the pages of *New Age* in 1955 and 1956, to suggest that the ANCWL was active in the area before 1959. How active, however, is not clear.
20. *Drum*, October 1959, 'Trouble in Natal'.
21. *Ibid.*
22. ANC (Tvl.): 'Annual Report of the Provincial Executive Committee', October 1959, pp. 13–15, FSAW II G7.
23. Yawitch, *op. cit.*, p. 4.
24. Kuper, *An African Experience*, p. 17.
25. *Drum*, October 1959, 'Trouble in Natal'.

20

'You Get Four Women, Get Your Friends . . . After That You Organise a Meeting': The Structure and Organisation of the FSAW

The FSAW was constituted as a federation of 'organisations or groups of females above the age of 18 years' and drew its membership entirely from its affiliated organisations. Because of its federal form, it depended on its executive committee, both national and regional, to maintain its identity as an organisation operating over and above its member organisations. The importance of the executive committees was exaggerated still further by the failure of the NEC to convene national conferences regularly. In terms of the constitution the national conference, representing all the branches, was the highest decision-making body in the FSAW and should meet annually 'if possible'. During the 1950s this never did prove possible, and only two conferences were held, in 1954 and 1956; the shaping of FSAW policy and its programme of action was, therefore, in the hands of its executive committees. These functioned at two levels, national and regional. Of the two, it was the regional committees that were the more important.

The constitution laid down that the next highest decision-making body after the national conference was the NEC. This was never a particularly effective body. The national president, Lilian Ngoyi, and secretary, Helen Joseph, both enjoyed considerable prestige within the organisation after their election to office in 1956. Most of their work for the FSAW was based on the Transvaal region, however, rather than on the NEC as such. Once the shift of head office to Johannesburg had taken place in 1956, the distinction between the national and Trsnavaal executives was frequently blurred, with the latter the more active body.

The reasons why the NEC was weak when based in Cape Town have already been discussed. The major weakness troubling it in Johannesburg after 1956 was that of poor communication with the regional committees. Distances were large, and postal communications were slow and, as the decade wore on, increasingly risky from a security point of view. There was no full-time organiser, and committee members could not afford to travel to other centres very often. To a request from Cape Town for a visit by Lilian Ngoyi, the Transvaal secretary replied:

> I wish to point out to you the difficulty confronting the President. She is a person with a big family to support and has nobody helping her. We feel that a three week visit means to her three weeks of having no money to support her family.[1]

As an organisation involved in the Congress Alliance, the FSAW was subject to the increasingly damaging restrictions placed upon the national liberation movement by the government in the 1950s in the form of police surveillance, harrassment of its leaders, bannings and intimidation. As a multiracial organisation, it struggled to convene meetings to suit all its members. Non-African women could not enter the African townships without permits; black women in the white suburbs in any capacity other than that of domestic worker or nanny were conspicuous and subject to official harrassment. As an example of how the laws of the land could upset the smooth functioning of the FSAW: in August 1957 Mary Moodley, chairwomen of the East Rand working committee, reported that she had been unable to attend an important branch meeting of the ANCWL in Benoni because of the problem of getting a permit to enter an African area. Her failure to attend the meeting exacerbated existing tensions between ANCWL and SACPO women in Benoni about the allocation of funds between the two groups.[2]

In convening national conferences there was the additional problem that in terms of the Urban Areas Act, no unqualified African could remain in a 'prescribed' (urban) area for longer than 72 hours without official permission. In organising the inaugural conference, its convenors decided to 'take a chance' and not apply for permits for the non-Johannesburg African delegates, for 'if permits were applied for, Saturday would be spent at the Pass Office and not at the Conference'. This decision involved taking extra precautions; for instance, ensuring transport for these women 'so there is as little chance as possible of their being picked up'.[3]

Many of the problems that hindered the FSAW's development as an organisation stemmed from the restrictions placed on women by their position within the family. A very large proportion of the women on its committees were married, with children to look after. For them it was often difficult to attend meetings; frequently, their only free time was late at night, when travel in the townships was particularly unsafe for women. In organising conferences, women's family commitments had constantly to be borne in mind. In early 1954, when discussions on when to hold the inaugural conference were still proceeding, Alexander suggested the Easter long weekend as being most suitable for the East London and Durban women. That was the easiest time for them to 'get away and leave the children at home'.[4]

Apart from their responsibilities as mothers, many women had uncooperative husbands who disapproved of or resented signs of too great an independence on the part of their wives. This 'backward attitude' of the men, as the FSAW termed it, was a real deterrent on women's political involvement and one the FSAW had constantly to fight against. In 1954, at the inaugural conference, Ngoyi's comments that had it not been for 'the husbands', many more women would have been present, drew cheers from the audience. The extent to which such attitudes could disrupt women's political effectiveness was manifested during the anti-pass demonstrations in Johannesburg in October 1958. There, as discussed earlier, it was the husbands of many of the arrested women who undermined their strategy of civil disobedience by bailing them out, before either the FSAW or ANC had come to a decision on what the best course of action would be. When women did have sympathetic and cooperative husbands, they generally still had to attend to domestic matters before they felt free to spend time on political work. Thus Virginia Mngomo's husband allowed her her freedom—but first she had to ensure that he had enough food and clean shirts and socks etc. laid out for the week.[5]

Not all the FSAW's organisational difficulties were external, however. Responsibility for failing to keep contact between the regions had also, on occasion, to be attributed to slackness on the part of the regional committees themselves. 'It is sickening how these people never acknowledge letters or report on anything', Ray Alexander had grumbled in mid 1955,[6] referring to the FSAW committees in Natal and the Eastern Cape, as well as the ANCWL contact in Kimberley. This situation did not improve substantially with the shift of the head office to Johannesburg. In 1959, Helen Joseph reported to the NEC that correspondence with the different regions was 'irregular'. In the case of the Eastern Cape, news of its activities came often via the columns of the newspaper *New Age*, rather than direct from the regional committee itself.[7]

Poor communications encouraged regional autonomy and a greater preoccupation with local rather than national campaigns and issues. Even the anti-pass campaign, though conceived of as a national campaign, was conducted with a high degree of regional initiative and local responsibility. The regional committees thus formed the organisational basis of the FSAW, determining, finally, its shape and effectiveness. They varied quite considerably in strength and character, as the following survey will show.

The regional Committees of the FSAW

As already described, the FSAW only succeeded in establishing four regional committees during the 1950s—in the Transvaal, Western Cape, Eastern Cape and Natal. In practice, the regions in which the committees operated were confined largely to the immediate vicinity of the city in which they were based, i.e. Johannesburg, Cape Town, Port Elizabeth and Durban. Of the four, the Transvaal and Western Cape were the two most solidly constituted regions. Committees were established soon after the inaugural conference and functioned throughout the FSAW's short history. The Eastern Cape and Natal committees were much less stable.

The Transvaal region, based on the Rand, the financial and industrial centre of the country, was by far the most dynamic of all four regions, although, because it is the only one for which extensive documentation survives, it is possible that one can exaggerate its dominance and relative strength. It was responsible for many of the FSAW's most dramatic protests of the 1950s—the two demonstrations to Pretoria in 1955 and 1956, the protest outside the Johannesburg City Hall in November 1958— and numerous smaller ones besides. It organised several major conferences which were generally very well attended.

Once the FSAW head office had been mvoed to Johannesburg in 1956, the Transvaal region's dominance within the FSAW became especially marked. Overlap of membership in the NEC and Transvaal regional executive was extensive: for some of the time Ngoyi and Joseph duplicated their respective positions as president and secretary in both the NEC and the Transvaal regional committee. Often it was the Transvaal regional committee, rather than the NEC itself, which made national policy decisions for the FSAW, for instance, in late 1959, the minutes of a Transvaal regional executive meeting record that the 'National President' led a discussion on what the role of the FSAW in the ANC's anti-pass campaign should be.[8]

Johannesburg was the heartland of the Congress Alliance and on the Rand the FSAW was in close (though not always harmonious) contact with the NCC of the Alliance and the other Congress organisations. The head office of the ANCWL was in Johannesburg, and overlap between ANCWL and FSAW committees, both regional and national, was considerable as well. After 1955, Lilian Ngoyi held the extremely important position of ANCWL national president, in addition to her posts in the FSAW. The overlap between the FSAW and ANCWL facilitated communications, but, at the same time, the very informality it encouraged led on occasion to confusion and some friction. This was evident in the anti-pass pledge campaign in 1951, when the Transvaal ANCWL accused the FSAW of by-passing its offices and communicating directly with its branches.

Such difficulties with the ANCWL, which arose from time to time, never proved serious. For the most part, the working relationship between the two organisations was good. The strength of the FSAW on the Rand lay in the ANCWL, as it knew full well. Women's League branches in Sophiatown, Alexandra and Orlando townships provided it with its strongest support. In a letter to the press in November 1955, Ngoyi spoke of the 'deep feelings of friendship and sympathy' that existed between 'women of different races'.[9] Several informants agree that amongst the women involved in the FSAW, these sentiments were widely shared. Where disagreements between the FSAW and ANCWL did arise, it was more often than not due to the intervention of the ANC itself—as in the case of the initial dispute about the form of the FSAW's membership. It was on the Rand that the FSAW was most assertive and active as an independent organisation amongst women—and on the Rand that tensions between it and male members of the Congress Alliance were most in evidence. Relations between the FSAW and the ANC are discussed more fully in the next chapter.

The difficulties that the Transvaal FSAW experienced in organising non-African women have been mentioned already. Nevertheless, the multi-racial character of the FSAW was most convincingly expressed there; COD and SACPO were probably stronger on the Reef than elsewhere in the country, while relations between the FSAW and Transvaal Indian Congress, its youth section in particular, appear to have been good. The youth section of the TIC always helped with the catering and cleaning at FSAW conferences. Beyond Johannesburg, efforts were made to set up additional local committees on the East Rand, the West Rand and in

Pretoria, although the attempt only took root in the East Rand, where a very active East Rand working committee was established. This was based primarily on SACPO members in Benoni. They were led by Mary Moodley, a large, warm-hearted woman, cheerful and dedicated to her work— 'Aunty Mary' to all who knew her.

Further afield, the FSAW's contact with women in the outlying towns and districts of the Transvaal was intermittent and unsatisfactory. Lack of a full-time organiser and inadequate communications made it very difficult to sustain contact, and it was dependent on the ANC network of branches for its links with country women. The FSAW was aware of the inadequacy of its links with the countryside and did make some attempts to reach women beyond the Reef. The most successful attempt was in January 1959, when S. Sibeko toured the Western Transvaal to advertise the forthcoming regional conference and recruit delegates.

Activities in the Western Cape were on a much smaller scale than in the Transvaal. The character of the Federation too was somewhat different —the African component was proportionally smaller and links with factory women, in the food canning industry in particular, stronger. The ANCWL was not as flourishing a body in the Western Cape as on the Rand. The scale of ANC and, hence, FSAW conferences and meetings was small compared to activities on the Rand. An ANCWL anti-pass conference in Cape Town in January 1955 drew only 80 delegates; one in February 1956, 81.[10] Both were lively meetings—'spirited' was *New Age*'s description of the 1956 meeting—but they hardly compared to similar meetings on the Rand where hundreds of women could be relied upon to attend. The failure of the ANCWL to mount any counter-demonstrations when the reference book units finally reached Cape Town in mid-1958 was a further reflection of its relative weakness in the Western Cape.

Part of the reason for this, it has been suggested, lay in the smaller African population and the greater residential insecurity of African women in Cape Town, particularly once the 'Eiselen Line' had been proclaimed in 1955. While the stringent influx control measures of the Western Cape provided a focal point for protests, in the long term this obstructed the emergence of a well-developed and stable organisation amongst women. Joseph has suggested that, while on the Rand the ANCWL formed the basis of the FSAW, in Cape Town it was the trade unions that were more important.[11] Certainly the role of trade unionists was very large in the Cape Town FSAW, though the ANCWL was not by any means unimportant. The links Ray Alexander had forged with the trade union movement proved strong. The only union formally to affiliate to the FSAW, the Food and Canning Workers' Union (including its African 'parallel' counterpart), was based in the Western Cape. Its officials figured prominently among the local Federation leadership—Liz Abrahams, Elizabeth Mafeking, Ruth Gottschalk. Through its branches the FSAW reached out into the small agricultural towns lying beyond Cape Town: Paarl, Wellington, Worcester, Stellenbosch. The Paarl and Worcester branches of the union, in particular, were in close contact with the regional committee of the FSAW.

Yet, outside of the union leadership, it is doubtful that many of the women working in the food processing factories were well-informed about the FSAW. As in the ANCWL, the affiliation of union members to the FSAW was automatic. There were no local FSAW committees in the Western Cape except in Cape Town. In Paarl, the area where the FSAW was probably best known, FSAW meetings were not separate from union ones. Any business of the Federation that needed to be discussed would simply be raised at the end of a union meeting.[12] Contact between the FSAW regional committee in Cape Town and union branches in the Boland towns was extremely informal, depending largely on the overlap of their respective committees. All regional functions of the FSAW appear to have taken place in Cape Town only. According to Abrahams, who lived in Paarl, whenever there was an important FSAW meeting or demonstration, delegates from Paarl, Stellenbosch and Worcester would travel to the city by bus to participate.

Outside the Food and Canning Workers Union, the following the FSAW had amongst 'Coloured' women was remarkably slight for a city where the bulk of the black population was fitted into this category. SACPO was not strong in Cape Town. It was rivalled by the strongly entrenched Non-European Unity Movement [NEUM]. The NEUM has been criticised for elevating to the level of non-negotiable principle the political strategy of boycott and non-collaboration. It was the strongest political movement among 'Coloured' intellectuals in the Western Cape in the 1950s. With its philosophy of boycott and contempt for 'collaborators', it managed to blunt the influence of the Congress campaigns within the Western Cape quite considerably. For the local FSAW this meant that access to a large and potentially important group of women was made extremely difficult.

The strength of the NEUM in Cape Town undoubtedly influenced the local FSAW committee to press for the principle of individual, rather than affiliated membership in 1954/55. In arguing the case, Alexander did not mention the NEUM directly, but she did refer to the 'Cape Coloured women' who would be excluded from participation if a federal form was adopted. Once the individual membership issue had been dropped, the FSAW in Cape Town made attempts to establish a 'League of Non-European Women' which would be able to affiliate to it. It organised an inaugural meeting at the Cape Town City Hall in June 1956, but nothing enduring materialised from it.[13] This was the third 'league' that leftwing women had tried to establish among 'Coloured' women in Cape Town since 1938. Previously there had been the 'Non-European Women's Suffrage League' of 1938 and a similarly titled league in 1948. All failed. 'Coloured' women, as a group, occupied an ambiguous position socially and economically, and this affected their political consciousness. They were more integrated into the labour force yet politically more marginal than either white or African women, a minority group who shared the language and culture of the dominant whites but were rejected by them as 'half-breeds', their inferiors. In turn, many working-class 'Coloured' people were sufficiently conditioned by racist ideology to reject Africans as culturally their inferiors. They thus could not easily identify with a political movement that called for equality for all and majority rule.

The white membership of the FSAW was smaller in Cape Town than on the Rand, where COD was at its strongest. However, in making contact with white liberal women's organisations—the Black Sash, NCW, some church groups—the FSAW had its greatest success in Cape Town. The Cape Association to Abolish Passes, established in 1957, was the only broad-based anti-pass committee established in the 1950s (although, as already mentioned, contact between the FSAW and the Black Sash did increase on the Rand after 1956). The Black Sash never agreed to affiliate to the FSAW in Cape Town, but the links established in the anti-pass committee proved enduring. After 1960 they were to gain in significance.

Since the FSAW in Cape Town is so poorly documented, it is difficult to explain why contact with the Black Sash and other white groups should have been easier in that city than elsewhere. The role of individuals seems to have been important. In this regard, the contacts Alexander had built up over many years with an extremely wide range of women's organisations in Cape Town, from the Union of Jewish Women to the Food and Canning Workers' Union, were particularly valuable. She herself had kept in touch with the NCW from the 1930s.[14] It is perhaps tempting for those who subscribe to the view that the Cape 'liberal tradition' has continued to infuse the social, if not the political, life in Cape Town, to take this as a further manifestation of that tradition. But the contact was too limited, the number of women it involved too small to amount to a significant interaction between women across colour lines. If it was a manifestation of the 'liberal tradition', it was equally a manifestation of the extent to which that had atrophied by the mid-twentieth century.

The third region of the FSAW, that of the Eastern Cape, which centred on Port Elizabeth, was far closer to Johannesburg in character than to Cape Town. This area is very poorly documented and few records of its day-to-day activities survive. Yet it had a reputation that still survives to the present day of being a very strong and dynamic ANC centre. The militancy that had characterised the Eastern Cape during the Defiance Campaign and prompted women leaders to launch the FSAW in 1953 remained true of this region throughout the 1950s. The level of political activity amongst women in the other Congresses was low, however, affecting the status of the FSAW regional committee. According to a report submitted to the NCC in 1956, COD in Port Elizabeth was 'weaker than any other area' while SACPO suffered from a 'generally inactive' membership.[15] Thus, although it was from Port Elizabeth that the original idea to launch the FSAW had come, a separate committee was not established there immediately after the inaugural conference. The first signs of a Federation committee, acting under the name of the 'Congress of Mothers' Committee', came only in September 1955, at a public meeting.[16]

The following month, in October, this committee sought formal affiliation with the FSAW.[17] Most of its support came from ANCWL members, with SACPO and the Food and Canning Workers' Union providing a sprinkling of additional members. Helen Joseph, who visited Port Elizabeth in 1956, was particularly struck by the militancy and commitment of the women she met. In her estimate, Port Elizabeth ranked second to the much larger Johannesburg as a centre for political activism amongst black women.[18] In 1962 a visitor from the WIDF echoed her views—'The women of Port Elizabeth are great fighters.'[19] The school boycott launched in 1955 against Bantu Education schools was particularly well supported. The anti-pass campaign too was vigorously pursued in the early years. In January 1956 a huge outdoor meeting was arranged by the 'Congress of Mothers'. Lilian Ngoyi was guest speaker, addressing the enormous gathering—6,000 people was *New Age*'s estimate—from the back of a parked lorry.[20] In view of the history of resistance in that area the failure of the ANCWL to launch a mass demonstration against the reference book units when they arrived in Port Elizabeth in mid 1958 was puzzling. Without detailed material on the organisation there, it is impossible to tell to what extent the ban on public meetings by Africans hampered it at the time.

Despite the reported high level of organisation within the ANC in the Eastern Cape, communications between the local FSAW committee and the head office in Johannesburg were poor. Just how poor was revealed in 1959, when Joseph reported to the NEC that for her information on developments in Port Elizabeth, she relied largely on newspaper reports. Nevertheless, although the lack of material on the FSAW in Port Elizabeth blurs one's picture, the impression gained from interviews and scattered references is that Port Elizabeth was a strong centre of activity. In concluding her report on the Eastern Cape to the NEC in 1959, Helen Joseph noted: 'Militant anti-pass campaigns are undertaken in the name of the Federation, mobilising both African and Coloured women in intense activity and solidarity.'[21]

The fourth FSAW region, Durban, was, by contrast, very weak and very unstable for most of this time. On several occasions over the years it ceased to operate altogether, although it always flickered back into life again. During 1954 and 1955 there was little, if any, FSAW activity. By March 1956, a group consisting of the ANCWL and 'loose groups' of Indian and 'Coloured' women had come together and were requesting affiliation to the NEC.[22] In June that year, Helen Joseph reported that a FSAW committee was functioning in Durban. Unfortunately her report (to the NCC) did not elaborate on the extent of this committee's activities, but her general comments on the strength of the Congress Alliance in the Durban area sketched out the limits within which the FSAW was operating: co-operation between the ANC and NIC was 'excellent', COD was extremely weak and amounted to little more than a handful of active individuals, SACPO was non-existent.[23] The basis of the FSAW in Durban was thus clearly the ANC and the Indian Congress.

For most of the 1950s both these organisations were weak. The NIC had gone into a decline after the Passive Resistance campaign of 1946. The number of branches represented at its annual provincial conference declined from 28 in 1947 to only 12 in 1959.[24] In 1956 the general secretary reported to the Natal provincial conference that since the Congress of the People (in 1955), branch activity had shown a 'steady decline', and no meaningful estimate of its membership was possible.[25] In the ANC in Natal, different factions had long divided the organisation. The ANCWL involved itself in some fierce and well-supported demonstrations against passes in 1955 and early 1956 but, by 1956, tensions within the organisation were already visible. In late 1956 these erupted into a disruptive power struggle amongst its leaders, which led to the expulsion of two senior executive members, the veteran Bertha Mkize and G. Kuzwayo.[26]

The ANCWL did maintain a branch network. Florence Mkhize, provincial organiser for the ANCWL during the 1950s, recalls how she used to recruit members and encourage new branches to form:

> I used to organise right through. . . I used to get a small group of women. The first thing was that they become members of the ANC, form a branch. . . You get four women, you get your friends, have a house meeting. There are 12 people, plenty. . . After that you organise a meeting.[27]

For most of the 1950s, however, Natal was the weakest FSAW region, and by 1959 the FSAW committee in Natal had foundered. 'No Federation Committee has yet been established but contact is maintained with the ANCWL, the Natal Indian Women's Congress and the COD', was how Helen Joseph reported on the Natal region to the NEC in March of that year.[28] Three months later the beerhall riots in Cato Manor exploded onto the scene. One effect of these riots and the subsequent disturbances in the countryside was to stimulate a resurgence of political organisation within Natal. The ANC and ANCWL experienced a marked upswing in membership and the FSAW, too, enjoyed a boost as a result. In the early 1960s, when elsewhere the organisation was struggling to survive, the FSAW in Natal experienced something of a revival—an indication of the degree to which women had been politicised by the events of 1959.

Outside the four major centres where it had its own committees, the FSAW depended totally on the network of ANC branches. In the larger towns where strong ANC branches functioned—Pretoria, Bloemfontein, Kimberley—communications between the FSAW and local women were reasonably good. Pretoria was very close to Johannesburg, and it was easy to involve it in activities arranged by the Transvaal committee. The NEC maintained a correspondence with the ANCWL in Bloemfontein that was at least as good, if not better, as its correspondence with the Port Elizabeth and Durban committees. Links with the smaller country branches were more difficult to maintain. The ANC had a showing in many of the smaller towns throughout the country, but the level of their membership, efficiency and activity fluctuated enormously. Frequently they were branches in name only. It is unlikely, too, that many ANC members in the more isolated regions were fully aware that the FSAW existed as a distinct body to which the ANCWL was affiliated.

In Queenstown, for instance, links between the local branch and the centre were fairly tenuous and only loosely maintained. According to Nomvo Booi, a member of the ANC in that town, the Queenstown branch of the ANC established no separate Women's League.[29] Men and women

belonged to a single organisation. Their branch had no close ties with either
East London or Port Elizabeth, the two large population centres nearest
them, although occasionally individual women from Queenstown attended
conferences at these places. She recalls that they kept informed about
developments in other centres by reading the newspapers. She had 'heard of'
the FSAW and knew that there were white women involved in ANCWL
campaigns—Helen Joseph, Ray Alexander. She knew that they 'were sympa-
thising'. But in Queenstown itself there was no social or political contact
between African and other racial groups. The small Indian community never
involved itself in Congress politics and involvement of whites was out of the
question: 'There was no chance with other racial groups—in small towns the
groups always stay apart.'

    In the densely populated reserve areas—where in 1951 some 46 per
cent of all African women were living—the ANC was barely represented
at all. Here, extensive and sustained political work amongst women by it
or the Women's League, or indeed, any other 'liberation' body (the NEUM
for instance), did not materialise during the 1950s. The ANCWL did
undertake some follow-up work in those areas where rural women themselves forced attention upon their situation—in Zeerust in 1957/58 and
later in Natal, in 1959. In both cases its involvement was in response to a
situation that had already blown up, generated by local people on their
own initiative. Neither the ANCWL nor the FSAW had a programme of
on-going politicisation and recruitment of country members.

    The attitude of the Federation towards rural women has already
been described. It was not oblivious to the importance of expanding its
work outside the towns; in 1956 the Transvaal region of the FSAW listed
the dearth of an organised movement amongst peasant women and its
own lack of contact with them as one of its major difficulties.[30] Time,
money and personnel were all at a premium, however, and the anti-pass
campaign in the cities absorbed most of its energies. At the same time,
government constraints made organisation in the rural areas increasingly
difficult. In 1958, for instance, a ban was imposed on the ANC in the
Marico (Zeerust) and Soutpansberg districts of the Transvaal. But the
neglect of the country areas was a major flaw in the ANCWL and the
FSAW. No mass organisation of women could ever claim to be representative unless it could count on rural support. The fundamental part
that women in the reserves played in reproducing the apartheid economy
made it particularly important that they be included in any women's
organisation that aimed at real political change in South Africa. The rural
disturbances in Zeerust and Natal both showed that there was no lack of
issues round which rural women could be organised. The problems lay
elsewhere, in penetrating the barriers erected by the state, by tradition
and by isolation.

Membership

Although it is possible to map out the areas covered by the FSAW, it is extremely difficult to give a rough estimate of the number of women it could claim as members by the end of the 1950s. Its affiliated organisations kept few reliable records of their own, and from all accounts, numbers fluctuated considerably over the years. In 1962 a visitor to the FSAW observed: 'The actual number of members of the FSAW has probably never been counted because the membership of the affiliated groups and organisations varies from time to time.'[31]

In 1952, when the Defiance Campaign was at its height, the ANC's official membership was estimated at about 100,000. By December 1955, however, according to one available figure, this had dropped to 28,700, little more than a quarter of the 1952 figure.[32] By the end of the decade, this had probably increased to some extent, but in 1959 the ANC admitted it was still far short of the target of 120,000 which it had set for itself at the 1958 conference. It reported that Natal was the only province to have achieved its target, of 15,000 people. The target for the Cape had been 50,000 and that for the Orange Free State 5,000; both provinces had failed to reach their goals. The Transvaal had been hampered by bannings of individual branches. By 1959 some 40 ANC branches had been banned, leaving a total of 87 branches still intact. The ANC executive reported that there had been approximately 6,000 members in the 40 banned branches, an average of 150 members per branch.[33] It is scanty evidence to build on, but the indications are that the paid-up membership of the ANC did not even approach 50,000 by the end of the 1950s.

What proportion of its members were women is hard to assess. If anything, the ANCWL was even less efficient about keeping statistics than the parent body. In 1959 the executive reported to the annual ANCWL conference that it 'is unable to give the correct membership of the ANCWL because no such reports were received from the respective provinces'. The report did claim, however, that 'since 1954 women have joined the ANC in great numbers.'[34] Political comment by *Drum* on the upswing in the numbers of women attending Congress meetings bears this statement out. It is highly improbable that the proportion of women in the ANC ever approached half during the latter part of the 1950s, given the position of women in society, but it was clearly on the increase throughout this period. It was a feature of the ANC that its membership always increased dramatically after a major political campaign (witness the impact of the Defiance Campaign), and political activity amongst women, with the anti-pass campaign, was extensive. The success of Natal's recruiting drive in 1959—the only province where the ANC achieved its allocated membership target—was undoubtedly related to the widespread unrest and demonstrations amongst African women in that province.

Information on women within the Indian Congress is much more sparse. As already mentioned, the SAIC had entered into a period of decline. As far as its female membership is concerned, Indian women, it has been said, were culturally probably the most suppressed group of women in South Africa. Their social and economic isolation during the 1950s was still marked. Such political activity as there was amongst them was confined to the districts of Durban and on the Rand and even there

was limited to individuals rather than groups. For the rest, both COD and
SACPO were tiny organisations with a membership of one or two hundred
at the most, confined largely to Cape Town and Johannesburg. Here, too,
the contribution of these organisations to the FSAW was limited very
much to that of individuals—although SACPO on the East Rand had a
particularly vigorous group of women supporters, under the sturdy leadership of Mary Moodley in Benoni.

To the four Congresses must also be added the Food and Canning
Workers' Union. Once again, records are sketchy, but it is unlikely its
membership ever exceeded several thousand during this period. Drawing
together all these sketchy fragments, one can reasonably conclude that
the outside limits of the formal membership of the FSAW at any one
time during the 1950s would have been in the region of 10,000 women.
This figure would have included a large proportion of women who were
members in name only. The core of active women was always small—
probably no more than a few hundred women across the country. And in
its day-to-day administration, as has already been pointed out, the FSAW
relied on an even smaller number of women.

From the above discussion it is clear that the FSAW membership was
based, overwhelmingly, on African women. While the contribution of non-
African women was important—it is difficult to think of the FSAW without thinking of Ray Alexander or Helen Joseph, for instance—in terms of
numbers it remained slight. For all the FSAW's stress on solidarity and its
own disavowal of the colour bar, it never managed to destroy the ethnic
barriers that were entrenched under apartheid and which separated women.
Its major campaign, that against passes for African women, had no general
appeal to non-African women apart from the handful who were already
politicised and active in Congress affairs. This campaign could not, on its
own, rally women who were not under the threat of passes themselves.
The FSAW thus remained conditioned by the dominant, colour-defined
political divisions in society. The goal of an organisation that would
'embrace all women, irrespective of race, colour or nationality' served as
an ideal; the fact that black and white women mixed freely in the organisation was a living example of the non-racialism that it espoused. The overall
lesson to be drawn from the FSAW's experience in recruiting members,
however, was that the interests of most black women and most white
women did not coincide. The FSAW proved that one could establish a
non-racial women's organisation, even though the structures of apartheid
society made it difficult. It did not prove that one could establish a
universal women's movement.

Therefore, given these limitations of size and regional distribution,
neither the FSAW nor its major affiliate, the ANCWL, could claim a mass
membership among South African women by the end of the 1950s.
Nevertheless, paid up membership alone was not a sufficient index of the
strength of the FSAW. While the membership figures for organisations like
COD and SACPO were an accurate indication of the support they enjoyed,
the same could not be said of the ANC. There were many in the African
townships who did not pay their annual subscriptions but yet considered

themselves ANC members. The same would have been true of the ANCWL. For all its organisational shortcomings, the FSAW could, on several occasions, rally enormous numbers of women. The mass gathering of women outside the Union Buildings in August 1956 testified to that— between ten and twenty thousand of them, at least as many as the number estimated to be the maximum for its entire membership. These women came from all the main cities and towns of South Africa and many of the smaller towns besides. FSAW conferences were always well attended. Regional meetings and demonstrations were, for the most part, well-supported, especially in the Transvaal. In November 1958 three to four thousand women from the Reef participated in the FSAW protest outside the Johannesburg City Hall and had it not been for police intimidation, it is likely the figure would have been higher. The Transvaal provincial conference in January 1959 drew in the region of 1,000 delegates, numbers of them coming from further afield than the Reef.

Within the limits already described—urban, Congress supporters— the range of women supporting the FSAW was impressive. The bulk of this support came from working-class women but there was a sprinkling of professional and university-educated women as well. Inevitably the small group of better educated and financially more secure women were influential at the executive level; they did not, however, deflect the FSAW away from its populist sympathies. It directed itself primarily to the black working class women and housewives, many of whom it drew into positions of leadership and authority within its committees; Dora Tamana, Annie Silinga, Katie White, Mary Moodley, Frances Baard, Liz Abrahams, Elizabeth Mafeking—these were no middle class women seeking personal 'liberation' and individual achievement. They were women who knew what it meant to go hungry, to work long hours for little pay, to be denied the security of a home, to suffer humiliation at the hands of employers and officials. They were fighting for a liberation that was broad-based, political rather than personal. Through them the voice of South African women was beginning to be heard.

Decision-Making Within the FSAW

It has been described how, in its day-to-day affairs, the FSAW relied heavily on a small group of extremely hard-working individuals to keep it functioning as an organisation. A very large part of the workload rested upon the secretaries, both national and regional. In the early years Alexander complained of a lack of initiative on the part of members of the NEC, then based in Cape Town, which meant that she needed to spend more time with them than she would have liked. This heavy reliance on the contribution of a single individual continued even once the FSAW had weathered its initial difficulties, and Helen Joseph assumed a very large responsibility for the ongoing administration of the FSAW as well, as national secretary after 1956 and, for much of the time, secretary of the Transvaal region too. Part of the problem lay in a lack of bureaucratic skills and experience on the part of many FSAW committee members. This increased the demands made on those women who did possess such skills, placing exceptionally heavy demands on a few people. Joseph, for instance, served on the executive committees of the FSAW (national and Transvaal) and COD, as well as holding a full-time job.

Women's lack of administrative skills was a product of several interacting and reinforcing factors. Sex, class and colour all conspired together to ensure that most members of the FSAW were poorly educated and had had scant opportunities to develop managerial skills. On the level of physical surroundings alone, black women were enormously disadvantaged. The average township house consisted of two or three rooms; families were large and the pressure on accommodation acute. Frequently, children were obliged to continue staying with their parents even after they were married and had children of their own.

Given a situation where class was demarcated largely (though not exclusively) on colour lines, the small number of white women within the FSAW were in a strong position to dominate at the administrative level. Because of their middle class position, they had the education and the opportunities to develop the skills which many of their black colleagues lacked. It was not mere coincidence that in the NEC elections of 1954 and 1956, the key administrative position of national secretary went on both occasions to white women. As members of the privileged white community, they enjoyed advantages denied most black women— education, mobility (Joseph's car, for instance), far greater financial security, comfortable and private working conditions. However, this polarity on colour lines should not be exaggerated. The trade unions, in particular, provided black women with a valuable training-ground for learning administrative skills and, as already mentioned, supplied the FSAW with some energetic and capable leaders.

More was at stake in the concentration of administrative responsibility than simply lack of expertise among FSAW members. As the 1950s wore on, the FSAW executives came under increasing pressure from the state, in the form of bannings of individuals, harrassment at meetings, intimidation by the police and security police. Inevitably this scared off potential recruits and increased the work-load on existing members.

Not only administrative matters, but general policy-making too was in the hands of a relatively small number of women (subject always to review by the ANC and the Congress Alliance's consultative committees). In the absence of regular annual conferences the executive committees were powerful and relatively independent bodies. At times the degree to which decision-making was centralised was overt. In 1955 an unsigned letter from Cape Town to an unidentified NEC member in the Transvaal was urging the importance of holding a conference, 'not on the scale of last year, but a conference of selected women' to iron out the difficulties facing the FSAW.[35] That same letter also expressed the dominance of the FSAW leadership in the shaping of policy more subtly. Talking about politicising new recruits, it stated that 'we must give them material to enable them to put forward things in the correct way although in their way.'

This centralisation did not pass without criticism, although it seems to have come mainly from outside the FSAW rather than from within. Accusations were levelled against it of high-handedness. At the time of the Congress of the People, one correspondent in *New Age* criticised the FSAW's meeting to discuss 'What Women Demand' for its lack of free discussion—there had not been enough debate from the floor, delegates had remained obedient to the leaders.[36] The following year, during the wrangle about the ratification of the FSAW's constitution, the COD executive also made some veiled comments about 'the cult of the individual', though later it retracted these remarks.[37] Committee members were not unaware of the importance of training new recruits to assume a more active and assertive role within the FSAW. This was a point that Alexander, in particular, stressed in the early years, and was also the reason why a joint-secretaryship was instituted in the Transvaal in 1956.

Yet while decision-making remained concentrated in the FSAW committees, this did not mean that the general membership of the FSAW never took the initiative. One very clear instance of the FSAW executive following rank-and-file example came in October 1958 in the anti-pass campaign in Johannesburg. There the decision to embark on a programme of civil disobedience came not from the top, but from what *Drum* called a 'ghost organisation' working amongst women in the different branches of the ANCWL.

Finances

Money was always a problem for the FSAW. Its inadequate financial resources were both an index of its weaknesses as an organisation and an inhibitory factor in its further development. Throughout, it operated on a shoestring budget, collecting money for its various campaigns largely on an *ad hoc* basis. The 1957 anti-pass campaign, for instance, was meant to be financed entirely from money collected from the women who signed the pledges—'pennies for pledges' was the FSAW slogan.

The FSAW had almost no financial resources of its own on which to operate. Probably at no stage did it ever have more than £15 or £20 in the bank. The only available reference to the NEC's funds, in the minutes of its 1959 meeting, reported that its account at that time stood at £7.5.1.[38] The total annual budget for the Transvaal during these years was always very small. Only once did it exceed £200. That was in 1958 and almost half of this sum was raised after the middle of October, when the FSAW was engaged in its fiercest anti-pass struggle in Johannesburg. The highest balance the Transvaal region carried over from one year to the next was a mere £13.18.10. That was in 1957/58. The smallest was 2/9 (between 1958/59).[39] Unfortunately budgets exist for the Transvaal region only—but this was the strongest and most active FSAW centre. In this connection, a startling example of the Federation's inefficiency and financial carelessness came at the end of 1958, when the Transvaal regional funds—

admittedly unlikely to be more than a few pounds by that stage—disappeared without trace. They 'went to one or two different people and got lost in transit and we never knew at which stage'.[40]

Raising money was a continual battle. The FSAW lacked a regular source of income. Affiliation fees from its member organisations were only £1.1s per branch per year and even then frequently not forthcoming; several times the FSAW was obliged to send out circulars reminding member groups about paying their fees. In 1959 the NEC reported that

> funds could not increase unless the promised branch donations of one guinea a year from the ANCWL were received regularly, for 1957 6 branches from the Eastern Cape, two branches from the Kimberley area and one donation from Durban had been received. Nothing had been received in respect of 1953.[41]

This depressing situation vindicated one of the arguments that had been put forward in their favour by the supporters of the individual membership camp. In April 1956, in raising the membership issue once again, the Cape Town-based NEC pointed out that an individual membership would bring in much more money for the FSAW, through members' subscriptions.[42] Political priorities (in this case relations with the ANC) took precedence over financial ones, however, and the matter was not pursued further.

The FSAW's ambiguous position within the Congress Alliance hindered its fund-raising attempts in other ways too. Many women did not see it as a separate body from the ANCWL, needing separate financial support. At the same time, the financial responsibility of the ANCWL towards the FSAW was not always clear. On occasion the ANC showed resentment because it felt the FSAW was encroaching on ANC territory in its fund-raising efforts. In 1959, Transvaal president Marcelle Goldberg felt obliged to clarify the position: 'Our policy has not been to accumulate funds but to see that money is raised for each campaign as it is undertaken for we do not compete with the affiliated organisations for financial support.'[43] This would seem to have been a case of turning necessity into a virtue—on other occasions the appeal for money was far more insistent.

Apart from affiliation fees, the FSAW was entirely dependent on donations and money it could raise by various fund-raising devices—cake sales, rummage sales, raffles, the sale of commemorative badges and pamphlets. Here too, the FSAW experienced difficulty in collecting money raised back from branches. At the NEC meeting in 1958 it was reported that 'large sums of money' were still outstanding from branches for sales of the booklet *Strijdom you have struck a rock*, a booklet that had been printed and distributed in early 1957 to commemorate the demonstration in Pretoria in August 1956.[44] Fourteen months later, by the time of the next NEC meeting, some of this money was still outstanding and the committee agreed that these amounts be 'written off'.[45]

No general meeting went by without a collection being made amongst the audience.

It does not help us to say quite a lot of things and yet we don't do it, it does not help us to say we are going to do this and we don't do it. It does not help us to do this work and yet we have not got any money.[46]

This was how one speaker urged women to donate money generously at a FSAW meeting in Johannesburg in May 1955. The sums realised were small. A successful meeting in the Transvaal would bring in £5 or £6. The provincial conference in January 1959, which was extremely well attended —by as many as 1,000 delegates, according to some reports—produced £10.13.10.[47]

Donations, an extremely irregular and unreliable form of support, were the largest single source of income for the Transvaal region in the period from August 1956 till December 1961—£98.12.6 out of the total of £703.3,11 that was raised in that time.[48] Most of this appears to have come from the wealthier members of the FSAW in COD, but women from the other Congresses did, on occasion, make contributions too. At no stage did the FSAW receive funds from abroad. The only financial assistance the WIDF ever contributed to the FSAW was for the air fares of Ngoyi and Tamana for their overseas tour in 1955.[49] (Although the FSAW retained a loose communication with the WIDF, it never affiliated to it.)

The FSAW attributed its financial difficulties to the general poverty of its members—that its support came from the 'lowest income group' in the country.[50] Undoubtedly this was true; as described earlier, black women formed the bulk of the FSAW's membership, and they were economically on the very bottom rung in society. Money was extremely tight; for most women it was a constant struggle to make ends meet. Nevertheless, this alone is not a sufficient explanation of why the FSAW struggled financially.

In 1955 Alexander pointed out perceptively that if African women could raise as much money as they did for the various churches to which they belonged, there was no reason why they could not raise enough to support one full-time worker for the FSAW.[51] A glance at some of the amounts of money raised at that time by African women's *manyanos* (women's church societies) confirms that substantial sums of money could be raised by women in the townships if they set their minds to it. According to a study on the *manyanos* by M. Brandel-Syrier, fund-raising formed a very large and successful part of these organisations' business. 'For most churches they are the fund-raising institutions and the churches could not exist without the women's financial help. This goes a long way to explain the power and status of the manyanos.'[52]

Thus, in 1953 the South Eastern Transvaal section of the Women's Missionary Society of the African Methodist Episcopal church raised £3,101 for the church. The following year, in 1954, the same group raised £2,074 at its national conference. On a similar scale, the women's fundraising committee of the Methodist church in the township at Evaton in the Transvaal raised £1,000 towards a new church building.

Clearly, then, an enormous fund-raising potential did exist amongst women in the African townships, the general poverty notwithstanding.

But while the *manyanos* were able to tap this, the FSAW did not. This raises some interesting questions about the differences between the two organisations, highlights their quite different standings in the community. As a political organisation within an undemocratic society, the FSAW was battling against the full weight of ideological pressures which frowned upon women, and black women in particular, involving themselves in political activity. It was a risky organisation for women to support financially; it was also not the sort of organisation business men would assist. By contrast, the church was widely regarded as a legitimate area for women (and for blacks) to work in. Religion also offers its adherents an immediate emotional and psychological release from the pressures of life under apartheid. B. Sundkler's study, *Bantu Prophets in South Africa*, has shown how for many blacks, male and female, the church operates as one of the few areas where they can be leaders without exposing themselves to the risks of political work. Religion is safe, politics is not—and the significance of that shows in hard cash terms.

The FSAW did not collapse because of lack of money. Invariably funds were found to finance its various campaigns, albeit sparingly, and volunteer work kept running costs to a minimum. Nevertheless, financial difficulties acted as a serious hindrance to its effectiveness as a political organisation.

Notes

1. Quoted in M. Benson, *Struggle for a Birthright*, p. 183.
2. M. Moodley, 'East Rand Working Committee Report', FSAW DI 2b.
3. FSAW correspondence, 3.4.54, FSAW BII.
4. FSAW correspondence, 8.2.54, FSAW BII.
5. Interview with V. Mngomo.
6. FSAW correspondence, 19.8.55, FSAW BII.
7. 'Minutes of the meeting of the NEC', 21.3.59, p. 3, FSAW BI.
8. 'Notes from the Regional Executive—Transvaal Executive Committee', FSAW DI.
9. Letter from L. Ngoyi to *Rand Daily Mail*, 2.11.55, FSAW CI 2.
10. *New Age*, 13.1.55 and 1.3.56.
11. Interview with H. Joseph.
12. Interview with L. Abrahams.
13. FSAW circular, 24.5.56, FSAW BII.
14. Interview with R. Alexander.
15. 'Report on a tour of the major centres of the Union, submitted to the NCC for discussion', p. 3, FSAW IIB.
16. *New Age*, 22.9.55.
17. Letter from secretary, 'Congress for Mothers' Committee' to FSAW, 22.10.55, FSAW CI 2.
18. Interview with H. Joseph.
19. WIDF, 'Report on a visit to South Africa sponsored by the WIDF, May–June 1962', p. 34.
20. *New Age*, 19.1.56.
21. 'Minutes of the meeting of the NEC', 23.1.59, p. 3, FSAW BI.
22. FSAW correspondence, undated letter from 'M', FSAW BII.

23. 'Report on a tour of the major centres of the Union, submitted to the NCC, for discussion', p. 4, FSAW IIB.
24. Johnson, *Indians and Apartheid,* p. 125.
25. *Ibid.,* p. 95.
26. 'Report of Natal Provincial Annual Conference of the ANC, 28–29 July 1956', p. 12, Treason Trial Exhibit no. 795.
27. Interview with F. Mkhize.
28. FSAW, 'Minutes of the Meeting of the NEC, March 21st 1959', p. 3, FSAW BI.
29. Interview with N. Booi.
30. 'Report to the WIDF', FSAW E.
31. WIDF, 'Report on a visit to South Africa, sponsored by the WIDF', p. 35.
32. 'Report from 15th to 19th December '55', a police transcript of the proceedings of the ANC annual conference, December 1955, Treason Trial Exhibit G 808.
33. ANC (Tvl): 'Annual Report of the Provincial Executive Committee', October 1959, pp. 13–15, FSAW II G7.
34. ANCWL, 'Executive Report', p. 2, in 'Annual Conference of the African National Congress Women's League', September 1959, FSAW II H7.
35. FSAW correspondence, 24.3.55, FSAW BII.
36. This criticism is spelled out and replied to in a letter from the Transvaal Regional Committee to *New Age,* 9.7.55, FSAW IIA.
37. See 'Extract from first letter from Cape Town read at meeting of NEC 20.8.56', FSAW A7. The NEC referred to here is that of COD, not the FSAW.
38. 'Minutes of the Meeting of the NEC', 21.3.59, p. 2, FSAW BI.
39. FSAW (Tvl), 'Financial Statements, 1956–59', FSAW DI 4, and 'Finances to 22.7.61', FSAW DI (1).
40. FSAW correspondence, 1.12.59, FSAW DI 4b.
41. 'Minutes of the meeting of the NEC', 21.3.59, p. 2, FSAW BI.
42. FSAW correspondence, 20.4.56, FSAW BII.
43. 'President's Report to the Provincial Conference', 27.1.59, p. 5, FSAW A13.
44. 'Minutes of the meeting of the NEC', 18.1.59, p. 2, FSAW BI.
45. 'Minutes of the meeting of the NEC', 21.3.59, p. 1, FSAW BI.
46. 'Women's Meeting held in the Trades Hall, 30 Kerk Street, Johannesburg on the 29th May, 1955', p. 17, Treason Trial Exhibit G 777.
47. FSAW (Tvl), 'Financial Statement for 1959', FSAW DI 4b.
48. Calculated from FSAW Financial Statements, FSAW CI 6, DI.
49. Interview with H. Joseph.
50. 'Report to the WIDF', *op. cit.,* FSAW E.
51. FSAW correspondence, 3.9.55, FSAW BII.
52. M. Brandel-Syrier, *Black Women in Search of God,* p. 70.

21

'The Equality of All Human Beings, of Both Sexes': Relationships Between the FSAW and the Congress Alliance

The FSAW's position within the Congress Alliance was not always clear. Partly this was a structural problem, relating to its federal nature and how it was integrated into the national liberation movement as a result. On the one hand, the FSAW was an independent body, with its own constitution and a set of aims which related specifically to women. On the other hand, all of its member groups, apart from the Food and Canning Workers Union (and even that was affiliated to SACTU) were auxiliaries or part of other, separate organisations to which they were ultimately responsible.

Because the FSAW was constituted on the basis of the member organisations of the Congress Alliance, its own ranking within that Alliance was not sharply delineated. Thus, as we have seen, even though it participated in all the Alliance's campaigns and was regarded by it as an organisation to which specific, women-oriented tasks could be allocated, the FSAW was never officially represented on the NCC, the highest co-ordinating body within the Alliance. Because of the informality that characterised the Congress Alliance, as well as the fact that, for at least part of the time, Joseph served on the NCC as a representative of COD, this exclusion did not mean isolation for the FSAW. It did, however, reflect the ambivalence felt by the male-dominated Congress Alliance on the role and scope of the women's movement within the national liberation movement.

The structural clumsiness of the FSAW led, on occasions, to complications about decision-making and the allocation of authority between it and the various Congress organisations. The dispute with members of the COD executive about the ratification of the FSAW's constitution at its second national conference in 1956 was a clear example of this. So too was the disagreement with the ANCWL about the manner in which the FSAW was conducting the anti-pass pledge campaign of 1957—that it was working directly with ANCWL branches instead of through the ANCWL executive.

The awkwardness of the FSAW's federal structure was not simply a matter of poor design. It had been imposed upon it by the ANC, using its superior authority within the Congress Alliance to prevail over the arguments of those within the FSAW who favoured an individual membership. The reasons for the ANC's stand throw light both on relationships between organisations within the Congress Alliance and on the standing of the women's movement within the national liberation movement in general and with the ANC in particular.

The FSAW was modelled on the multi-racial and loosely federal structure of the Congress Alliance. The ANC's insistence on this was based on its fears that a unitary women's organisation would compete with the ANCWL for membership as well as prove too independent of ultimate Congress control. The position the ANC adopted with regard to the FSAW, in 1954/55, was consistent with the stand it had already taken on the composition of the Congress Alliance. Although committed to cooperating with other political organisations with which it shared 'common objectives and. . . methods',[1] the ANC had always insisted on its separate identity as an African political party. It had never been prepared to surrender its independence and authority to combine with its political allies in a single, non-racial organisation. In the 1940s, discussions between the ANC and AAC towards achieving closer unity had foundered at least partly because the ANC insisted that they form an exclusively African organisation, which could then cooperate with other non-African political groups. At the time Mr A.P. Mda of the ANC said: 'We should appeal to Africans as such, to unite as Africans. An African United Front would not be opposed to an alliance with other oppressed groups, organised in their national organisations.'[2] The ANC retained this approach towards the Congress Alliance in the 1950s: 'Co-operation will always be on the basis of equality and mutual respect for the individuality and identity of our organisations.'[3]

In effect, the ANC was upholding the dominant colour-conscious ideology of ethnic exclusivism and 'racial pride' which, under various guises, had informed South Africa's political life since 1910. The ANC of the 1950s took its stand on a vision of a 'multiracial, corporate society'. Although it attacked discrimination on the grounds of colour, it accepted colour-based group identification as a basic factor in South Africa's political life. In working towards its goal of a multiracial society, it saw itself as a vanguard organisation representing the African majority of the population. It was not prepared to abandon its ethnic integrity and position of leadership to a non-racial political party.

> Since its inception the ANC accepted South Africa as a multi-racial society in which all racial groups have the right to live in dignity and prosperity. In fact the ANC was founded in order to unite the African tribes into a political force in order to demand full democratic rights within the multi-racial framework of our society.[4]

During the 1950s the ANC successfully maintained this viewpoint in the face of criticism coming from both the Africanist faction and leftwing members of the Congress Alliance (within COD in particular). The Africanists, later the PAC's, criticism of the Alliance's multiracial construction has been outlined already. They were more concerned about white dominance in the Alliance than non-racialism. In the late 1950s, however, provoked in part by the Africanists' accusations of apartheid within the Alliance, some COD members took up their criticisms. They raised the question of transforming the Congress Alliance into a unitary national liberation organisation.[5] Their tentative overtures in this direction were not successful; the ANC, by far the largest and politically most significant of the Congresses, was too powerful for its objections to be overruled.

As in the Congress Alliance, so too in the FSAW, the ANC's insistence on a multiracial structure carried the most weight when the membership question was being discussed. In this case it was not prepared to expose the ANCWL either to competition from another women's organisation or to the risk of being absorbed in a non-racial movement outside its control. In 1955 the FSAW had accepted that without the ANCWL it could never hope to be more than a peripheral organisation within the national liberation movement. Since it felt that the first priority of the women's movement was to achieve victory for the national liberation movement, it accepted the limitations of the federal structure imposed upon it by the ANC.

The relationship between the FSAW and ANC did not, however, fit simply into the general pattern of ANC-Congress Alliance interaction. More was at stake than a straightforward tussle for power between two political organisations, even though this played its part. A large source of tension, over and above the points already raised, was that the FSAW was an organisation of women and, as such, a challenge to prejudices against women's political autonomy and adulthood, prejudices which were deeply rooted within the ANC and Congress Alliance. An overly independent and non-racial women's movement threatened not only ANC hegemony within the Congress Alliance; it threatened male hegemony within the Alliance as well. This ambivalence on the part of the men wove itself in and out of most of the ANC's dealings with the FSAW and ANCWL. The range of attitudes the ANC displayed towards the political work of the women was wide and its approach often inconsistent —sometimes admiring and supportive, at other times (occasionally at one and the same time) uneasy, resentful and anxious to assert male control.

The formation of the FSAW in 1954 was generally welcomed and encouraged by the various Congress bodies. Certainly at a theoretical level they recognised the importance of mobilising women for the political struggle. This the national liberation movement had already accepted in the 1940s; by 1954 few would have openly questioned it. The ANC also conceded that for women to be able to take part in political work more actively, some restructuring of traditional relationships between men and women was necessary. In this vein, the ANC executive declared in 1955:

> We know that we cannot win liberation or build a strong movement without the participation of the women. We must. . . make it possible for women to play their part by regarding them as equals and helping to emancipate them in the home, even relieving them of their many family and household burdens so that women may be given an opportunity of being politically active. The men in the Congress movement must fight constantly. . . those outmoded customs which make women inferior and by personal example must demonstrate their belief in the equality of all human beings, of both sexes.[6]

As had characterised the entire history of the women's movement within the national liberation movement, however, in practice both actions and attitudes often lagged far behind accepted principles. Advances had been made since the days when politics was unquestioningly assumed to be a male domain, but by the end of the 1950s, the national liberation movement had yet to grant women a full and unequivocal recognition of their rights as equals of men.

This lag between theory and practice was most marked at the level of the ANC rank and file. Many male members of the ANC were deeply conservative and traditionalist in their attitudes towards women. Indeed, as already pointed out, for many African men their chief reason for opposing passes for women was that the government was thereby usurping their authority over 'their' womenfolk. For both men and women, passes for women posed a threat to the stability and security of the home. Associated with that there frequently went a tenacious conviction that women's proper place was in the home and nowhere else and that within the home their correct status was one of subordination to men.

The debate on birth control at the FSAW's meeting to discuss 'What Women Demand' in May 1955 revealed how strong was the belief in women's subordinate position within the family in Congress circles. Many women present expressed apprehension at what their husbands' reactions to contraception would be. By freeing women's sexuality from their reproductive role and at the same time allowing women control over so large and important an area of their lives, contraception threatened the already declining authority of the husband within the patriarchal family. The jocular dismissal with which some male Congress members greeted this debate—that this was not the stuff of politics—testified to a limited perception of what women's emancipation entailed amongst at least some members of the national liberation movement. These men were content for women to be organised to assist the men, to fight for equality and an end to discrimination in general terms. The question of sexual equality and sexual discrimination, however, raised disturbing questions and placed in jeopardy one of the few areas where black men were assured of a position of relative power and prestige, the patriarchal family. Thus many Congress members either refused to take such questions seriously or resisted including them within the programme of the national liberation movement.

It was rare for male resistance to female political achievement to assume overt forms within the Congress movement of the 1950s. Attitudes were more often equivocal, resistance finding expression in a general passivity on the part of Congress men towards the political campaigns of the women rather than in an active opposition. The most serious manifestation of this was in the anti-pass campaign. While men applauded the women's campaign, few joined in, despite constant urgings from the FSAW, ANCWL and senior ANC members themselves. Something of the conflicting emotions generated within the ANC by the women's campaigns and demonstrations of the 1950s—the admiration tinged with unease—were captured by a comment that concluded a *Drum* article on the October

1958 disturbances in Johannesburg: 'Meanwhile the men have stood by looking on bewildered and stunned. And as one of them said: "God, the women are showing us something".'[7]

It was also rare for the issues involved to be publicly discussed. The *Sechaba* article, 'Don't Stifle the Work of the Women's Federation', which appeared in 1956, was an unusually direct discussion of male opposition to women's political activism. In supporting the work of the women's organisations, this article criticised 'some Congress members' for not voicing openly their doubts and misunderstandings about the form and scope of the women's movement.[8] The fact that such an article was necessary indicated the extent to which resentment towards the FSAW clouded the surface of apparent ANC support.

The FSAW experienced greatest difficulty with the Transvaal provincial executive of the ANC. The Transvaal ANC was, from all accounts received, far less generous in its support and enthusiasm for the women's organisation than the national or other provincial branches. In the absence of detailed information on the relationships between the Federation and ANC executives in the other areas, it is impossible to be sure why the Transvaal region particularly should have proved the most difficult region of the ANC for the FSAW to work with. The fact that the Rand was the centre of both FSAW and ANC activity could have been a factor—any of the general tensions that existed between the two organisations would be exacerbated by the greater pressure of events in that region. The Transvaal was also the home-base for the Africanist faction within the ANC. Whether there was any link between the Africanists' brand of exclusive African nationalism and the Transvaal ANC's form of anti-feminism, however, remains a speculative (though intriguing) question.

As the decade wore on and women came more and more to the fore in the anti-pass campaign, the prestige and status of women within the Congress Alliance and the ANC definitely increased. The FSAW was an educative force within the Congress Alliance. Its very existence ensured that the contribution of women to the liberation struggle could not be overlooked but had, instead, to be considered and reassessed. The election of Lilian Ngoyi to the ANC national executive in 1955 was one sign of a greater respect for women. Another was the ANC's decision to commemorate August 9th as 'Women's Day' in honour of the massive demonstration staged by the FSAW and ANCWL in Pretoria in 1956. In a speech in 1959 Chief Lutuli, national president of the ANC, emphasised that all offices in the ANC were open to everybody, male and female, on the basis of merit: recognition and promotion would be based on equality between the sexes.[9]

Generally, the national leadership of the ANC adopted a more sophisticated approach to the FSAW than rank and file members. It was openly supportive of the women so long as they did not trespass on its territory or usurp its authority. The article, 'Don't Stifle the Work of the Women's Federation', was adamant that the FSAW was a 'full-blooded member of the freedom movement and must not be regarded—or treated—as a step-child'. Nevertheless, even the ANC national executive saw at least part of the work of the FSAW and ANCWL in very conventional terms. Women's political priorities were regarded as centring on domestic issues, a perspective which the FSAW itself generally shared. Hence the allocation of the Freedom Charter clause dealing with 'houses, security and comfort' to Helen Joseph for discussion at the Congress of the People in 1955. Of all the clauses, this was regarded as most appropriately 'women's work'. Hence, too, the delegation of accommodation and catering arrangements for major national conferences—the Congress of the People in 1955, the National Workers' Conference in 1958, the National Anti-Pass Campaign in 1959—to the women's organisations. In a recent publication, Hilda Bernstein (Hilda Watts) recalls that while the ANCWL of the 1950s was 'a means of organising women for the national liberation struggle', it also served as 'a means of obtaining the usual work out of the women—feeding and finding accommodation for delegates to conferences and similar work'.[10]

At the same time, traces of the ambivalence that characterised much of the ANC's dealings with the women's organisations at the rank and file level could be detected at the national leadership level as well. In June 1958 Chief Lutuli was asked in an interview by *Drum* if it were not true that women were playing a 'much bigger—perhaps the crucial part' in Congress politics. His reply toned down any suggestion of women competing with men politically:

> There are signs that women are beginning to play an effective part in politics. I cannot visualise a situation in which the movement will be overwhelmingly feminine, but they will play a very important part. More and more African women will not only actively but in silent ways contribute to the struggle.[11]

The hint of unease that women might be challenging the traditional leadership position of men was present more strongly in a statement Lutuli issued the following year, on the occasion of 'Women's Day'. He began by paying tribute to the courage and initiative displayed by women in the anti-pass campaign: 'They are pairing effectively with their menfolk. At times they seem a length ahead of men. This is all for the good.'[12] Later in the same message, however, the political assertiveness of women became a stick with which Lutuli chided the men of the ANC for their own failure to contribute actively to the anti-pass campaign: 'Women are putting men's traditional dignity and so-called superiority in jeopardy. Do African men of our day want to play second fiddle to women?'[13] Clearly, this was an unacceptable proposition.

Relationships between the FSAW and Congress Alliance were thus complex. The conduct of the anti-pass campaign, the major campaign on which the FSAW embarked, brought out many of the tensions, both structural and ideological, as well as the ambiguities that marked this interaction. In seeking to understand why male support for the anti-pass campaign was never strongly forthcoming, one can advance several reasons —the internal dissensions and the organisational weaknesses plaguing the ANC, the fact that men already carried passes and thus lacked the same psychological motivation that women, confronted with a new and alarming threat to their position, possessed. No analysis will be complete, however, without taking into account the ambivalence that many Congress men felt towards women in politics, and the extent to which this determined that the anti-pass campaign would remain a predominantly female and, therefore, limited political campaign. Despite continued urgings from the FSAW, NCC and the ANC executive, the anti-pass campaign of the 1950s was, in the final analysis, regarded as a sectarian 'women's issue' by the general membership of Congress Alliance; it was not accorded full status as a common political campaign. Few men were prepared to work under or even alongside women. While women might be 'pairing effectively with their menfolk', the same could not be said wholeheartedly in reverse.

Relationships between the FSAW and the Congress Alliance were, of course, a two-way stream. The FSAW itself, though far clearer on the need for women to participate actively and as equals in the national liberation movement, was not always consistent on the question of what women's political role should be. Its attitude towards the ANC and that body's attempts to dominate it, swung between criticism and conciliation, adding to the complexities of their relationship.

In 1954 the 'Women's Charter' had outlined what the FSAW regarded as the double responsibility facing the women's movement—allegiance to the national liberation movement and participation in its campaigns on the one hand; commitment to the emancipation of women from their inferior position in society on the other. This duality of purpose the FSAW continued to uphold throughout its short career. Ultimately, however, it never doubted that its first responsibility was to the general liberation struggle, by blacks, against the white supremacist state. Not till that had been won could most women expect to free themselves from sex-based discrimination:

> The fundamental struggle of the people is for National Liberation and. . . any women's organisation that (stands) outside this struggle must stand apart from the mass of women. . . this statement does not in any way mean that the Federation of South African Women was not concerned with the problem of women's rights, and that it did not strive for the emancipation of women. . . what was realised was that it would be impossible for women to achieve their rights as women in a society in which so many fundamental rights were denied to both men and women by virtue of their sex.[14]

Any conflict that threatened the unity of the national liberation movement should, therefore, be avoided. At the same time, the senior position of the ANC within that movement, as leader of 'the mass of women' should be respected. For this reason, the FSAW tended to downplay friction between it and the other Congress bodies. 'I would like to remind you that the Federation. . . is not an organisation set up in opposition to those already existing organisations,' Transvaal president Marcelle Goldberg stressed in her report to the provincial conference of the FSAW in January 1959.[15] As the anti-pass campaign wore on, the FSAW also appeared anxious to appease fears amongst ANC men that the women's campaign was in some way reflecting poorly on their (the men's) virility. Lilian Ngoyi's speech to the annual ANCWL Conference in 1959, cautioning her audience against the 'impression' that 'seems to be gaining ground', that the women were 'courageous and militant', the men 'frightened and timid', reflected these concerns.[16] Partly Ngoyi's views corresponded with the conscious, political choices the FSAW had made concerning the priorities facing the women's movement. Yet these conscious beliefs were buttressed by other, often less conscious attitudes which reflected the extent to which the FSAW itself had been influenced by patriarchal ideology. This also played a part in making it more amenable to ANC authority than it might otherwise have been.

In its general approach, the FSAW was committed to the full emancipation of women from their subordinate position in society. This the 'Women's Charter' and its 'Aims' had made clear. Nevertheless, partriarchal ideology ran deep and was not confined to male members of the Congress Alliance only; the FSAW, too, was conditioned by it. Many of the women involved in the FSAW and the ANCWL accepted that women were, in some way, subordinate to men, their responsibilities primarily domestic, and their political contribution supportive rather than innovative. The conservative defence of home and custom which had characterised much of the protests by rural women during the 1950s helped shape urban women's anti-pass protests too: 'Verwoerd is to break our homes with this [sic] pass laws', commented one woman at an ANCWL meeting at Moroka township, Johannesburg, in 1955.[17]

Within the FSAW, the degree to which the importance of the battle against sex discrimination was stressed varied from woman to woman and from occasion to occasion. Even amongst the FSAW leadership, where women's rights and the abolition of sex discrimination were strongly endorsed, women's domestic role as wife and, more often, mother was continually being stressed. Frequently 'mother' and 'woman' were interchangeable terms in the FSAW rhetoric. The memorandum against the pass laws which the FSAW submitted to the Mayor of Johannesburg in November 1958 illustrated this:

> We say to you, and we speak from our hearts as mothers, whatever our race, that the pass system is in itself a crime against humanity; to inflict it upon women is an even greater crime—a crime against motherhood.[18]

Such sentiments reinforced those views that women's primary identification was domestic and maternal, and in this way contributed to the often unconscious reservations about women's political autonomy that existed within the Congress Alliance.

In addition to the above factors, the pressure of events on the Congress Alliance in the 1950s meant that such contradictions as did exist between men and women within it were often pushed to one side. Not only were they overshadowed by that common threat which all the national liberation organisations of the 1950s were facing from an increasingly totalitarian state; the FSAW was also preoccupied with the immediate demands of planning and organising the anti-pass campaign, and most of its energies were channelled into that. As a result, it had little time in which to develop its general understanding of the subordinate position of women in society into a clear critique of male/female relationships within the Congress Alliance. This made it less critical of male dominance in practice than many of its statements about women's emancipation would suggest.

Yet the extent to which the FSAW was prepared to accept a junior position within the Alliance should not be exaggerated. For all the qualifications on its stand on women's rights that undoubtedly coloured both its outlook and its activities, the FSAW never regarded itself as a mere tea-making appendage to the Alliance. It saw women as political actors in their own right and, within the limits already described, defended its own decision-making powers and autonomy strongly. In the long term, it was clearly committed to the ideal of a society where neither sex nor colour would serve as criteria for discrimination against individuals. Moreover, as an activist body above all, it was critical and impatient of passivity in other organisations and ready to resist attempts to curb its own initiative.

Finally, political involvement for women in the 1950s generally had a radicalising effect on their perceptions of themselves and their place in society. Women in the FSAW were encouraged to assume greater responsibility and independence; the short-term success of many of their campaigns made them value their own political contribution more highly as well as view the performance of other Congress organisations more critically. In this regard, one effect of the FSAW on its members was to encourage the trend towards greater female independence and *de facto* authority within the urban African family of the 1950s. 'The women of Africa are on the march', a woman from Zeerust had commented in 1957. Her metaphor was an apt one. Whether consciously or not, women in the FSAW were moving beyond the traditional boundaries that formerly had circumscribed their lives.

Notes

1. From 'Programme and Policy', *African National Congress Handbook*, p. 5, FSAW II G2.
2. 'Minutes of the Joint Meeting of the National Executive Committees of the ANC and the AAC, April 17–18, 1949', in Karis and Carter, *From Protest to Challenge*, vol. II, p. 383, Document 70(a).
3. 'Programme and Policy', *African National Congress Handbook*, p. 5, FSAW II, G2.
4. ANC, 'Report of the 46th Annual National Conference, December 1958', p. 26, FSAW II G.
5. For instance, an article by P. Rodda, 'The Africanists cut loose', in *Africa South*, vol. 3, no. 4, July-September 1959.
6. '43rd National Conference of the ANC held in Bloemfontein from the 17th–19th December, 1955', p. 10, Treason Trial Exhibit G 809.

7.   *Drum,* December 1958, 'The Battle of the Women', p. 22.
8.   'Don't Stifle the Work of the Women's Federation', pamphlet reprinted from *Sechaba,* September 1956, FSAW E.
9.   'Chief Speaks: A message by Albert J. Lutuli', 9.8.59, p. 3, FSAW A14.
10. H. Bernstein, *For their Triumphs and For Their Tears,* p. 43.
11. *Drum,* June 1958, 'Lutuli Talks', p. 59.
12. 'Chief Speaks: A message by Albert J. Lutuli', 9.8.59, p. 3, FSAW A14.
13. *Ibid.,* p. 4.
14. Statement by Helen Joseph, *Treason Trial Record,* vol. 66, p. 13996.
15. 'President's Report to the Provincial Conference, 27.1.59', p. 1, FSAW A13.
16. 'Presidential Address', p. 2, in 'Annual Conference of the African National Congress Women's League', FSAW II H7. The full quote appears in chapter nineteen.
17. 'Copy of notes made by N/D/Const. Phillip Maskanya at a meeting of the ANCWL held at Moroka, on 23.10.56', p. 2, Treason Trial Exhibit G 850.
18. 'Memorandum on the Pass Laws', FSAW CI 6.

22

'Freedom Does Not Come Walking to You – It Must Be Won': Sharpeville and the Decline of the FSAW

The FSAW plans for 1960 were abruptly disrupted by the momentous events that rocked the country in the wake of the Sharpeville shootings on the 21st March 1960. Sharpeville—where sixty-nine people were shot dead when police opened fire on a large gathering of unarmed demonstrators—was an epoch-making event. The very name has become synonmous with police repression in South Africa. The demonstration which precipitated the shootings was partly a result of the rivalry ensnaring the ANC and the PAC. After the ANC's abortive stay-at-home in April 1958, political tension in the country built up steadily to a crisis point. In 1959 the ANC called for a gradual escalation in its on-going anti-pass campaign, to culminate in demonstrations across the country on the 31st March 1960. While preparations for this were going on, the PAC launched a counter-demonstration. It pre-empted the ANC by calling for mass demonstrations against passes on the 21st of March—ten days ahead of the ANC schedule.

These demonstrations were planned as a massive showing of civil disobedience. Men and women were asked to present themselves outside their local police stations, without their reference books, to court arrest. The gathering outside the Sharpeville police station was in response to this call. Until the police opened fire, it was only one of many such demonstrations across the country; then came the shots, the deaths, and the name Sharpeville was thrust into the history books. News of the deaths flashed rapidly around the world, provoking a storm of condemnation internationally. Inside South Africa, Sharpeville triggered off the inevitable crackdown on the national liberation movement that the government had been threatening for some time. In the aftermath, the government moved quickly to stamp out black opposition groups. It declared a state of emergency, rounding up and detaining hundreds of political leaders throughout the country. In April 1960 the government followed this up by banning the ANC and the PAC as lawful political organisations. With this act fifty years of non-violent struggle by the ANC—at first conciliatory, constitutional, later confrontational and extra-legal, but always peaceful— was brought to nothing. Both the ANC and the PAC were driven underground. From there they were forced to review their strategies and adopt alternative methods of resistance.

The immediate effect of the banning and detentions on the national liberation movement was catastrophic. The Congress Alliance was plunged into disarray. It took months for it to regroup and begin the painful process of adjustment to the new political situation. By mid-1960, its former strategy of mass demonstrations and civil disobedience had clearly failed to bring about political change. Yet it was reluctant to abandon non-violence. A year after the ANC had been banned, the Congress group was still trying to pressurise the government to negotiate with it by means of a nationwide 'stay-at-home'. The stay-at-home, called for the 31st May 1961 (the day South Africa became a republic and left the Commonwealth), was a failure. Only afterwards, in mid-1961, did Congress leaders finally abandon non-violence as a principle and make the momentous decision to turn to violent methods of resistance. During 1961 both the ANC and PAC established military wings—*Umkhonto we Sizwe* [ANC] and *Poqo* [PAC]. The first act of sabotage by the ANC followed in December 1961. Even though it had thus accepted violence as a means of struggle, it was still committed to tactics which avoided loss of life. The first acts of sabotage were against buildings and strategic installations such as electric pylons. Armed guerilla warfare came only later, in the mid 1960s.

The Unlawful Organisations Act of 1960, which created the machinery to ban the ANC and the PAC, was only one strand in an ever-spreading net of security legislation that the government pushed through a pliant parliament. The Defence Amendment Act, the Police Amendment Act, the Indemnity Act, the General Laws Amendment Act, the Welfare Organisations Amendment Act, all of 1961, extended the coercive powers of the state, narrowed the scope of legal opposition, and concentrated still greater powers to ban, prohibit and rule by proclamation in the hands of the Prime Minister and his cabinet. In 1962 the government enacted an even tougher series of amendments to the existing security legislation to deal with the threat of sabotage. The General Laws Amendment Act of 1962—the Sabotage Act, as it soon became known—equated sabotage with treason, conviction of which can carry the death penalty. It also drastically increased the restrictions imposed on individuals banned in terms of the Suppression of Communism Act, and created a new, extra-judicial form of restriction, house-arrest. A person placed under house-arrest is confined, at the discretion of the Minister of Justice, to his or her house for specific periods, generally outside of working hours during the week and for the whole of the weekend. Shortly thereafter, all public gatherings other than religious were prohibited in two of the most famous sites for political rallies, the Johannesberg City Hall steps and the Grand Parade in Cape Town. During 1962 COD was banned as an organisation. In 1963 the Congress Alliance suffered a further and very severe blow when many of its top leadership were arrested and subsequently brought to trial for sabotage. Eight of these people, including Nelson Mandela, Walter Sisulu, Govan Mbeki and Dennis Goldberg, were sentenced to life imprisonment.

Regrouping in the FSAW

The immediate impact of these events on the FSAW was devastating. 'The Federation was a child of its times', recalls Helen Joseph—a child of the 1950s.[1] In structure, tactics and outlook it remained rooted in that decade. In the long run it failed to survive the radical changes of the early 1960s. Its position in the polarised political climate after Sharpeville became more and more untenable. Although never banned itself, it remained an ally of an organisation that had been driven underground and had adopted illegal methods of resistance; an organisation, moreover, that the FSAW regarded as its political senior and which supplied it with the bulk of its membership. At the same time, the FSAW's freedom to act as a legal political organisation was curtailed drastically after 1960 by banning actions against its leaders, by political trials and restrictive legislation. It was clear that any signs of serious opposition would be ruthlessly suppressed by the government; the area in which the FSAW could manoeuvre had been viciously restricted.

In the short term, however, the FSAW managed to rally its resources and survive the immediate crisis of 1960. At first, the political upheavals after Sharpeville left it in a state of confusion, its executive dispersed, its projects abandoned. In the Transvaal, the one region for which reasonable records survive, no executive meetings at all were held between late 1959 and early 1961. During the state of emergency, many of the top leaders in the FSAW were detained, including Helen Joseph and Lilian Ngoyi, while those who were not rounded up went into hiding and temporary retreat. The banning of the ANC and ANCWL was an even more damaging blow to the organisation. At a single stroke it was stripped of most of its membership. The 1954 decision to base the FSAW on an affiliated rather than an individual membership now acquired a new significance—though had the FSAW ever developed a mass individual membership of its own, there can be little doubt that, sooner or later, it would have been banned outright itself.

1960 was a grim year, but by 1961 the FSAW was showing signs of revival. The spirit of optimism and perseverance, so characteristic of it in the 1950s, was not quashed. The first priority of its leaders, once they had emerged into political circulation again, was to reorganise its membership and try and recoup the losses caused by the banning of the ANCWL. In late 1960 or early 1961 the NEC called a meeting—its first after Sharpeville—where it discussed ways of rebuilding the shattered structure of the Federation. Its conclusions were reported to a meeting of the Transvaal regional executive in February 1961:

> Efforts to be made to build Federation on stronger basis. To organise among all sections, not only African women. Importance of approach to Trade Unions, churches and other bodies emphasised. Regions urged to organise Regional Conferences.[2]

It was decided, as a first step, that the FSAW should establish community-based clubs amongst African women. These would then be able to affiliate to it in the place of the banned ANCWL. During 1961, the regional executives made strenuous efforts to get these going and redirect ex-members of the ANCWL into them. The clubs—called 'Save our Families

Clubs'[3] —were seen as a direct replacement of the ANCWL's branch organisation. Despite the knock the FSAW had received by having the ANCWL banned it still did not change over to an individual membership. In the absence of any record of the discussion that surrounded the decision to form clubs, it is difficult to know why this opportunity of restructuring the membership was wasted. During the 1950s, as described in previous chapters, the FSAW had encountered many problems because of its clumsy federal form—problems to do with procedure, problems to do with money. The banning of the ANCWL showed how damaging government action against an affiliated organisation could be, and also removed the major obstacle the Cape Town committee had faced when lobbying for an individual membership in 1954/55, the ANC. Possibly the task of reorganisation that that would require was too taxing at a time when the FSAW was so weak. Possibly, too, its leaders felt that such a step would merely hasten the banning of the FSAW itself.

Initial results of the drive to establish clubs were encouraging. In July 1961 the Transvaal FSAW reported that 17 such clubs had affiliated.[4] By mid-1962 there were 72 clubs affiliated to the Federation—30 in the Transvaal, 18 in Natal and 12 each in the Western and Eastern Cape.[5] The fact that the Natal region had the second highest number of clubs affiliated to it testified to the strong politicising impact of the disturbances of 1959 on the women of that province. Previously it had been the most sluggish of the four FSAW regions. After 1959 it coped better with the crisis of Sharpeville and the ensuing events than either the Eastern or the Western Cape regions.

By 1961 all four FSAW regions were functioning again. The Transvaal was still the most dynamic, and throughout 1961 the Transvaal executive met regularly. Minutes survive for meetings held in February, March, April, June and July. The tone of these meetings was business-like. The committee discussed numerous projects—study groups, a national newsletter (which appears to have been achieved for a few months at least), raising funds to employ a full-time organiser. The need for a paid member of staff who could work full time was more urgent than ever but the difficulties in finding the funds to employ someone were even more acute. In November 1961 Helen Joseph described the FSAW's weak financial position and its effects thus:

> The Federation is in serious financial difficulties and if we are to maintain our existence and develop as we should, and indeed as we know that we can, the finances have to be found to keep our activities going and to pay the expenses of having an organiser, which we know to be essential for our progress.[6]

The FSAW continued to make overtures to the Liberal Party, Black Sash and NCW. Now that the ANCWL had been banned, it was more anxious than ever to broaden its base and draw in other organisations. The FSAW in Cape Town, with its longer history of contact with liberal white women's organisations, achieved the most success in this area. By 1962 it was assisting the Black Sash to run a bail office for offenders. It was in contact with the more conservative NCW and an unidentified group of Quakers as well.[7] Yet although a greater degree of cooperation appeared possible on specific issues, notably that of civil rights, this still fell short of affiliation.

By the second half of 1961 there were promising signs that the FSAW had recovered from the slump of 1960. In August 1961 the Transvaal organised a regional conference to coincide with the anniversary of Women's Day. They publicised the event extensively, distributing 22,000 leaflets to advertise the meeting beforehand—'of which 1,000 are for Indian women and 1,000 for Coloured women'.[8] They also organised numerous meetings all over the Rand to publicise the event. FSAW speakers visited towns as far afield as Ermelo, Bethal, Vereeniging and Nigel. The arrangements to commemorate Women's Day showed a marked continuity with the pre-Sharpeville period. They included the sale of commemorative badges, a poster demonstration on the City Hall steps and a memorandum on 'rents, arrests and housing' to be handed in to the mayor.[9]

The most impressive sign of recovery came in September 1961 when the FSAW staged its third national conference in Port Elizabeth. From all reports it was a success. The conference was attended by over 400 delegates, women from Cape Town and the Rand travelling to Port Elizabeth by hired bus. The hall where the conference was held was crowded with additional guests, its 2,000 seats filled to capacity, according to a report in *Drum*.[10] The size of the gathering was proof that the FSAW still had a sizeable following, although the open presence of Special Branch policemen—equipped with tape recorders—was a forceful reminder of the restrictions under which it operated.[11]

The conference was clearly a major political event for the embattled national liberation movement. *Drum* described it as 'the first big-scale political meeting and the first open sign of political activity since the end of May demonstrations'.[12] It appears to have generated the characteristic enthusiasm and spirit of earlier meetings. Mary Moodley remembers it favourably as a 'good' conference;[13] to the women present the possibility that this would prove the last national conference of the FSAW was too remote to consider.

At the meeting both Ngoyi and Joseph were re-elected to their positions as national president and secretary respectively, a mark of the high status they enjoyed within the organisation. The conference also reaffirmed the FSAW's stand on several issues. Resolutions were passed condemning the pass laws, the Bantu Authorities Act and Bantu Education. The meeting confirmed the FSAW's commitment to equal rights for women. In addition, it called for the lifting of the bans on the ANC and PAC and a stop to arbitrary arrests, prolonged trials and bannings. In her presidential report Lilian Ngoyi's assessment of the political situation in South Africa was sober but not downcast: 'Freedom does not come walking towards you—it must be won. As women we must go on playing our part.'[14]

By September 1961 the banned ANC had already begun to plan its first act of sabotage. The FSAW, however, remained committed to non-violence as a strategy. As a legal organisation it could hardly have done otherwise. More than mere legalism was involved, however; as in the 1950s, belief in peaceful methods of change was strongly entrenched among its members. At the national conference Lilian Ngoyi attacked the pistol clubs that had proliferated among white women in the aftermath of Sharpeville as a 'disgrace to womanhood'.[15] The clubs were an indication both of the highly charged political situation that prevailed and the degree to which white women identified themselves with the maintenance of the *status quo*. For Ngoyi they were an ugly reminder of the violence the FSAW wanted to avoid. 'How can there be peace in a country with these clubs?' she demanded.

In retrospect, the confidence and energy displayed by the FSAW at this time appears remarkable in view of the enormous odds stacked against it. It was in a state of siege. The minutes of Transvaal executive meetings tell the story graphically: the style of writing is far more cryptic than before, the women attending are referred to by initials only, never by name. The security situation was such that direct and open communication between the head office and the regions was extremely difficult to arrange. The coordinating and supervisory role of the NEC declined still further in relation to the regional committees as a result. None of these problems were new—although intensified—and by themselves they need not have destroyed the FSAW. What finally killed it was the annihilation of its leadership. As soon as the organisation showed itself capable of holding well-attended and effective meetings and conferences again, the government stepped in and began, systematically, to pick off the most important office-bearers.

In October 1961, a month after her outspoken speech to the FSAW conference, Lilian Ngoyi was banned and subsequently confined to the Johannesburg township of Orlando for five years. A similar order was served on Florence Matomela, one of the founding members of the FSAW and a major source of its strength in the Eastern Cape.[16] During 1962 the tempo of repressive action against FSAW leaders by the state quickened. In April 1962 Helen Joseph's original banning order, imposed in 1957, expired, but within a few months (during which time she resumed public political work vigorously) she was banned once again. This time she was compelled to sever all links with the FSAW. In addition she became the first person to be subjected to house-arrest. For all three women, their bannings marked the beginning of years of harrassment by the state. There was no let-up in the pressure on them. Helen Joseph remained under house arrest for ten years—ten years during which she could never leave her house at night or over weekends and, even more isolating, never have visitors to see her at her home. Lilian Ngoyi was banned and 'listed' as a communist until her death in March 1980. Florence Matomela was charged with 'furthering the aims of the ANC' and sentenced to five years' imprisonment in 1963; she died soon after her release, in June 1969.

The loss of three of its most senior and respected office bearers was a fatal blow to the FSAW. Nevertheless, it did not collapse immediately, continuing to function on the Rand, in Port Elizabeth, Durban and Cape Town. In mid-1962 the WIDF sent out a representative to assess the situation within the FSAW and report back on her findings. She visited all the major centres and met with the most important leaders. She was struck by the lack of pessimism, 'despite the fact that there is no underestimation of the present strength of the Nationalist government'.[17] 'At the moment we have been stunned by the terrible implications of the Sabotage Act but we shall recover and nothing will daunt us,' Lilian Ngoyi told her when she went secretly to visit her in Orlando Township, Soweto.[18] Florence Matomela was equally undeterred by her banning order: 'Never mind the wind and the rain, we'll fight,' was her comment.

Women were even discussing plans for the next national conference which they wished to hold in 1963. One of the main topics on the agenda for that meeting was a 'Women's Bill of Rights':

> The thinking behind the compilation of such a bill is that although the Federation is an integral part of the Congress Alliance and subscribes to the Freedom Charter, it is felt that there is a special need for a Bill detailing the special demands of women which will have to be met in any democratic state.[19]

Unfortunately the WIDF report does not make it clear where this suggestion came from, and in what way this 'Bill of Rights' would have differed from or expanded upon the 'Women's Charter' of 1954. Further comments in this report on the relationship between the FSAW and the ANC made it clear that the FSAW was still fighting male domination.

> The national leadership of the ANC has agreed that the FSAW shall have an independent political existence but it is not always easy to get this across in some areas. In one, for instance, the women found that they had to get the men to endorse all their arrangements and while this may have been partly the tightening up of general political control. . . the women nevertheless felt they were being subjected to too much male domination.[20]

During 1962, both the Transvaal and Natal regions held provincial conferences. Helen Joseph managed to attend the Natal conference in the short period of respite she enjoyed between the ending of one banning order and the beginning of the next, more severe, one. Her own impression of the conference was that it was not well organised and did not compare with meetings arranged on the Rand.[21] Nevertheless, in view of the dismal record of the FSAW in Natal in the 1950s, the fact that the conference was held at all, and at that time in the FSAW's history, was remarkable.

By the end of 1962, however, the strain on the FSAW's leaders and resources was showing clearly. The government's strategy of restricting individual leaders was destroying the FSAW as effectively, if more slowly, as an outright banning order. In the next two or three years more and more of the organisation's most experienced and dedicated members were removed from office by banning orders, arrests and, as the pressure

mounted, exile. Albertina Sisulu, Mary Moodley, Amina Cachalia, Liz
Abrahams, Ruth Matseoane, Bertha Mashaba, Violet Weinberg, Frances
Baard. . . the list of restricted leaders is a lengthy one. In 1965
Ray Alexander went into exile in Zambia. Other political leaders were
forced to follow suit. In her book on 'Women in apartheid South Africa',
For Their Triumphs and For Their Tears, Hilda Bernstein (Hilda Watts),
herself in exile in Britain, lists 90 women who have been imprisoned on
political charges between 1960 and 1975, 105 women who have been
banned and six women who have been banished. Very many of these cases
belong to the early 1960s, including women of the FSAW.

> Women were prosecuted on a wide variety of political charges including treason,
> terrorism, sabotage, membership of or assistance to a banned organisation,
> helping people to escape from the country, recruiting guerillas, breaches of
> banning orders and similar charges. Among those who have served jail sentences
> are women of all colours and all ages and religions. There have been young
> girls, many mothers, and grandmothers, some over 70.[22]

As the pressures against the FSAW continued to mount, its general
following dwindled very rapidly. By the mid 1960s it consisted of little
more than a handful of committed, but embattled committee members.
Under these circumstances, it proved impossible to hold another national
conference in 1963 as was originally intended. The Transvaal provincial
conference, in August 1962, was the last meeting of any size convened by
the FSAW; thereafter its decline was rapid. An undated typescript history
of the FSAW, written probably in the mid-1960s, showed some of the
fighting spirit that had always characterised the FSAW. It refused to
concede that the FSAW had disappeared from the political scene but
admitted that it had 'become impossible for the Federation to continue
to function as an organisation although it has never been banned nor did
it ever dissolve itself.' Nevertheless, it concluded on a positive note: 'From
time to time, on historic funeral occasions, the women of the old Federation still emerge as a body wearing their Federation uniforms.'[23]

There is no single date which marks the collapse of the FSAW. It was
a cumulative process rather than a sudden event. Perhaps 1st February
1963, the day on which it became compulsory for all African women to
carry reference books, can be taken as a symbolic date for the ending of
the FSAW. When this date was gazetted, the FSAW realised that its members did not have the resources or the numbers to resist taking out reference books any longer. Grimly, reluctantly, it instructed those women
who were still without books to submit. To continue to defy the law at
that stage would have been futile. It would have exposed resisters to
unnecessary arrest and weakened the women's organisation still further.
Not all women could bring themselves to comply with these instructions.
Frances Baard, for instance, could not accept the idea of carrying a reference book after so many years of fighting them, and stubbornly refused.
In 1969, after having served a 5 year jail sentence under the Suppression
of Communism Act, she was still without a book. She was arrested soon

after her release because of this and sent back to jail for a further fourteen days. 'I said in court: "I don't want it. I am prepared to go to jail."'[24] Only later, after her release once again, did she finally bow to the pressure and accept that 'terrible document—under protest'. For her and the other women who had held out against reference books for so long, it was a painful and bitter experience to submit in the end.

Individual protests apart, by 1963 the anti-pass campaign had finally been brought to a close. So too had an era in the history of political organisation amongst women in South Africa. Yet if the FSAW had been crushed, the spirit and commitment of the women who had led it had not been broken. Those who went into exile took this spirit with them and fed it into the women's section of the ANC in exile. Those who stayed behind continued to work for the cause of national liberation in whatever way they could. The ideas of the FSAW were never destroyed. After a period of apparent dormancy in the late 1960s—the result of the massive crackdown of the previous years—women began to regroup in the 1970s. They turned to the history of the FSAW for inspiration, picking up on the 'Women's Charter' and the FSAW's 'Aims'.

In 1975 a small group of black women established a short-lived Black Women's Federation. They drew heavily on the 'Women's Charter' in their own statement of position, with one major difference. Whereas the FSAW had committed itself unequivocally to an organisation that was open to all who subscribed to its aims, the Black Women's Federation was, as its name made clear, open to black women only. It allied itself to the Black Consciousness Movement then strongly entrenched among black students and professional groups. The Black Women's Federation was not given time to prove whether it could establish a broad-based, populist movement or not—it was banned with other black consciousness organisations in October 1977.

Not all the women of the FSAW who were still active politically were happy about adopting a black consciousness line. In more recent years, there are signs that their viewpoint is prevailing and talk of reviving the FSAW or at least reactivating women's organisations along similar lines can sometimes be heard. The numbers involved are small, the obstacles to organisation enormous—but it is apparent that the embers of the FSAW are still glowing and may yet produce a spark.

As a political organisation, the FSAW broke new ground amongst women in South Africa. There were three main aspects to its programme which distinguished it from other contemporary or earlier national women's organisations—its commitment to the emancipation of women, its commitment to the national liberation movement and, related to both of these, its multiracialism.

Before the FSAW, almost all other women's organisations, from left to right across the political spectrum, had been organised as mere auxiliaries to parent, male-dominated bodies and had been seen chiefly in a 'tea and typing' capacity. The ANCWL itself had been formed in this mould. The one qualified exception to this general pattern had been the white women's suffrage organisation, the WEAU. This, however, had had a limited political programme and, with the passage of the Women's Enfranchisement Act in 1930, it had disbanded. The FSAW was thus the first national women's organisation to include a comprehensive programme for the emancipation of women along with its general political programme—and to take up this issue with its male colleagues. For all the qualifications that tempered its stand on women's emancipation in practice, it represented a real and serious attempt to incorporate women into the political programme of the national liberation movement on an equal footing with men; for this alone, it warrants recognition.

The FSAW also rejected the colour-consciousness that had permeated other women's organisations. This flowed inevitably from its more develop-ed feminist consciousness, which reinforced and expanded upon the multi-racial tradition already present within the Congress Alliance. Because women were seen to suffer serious disabilities on account of their sex, the FSAW could envisage the possibility of a universal women's movement aimed at removing those disabilities and cutting across existing colour lines in society. While directing its attention to the problems facing the black majority of women in South Africa, it continually addressed itself in much broader terms to all women. 'No woman can be free while her sister is in chains', claimed one FSAW document in 1959.[25]

In claiming this unity, the FSAW exposed itself to the contradictions facing any women's movement with universalist aspirations in South Africa. As it was to discover after 1954, all women in society do not share a common experience or identity. The divisions of colour, irrational and discriminatory though they appeared to the FSAW, correspond to more complex relationships of power and wealth and it was these, ultimately, that determined the nature of women's varied political allegiances. Throughout the twentieth century the primary identification of women had not been with their sex, but with their colour group; this was as true of women in the 1950s as it had been of women at the time of the Bantu Women's League. The diversity of women's experience found expression in the diversity of the political positions found amongst them. The FSAW in the 1950s represented one particular direction that women's political involvement had taken. Even though it envisaged the establishment of a broad movement, open to all women, it was certainly not representative of all women politically.

The commitment of the FSAW to the national liberation movement was in itself an indication of the primacy of non-sex-related issues for women in South Africa. In linking the women's movement to the national liberation movement, it reflected—and chose to reflect—the political priorities of the majority of South African women. In speaking of the rights of all women, it was, in fact, attacking the basis of the South African state in which the dominant interests of most white women were vested. Those few white women who were involved in it, though playing an important part and strengthening its commitment to a multi-racial society, were not representative of their group.

And yet, in linking up black and white women in a single organisation, the FSAW was making an important statement, at the time and to future generations. 'It was a struggle which can never be forgotten, women having a unity, black and white', Florence Mkhize has said.[26] The FSAW establish- ed that racism is not universal and endemic in South Africa, that it can be breached, that what is important is not the colour of one's skin but one's understanding of the forces of exploitation in South Africa, and one's commitment to their overthrow. The FSAW never rejected white women who had made that commitment but welcomed them as allies. Its entire history was a vindication of its faith in the non-racial ideal.

In many ways the programme of the FSAW, as set out in the 'Women's Charter', was in advance of the thinking of most of the women to whom its appeal was directed. Yet in organising within the FSAW, women were coming into contact with new perspectives. The horizons of the female world were widening, new patterns of behaviour emerging. At the same time, the broadening out of black resistance to include women introduced a new dimension to the political struggle being waged against the white supremacist state. The anti-pass campaign revealed clearly the potential source of strength for the national liberation movement that women represented.

It was a potential that in the 1950s, however, was only suggested, never realised. In many ways, the history of the anti-pass campaign was the history of the FSAW; the defeat of that campaign was the defeat of the FSAW too. Formed in 1954, its peak period came between late 1955 and the end of 1958, when the campaign against passes was in full swing. Although neither the FSAW nor the ANCWL could claim responsibility for all the anti-pass protests mounted by women during this time, their role in directing, articulating, and encouraging their resistance was sub- stantial. By 1959, however, the campaign was losing its momentum in the face of the escalating government repression, and in the early 1960s it was finally broken. With the enforcement of the compulsory carrying of passes by women in early 1963, the FSAW lost its major rallying point amongst women. Its own eclipse after 1963 followed quickly.

Yet despite the short lifespan of the FSAW—little more than eight or nine years—it remains a significant organisation in the history of women's political activity in South Africa. Its failures, as much as its successes, cast light both on the position of women in the 1950s and early 1960s, as well as on the problems faced by any organisation aiming to improve the position of women in South Africa. It was an organisation working towards a society free from any form of discrimination, whether on the grounds of sex, colour or class. As such, it was a pioneering organisation amongst women. In stressing that women needed to organise as a group to fight against those 'customs and conventions' which kept them in a position of inferiority to men, it was a pioneering organisation within the national liberation movement too. Although conceding priority to the national liberation movement, it did not lose sight of the necessity of the women's movement if full equality for women was to be won. The women's struggle, it argued, is more than 'just the struggle of the non-European people of South Africa for freedom, justice and security': it is a 'struggle within a struggle, which transcends them. . . a struggle which will continue long after freedom has been won. . .'[27]

The legacy of the FSAW is one of an open-hearted belief in a free and non-racial society. It is one of optimism that such a society will be attained—and of a dogged commitment to the struggle that that involves. It is a legacy of hope and of courage. 'Tired?', Frances Baard replies when asked if the long struggle of the 1940s and 1950s, as well as her years in jail, have not worn her down.

> I don't know what you mean by 'tired'. I can't give up because the spirit is still there. I can't help it, even if I wanted to give up. Although I can't do everything physically, the spirit still wants what I always wanted.[28]

Notes

1. Interview with H. Joseph.
2. FSAW, 'Minutes of the meeting of the Tvl. Regional Committee', 11.2.61, FSAW DI.
3. FSAW, 'Minutes of the meeting of the Tvl. Regional Committee', 22.7.61, FSAW DI.
4. *Ibid.*
5. WIDF, 'Report on a visit to South Africa sponsored by the WIDF', p. 33. Unfortunately there seems no way of knowing what the average membership of these clubs was.
6. FSAW correspondence to Jabavu 'Save our Families Association', 22.11.61, FSAW DI 3.
7. WIDF, 'Report on a visit to South Africa', *op. cit.,* p. 25.
8. FSAW, 'Minutes of the meeting of the Tvl. Regional Committee', 22.7.61, FSAW DI.
9. *Ibid.*
10. *Drum,* October 1961, 'The Women Speak Up', p. 47.
11. *Ibid.*
12. *Ibid.*
13. Interview with M. Moodley.
14. *Drum,* October 1961, 'The Women Speak Up', p. 47.
15. *Ibid.*
16. 'Never mind the wind and rain—we'll fight', paper clipping, FSAW FII.
17. WIDF, 'Report on a visit to South Africa sponsored by the WIDF', p. 28.
18. 'Never mind the wind and rain—we'll fight', FSAW FII.
19. WIDF, 'Report on a visit to South Africa sponsored by the WIDF', p. 38.
20. WIDF, 'Report on a visit to South Africa sponsored by the WIDF', p. 33.
21. Interview with H. Joseph.
22. H. Bernstein, *For Their Triumphs and For Their Tears,* p. 50.
23. 'Federation of Women', p. 3, FSAW FII.
24. Interview with F. Baard.
25. Pledge of support from the FSAW for the anti-pass struggle of African women, nd, c. March 1959, FSAW CI 7.
26. Interview with F. Mkhize.
27. 'A way to a better South Africa: Women have an important part', by 'A Woman Leader', article for *Golden City Post,* September 1957, FSAW E.
28. Interview with F. Baard.

APPENDIX A
Women's Charter and Aims

Preamble: We, the women of South Africa, wives and mothers, working women and housewives, African, Indians, European and Coloured, hereby declare our aim of striving for the removal of all laws, regulations, conventions and customs that discriminate against us as women, and that deprive us in any way of our inherent right to the advantages, responsibilities and opportunities that society offers to any one section of the population.

A Single Society: We women do not form a society separate from the men. There is only one society, and it is made up of both women and men. As women we share the problems and anxieties of our men, and join hands with them to remove social evils and obstacles to progress.

Test of Civilisation: The level of civilisation which any society has reached can be measured by the degree of freedom that its members enjoy. The status of women is a test of civilisation. Measured by that standard, South Africa must be considered low in the scale of civilised nations.

Women's Lot: We women share with our menfolk the cares and anxieties imposed by poverty and its evils. As wives and mothers, it falls upon us to make small wages stretch a long way. It is we who feel the cries of our children when they are hungry and sick. It is our lot to keep and care for the homes that are too small, broken and dirty to be kept clean. We know the burden of looking after children and land when our husbands are away in the mines, on the farms, and in the towns earning our daily bread.

We know what it is to keep family life going in pondokkies and shanties, or in overcrowded one-room apartments. We know the bitterness of children taken to lawless ways, of daughters becoming unmarried mothers whilst still at school, of boys and girls growing up without education, training or jobs at a living wage.

Poor and Rich: These are evils that need not exist. They exist because the society in which we live is divided into poor and rich, into non-European and European. They exist because there are privileges for the few, discrimination and harsh treatment for the many. We women have stood and will stand shoulder to shoulder with our menfolk in a common struggle against poverty, race and class discrimination, and the evils of the colour-bar.

National Liberation: As members of the National Liberatory movements and Trade Unions, in and through our various organisations, we march forward with our men in the struggle for liberation and the defence of the working people. We pledge ourselves to keep high the banner of equality, fraternity and liberty. As women there rests upon us also the burden of removing from our society all the social differences developed in past times between men and women, which have the effect of keeping our sex in a position of inferiority and subordination.

Equality for Women: We resolve to struggle for the removal of laws and customs that deny African women the right to own, inherit or alienate property. We resolve to work for a change in the laws of marriage such as are found amongst our African, Malay and Indian people, which have the effect of placing wives in the position of legal subjection to husbands, and giving husbands the power to dispose of wives' property and earnings, and dictate to them in all matters affecting them and their children.

We recognise that the women are treated as minors by these marriage and property laws because of ancient and revered traditions and customs which had their origin in the antiquity of the people and no doubt served purposes of great value in bygone times.

There was a time in the African society when every woman reaching marriageable stage was assured of a husband, home, land and security.

Then husbands and wives with their children belonged to families and clans that supplied most of their own material needs and were largely self-sufficient. Men and women were partners in a compact and closely integrated family unit.

Women who Labour: Those conditions have gone. The tribal and kinship society to which they belonged has been destroyed as a result of the loss of tribal land, migration of men away from the tribal home, the growth of towns and industries, and the rise of a great body of wage-earners on the farms and in the urban areas, who depend wholly or mainly on wages for a livelihood.

Thousands of African women, like Indians, Coloured and European women, are employed today in factories, homes, offices, shops, on farms, in professions as nurses, teachers and the like. As unmarried women, widows or divorcees they have to fend for themselves, often without the assistance of a male relative. Many of them are responsible not only for their own livelihood but also that of their children.

Large numbers of women today are in fact the sole breadwinners and heads of their families.

Forever Minors: Nevertheless, the laws and practices derived from an earlier and different state of society are still applied to them. They are responsible for their own person and their children. Yet the law seeks to enforce upon them the status of a minor.

Not only are African, Coloured and Indian women denied political rights, but they are also in many parts of the Union denied the same status as men in such matters as the right to enter into contracts, to own and dispose of property, and to execise guardianship over their children.

Obstacle to Progress: The law has lagged behind the development of society; it no longer corresponds to the actual social and economic position of women. The law has become an obstacle to progress of the women, and therefore a brake on the whole of society.

This intolerable condition would not be allowed to continue were it not for the refusal of a large section of our menfolk to concede to us women the rights and privileges which they demand for themselves.

We shall teach the men that they cannot hope to liberate themselves from the evils of discrimination and prejudice as long as they fail to extend to women complete and unqualified equality in law and in practice.

Need for Education: We also recognise that large numbers of our womenfolk continue to be bound by traditional practices and conventions, and fail to realise that these have become obsolete and a brake on progress. It is our duty and privilege to enlist all women in our struggle for emancipation and to bring to them all realisation of the intimate relationship that exists between their status of inferiority as women and the inferior status to which their people are subjected by discriminatory laws and colour prejudices.

It is our intention to carry out a nation-wide programme of education that will bring home to the men and women of all national groups the realisation that freedom cannot be won for any one section or for the people as a whole as long as we women are kept in bondage.

An Appeal: We women appeal to all progressive organisations, to members of the great National Liberatory movements, to the trade unions and working class organisations, to the churches, educational and welfare organisations, to all progressive men and women who have the interests of the people at heart, to join with us in this great and noble endeavour.

Our Aims

We declare the following aims:

This organisation is formed for the purpose of uniting women in common action for the removal of all political, legal, economic and social disabilities. We shall strive for women to obtain:

1. The right to vote and to be elected to all State bodies, without restriction or discrimination.
2. The right to full opportunities for employment with equal pay and possibilities of promotion in all spheres of work.
3. Equal rights with men in relation to property, marriage and children, and for the removal of all laws and customs that deny women such equal rights.
4. For the development of every child through free compulsory education for all; for the protection of mother and child through maternity

homes, welfare clinics, creches and nursery schools, in countryside and towns; through proper homes for all, and through the provision of water, light, transport, sanitation, and other amenities of modern civilisation.

5. For the removal of all laws that restrict free movement, that prevent or hinder the right of free association and activity in democratic organisations, and the right to participate in the work of these organisations.

6. To build and strengthen women's sections in the National Liberatory movements, the organisation of women in trade unions, and through the peoples' varied organisation.

7. To cooperate with all other organisations that have similar aims in South Africa as well as throughout the world.

8. To strive for permanent peace throughout the world.

APPENDIX B

Women known to have attended the inaugural conference and the organisations which they represented.

Cape Town and area:
1. Dora Tamana—ANCWL, Retreat Women's Vigilance Association.
2. Esther Nose—Retreat Women's Vigilance Association.
3. Emma Razone—Nyanga Women's Vigilance Association.
4. Albertina Gwenkane—Nyanga Women's Vigilance Association.
5. Rosie Mpetha—Nyanga Women's Vigilance Association.
6. Annie Silinga—ANCWL, Langa Women's Vigilance Association.
7. Winifred Seqwana—ANCWL, Langa Women's Vigilance Association.
8. Gladys Smith—Cape Housewives' League.
9. Katie White—Guardian Christmas Club.
10. Hetty McLeod—Cape Factory Workers Committee.
11. Hilda Lotz
12. Freda von Rheda—Food and Canning Workers Union.
13. Mabel Jones—African Food and Canning Workers Union, Worcester.
14. Elizabeth Mafeking—African Food and Canning Workers Union, Paarl
15. Betty Kearus/T. Steenkamp—African Food and Canning Workers Union, Paarl.
16. Ray Alexander—COD.
17. Cecilia Rosier—COD.

Cradock:
1. Cecilia A.N. Kuse—ANCWL.

Durban:
1. Fatima Meer—SAIC.
2. Bertha Mkize—ANCWL.
3. Henrietta Ostrich—African Women's Association.

East London:
1. Martha Nqxesha—African Food and Canning Workers Union.

Johannesburg:
1. Hetty du Preez—Garment Workers' Union, no. 2.
2. Lilian Ngoyi—ANCWL.
3. Rica Hodgson—COD.
4. Rahima Moosa—SAIC.
5. Helen Joseph—COD.
6. Ida Mtwana—ANCWL.
7. Josie Palmer—Transvaal All-Women's Union.
8. Hilda Watts—COD.
9. Amina Cachalia—SAIC.

Kimberley:
1.   Sister M.F. Thompson—ANCWL.

Port Elizabeth:
1.   Florence Matomela—ANCWL.

APPENDIX C

'What Women Demand', compiled in preparation for the Congress of the People, 1955. FSAW II A.

We Demand
Four months maternity leave on full pay for working mothers.
Properly staffed and equipped maternity homes, ante-natal clinics, and child welfare centres in all towns and villages, and in the reserves and rural areas.
Day nurseries for the children of working mothers.
Nursery schools for the pre-school children.
Birth control clinics.

We demand these for all *mothers of all races.*

We Demand
Compulsory, free and universal education from the primary school to the University.
Adequate school feeding and free milk for all children in day nurseries, nursery schools, and primary and secondary schools.
Special schools for handicapped children.
Play centres and cultural centres for school children.
Properly equipped playgrounds and sportsfields.
Vocational training and apprenticeship facilities.

We demand these for all *children of all races.*

We Demand
Proper houses at rents not more than 10 per cent of the earnings of the head of the household.
Indoor sanitation, water supply and proper lighting in our homes.
The right to own our own homes and the land on which we build them.
The right to live where we choose.
Housing loan schemes at low rates of interest.
Lighting in our streets.
Properly made roads and storm water drainage.
Adequate public transport facilities.
Parks and recreation centres.
Sportsfields and swimming pools.
Public conveniences.

We demand these for all *people of all races.*

We Demand
Better shopping facilities, particularly in the non-European townships.

More dairies, and full supplies of pasteurised whole milk.

Mobile vegetable markets.

Subsidisation of all protective foods: Bread, Meal, Meat, Milk, Vegetables and Fruit.

Controlled prices for all essential commodities: Food, Basic Clothing, Fuel.

Fair rationing of essential foods and fuel when in short supply.

We demand these for all *people in all places.*

We Demand

The right of *all* people to own and work their own farms.

The development of all uncultivated land.

The fair distribution of land amongst *all* people.

The mechanisation of methods of food production.

The scientific improvement of land by:

      a. Irrigation and intensive farming.

      b. Control of soil erosion and improvement of the soil.

      c. Supply of seed to all people producing from the land.

Efficient organisation of the distribution and marketing of food.

We demand sufficient food for all *people.*

We Demand

More and better land for the reserves.

Schools for children living in the reserves.

Maternity, medical and social services in the reserves.

Shops and controlled prices in the reserves.

Planned agricultural development of the reserves.

The abolition of migratory labour which destroys our family life by removing our husbands and which destroys their health through the conditions of their labour and the compound system.

We demand that the reserves become food producing areas and not reservoirs of cheap labour.

We Demand

The transfer of trust farms to the ownership of the African people.

The abolition of convict farm labour.

The payment of minimum cash wages for all men and women on farms.

The abolition of child labour on the farms.

The abolition of the 'tot' system.

Free compulsory universal education for all children in rural areas.

Paid holidays for all farm workers.

The inclusion of farm workers in all industrial legislation.

We demand these rights for all *people in the rural areas.*

We Demand
That equal invalidity and old age pensions be paid for people of *all* races.
Homes and proper care for *all* aged and sick people.
National medical services for *all* sick people.
Adequate and equal hospital services for *all* people.
Increased cost of living allowances adequate to meet the rising cost of living.
That all African workers in all spheres of employment be covered by unemployment insurance and illness allowances.
The consolidation of part of the cost of living allowance into basic wages.
That no person be required to carry a pass or reference book.
Equal rights for *all* people.

We demand these fundamental rights for all *people.*

We Demand for all *women in South Africa*
The right to vote.
The right to be elected to all State, Provincial or Municipal bodies.
Full opportunities for employment in all spheres of work.
Equal pay for equal work.
Equal rights with men in property, in marriage, and in the guardianship of our children.

And together with other women all over the world.

We Demand
The banning of atomic and hydrogen bombs.
The use of the atom for peaceful purposes and the betterment of the world.
That there shall be *no more war.*
That there shall be *peace and freedom for our children.*

BIBLIOGRAPHY

I. Unpublished Documentary Material

1. *The Federation of South African Women's Papers*, South African Institute of Race Relations, Johannesburg. (FSAW reference in the text.)

   These papers cover the years between 1954 and the early 1960s, with the earlier period more richly documented than the later. Most of the material is concerned with the Transvaal region of the FSAW. As well as papers of the FSAW itself, the collection also includes some material from organisations with which the FSAW was in contact, including the ANCWL and other organisations within the Congress Alliance; the Liberal Party; the South African Peace Council. Material includes correspondence, literature to do with various campaigns—pamphlets, memoranda on the pass laws, reports, work schedules—conference agendas and reports, press statements, speech notes, biographical sketches, some financial statements and minutes of meetings.

   In addition, the following papers of the FSAW, which do not form part of the above collection, were also consulted:
   —'Draft Constitution' in *Papers of the Natal Indian Congress* (20.18), Unisa Documentation Centre for African Studies, Accession no. 105.
   —'Report of the First National Conference of Women held in the Trades Hall, Johannesburg, South Africa, April 17th, 1954', South African Library, Cape Town.
2. 'The History of the ANC Women's League and the role of Women', anon., n.d., carbon type-script. Private collection, possessor to remain anonymous.
3. Hoover Institution Microfilm Collection, *South Africa, a collection of miscellaneous documents, 1902-1963*, Reel 8.
4. NCAW papers in *Rheinhallt-Jones Papers*, Organisations, University of the Witwatersrand.
5. People's Food Council, 'Circular', 11/3/44 and 16/11/44 in *A.B. Xuma Papers*, Box 440311 and 44116a, University of the Witwatersrand.
6. WIDF, 'Report on a visit to South Africa sponsored by the WIDF, May-June 1962'. Private collection, possessor to remain anonymous.

II. Official Records

A. Court Records

Regina vs. Faried Adams and Others, record of arraignment to conclusion (Aug. 1959-Mar. 1961).
Vol. 66, 67, 68, 69, 70, 84 and collection of documents of some of the exhibits used in the Trial (*Treason Trial Record*). South African Institute of Race Relations, Johannesburg.

B. *Parliamentary Debates*

House of Assembly Debates, 1930, 1937, 1950, 1952, 1955, 1957.
Senate Debates, 1950, 1952.

C. *Reports of Commissions and Departmental Committees*

Bantu Affairs Commission, *Report,* 1957-1961, UG 36-61.
Dept. of Native Affairs, *Annual Reports,* 1919-1921, 1935-1936, 1944/45-1954/57.
Native Affairs Commission, *Annual Reports,* 1945/46-1956.
Social and Economic Planning Council, *The Economic and Social Conditions of the Racial Groups in South Africa,* Report no. 13, 8/5/48, UG 53-48.
South Africa, *Industrial Legislation Commission,* 1951, UG 62-51.
——————, *Report of the Inter-Departmental Committee on the Social, Health and Economic Conditions of Urban Natives,* 1942.
——————, *Report of the Inter-Departmental Committee on the Native Pass Laws,* 1920, UG 41-22.
——————, *Report of the Native Farm Labour Committee,* 1937-39 (Pretoria), 1939.
——————, *Report of the Native Laws Commission,* 1946-48, UG 28-48.
——————, *Report of the Senate Select Committee on Natives (Abolition of Passes and Coordination of Documents) Bill,* SC 2-52.
——————, *Summary of the Report of the Commission for the Socio-economic development of the Bantu areas within the Union of South Africa,* UG 61-55.

D. *Census and Statistics*

Bureau of Census and Statistics, *Union Statistics for 50 Years* (Pretoria, 1960).
South Africa, *Census of Industrial Establishments,* 1937-38.
——————, *Industrial Census,* 1951-52, Special Report, no. 206.
——————, *Official Yearbook of the Union,* no. 2, 1918.
——————, *Census of the Union of South Africa, 1911,* Part 5, UG 32d-1912.
——————, *Third Census of the population of the Union of South Africa, 1921,* Part 6, UG 37-1925.
——————, *Sixth Census of the Population of the Union of South Africa, 1936,* vol. 7, UG 11-1942; vol. 9, UG 12-1942.
——————, *Population Census, 1946,* vol. 5, UG 41-1954.
——————, *Population Census, 1951,* vol. 1, UG 42-1955.
——————, *Population Census, 1960,* no. 8.

III. Newspapers and Periodicals

A. Newspapers

A.P.O., 1909-1917.
Forward, 1924, 1925, 1927, 1928.
Guardian, 1937-1952.
    Subsequently: *Clarion*, 1952.
              Advance, 1952-1954.
              New Age, 1954-1958.
The International, 1919-1923.
Umsebenzi/South African Worker, 1930-1937.

B. Limited editions of newspapers consulted

Cape Times, 1955, 1956.
Miscellaneous collection of newspaper cuttings, 1958-1963, including cuttings from *The Star, Rand Daily Mail, Golden City Post* (Private Collection).
Natal Mercury, 1911.
Die Vaderland, 1955, 1956.

C. Periodicals

Drum, 1951-1963.
Fighting Talk, 1952-1958.
Women's Outlook, Aug. 1921.

IV. Pamphlets

Close, R., *New Life* (Cape Town, Food and Canning Workers Union, 1950). South African Library.
Communist Party of South Africa, *Communists in Conference, the 1943-44 National Conference of the Communist Party of South Africa* (Cape Town, 1944). South African Library.
Empire Group of South Africa, Cape Area Branch, *Franchise Rights and Wrongs* (Cape Town, 1931). South African Library.
FSAW, *Strijdom. . . You have Struck a Rock* (1956). South African Library.
FSAW and ANCWL, *Women in Chains* (c. 1956). South African Library.
Seccombe, W., *The Housewife and her Labour under Capitalism* (London, n.d., c. 1974/75).
South African Institute of Race Relations, *African Family Life* (Johannesburg, 1968).
Treharne, M., *History of the National Council of Women of South Africa, 1909-1948* (Cape Town, 1948).
Wix, E., *The Cost of Living* (South African Institute of Race Relations, Johannesburg, 1951).

V. Books

Andrews, W.H., *Class Struggles in South Africa* (Cape Town, 1940).

Benson, M., *The Struggle for a Birthright* (Harmondsworth, Penguin, 1966).

Bernstein, H., *For Their Triumphs and For Their Tears* (London, 1975).

Brandel-Syrier, M., *Black Women in Search of God* (London, 1962).

Carnegie Commission, *The Poor White Problem in South Africa, Report of the Carnegie Commission*, vols. 1, 5 (Stellenbosch, 1932).

Carroll, B.A. (ed.), *Liberating Women's History* (Urbana, Chicago, 1976).

Cope, R.K., *Comrade Bill: the Life and Times of W.H. Andrews, Workers' leader* (Cape Town, 1944).

Davidson, B., *Report on Southern Africa* (London, 1952).

Davies, I., *African Trade Unions* (Harmondsworth, Penguin, 1966).

du Toit, B., *Ukubamba Amadolo; Workers' Struggles in the South African Textile Industry* (London, 1978).

Feit, E., *African Opposition in South Africa* (Stanford, 1967).

Forman, L. and Sachs, E.S., *The South African Treason Trial* (London, 1957).

Geffen, I.A., *The Laws of South Africa affecting women and children* (Johannesburg, 1928).

Gibson, R., *African Liberation Movements* (Oxford, 1972).

Gollock, G.A., *Daughters of Africa* (London, 1932).

Harrison, W.H., *Memoirs of a Socialist in South Africa, 1903-1947* (Cape Town, n.d.).

Hooper, C., *Brief Authority* (London, 1960).

Horrell, M., *Action, Reaction and Counteraction* (Johannesburg, 1963).

——————, *Legislation and Race Relations* (Johannesburg, 1971).

——————, *Racialism and the Trade Unions* (Johannesburg, 1959).

——————, *South Africa's Workers: Their Organisations and Patterns of Employment* (Johannesburg, 1969).

Joseph, H., *If this be Treason* (London, 1963).

——————, *Tomorrow's Sun* (London, 1966).

Karis, T. and Carter, G.M. (eds.), *From Protest to Challenge, a documentary history of African politics in South Africa, 1882-1964*, vols. 1-4 (Stanford, 1973).

Karis, T., *The Treason Trial in South Africa: a Guide to the Microfilm Record of the Trial* (Stanford, 1965).

Keiskammahoek Rural Survey (Pietermaritzburg, 1952): vol. II, Hobart Houghton, D. and Walton, E.M., *The economy of a Native Reserve;* vol. III, Wilson, M., Kaplan, S., Maki, T. and Walton, E., *Social Structure.*

Kuper, L., *An African Bourgeoisie: Race, Class and Politics in South Africa* (New Haven, 1965).

——————, *Passive Resistance in South Africa* (New Haven, 1957).

Lessing, D., *A Ripple from the Storm* (London, 1965).

Lewis, T.H. (ed.), *Women of South Africa* (Cape Town, 1913).

Little, K., *African Women in Towns: an Aspect of Africa's Social*

Revolution (Cambridge, 1973).

Michelman, C., *The Black Sash of South Africa; a case study in liberalism* (London, 1975).

Mitchell, J., *Women's Estate* (London, 1971).

Patterson, S., *Colour and Culture in South Africa* (London, 1953).

Pauw, B.A., *The Second Generation: a Study of the Family among Urbanised Bantu in East London* (Cape Town, 1963, revised 1973).

Plaatje, S., *Native Life in South Africa,* (New York, 1969).

Rosaldo, M.Z. and Lampere, L. (eds.), *Women, Culture and Society* (Stanford, 1974).

Roux, E., *S.P. Bunting, a Political Biography* (Cape Town, 1944).

_____, *Time Longer than Rope* (Madison, second ed. 1964).

Sachs, E.S., *Rebels' Daughters* (London, 1957).

Sampson, A., *The Treason Cage* (London, 1958).

Schreiner, O., *The Story of an African Farm* (London, 1883?).

_____ ,*Women and Labour* (London, 1911).

Simons, H.J., *African Women, their Legal Status in South Africa* (London, 1968).

Simons, H.J. and Simons, R.E., *Class and Colour in South Africa, 1850-1950* (Harmondsworth, Penguin, 1969).

Solomon, B., *Time Remembered* (Cape Town, 1968).

South African Institute of Race Relations, *Survey of Race Relations* 1951/2-1963 (Johannesburg).

Sundkler, B.G.M., *Bantu Prophets in South Africa* (London, 1961).

Walker, I.L. and Weinbren, B., *2000 Casualties: A History of the South African Labour Movement* (Johannesburg, 1961).

Walshe, P., *Black Nationalism in South Africa: A Short History* (Johannesburg, 1973).

_____ , *The Rise of African Nationalism in South Africa: The ANC 1912-1952* (London, 1970).

Wilson, M. and Mafeje, A., *Langa: A Study of Social Groups in an African Township* (Cape Town, 1963).

Wilson, M. and Thompson, L.M. (eds.), *The Oxford History of South Africa,* vol. II (Oxford, 1971).

Wolton, D., *Whither South Africa?* (London, 1947).

Reference

Cooper, B. (comp.), *Bibliography on the Trade Union Movement in the Union of South Africa, 1920-1951* (Cape Town, 1953).

Dubow, R. (comp.), *The Status of Women in South Africa: A Select Bibliography* (University of Cape Town, 1964).

Gordon, M. (comp.), *Trade Unionism in South Africa, 1952-1966: A Select Bibliography* (University of the Witwatersrand, 1968).

Kratochvil, L. and Shaw, S. (comp.), *African women: A Select Bibliography* (Cambridge, 1974).

Perlman, M. and Moal, M.P., 'Analytical Bibliography' in Paulme, D. (ed.), *Women of Tropical Africa* (London, 1963).

Rosenthal, E. (comp.), *Southern African Dictionary of National Biography* (London, 1966).

Skota, T.D.M., *The African Yearly Register* (Johannesburg, 1931).

VI. Articles and Printed Papers

Ainslie, R., 'Dora Tamana' in *Spare Rib*, Sept. 1975.

Brain, J.L., 'The Position of Women on Rural Development Schemes in Tanzania' in *Ufahamu*, vol. VI, no. 1, 1975.

Burkett, E.C., 'In Dubious Sisterhood: Race and Class in Spanish Colonial South America' in *Latin American Perspectives*, vol. IV, nos. 1 and 2, 1977.

Carter, D., 'The Defiance Campaign—a comparative analysis of the organisation, leadership and participation in the Eastern Cape and the Transvaal' in University of London, Institute of Commonwealth Studies, *Collected Seminar Papers on the Societies of Southern Africa in the 19th and 20th Centuries*, vol. II, Oct. 1970-June 1971.

Davenport, T.R.H., 'African Townsmen: South Africa's Natives (Urban Areas) Legislation Through the Years' in *African Affairs*, vol. 68, no. 271, April 1969.

——————————, 'The beginnings of urban segregation in South Africa', Occasional Paper no. 15, Institute of Social and Economic Research, Rhodes University, Grahamstown, 1971.

Deere, C.D., 'Changing social relations of production and Peruvian peasant women's work' in *Latin American Perspectives*, vol. IV, nos. 1 and 2, 1977.

Fairbairn, J., 'Zeerust: a profile of resistance' in *Africa South*, vol. 2, no. 3, April-June 1958.

Farrag, A.M., 'The occupational structure of the labour force: patterns and trends in selected countries' in *Population Studies*, part I, July 1964.

Feit, E., 'Urban revolt in South Africa' in *Journal of Modern African Studies*, vol. 8, 1970.

Gordon, A.D., Buhle, M.J. and Dye, N.S., 'The Problem of Women's History' in Carroll, B.A. (ed.), *Liberating Women's History* (Urbana, Chicago, 1976).

Hellman, E., 'The African Family Today' in South African Institute of Race Relations, *African Family Life* (Johannesburg, 1967).

Horrell, M., 'The "Pass Laws" ' in South African Institute of Race Relations, Fact Paper no. 7, 1960.

Hunter, M., 'The effects of contact with Europeans on the status of Pondo women' in *Africa*, vol. VI, 1933.

Jarrett-Kerr, M. and 'an African nurse' (pseud.), 'Apartheid in Nursing' in *Africa South*, vol. 3, no. 1, Oct.-Dec. 1958.

Joseph, H., 'Women and Passes' in *Africa South*, vol. 2, no. 2, Jan.-Mar. 1958 and vol. 3, no. 3, April-June 1959.

Lebeuf, A., 'The role of women in the political organisations of African societies' in Paulme, D. (ed.), *Women of Tropical Africa* (London, 1963).

Legassick, M., 'Legislation, ideology and economy in post-1948 South Africa' in *Journal of Southern African Studies*, vol. 1, no. 1, 1974.

Lewin, J., 'The legal status of African women' in *Race Relations Journal*, vol. 26, 1959.

Mait, J., 'Cold Comfort for Josie in Moscow' in *Drum*, June 1975.

Bowbey, J., 'Introduction' to 'Afrikaner women of the Garment Union during the thirties and forties' in *South African Labour Bulletin*, vol. 2, no. 4, 1975.

Mbilinyi, M., 'The "new woman" and traditional norms in Tanzania' in *Journal of Modern African Studies*, vol. 10, no. 1, 1972.

McPherson, J., 'We need more women in South African public life' in *The Outspan*, 15/3/46.

Meer, F., 'African Nationalism—Inhibiting Factors' in Adam, H. (ed.), *South Africa, sociological perspectives* (London, 1971).

Michelman, C., 'The Black Sash, South Africa's stubborn liberals' Paper presented at 14th annual meeting of the African Studies Association, Denver, Colorado, U.S.A., May 1971.

Morris, M., 'The development of capitalism in South African agriculture; class struggle in the countryside' in *Economy and Society*, vol. 5, no. 3, 1976.

Mullings, L., 'Women and economic change in Africa' in Hafkin, J. and Bay, E.G. (eds.), *Women in Africa* (Stanford, 1976).

Mvubelo, L., 'Comment' on Scheepers, A., 'The Garment Workers face the Challenge' in Thomas, W.H. (ed.), *Labour Perspectives on South Africa* (Cape Town, 1974).

Ngcobo, S., 'The Urban Bantu family as a unit' in *Race Relations*, vol. 14, no. 4, 1947.

O'Barr, J.F., 'Making the invisible visible: African women in politics and policy' in *African Studies Review*, vol. 18, no. 3, 1975.

Robinson, S., ' "Our Women are a rock"—Women and the politics of liberation in South Africa' in *Ufahamu*, vol. 6, no. 1, 1975.

Rodda, P., 'The Africanists cut loose' in *Africa South*, vol. 3, no. 4, July-Sept. 1959.

Scheepers, A., 'The Garment Workers face the challenge' in Thomas, W.H. (ed.), *Labour Perspectives on South Africa* (Cape Town, 1974).

Simons, H.J., 'The status of African women' in Smith, P. (ed.), *Africa in Transition* (London, 1958).

Sisulu, W., 'Congress and the Africanists' in *Africa South*, vol. 3, no. 4, July-Sept. 1959.

Trapido, S., 'South Africa in a comparative study of industrialisation' in *The Journal of Development Studies*, vol. 7, no. 3, April 1971.

Van Allen, J., 'Aba Riots or the Igbo Woman's War?—Ideology, stratification and the invisibility of women' in *Ufahamu*, vol. 6, no. 1, 1975.

——————, ' "Sitting on a Man": colonialism and the lost political institutions of Igbo women' in *Canadian Journal of African Studies*, vol. 6, no. 2, 1972.

van der Horst, S., 'Labour' in Hellmann, E. (ed.), *Handbook on Race Relations in South Africa* (London, 1949).

van der Horst, S., 'Women as an economic force in Southern Africa', reprinted from *Proceedings of Joint Regional Conference of South African and Rhodesian Associations of University Women,* Centre for Inter-Group Studies, University of Cape Town, 1976.

Walker, C., ' "We Fight for Food"; Women and the "Food Crisis" of the 1940s' in *Work in Progress,* no. 3, Jan. 1975.

Weiskoff, F.B., 'Women's Place in the Labour market' in *American Economic Review,* vol. 62, no. 2, 1972.

Wipper, A., 'African Women, Fashion and Scapegoating' in *Canadian Journal of African Studies,* vol. 6, no. 2, 1972.

——————, 'The politics of sex; some strategies employed by the Kenyan power elite to handle a normative-existential discrepancy' in *African Studies Review,* vol. 14, no. 3, 1971.

——————, 'The Roles of African Women, Past, Present and Future' in *Canadian Journal of African Studies,* vol. 6, no. 2, 1972.

Wolpe, H., 'Capitalism and Cheap Labour-power in South Africa; from segregation to apartheid' in *Economy and Society,* vol. 1, no. 4, Nov. 1972.

——————, 'The theory of internal colonisation: the South African case' in University of London, Institute of Commonwealth Studies, *Collected Seminar Papers on the Societies of Southern Africa in the 19th and 20th Centuries,* vol. 5, Oct. 1973-March 1974.

VII. Unpublished Theses and Seminar Papers

Fransman, M., *A discussion on some issues related to the South African social formation* (photocopy, 1975?, in University of Cape Town Library, Special Collections Division).

Johns, S.W., *Marxism-Leninism in a multi-racial environment; the origins and early history of the Communist Party of South Africa, 1914-1932* (microfilm, unpubl. Ph.D. thesis, Harvard University, 1965).

Johnson, R.E., *Indians and Apartheid in South Africa: the failure of resistance* (microfilm, unpubl. Ph.D. thesis, University of Massachusetts, 1973).

Kros, C., *Urban African Women's Organisations and Protests on the Rand from the years 1939 to 1956,* (unpubl. B.A. Hons. thesis, University of Witwatersrand, 1978).

Ladlau, L.K., *The Cato Manor Riots, 1959-1960* (unpubl. M.A. thesis, University of Natal, 1975).

Legassick, M., *Class and nationalism in South African protest: the South African Communist Party and the "Native Republics" 1928-34* (photocopy, n.d., in Univ. of Cape Town Library, Special Collections Division).

Lewis, D., *African Trade Unions and the South African State, 1947-1953* (unpubl. paper, Cape Town, 1976).

Mackintosh, M., Marpeth, R., Halpern, P., Langton, P., *The Hardest Work of All: women and the process of industrialisation,* (mimeo, paper presented to the British Sociological Association, n.d. c. 1974/75).

Mackintosh, M., *The Study of Women in Society* (mimeo, 26/8/74).

Morris, M., *Apartheid, Agriculture and the State: the farm labour question* (unpubl. paper presented to SALDRU Farm Labour Conference, Cape Town, Sept. 1976).

Stone, C., *Industrialisation and Female Labour Force Participation: Coloured women in the Cape Peninsula* (unpubl. research paper, Centre for Inter-Group Studies, Univ. of Cape Town, May 1975).

—————, *Women and Production* (paper presented at the NUSAS Women's Seminar, Stutterheim, 1975).

van der Ross, R.E., *A political and social history of the Cape Coloured People, 1880-1970* (manuscript, Cape Town, 1973).

Walker, C., *The Federation of South African Women* (paper presented at Conference on the History of Opposition in South Africa, Univ. of the Witwatersrand, Jan. 1978).

—————, *The Woman's Suffrage Movement in South Africa* (B.A. Hons. thesis, Univ. of Cape Town, 1974).

Wells, J., *Interview with Josie Palmer* (South African Institute of Race Relations, Johannesburg, Oct. 1977).

Yawitch, J., *Natal 1959—the Women's Protests* (paper presented at Conference on the History of Opposition in South Africa, Univ. of the Witwatersrand, Jan. 1978).

VIII. Interviews

These interviews were conducted between July 1976—December 1977.

Liz Abrahams
Ray Alexander
Frances Baard
Nomvo Booi
Amina Cachalia
Helen Joseph
Florence Mkhize
Virginia Mngomo
Mary Moodley
Lilian Ngoyi
Dora Tamana
Katie White

INDEX